D0358717

THE NORMAN CONQUEST

The Norman Conquest

D J A Matthew
Lecturer in History in the University of Liverpool

B T Batsford Ltd
London

This book was written especially for my mother and father who, though unfamiliar with historical scholarship, gave me the initial encouragement to study

By the same author

The Norman Monasteries and their English Possessions

First published 1966

Made and printed in Great Britain by
William Clowes and Sons Ltd London and Beccles
for the publishers
B T BATSFORD LTD
4 Fitzhardinge Street London W1

Preface

No argument could persuade thoughtful persons, particularly in the year of the ninth centenary of the battle of Hastings, that there was an unsatisfied demand for works on the Norman Conquest. Only in the reading can this book establish its value, for the subject matter has never been neglected. I have not set out to tell again the story of the Conquest or of the three Norman kings, and I hope that I will not be found to have assumed to much familiarity with events, characters or interpretations. My intention has been to write an essay on the meaning of these events and their bearing on the history of England. In doing so, I have been guided by three considerations.

In the first place I have concentrated on the particular men concerned, in order to avoid generalising about whole groups of characters. Though this may give the impression of superficiality, the personal approach is in least danger of distorting the historical picture, when, as here, important changes affecting a whole society were brought about by comparatively few men. To bring out the individual characters I have drawn heavily on those contemporary records that also focus attention on leading figures. The special importance of the original sources is that they are now the only means we have of making direct contact with the men of that period.

It has been my second principal aim to bring out the merit and the interest of these sources. There are, however, many matters of interest to us now that were of little concern to writers then, and many readers may think that my presentation of events through eleventh-century records ignores whole sections of the community, like the peasantry. In a book of these proportions however, a great deal has had to be omitted and it seemed more useful to concentrate on what could be more certainly known. Readers interested in particular analysis of such records as Domesday book must turn to specialised studies.

My third principle has been to concentrate on achievement, rather than destruction in the Norman period, on the assumption that the reader of an essay of interpretation may reasonably expect a discussion of the more lasting interest of the Normans and not a chronicle of their misdeeds. I do not consider this to be white-washing them, even if the emphasis has been put upon how they changed their world and brought a different kind of England into being. All periods are full of calamities as well as of good deeds, but, to my mind, it is more useful for histories to concentrate on achievements especially when, so long after the events, there is no further point in taking sides.

This work has been constructed on the foundations laid by generations of scholars. My references to published work can only indicate a fraction of my indebtedness to the whole host of writers who have preceded me. I should, however, like to conclude by acknowledging the influence of those who have helped me personally. With my friends, Dr Peter Carter, Dr Henry Mayr-Harting and Mr Norman Blake, I have been able to establish in conversation the living interest of matters that can easily seem remote and arid. Moreover, by introducing me to ideas and books otherwise unknown to me, they led me on to problems and solutions that I could not have found alone. I have incurred a different but no less personal debt to my seniors. Mr J. M. Wallace-Hadrill, who first made me want to study medieval history, showed me the value and meaning of real scholarship and how to set about understanding the basic texts of *Stubbs' Charters*. Professor R.W. Southern, who guided my later explorations into the byways of Norman history, showed me how, by contemplation of the texts, they may become a place for meeting the minds of men from other ages. Lastly, Professor C. N. L. Brooke has selflessly advised and commented upon a succession of drafts and by encouraging enthusiastic study of medieval history in his department at Liverpool has made it a congenial place for the composition of this essay. To these scholars I owe my faith that the study of the middle ages is one of the more humane sciences. I would like to hope that they could find a little evidence here of their own teaching and wisdom.

Rome, Quinquagesima, 1966 — D.M.

Contents

The Illustrations

The Author and Publishers would like to thank the above-mentioned museums and libraries for permission to reproduce the illustrations from the MSS in their possession.

Part One

Before the Conquest

1 England before the Norman Conquest

The Wealth of England

Sea journeys are still the best way to savour the taste of travel—the wind and water in mid-ocean, the strangeness of other lands in foreign ports. But in few corners of the modern world—such as the archipelagos of the Aegean or south-east Asia—is transport by sea not only the most attractive, but also the easiest and the most natural method. It was not the aeroplane but the modern rail and road communication systems over land that first deprived ships of their ancient superiority in transport. So long as it was simpler to carry bulky cargoes, and great numbers of people, by water, those with easy access to waterways maintained better links with distant lands than with men living in the same country. This was particularly true of England in the eleventh century. Though small and relatively well organised with several major roads, as an island penetrated by many sea-channels and rivers it was exceptionally well placed both to launch its produce overseas and to draw into the heart of the island peoples from all over the north-east Atlantic ocean. Travel by water was relatively rapid; whereas the Conqueror sailed across the Channel overnight, Harold rode two days to reach Hastings from London. This was because there were no natural obstacles other than the elements to contend with.

The relative merits of these different methods of travel were appreciated at the time: Goscelin (a Fleming who lived in England most of his adult life) gives a charming description of an effortless journey made down the Thames,[1] but without counting the days; from Abingdon the monks found the roundabout journey by river to London too slow, so they travelled overland; but it was wearisome and they welcomed the gift of a house at Colnbrook eighteen miles from London, where they could rest after a long day's ride.[2]

Most writers committed themselves to journeys by sea with much foreboding, but Goscelin could also see the pleasure of a trip when 'the west wind filled the sails and the ship sped through the swelling waves like a plough, and the exalted thoughts of the saintly passenger flew ahead, even before the pennants in the wind'.[3]

The sea had its own hazards, natural and otherwise, but they did not reduce the advantages of sea-transport. Pirates, who figure in many sea-stories of the eleventh, as of other centuries, were necessarily parasites, and could only profit if regular commerce flourished in spite of them. Merchants took the risk of meeting them. They stood an even chance in an open fight on the high seas, where pirates had no special advantages. Fresh winds, mists and storms could be used as much by merchants to escape from a dangerous encounter as by pirates to surprise merchant vessels.[4] One pirate ship, foiled of its chance to capture a vessel making for home, had to try and retrieve its fortune by brazenly entering the port of Fécamp and seizing the ship at the harbour side, while the crew warmed themselves in a quayside shelter after the bitter winter journey.[5] Unsuccessful pirates naturally figure more often in stories of miraculous escapes than the successful ones, but all piracy depended more on luck than special talents. Even merchants occasionally profited from piratical actions. Those in the port of Bristol, who succeeded in luring unwary persons aboard their ships to examine merchandise, might set sail unexpectedly and sell their passengers as slaves in Ireland. The slave trade was denounced by bishop Wulfstan of Worcester,[6] who knew of the activity of slavers round the Severn estuary. Kings declared slaving to be illegal, but Englishmen captured and sold one another for profit, if they could.[7] They must have been numerous amongst the pirates as well, for English was a language of diplomacy in treating with them over ransoms. No clear division between commerce and piracy faithfully reflects eleventh-century realities. The bold Vikings themselves were both merchants and pirates, showing one face to their customers and the other to their victims.

The heavily indented coastline of western Europe offered many harbours and channels of access to the heart of the land mass. Merchants and pirates showed the way to, or followed in the wake of, whole groups and tribes who had left one land for another as unsolicited, or often undesired, immigrants. At different times, under Alfred, Edgar and Edward the Confessor, English kings commanded navies to protect the coast-lines, but, however useful they may have been on occasion against specific enemies, they could not be deployed to patrol the seas regularly or bar all possible ports of entry.[8] The Scandinavians had cast their net around the British Isles. They had settlements in the west, at Dublin and in the Hebrides; in the north they were established as close as the Orkneys as well as in the deeper ocean; in the east they traded at York, London and Rouen. Eastern England had been drawn into extensive trading across the North Sea or the straits of Dover; here were found the principal towns and ports, which were enriched by merchants from overseas. At St Ives in Huntingdonshire, men from as far away as Cologne, Saxony and Venice laid their offerings on the shrine of the wonder-working saint.[9] But London was the chief port that drew merchants up the Thames to anchor near the bridge where the major roads of Roman Britain still converged.

London had been important commercially for centuries, but it acquired a political significance in the eleventh century.[10] Though earlier kings of England had been crowned at Winchester in the old capital of Wessex, Harold was the first king to be crowned at Westminster and his successors followed the precedent. The ostensible reason for this was the site of the Confessor's monastery, but the Confessor's own choice for Westminster as the site of his church to St Peter shows that he wished to settle his monks and his residence near London. At the other end of the city, overlooking the port itself, the Conqueror built his castle—the Tower. The kings of eleventh-century England established themselves around the most important trading port of their kingdom; between the limits defined by military and monastic protection, London over the succeeding centuries developed its claim to become the capital city. Before it became the national capital, it was already a proud international city of commerce, protected by its Roman walls, probably reinforced at this time, and capable of fielding its own military contingents.

Men from as far away as Sussex might be obliged to contribute to necessary building operations on the bridge there. It had become so urban that the citizens acquired the right to hunt in the neighbouring counties. Trade was its main activity, some of which, if not all, was in the hands of foreigners. Flemings and Rhinelanders brought cloth from Bavaria, fine linen, coats of mail, Rhenish wine and goods from distant Constantinople. They had wharves in London from the tenth century and had royal protection for travelling to trading fairs all over England. There were Scandinavians and Russians. Men of Rouen had depots at the end of the tenth century and by the early twelfth century there were branches of business from Champagne, the greatest fairground of Europe. After the Norman Conquest, one of the richest Norman business-men acquired property in the three major ports of the new dominion: Rouen, Caen and London.[11] The importance of London to the money market is proved by the centralisation of die-cutting for the king's coins in London, though coins continued to be struck in provincial cities with the king's dies. Commerce also encouraged industry. A greater variety of trades and a greater number of craftsmen than for any other city of England crowded within its walls. No wonder that, after the battle of Hastings had annihilated England's best army, the Conqueror prowled round London until the citizens and England's leaders admitted him as king to Westminster, or that the Conqueror issued to the Londoners the first of his confirmations of ancient privilege.

The only English cities comparable in importance were Winchester, the ancient royal capital where kings still kept their treasure in the eleventh century, and Canterbury, whose archbishop enjoyed the dignity of presiding over most of the sees of England. Both these cities were almost as closely related to the sea as London itself. In the reign of Harold I, the men of Winchester could expect troops of their Danish allies to come by ship up the Itchen[12] and Canterbury was easily reached from Dover. The three principal cities of England probably maintained their best contacts with one another by water rather than by land, though Canterbury lay on the Roman road from London to Dover.

The major roads of eleventh-century England were an important asset to the kingdom: Watling Street, Ermine Street and the Fosse Way[13] should have been broad enough for sixteen horsemen to ride abreast, and the sides were cut back to prevent ambushes.[14] Over these roads alone was the king sure enough of his power to offer protection to merchants and travellers. The state of other roads can only be guessed at. When bishop Ethelwine of Durham tried to escape to Lindisfarne in a great hurry with the precious relic of St Cuthbert's body, he travelled in winter about one hundred miles in four days.[15] Hardly much quicker was Harold's march from London to Hastings on the eve of the battle, though it is calculated that he could travel on the Roman road to Yorkshire and back much faster. Travelling by road could rarely have been more rapid than forty miles a day with the swiftest horses; men with packages travelling by local paths might have done as little as ten miles a day. No part of England was so impeded by natural obstacles like woods or marshes as to make passage impossible, but it was slow and painful. With patience and good supplies the Conqueror's army crossed the Pennines in winter between Yorkshire and Chester; only the wastes of Snowdonia defeated Rufus's army. England was, by eleventh-century standards, a penetrable country, well linked by major roads and lying at the centre of a commercial network that added to its own natural prosperity.

The foreign merchants and visitors, as well as conquerors, were well placed to assess the wealth of the country and probably never tired of admiring this demi-paradise. The Fleming Goscelin described his adopted land with enthusiastic rhetoric. Like other examples of this type, his description is based on the first chapters of Bede's *Ecclesiastical History*, but, whereas Bede is sober and scientific, Goscelin, as an outsider, allows his admiration to overflow in eloquence. For the thousands of inarticulate men, who discovered the wealth of England in the eleventh century, Goscelin's own words set down what the sharp-eyed merchants and the painstaking settler had experience of.

> You must know that all earthly riches and delights, which in other places exist only individually, are here found gathered together. It is an imperial kingdom governed royally by Roman Caesars whose boast it was to have a throne both here and at Rome. The generous earth produces bountiful harvests not only from indigenous grains and fruits, but also from species introduced from Greece and exotic climes. On all sides it luxuriates in fruitful fields, verdant meadows, wide

> plains, fertile pastures, milky herds and horses apt for warlike pursuits. It is watered by bubbling springs, rising streams, majestic and famous rivers. Watercourses teeming with fish and fowl and conveniently adaptable for the use of town and country are continually agitated by the traffic of ships. There are abundant groves and forests. Fields and hills are covered with vegetation, fruits and trees, and they abound with all sorts of game. There are chestnut woods fit for the banquets of gods; the vineyards rival not only those of France and Italy but also of Greece and Carthage. There are salt springs; warm baths are fed from hot springs and streams. What shall I say of the riches of the sea, not only in commerce, but in all the kinds of fish which enrich and distinguish this kingdom? Amongst these diverse and great riches of the sea, dolphins, seals and enormous whales may be taken. Shellfish provide red and purple dyes which keep their resplendent colours and are never impaired by sun or rain, whilst other dyes change and fade with age. Within these shellfish, great pearls of brilliant sheen are found in different colours: red, green, purple, blue, aquamarine but the greatest number are white. By the skill of jewellers they are set with precious stones in gold to adorn the church. Even more resplendent is the gold cloth woven by English maidens. Chosen by kings and bishops, it glows with its red and purple hues. Splendid pearls and marguerites with exquisite gems sparkle against the golden thread—a radiant conjunction of artistic excellence. Through these pearls Britain in the west claims kinship with oriental India. This land also has great quantities of amber: purple, wax-coloured, white and green. There are rich veins of metal: copper, iron, lead, tin, silver and gold. Admire too, its rocks and towering cliffs, its churches and ramparts of great stone blocks, decorated with native marble.[16]

Goscelin calls attention not only to the natural riches of England but also to the skill some native craftsmen showed in using them. The importance of the sea, both for bringing foreign products into the country and for yielding up fish and pearls, and the significance of the waterways are also well brought out by Goscelin. He emphasized that what made England a paradise was the incredible variety of its riches; what was introduced from outside only complemented its natural resources.

England was prosperous because it was not dependent on any one particular source of wealth. Less cultivated minds than Goscelin's appreciated above all the visible, glittering wealth of England. The easy conversion of natural resources into gold and silver is the most precocious aspect of England's economic development in the eleventh century. In the few years from its foundation by Harold to the Norman Conquest, Waltham abbey accumulated precious church ornaments that alone represented a fortune: seven reliquaries, three of gold; four gospel texts enriched with gold, silver and gems; four great gold and silver censers; six candelabra, two of gold, four of silver; three great cruets, of gold and gilded silver worked by Greeks; four golden crosses with silver and gems; one cross cast from fifty marks of silver; two gold and three silver chalices; four altars with relics, one of gold, and three of gilded silver; one wine horn worth one hundred shillings; ten reliquaries, one of two marks of gold and gems, the others of gold and gilded silver; two precious bells; five priest's vestments, very precious with gold and silver; four chasubles of gold and gems, one worth more than twelve marks of gold; two capes of gold and gems and two women's saddle cloths woven with much gold thread.[17] The monastic churches of England were exceptionally rich in objects of this kind. In addition, their landed wealth amounted to about an eighth of the estimated value of the whole country. Monks and other rich men were able to turn their resources easily into gold, silver and jewels. Kings were able to realise their revenues in money, strike coins, levy taxes, buy off enemies and spend money as they desired. England was not only rich; its riches could easily purchase whatever seemed desirable.

The wealth of England is more easily described than explained. Goscelin suggests that the economic exploitation of all the natural resources, including woodland, waterways, mines and fields, was the real cause of prosperity. William of Poitiers comments on its abundance of grain as well as its supplies of gold. Varied agriculture would be the soundest basis of the economy.[18] The country was well populated with settlements at no great distance from one another, except in the extremities of the south-west and north of the Humber. East Anglia was more densely populated than other parts of the country. It had received more recent immigrants in great numbers across the North Sea. The small towns of eastern England must generally have derived their prosperity from exchange of agricultural produce. At Norwich, Ipswich and Colchester the burgesses were a social group quite distinct from the 'bordars' or poor agricultural workers, and the reciprocal relationship of town and country implies a specialisation in the economy. There was also regional diversity in the agricultural pattern. Sheep were kept in downland and in marshes, for the wool clip was already important to the Flemish weaving towns. Ewes' milk and goats' milk were turned into cheese that was appreciated in Normandy; water-meadows for dairy cattle were not evenly distributed, and dairy herds not necessarily common, but oxen were the normal plough-beasts. Local factors must have influenced economic organisation to a degree that can only be guessed at, but regional differences in wealth and society can be pointed out. Eastern England, more densely populated, had a larger proportion of 'free' peasantry than other parts of England: peasants paying taxes on their own account, rentpayers owing few agricultural services to landlords, freemen of equal legal standing who attended the public law-courts. In the west of England there were fewer men of this type; there, it was common to pay taxes through the lord who assumed such public responsibilities, extracting services as well as payments from his tenants and dispensing justice in his court. Differences of status at law only came to have important general consequences when royal justice in the twelfth century became an instrument of political change; in the eleventh century the tangible differences of wealth and extent of landed estate had more meaning. The free peasants of the east were often poorer and cultivated smaller estates than some richer dependent peasants of the west. Even more striking, however, were the great differences in wealth within groups of the same region. Some freemen of the east prospered with their freedom; others fell into debt or diminished their estates by division among heirs. Some prosperous 'villeins' of the west had bigger teams of plough beasts than their neighbours. The inequality of wealth in the same social class is a notable, and perhaps surprising, aspect of eleventh-century England. It was true of all classes. Of forty monasteries owning one-eighth of landed wealth, the seven richest owned more than half; of fifteen bishoprics owning one-ninth of landed wealth, the ten poorest enjoyed hardly more than a mere third. It is more difficult to account for the distribution of secular wealth until after the Conquest, but it is unlikely that the range of fortunes was any less great. Noblemen favoured by relationship to the royal family or befriended by kings like Canute and the Conqueror amassed estates and fortunes that placed them in an entirely separate category from poorer men of noble birth. England was a rich country but its wealth was unevenly distributed regionally and socially. Probably the very ease of conversion of natural wealth into money helped to accentuate the differences.

The Unity of England

The wealth of England impressed the Danes of the late tenth century when the English king bought off their attacks by giving them great quantities of gold raised by taxation from his subjects: the Danegeld. The ability of the king to levy public taxation at this time is evidence of the very high degree of government and administration in the country. The king's control of the minting of money is the natural complement. Compared to other eleventh-century kings, the English exercised real power and commanded greater resources. They considered themselves to be emperors and rather pompously used the styles of the emperor at Constantinople as appropriate. In the tenth century, king Athelstan, who received the formal submission of princes of western Britain, called himself 'basileus' and when the Conqueror returned to Normandy in 1067 he exuberantly recorded in a charter that by his conquest he had become a 'basileus' himself. Constantinople, though far away, was not out of range. At the time of the Conquest itself a modest English thegn and his wife were planning a journey there,[19] and after it many exiled men of his rank naturally sought employment in the armies of the eastern emperor. Monks and other clergy from England on the pious journey to or from Jerusalem visited it.[20] Cult objects for churches were made by Greeks and the Conqueror's crown was modelled on that of the emperor.[21] The aping of ancient and respectable authority did not cover a sham government. It represented an awareness of what was fitting. In this respect the English 'empire' was as credible as the 'German', for the English kings did govern in a recognisably 'imperial' manner.[22] They had administration enough to raise taxes; they had army enough to command the respect of their enemies.

The effectiveness of govenment in the eleventh century still depended on military success and nothing has done more to discredit the reputation of Engish society than the single defeat at Hastings in 1066. The fact that the English king had shown his own capacity to lead, and the ability and courage of his soldiers to fight, only three weeks earlier at Stamford Bridge, has too often been minimised. At that battle, Harold's unseasoned troops had defeated the king of Norway, a former captain of the imperial guard at Constantinople (and bold lover of an empress) famed for his technical mastery of the art of war. England did not decline as a military power in the eleventh century and kings were expected to display military abilities as well as to offer the blessings of peace and justice. Even Edward the Confessor, the most pacific of eleventh-century kings, was presented as a man of military distinction to his contemporaries. Some of his coins display him as a martial figure;[23] the Anglo-Saxon chronicler speaks of him as 'noble in armour, a king of excellent virtue, pure and benign, Edward the noble protected his fatherland, his realm and his people'. The king also commanded a navy. King Edgar in the tenth century may have devised a system of raising ships with which to patrol the British seas;[24] Edward the Confessor mobilised a fleet in the channel at the behest of his continental allies; Harold's fleet lay off the Isle of Wight during the summer of 1066 to intercept the Conqueror's invasion force. How exactly military and naval forces were raised before the Conquest is a matter of learned controversy, principally because our sources of information are so slight.[25] There was a general obligation of service, known as 'fyrd' duty, which was owed by all land, and performed by a man of the estate or his deputy. In the tenth century English kings from Edward the Elder onwards were engaged in fairly frequent wars, first against the area settled by the Danes under Alfred and later on the western and northern borders of reunited England. The frequency of warfare and the degree of military skill required probably made it necessary to provide for a more professional military service, either to supplement or to replace the old service, at least in some places. The king's fighting men, or thegns, were assigned estates by landlords and in return they performed military duties. In the eleventh century Canute and his successors used the landless fighting men of their household as the core of their armies. The different types of soldier, of armament and service, and the varying burdens upon the population to contribute to the army, created a very confused institutional pattern, which was not necessarily reflected in campaigns. Harold Godwinson, faced with foreign invasion in 1066, could mobilise troops to watch along the south coast during the summer. They remained at the ready until the first week in September when their food supplies ran out and they had to return to their homes, and presumably helped there with the harvest. At the same time he had a professional mounted army at his disposal which could advance from the south of England to Yorkshire at the first word of the Norwegian invasion, and there inflict a heavy defeat on the invaders within hours of arriving after a long journey. Harold could withdraw this same force, depleted but no doubt reinforced, and expect the same success against the Normans in the south after the long journey south. In the north itself, the earls of Northumbria and Mercia could field soldiers to beat back small parties of invaders by sea, and also put a large army into battle against the Norwegians within two weeks or less of the Norwegians' invasion. The earls must have had household troops of their own, as Harold had, and both campaigns deployed troops raised by shire levies. The actual details of organisation cannot now be reconstructed, but it is obvious that the military forces of pre-Conquest England were considerable, that the commanders were watchful and able to act swiftly and had some reason to be confident of their powers to repel foreign soldiers. The soldiers themselves were of comparable skill and equipment to those of the continent. Harold had fought in Normandy with the Conqueror and received arms from him, arms which he had shown that he knew how to use; his brother Tostig, former earl of Northumbria, fought with the Norwegians. The English troops, it is said, did not customarily fight on horse-back, though some of them at least rode to battle; but the Conqueror himself also fought on foot when his horses were killed, though his men were surprised by this.[26] It is even possible that the reason why the Norman cavalry was so much in evidence at Hastings was that the English were placed on the crest of a hill and that only horses provided the speed or cover needed to carry the Normans within range of personal contact with the enemy. Fighting in Normandy was often a question of sieges and technical invention, rather than pitched battles between cavalry forces. At least in 1106 the Normans, like the English in 1066, fought on foot. The significant differences between the English armies before the Conquest and their foreign enemies were slight and even the Norman cavalry fled in disarray before the English defence in the opening phases of Hastings itself.

The English kings could therefore use an army effectively in battle. Nevertheless, English kings were not always successful in warfare. In particular England was unable to defeat the Danes at the beginning of the eleventh century, and a Dane, Canute, became king of England and his sons reigned after him in turn. This defeat is the more striking because in the great struggle with the Danes under Alfred and his son, despite the initial Danish victories, the English royal line had never been completely overwhelmed and eventually the English military successes against the Danish invaders had led to the emergence of a powerful English kingship. Yet this kingship, so much more ceremonious under Edgar than under Alfred, was unable to defeat the second waves of invaders in the time of Edgar's son, Aethelred II. However important the resources of kingship, the personal qualities that each holder brought to his office were indispensable. The wealth and valour of the English were there to be used by Aethelred II, but he was personally incapable of taking advantage of them. He was militarily incompetent and he did not make up for his deficiency with political skill. He was irresolute, rash and untrustworthy; other people could not cover up for his personal failings. The monarchy had become powerful because of its military leadership, and military success it had to have to survive. Up to a point the king could rely on loyal generals, but ultimately he would find himself either dependent on their good faith or in political conflict with their ambitions. The English were not equipped in the eleventh century to divide their loyalty between the head of state and the military hero. The king must be both, if the kingship was to be worth anything to the people.

When the king was irresolute and unsuccessful and the normal sanctions of government broke down, the English were thrown back on their basic social resources. In a military society, as it was in the eleventh century and had been for centuries, the most natural of all social bonds, apart from blood-relationship, was the association between a soldier and his commander, which, in the small units of these armies, was the bond between a man, or vassal, and his lord. It was a relationship of honour created by an oath sworn by the vassal to his lord; in this society a man was honourable and 'moral' in so far as he kept his oath, and served his lord faithfully even to death. The lord in return offered protection so that the vassal could thereby acquire both a respected place in the community and a means of satisfying his ambition. It was not essentially an association of mutual self-interest but of honour. It gave men the sense of belonging to a community; it gave them a goal in life and a code of behaviour. Inevitably there were untrustworthy men who betrayed their lords, their oaths and their own honour. This no more proves that trust and loyalty were words of resounding hollowness than the frequency of adultery annihilates the value of marriage. The moral code of honour survived the frequent and flagrant breaches of it and praise of honourable and oath-worthy men became both profounder and more affecting as men of high principle became rarer.

This loyalty to the lord was a personal sworn loyalty to an individual. As the basis of all social relationships, the swearing of oaths of loyalty and obedience was surrounded with all the solemnity of religious ceremony known in the eleventh century. The respect with which the king himself was viewed was also closely related to this concept, because, by a law of king Edmund in the tenth century, all English freemen took a solemn oath of loyalty to the king as a specific act of commitment.[27] When the king died, new oaths had to be sworn to his successor. This loyalty to specific rulers was the only eleventh-century equivalent of duty to the state and the unity of the state depended upon the oaths. When the king died, 'loyalty' foundered until it was renewed by a fresh act of loyalty. Essentially public duty was conceived in terms used for other social obligations and only differed from other loyal oaths in two respects: all men took the same king as lord and breaches of the oath were not merely immoral, but illegal, and would be punished. The strength of the king could therefore be calculated from his power to punish those who violated their oaths.

By this test, the government of Aethelred II was weak. The king failed to command respect, he failed to defeat his enemies, the Danes and their king Sweyn. The Danish king occupied part of the country and bid for control of the rest. Englishmen in prominent positions found that their lord the king gave them no help or protection and that they had to fend for themselves. For want of an English lord they had to take a Dane. They were reluctant to do this, but their attachment to an English lord had been a mere matter of sentiment—they preferred their own Christian ruler to a foreign, pagan or quasi-pagan chief; but they did not feel that they were betraying their country: they owed only a personal loyalty and exchanged it with reluctance for another personal one. The bond of lord and vassal was not the same as the bond of king and subject and lay quite outside the modern notions of the duty of native-born men to their state.

The freemen who dealt in the social ramifications of lordship were not playing irresponsibly with the well-being of the community and the natural instincts of the great majority of the population were not being sacrificed. All that free Englishmen had in common in the eleventh century was their obligation to swear allegiance to the king. The king was not merely a symbol of their unity, he was the instrument of it. Englishmen did not have the vaguest sense of the existence of common institutions of government or law. Had they considered such matters in the light of political bonds, they would have emphasised regional differences justified by law.

The regional differences had crystallised in the eleventh century into legal distinctions which had become more important than the original racial elements of which the regions had been composed. Men of each region were entitled to be judged by their own laws and were faithful to these codes and jealous of their integrity. The outstanding difference was the contrast between the English areas and the Danelaw. The Danelaw stretched north of the Thames to the Scottish border covering the eastern half of the country with some of the best agricultural land, the highest urban density and the best trading connections overseas. It was not inhabited only by men of Danish descent, but, however few the original Danish settlers had been, they had won recognition for their own laws and customs over the whole area, within the relatively short time between their occupation of the area in the mid-ninth century and their acceptance of English overlordship under Edward the Elder. For the men of this region, their laws and customs were worth defending and the difference between them and other men of England was entirely dependent upon it, for there was no 'political' authority in the Danelaw to justify or sustain it. The differences between English areas, like Mercia and Wessex, may seem very small now, from a legal point of view, but they had originally been separate and rival kingdoms and the areas remained subject to different 'earls' in pre-Conquest England so that political loyalties to the region survived. The *Anglo-Saxon Chronicle* records of Canute that he crossed the Thames into Mercia at Cricklade, as though he were crossing the frontiers of a foreign land.[28] Long after the Conquest, differences between Mercia and Wessex still seemed important. It is not for us to deride such men for their parochial horizons.

Regional differences also had geographical justification. Most regions had their own coast-line which drew their economic life to different parts of the ocean. Wessex was more concerned with Channel traffic and Kent had a special concern with the straits of Dover and the people of Flanders; Mercia tended to be drawn towards Ireland through the port of Chester; the Danelaw looked across the North Sea. The majority of men, who lived and died in their own part of the country and knew at the most the area of their own shire, were probably not even aware of regional loyalties: when summoned to fight the 'national' enemy in their shire force, it was usually under their local leaders and for the safety of their own locality.

In the eleventh century, the regional loyalties had been given the opportunity to acquire a political expression by Canute who divided the country into great earldoms: Wessex, Mercia, East Anglia and Northumbria, over which very powerful men were appointed as earls or 'viceroys'. From one point of view this may seem to be an unwise concession to the separatist spirit, but it is interesting that Canute and Edward the Confessor were both powerful enough to appoint strangers to the regions as earls, and that in practice the earls by their personal relationship to the king and their position regionally were well placed to reconcile royal and regional interests. When in 1065 all the men of Northumbria unanimously repudiated their earl,[29] Tostig Godwinson, whom the king had appointed, and chose another as their own earl, it was the appointment not of a man of Northumbria but of the younger son of another great earl, from Mercia, which they asked the king to approve. Though regional feeling was not so separatist as to insist on a local earl, it spoke with a common voice that the king could not lightly decline to hear. Nevertheless the region was loyal to the king to the point of deferring to his formal powers of confirmation.

On this loom of relationships, lords and vassals on the warp, regional and national on the woof, were woven the political affairs of pre-Conquest England. The sense of a national policy and national situation was not something natural to the ordinary Englishman. It was more commonly felt by those whose interests brought them in touch with royal affairs and by those whose estates were not confined to one part of the country and these were in general the great noble families of England. Some of these families were descended from younger branches of the royal house of Wessex, who had acquired political and military responsibilities in the tenth century, but those who mattered in eleventh-century England were the families whose positions had been confirmed by Canute at the time of the creation of the earldoms. In particular, Godwin, made earl of Wessex, dominated English politics until his death: his sons Swegn, Harold, Tostig, Gyrth and Leofwine became earls and his daughter became queen of England. The most powerful rival of the Godwinsons was the family of Leofric of Mercia. Aware though they were of the common problems of England these families did not develop a sense of national loyalty to strengthen the royal position. They thought of family interests and dynastic loyalties first. If they quarrelled within the family, as Tostig and Harold quarrelled in 1065, it was for private reasons, not national ones. But their world was not a narrow one. Beyond the family they saw the international scene in which they figured as prominently as the king. The Godwinsons sought foreign brides. Harold was a visitor at Bruges, in Normandy and at Rome.[30] The earl of Mercia, Aelfgar, was no more stay-at-home than his rival Harold. When his son fell sick and died at Reims, Aelfgar invited the monks there to hold a valuable estate in distant Shropshire out of gratitude for their charitable care of the young man. The great men inhabited the wide world not as mere citizens of a small kingdom, but in their own right. In a moral work, Goscelin[31] describes the unhappiness of a young girl of noble birth who was married to a foreign husband and lived amongst people of barbarous ways and unknown languages, but he consoles such brides with the reflection that it has always been the same. The Israelites had been exiled in Egypt and the Trojans in Italy. By the intermarriage of strange peoples, the population was constantly modified. A girl born in England could be English even if her father were Danish and her mother from the Rhineland. The mixture of peoples in the upper ranks of society can easily be traced by intermarriage amongst foreign families. Given the basically local character of society, once the well-born began to look beyond their own immediate interests, they did not automatically develop a respect for a national unity; on the contrary, they entered into international society.

Some of the better-educated clergy had their own reasons for thinking more often about English unity, and were capable of defending it without renouncing their profound respect for the apostolic see at Rome. Bede had tried to describe the conversion of the whole of England to Christianity: the unity of the English people in the church was older than their unity under monarchy. For a century after the conversion the archbishop of Canterbury had been the single leader of Christian England; even the belated creation of an archbishopric of York, which nominally split ecclesiastical authority, impaired no existing political union, and in practice Canterbury's lead was uncontested. However, once York had become a great Danish city, as it was from the tenth century, it appeared to threaten Canterbury's undisputed sway. This provoked at Canterbury a spirited defence of Augustine's primacy and the unity of Britain. Although it was founded on Canterbury's own pretensions, it took the form of pleading political considerations. Within such limits, the Canterbury clergy did have a more enlightened sense of the unity of England. The church exalted the monarch by its ceremonies of coronation and by its repeated comparisons of the monarchy with that of the Old Testament, which had been given by God to govern his chosen people. The higher clergy were the men least attached to regional loyalties; regional law was no concern of those who enjoyed a special status at law as clergy and they assumed pastoral charges anywhere in the land. Educated in the international traditions of the church, they were better equipped intellectually to reject the partial loyalties that undermined the monarchy. The

Anglo-Saxon Chronicle, written in different monasteries up and down the country, concentrated with remarkable consistency on national events. Though regional variations occur, they never obscured the writers' genuine appreciation that England's problems were one.

The most striking occasion for testing this sense of patriotism came in 1051–52 when the king, Edward the Confessor, quarrelled with his father-in-law, earl Godwin.[32] It is assumed that the quarrel was connected with the king's desire to favour foreigners. The author of the *Chronicle* alleges that both sides had such a sharp appreciation of national unity that they deliberately renounced the possibility of settling their dispute by battle, in case civil war should leave the country open to invasion and bring ruin upon themselves, and that the Godwinsons went into exile to save the country. Having ascribed the best motives for their exile to the Godwinsons, the chronicler goes on to show that, the following year, they did not scruple to risk plunging the country into turmoil by returning with a show of force and obliging the king either to pardon them, or to start a civil war himself. The Godwinsons' numerous rivals and enemies at court might have acknowledged their patriotism in 1051 but could not have done so in 1052. Their enemies, at least, on both occasions would have ascribed their actions to calculation of their own best self-interest. What is most remarkable is that the chronicler should try to pass off the Godwinsons as self-denying patriots. He was probably a man of Canterbury, certainly one of Wessex, who himself favoured the family of the earl. But outside Wessex the presumption of the Godwinsons to dictate to the king in the national interest would seem hypocritical. The national interest was loyalty to the king and trust in his lordship. To aim at correcting the king's policy was to plan his overthrow and aspire to his lordship. The other noble families of England saw the Godwinsons as ambitious upstarts, with no more title to the throne than they had, and Harold Godwinson proved them right when he took the crown in 1066. How durable was his kingship?

England and the Continent

England was wealthy and well able to supply a military king with the resources that he needed to defend his government and keep his people from foreign domination, but in order to maintain English independence the king, even in the eleventh century, needed foreign allies. It was not merely that English economic prosperity was intimately involved in overseas trade. Pressure of invaders from Scandinavia in particular had become so heavy by the year 1000 that all the many resources of kingship, army, navy and coastal defences did not suffice to prevent landings and settlements unless the king could expect cooperation from neighbouring continental rulers. Though it is easy, by studying English institutional history, to become convinced of the essential continuity of English government at least up to 1066, to contemporaries eleventh-century England seemed dominated by foreign powers. King Sweyn of Denmark, who descended on England as an enemy of king Aethelred and succeeded in gaining grudging, but genuine, support from Aethelred's nobility, was succeeded by his son Canute. Canute's support came chiefly from southern England and for a time he had to share England with Aethelred's son, Edmund Ironside, unexpectedly strong in the Danelaw. When Edmund died within a few months, Canute became king of the whole of England, as well as of Denmark, and the other heirs of Aethelred were banished to the continent. Canute had already lived in England for several years and had been regarded by many leading men as the enemy of their natural lord. When he became king, such men were at his mercy. If ever England lay at the feet of a conqueror in the eleventh century it was in 1016.

From the reign of Canute onwards, it was obvious to foreign powers that England was capable of being subjected to foreign domination and in this context the Norman success in 1066 only seemed like the exchange of one yoke for another. The problem of the Conquest would be to explain why the Normans were in the long run more successful than the Danes in holding on to England, rather than to ask why England was unable to preserve its own complete independence. Both questions clearly belong together, but the survival of English independence was doomed not in 1066 but in 1016. The origin of the problem was in Aethelred's reign.

The contrast between the success of Alfred and Edward the Elder in subduing and controlling the Danes and the failure of Aethelred to defeat king Sweyn has already been presented. Part of the explanation of this contrast can be found in the changed situation on the continent itself. In Alfred's time,[33] the English had drawn both comfort and practical advantage from the fact that the Viking fleets raiding in the Channel were attacked not only from England but from the Carolingian empire itself and that the Viking armies had to reckon with Frankish as well as English opposition. But whereas with this initial advantage Edward the Elder could turn and deal effectively with the Danes of eastern England, the last Carolingian rulers failed to obtain a long-term recognition of their authority over the Danish settlers in northern France. The Scandinavian leader, Rollo, who accepted part of Normandy from Charles the Simple in 911, extended his influence over the rest in the succeeding years and a distinct region, or duchy as it came to be called, developed slowly in the tenth century. During the reigns of the powerful English kings Aethelstan and Edgar, Normandy still counted for relatively little: it was confused and anarchic and its military interests were absorbed in the campaigns of the Capetian dukes of France, whose influence in the duchy had superseded that of the last Carolingians. In 987 the Capetians became kings of France and drew the Normans into general French politics; at the same time the Norman rulers began to develop special political interests of their own. In the final years of duke Richard I, they began to cooperate with a new wave of Viking raiders. When the young Aethelred was king, therefore, he found that the southern shore of the Channel did not cooperate in his efforts to keep the seas clear of Vikings, as it had cooperated with his ancestor Alfred a century earlier. The enmity of the southern coast of the Channel considerably reduced the capacity of the English king to defeat his enemies.

Aethelred's government was so alarmed by the Norman alliance with the pagan Scandinavians that it appealed to pope John XV (985–996) to persuade the Normans to sever their unholy connection.[34] The Capetian kings had no power to discipline the Normans and the pope's influence could be only moral. The conversion of the pagans to Christianity, which came about in the next few years, anyway destroyed the basis of the papal case and would have left the duke's conscience clear, had it troubled him. In fact duke Richard II continued to cooperate with the Viking invaders. As late as 1014 he entertained at Rouen a host on its return from a raid of devastation in north-west France.[35] The motives for his alliance are not easy to discover. Maybe he feared for his own duchy and preferred to accommodate wilful and dangerous men in the hope of turning their energies elsewhere. It is likely that the Normans derived other advantages from this alliance. The duchy seems to have had unprecedented supplies of hard cash under Richard II; the Viking raiders, who brought back the booty of war and trade and who wintered and refitted in Normandy, could have been the source of it. The practical advantage of the alliance might have seemed more obvious because there was already a sense of kinship between the Scandinavians and the descendants of the Scandinavian settlers of 911. Whatever variety of courses prompted the Normans to it, the alliance was deep-rooted enough to defy moral and religious pressures.

In these circumstances it is only to be expected that Aethelred's government would have pleaded in vain with the duke. Nevertheless in 1002, he consented to the marriage of his sister Emma to Aethelred. Presumably in the confidence that this Norman alliance gave him, Aethelred ordered the famous St Brice massacre of the leading Danes of England, which prompted king Sweyn of Denmark to campaign in person to avenge his sister, one of the victims. Whether the marriage and the massacre were related in this way or not, they cancelled one another out. The advantage of the marriage counted for nothing in the struggle with the Danish king in England and it must very quickly have become obvious to Richard II that there were no advantages for him in the alliance with the desperate Aethelred. Had Emma herself pleaded with her brother to help her husband, the case might have been different, but it is probable that Emma became indifferent to her husband. A later admirer omitted to mention this relationship in the *encomium* which he wrote for her, as though Emma had no wish to be reminded of Aethelred's existence.[36] Why Richard II ever consented to the marriage in the first place is not known, but the marriage did not materially help Aethelred;

Richard never cooperated with him against the Vikings and the extent of his feeling for the king was to receive him and his family when he was driven into exile in 1013.

The importance of trying to obtain the friendship of Normandy had however been shown and every English king thereafter (with the two exceptions of Harold I and Harold II) attempted to obtain Norman support or neutrality. By Aethelred's reign England was obviously vulnerable and sensible precautions had to be taken in the south. Immediately after he became king, Canute invited Aethelred's widow Emma to become his wife, and she became the mother of his legitimate heir to the Scandinavian empire, Hardacanute. She was also the mother of Hardacanute's successor, Edward the Confessor, and it was through Emma that the Conqueror was related to Edward. Emma could not, of course, transmit any claim to the English throne, but she was a political personage of importance in English politics from her first marriage in 1002 until her death in 1052. She was a formidable old lady by the time her first son, the Confessor, went down to Winchester to seize her property. Her headstrong individuality makes it difficult to believe that she either advocated Norman interests in England or tactfully justified English policies in Normandy, but nevertheless she represented the truth that English kings of the eleventh century had realised the need to take Normandy into account.

Norman influence on England is not the same as Norman government. Canute and Hardacanute, though they valued their connection, were Scandinavian rulers, not Norman puppets. Canute showed that union with Denmark was a perfectly viable form of government. It was not an arbitrary association of states because Canute made a political reality out of the common economic interests of the northern seas, and was the common lord of Danes scattered over the whole area, who were united by language, literature and culture. The extent to which even the English shared in this Scandinavian world may be guessed from their own literature: *Beowulf* is an Anglo-Saxon poem about a Scandinavian hero. It is also said that Edward the Confessor, the least Danish of English rulers, was fond of telling old Norse tales and recounted the story of Olaf, the greatest of kings, every year at Easter to his bodyguard.[37] By bringing the English and the Danes into a common political society, Canute was not doing violence to the realities on which politics are based. His Danish heirs expected that his personal achievement could be repeated. In fact this Scandinavian unity foundered in 1042 and it was never renewed after the long reign of the Confessor and the Norman Conquest.

The reign of the Confessor has seemed to prove that England was capable of avoiding the disagreeable fate of belonging either to a Scandinavian or a Norman empire in the mid-eleventh century. The Confessor became king by a national renewal of confidence in the old English royal house for he was 'a flower sprung from the root of ancient kings'. The collapse of government under his father had been repaired and strengthened by Canute; the great earls and regions were generally dutiful and submissive; the king was respected and was fortunate in not being put to the extreme military test, though he showed himself energetic and full of authority at times of danger. Yet this national king appeared to the Godwinsons to favour Normans too much in his own lifetime and intended after his death that his kingship should pass to his Norman cousin. Why is it that a king sustained by patriotic men and himself born to the ancient house of Wessex should betray the very basis of patriotism by looking for a foreign king to succeed him in England? The Confessor was not so bemused as his later admirers. He knew that the position of king did not really depend on patriotic sentiment and he evidently realised that foreign politics were perhaps even more important to England's well-being than composing the rivalries of the great families of earls themselves.

In 1035, when Canute died, his son by an irregular union, Harold, was chosen king, in the absence of Hardacanute who was in Denmark. Harold had an English mother, but his bastardy in the eyes of the church should have been a sufficient reason to discredit his claim to the throne. By usurping the claims of his half-brother Hardacanute in Denmark he risked losing Danish support. His success in obtaining the throne and the treasury at Winchester, together with the support given him by Godwin who was earl of Wessex, suggest that Godwin had been instrumental in making him king. When Aethelred's younger son by Emma tried to invade England, it was Godwin who made him a prisoner and who was later held morally responsible for his death. The elder brother, Edward the Confessor, also tried to enter England and was repulsed at Southampton by English forces. The Normans thought that the English remained loyal to Harold out of fear that the Danes would rush to his support if Edward aimed to make himself king.[38] Less than seven years later, however, Edward did become king. The only probable explanation of this change of heart in Wessex is that, whereas Edward was opposed by Godwin in 1035, he was not in 1042. It was not that patriotism had revived; five years of Harold's allegedly tyrannous government had not made it distasteful for the English to receive Hardacanute in 1040: the 'Danish' element was still strong in English politics. Hardacanute, when he became king, immediately invited his half-brother Edward to return to England and when the king died Edward was his natural successor.

The election of Edward as king in 1042 may be seen as a restoration of the old English line. But Aethelred, a king of unhappy memory, had been dead for nearly thirty years, since when a new generation had grown up with Canute's Scandinavian world, its extensive alliances abroad and its earldoms at home. Such a restoration could only be a sentimental reflection. It was not as the son of Aethelred that Edward became king, but as brother to Hardacanute, as son of Canute's widow Emma, and as protégé of earl Godwin, whose daughter he married in 1044. Norman writers also stress that Edward had Norman help and, though this was probably inspired by a wish to emphasise Edward's indebtedness to the Normans, it is certain that Godwin also thought that Edward was too much inclined to favour Normans. Edward, later, developed his own policy as king and tried to break out of the fetters in which Godwin had confined him. As the reign lengthened out, he became more sure of himself, his government perhaps began to emphasise its legitimist character rather than its Danish structure and Edward thought that he could act on his own initiative. A clash between the king and Godwinsons produced the threat of civil war in 1051–52 and the king showed not only that he was powerful enough to exile the powerful earl but also that he had the support of the earl's rivals, the other earls of England. He was not, however, powerful enough to keep them in exile and when readmitted to favour in 1052, they appeared to have consolidated their hold. The king's Norman friends, or many of them, were banished; he was obliged to take back his queen, whom he had over-hastily banished to a nunnery in 1051; and he never again showed any sign of political initiative, leaving government, apparently, to Harold Godwinson.[39] The power of the Godwinsons to make kings in England from 1035 reached its culmination when Edward died and Harold took the throne himself.

Many historians have seen the house of Godwin as representing a patriotic policy. They raised native sons to the kingship, Harold I, Hardacanute, Edward the Confessor: when other candidates failed in 1066 they offered one of their own house, Harold II. This policy could however be successful only if foreign powers could be kept at bay and native rulers were strong enough to command acceptance. Harold thought that he was able to do this and was prepared to do without foreign allies. In spite of his great courage and ability the invasion of forces from Norway and Normandy in September 1066 did in fact overwhelm him. It is probable that the Confessor's different policy was devised to meet this situation, because he did not think that England could withstand pressure from outside. The Confessor could have reflected on his own father's weakness, exposed to hostility from both Richard II and Sweyn of Denmark; he had also lived with foreign rulers for nearly thirty years and watched England and its situation from the point of view of the continent. He was not trained or educated in England after his tenth year, at the very oldest. He was a man whose fortune was made by the Godwinsons, but who by no means accepted that they were essential to his survival. He clearly thought that Norman help would be sufficient to protect him from them, and in one sense his policy was proved a failure: the Normans did not save him from the ignominy of having to pardon his enemy and he retired from politics. But what had proved a failure in 1052 was not foredoomed in 1066. The Confessor's policy had been to rule England with foreign alliances; the Godwinsons' policy was to rely on their own native resources. In the conditions of 1066, the Confessor's policy was successful and Harold's failed.

It could be objected that the Confessor's policy was a mere whim to favour his Norman relative, rather than a shrewd calculation of what was possible, and that the Godwinsons had shown that they were able to maintain the independence of England by raising a succession of kings of their own after 1035. In practice they themselves realised that they needed foreign allies. Whatever part they had played in raising Harold I to the throne, his successor Hardacanute had sailed from Flanders and claimed the throne as his father's heir. He had legitimist support that the Godwinsons could not challenge. Though they were lucky to have Edward as his successor, a man without a party of his own in England, their influence over him did not prevent their exile in 1051 and then they too found that Flanders was near and could be a place for launching their own comeback. Tostig Godwinson married the count of Flanders' daughter; Harold Godwinson cultivated his connections there; both found it expedient to make their way to Rome and to keep on good terms with the papacy. English rulers, whatever their self-confidence and power, could not altogether ignore the need for foreign friends. Harold I had indeed governed with no foreign connections, but he had been lucky to face only the small invasions of Aethelred's sons and owed his throne to the power of Godwin to control Wessex. Once Edward the Confessor had interested the Norman duke in succeeding to the English throne, could the power of the Godwinsons keep out the massed effort of the whole Norman duchy?

Edward's decision to nominate William of Normandy as his successor in 1051 introduced a new factor into English politics that was quite independent of the role played by Normandy since 1002. The Confessor's choice of candidate was entirely free. Had he chosen merely a man with influence across the Channel, he could have looked to Eustace of Boulogne, his brother-in-law, or to the counts of Flanders, descended like himself from Alfred of Wessex. A prince of this region would assure control of the narrow seas, and could easily dominate the three key cities of London, Canterbury and Winchester. He turned to William because William by 1051 was not merely his cousin, but was young, had shown himself to be an able military leader, and a politician who had already negotiated the Flemish alliance that would make entry into England easier. If he held both shores of the Channel, he would be better able to control the Danish fleet. The Confessor did not fancy a Scandinavian successor, probably for emotional reasons. His line had been ousted by the kings of Denmark and his own foreign connections were to the south. He was a kinsman of Henry I of France and related to the emperor Henry III of Germany. His exile had been spent in

Normandy and the regions of northern France and perhaps in the Rhineland. From the lands that he knew, he picked the young man he considered capable of proving a good ruler.

What right however had the Confessor to choose his successor in this arbitrary way and make the nobility swear allegiance to him? Surely, there were fixed rules or norms of succession to the throne that limited the free choice of rulers? During the tenth century, when the house of Wessex ruled all England, all the kings were chosen from the royal family, not always raising the oldest legitimate son to the undivided throne, but in practice preventing the elevation of outsiders. The great men made the choice on practical grounds, fitness for office and degree of kinship, but in normal circumstances the obvious candidate obtained general recognition on the designation of his father. The candidate, having established his claim, acquired a right to the throne and he was anointed and crowned king by the church, which emphasised that he had been chosen by God as Saul and David had been chosen. By 973, the date of the first recorded anointing ceremony, it had become essential to kingship, and this reduced the significance of the political preliminaries of election and recognition. The emphasis on God's choice of the ruler and the king's divine mandate gave the king a new type of authority while he lived.

In practice the king still needed to be a good lord and a successful general, and all the blessings of the church could not save Aethelred from exile or prevent the general recognition of Canute as lord and king in 1016. Not only were Aethelred's other children set aside in Canute's favour, but also the heir of Edmund Ironside stood no chance against the Dane. Canute had no claim to the throne by blood, and it is doubtful whether his marriage to Emma, Aethelred's widow, was seen as a means either of establishing kinship to the late king or of strengthening his kingship by her previous queenship. But, though Canute had entered upon his kingship by an unprecedented step that seemed to impose itself in 1016, he never attempted to rule otherwise than in the tradition of his predecessors. He was succeeded by his two sons, whose claims to the throne were their relationship to the late king. Hardacanute seems to have named his brother Edward as his heir and to have made his followers swear to accept him as such. There was therefore an idea that the king had authority to name his successor, probably on the same legal grounds that enabled Anglo-Saxons to will away their property.[40] In normal circumstances a man would choose his sons as his heirs, but if he had no sons he would choose others of his kin.

Since loyalty to the king himself was secured by oaths, it was natural that the king should attempt to secure respect for his 'will' by making men swear to accept his nominated heir as such during his life-time. When the Confessor himself was born, Aethelred forced men to take an oath to recognise the infant as his heir; this Aethelred did to keep out his other sons by his previous marriage. The legality of this step may be contested. Did the king have the right to 'disinherit' the obvious heirs? In practice this oath did not prevent the succession of Edmund Ironside. Was this an exceptional case, because the Confessor, then only a boy, could not, as Edmund could, rally the army against the Danes? In fact the choice of Edmund in exceptional circumstances was entirely unhampered by the swearing of this oath to his younger brother. A century later, Henry I made his great men swear to accept his son William as heir, in preference to the son of his elder brother Robert, and later after William's death, to recognise his daughter Mathilda as heir in preference to other candidates. At Henry's death, his nephew Stephen, though he had sworn, was chosen king and recognised by the church, and his perjury was not then held to be an impediment to his government. All these instances are relevant to the problem of the Confessor's nomination of William of Normandy.

Like his father before him, Edward thought he had the right to name his successor. His nobles did not contest this right, though they did not like his choice. They could not even refuse to swear. The Godwinsons swore and gave hostages to William as a guarantee of their good faith. But what was sworn to the command of one king, lost its power to bind men on his death. Just as allegiance to the state was suspended when the power of the oath was broken by the king's death, so too the oath to his successor had none of the force of the oath of lord and vassal, and none of the legality of oaths to the consecrated king. If another candidate could be chosen by God and confirmed by the church and could obtain from men the oath of loyalty due to the crowned king, his position was much stronger than that of any man singled out in a previous reign as heir. For this reason, Stephen, as crowned king, was always in a stronger position than Mathilda. These oaths sworn in the previous king's reign gave a candidate a claim to the throne, a claim perhaps slightly stronger than seniority of birth itself, but claims had to be presented and the right established and such a right could only become clear in the circumstances of the time. The claims of the Confessor, such as they were, had been set aside in 1016 in favour of Edmund; the claims of Mathilda were set aside in favour of Stephen in 1135; and in 1066 the claims of William of Normandy were set aside in favour of Harold Godwinson. What Edward could do, he had done: he had given William a claim to the throne. It was up to him to prove his right.

2 Normandy

The Normans

The Normans of the eleventh century would have considered it only natural that historians should study and admire them. They were proud of themselves[1] and aware of their identity as a group apart, though others could be easily assimilated into their violent and self-assertive society. Their tenth-century reputation as Godless pillagers of northern France earned them bitter notices in monastic chronicles, but not until the reign of Richard II (996–1025) did they apparently take any interest in recording their own deeds for posterity. Richard had to go outside the duchy to find Dudo the canon of St Quentin to compose a legendary book about the deeds of his ancestors.[2] The taste for this kind of literature caught on in the eleventh century to the point where the Normans' desire to be remembered in history became a motive for their increasingly ambitious exploits. Several malicious writers later referred to the Normans' avidity for doing something memorable to account even for such trivial actions as Herfast's removal of his see from Elmham to Thetford, and greater men expected their conquests of proud and wealthy peoples to bring them renown. By the end of the eleventh century, their military successes had created a Norman commonwealth with dominions in the Anglo-Norman realm, in southern Italy and Sicily and in the Holy Land at Bohemond's Antioch. Like later colonials, the Normans were mindful of the old country, even if they preferred the new. They generously donated their wealth to the churches of their homeland,[3] helped distant or disreputable relations to make their fortunes and entertained their sovereign with respect and ostentation, as when duke Robert II lingered in Sicily on his return from the First Crusade. The Normans did not scruple to admit that their riches and lands had been won by feats of arms and gloried that brave men of good family and no fortune like the sons of Hauteville should snatch the blessings of Providence from the Greeks and the infidel in southern Italy. Nor did the Normans profess any bigoted faith to justify their crusade. At first their campaigns had roused the imperial popes, like Leo IX, to defend the interests of the German and Greek emperors in Italy against them; later, when popes allied with the Normans, the rough soldiers of Guiscard, who rescued Gregory VII from Rome, did not adopt any hypocritical respect for the Holy City, and they sacked it with pleasure.

The Normans who set about making their fortunes in lands held by the Saracens, consistently tolerated the religion of their subjects and adopted the civilisation of Greeks and Arabs for their own advantage. Whether they learned their tolerance from their subjects or brought their own genius for assimilation from the north, the Normans developed the characteristic virtues of empire-builders which are not always found in mere conquerors. They arrived hard-headed and clannish; they became cultured and sceptical.

The spread of Normans across Europe in the eleventh century could have been a mere response to favourable conditions on the part of unscrupulous adventurers. Conditions in their homeland also played a part in determining their course. In the tenth century the Normans under the 'duke' engaged in the military campaigns of the Capetian duke of the Franks, who became king of France in 987; but after the Normans had participated in the French king's expeditions to Burgundy in 1006, the Normans rarely helped their king. Capetian influence over their barons generally dwindled to ceremonial occasions in the eleventh century. Instead, the Norman counts were drawn into the political debates of the Scandinavian world. In Normandy itself some men succeeded in taking the affairs of the duchy into their aristocratic hands; the others, less successful or less well connected, had either to accept subordinate roles in Normandy or opportunities elsewhere. The sons of Hauteville went to Italy to make their fortune at a time when their relative poverty had become a slur on their reputations.

Who were the Normans? They were the people of the duchy which achieved its special character in the reign of duke Richard II. The first duke, Rollo, who had obtained a concession of lands in 911, had extended his territory beyond the limits of the original grant, but his successors, William Longsword and Richard I, never played a very prominent role and the duchy remained undistinguished. The Scandinavian colonisation had been thin. Their language and customs were quickly replaced by those of the more numerous Gallic inhabitants. By the end of the tenth century the bishops of western Normandy (where the pagan settlement had been densest) had returned to their sees and it was as nominal Christians, of military bravery but dreaded cruelty, that the Normans emerged as figures of European importance. Their long period of quiescence may have been a period of germination, but the identifiable Scandinavian element in their character and institutions is so slight, that it seems more natural to explain their qualities in terms of the situation in the duchy under Richard II himself.

A later legend of Richard II recounted how, shut up in a tower, he went over his accounts with his officials.[4] The historical justification of this picture is that Richard was the first duke to have left proof of his interest in money.[5] Merchants of Rouen had wharves in London; monks too were spending money freely for the purchase of estates and the province began to support a number of lavish religious houses. The duke himself afforded money for an elaborate monastery at Fécamp for the heavenly salvation of his family. His association with the Scandinavian pirates as merchants, or 'paying guests', probably explains the unprecedented liquid wealth of Normandy and the interest shown in Normandy at this time by less favoured neighbours, the Angevins and the Bretons. Richard himself acted independently of his Capetian overlord. He broke the old custom of alliance with the Capetians by marrying a Breton princess and his sister married English kings. He dealt independently with the papacy, yielding only for an instant to suggestions that he sever his friendship with England's pagan enemies. He himself received from the pope a privilege for his monastery that pushed the abbot, the great William of Volpiano, also abbot of Dijon, into second place. Richard II and his Normans already played the cool and impudent role of their successors. There is no hint of this character in the anecdotes about their predecessors.

The chief institutional importance of Richard's reign is the appearance on the Norman frontier of his half-brothers, all styled 'count' and established in military castles, a military innovation that was proving its importance in Anjou at this time.[6] Ralph at Ivry, Robert at Evreux (he kept the county and later passed it to his sons even after becoming archbishop of Rouen), Godfrey at Brionne, William at Eu and Robert at Mortain,[7] managed the frontier—or marcher—regions by assuming important military powers. It is probable that they exercised Richard's own powers in their regions. The counts of Evreux, Eu and Mortain all enjoyed the rights of 'the forest' which the count normally reserved for himself: the others may have done the same.[8] Richard made no difficulties about conceding this privilege and his formal authority over them did not in practice mean much. His brother Robert certainly asked for 'ducal' approval of a grant of customs from the county of Evreux to Jumièges as though the duke had power to refuse it.[9] But it is more worth noticing that Richard was apparently indifferent to the distribution of former ducal customs and privileges not only to the counts but to their favourites. Richard's brothers were free to act independently of him, and made no effort to conserve the rights that they exercised and Richard did nothing to prevent the fragmentation of authority.

This conclusion is surprising because Richard himself, compared to his predecessors, seems exceptionally prominent, active and successful. In one sense, the powers exercised by his brothers extended ducal influence where it had not previously existed at all, though this impression may be due to the absence of earlier information about the frontier regions. Had they been ruled directly by the duke's officials, indirectly by loyal subordinates or been subject to persons not formally connected with the ducal court at all? Whether or not Richard II had more authority than his predecessors, it was exercised differently. Richard and his brothers were all technically 'counts' and if the province was better or more governed in the eleventh century it was only so long as the counts cooperated in a common enterprise of government. If the duke exercised a leadership of his aristocratic federation it must have been independently of his official status, and a matter of personal political success.

The new vigour of Normandy in the eleventh century was first demonstrated by the new counts, not by the duke. What was the importance of this office of count, originally devised in the Carolingian empire for purposes of defence and local government? In spite of the withdrawal of Carolingian government from Normandy after the late ninth century, the local government districts, or *pays*, survived as units of administration into the eleventh century,[10] when the *vicomtes* first appear as local ducal officials, often handing on their offices to their sons in the main parts of the duchy. This fact alone would suggest that during the tenth century, of which nothing is known, the rudiments of administration survived, or at least, which is equally important, that the Norman rulers had introduced no lasting innovations of their own. It is entirely speculative to suppose that the Norman rulers controlled these officers. But when Richard II appointed his half-brothers to the position of count in the marches, it is unlikely either that he parted with important authority in the borders, or that he at last obtained existing offices for members of his family. The significance of the appointments is that the old authorities of Carolingian Neustria began to pale beside the new luminaries of the Norman duchy. These men were originally members of the duke's family and family connections were their characteristic interest and pride, but they did not establish a common ducal authority. They showed how little they cared for the ducal authority by their way of competing later for the ducal title.

The consequences of these family settlements on the border were damaging to the ducal position as soon as Richard II died. His son, Richard III, was murdered within months of his father's death. His brother, Robert count of Hiémois, the wildest of the march counties, seized the duchy and forced Richard's infant son Nicholas to become a monk in the family monastery of Fécamp. In his turn, Robert was unable to prevent his uncle Robert, archbishop of Rouen, count of Evreux, from becoming the real ruler of the duchy.[11] Abandoning his powerless role, he undertook a pilgrimage to Jerusalem, from which he never returned. The archbishop replaced him, when his death was known, by his bastard infant son William, who clearly had no legal title which the church could endorse. His minority was a period of scandal and horror. His relations, friends and tutor were murdered. His wishes and will counted for nothing except as the barest veil of private interest.

These events had been made possible by the situation created under Richard II, when the counts had acquired privileges and responsibilities that made them aggressive. The creation of these counties was nothing but a means of satisfying the duke's relations and coping with the military problem of the frontier, for there is no evidence that the counts in any way contributed to the duke's own authority. The counts' position on the frontiers in their castles proves that from the first their real purpose was military. The encouragement of Norman military prowess at this time was the most decisive factor in shaping the Normans themselves in the eleventh century. No doubt Normans had fought previously and ferociously in Capetian armies, but the Norman knights, the castle, the defence of Norman frontiers and the expansion of Norman interests in the eleventh century are not the mere discharge of obligations by an aggressive expansion of Norman families on their own account. This movement was released by the new counts.[12]

The counts needed active military men around them to defend the landed frontiers against those numerous enemies who were excited by the prospect of plundering the rich province. In the north, the count of Eu faced the counts of Ponthieu, uneasily subordinated only in the mid-eleventh century. In the west, the count of Mortain had to contain the restless Bretons in the uncertain frontier lands where the monks of Mont Saint Michel wisely prayed for both sides. To the south, where the Angevins were consolidating the first feudal empire in the Loire valley, the counts of Hiémois held a position of doubtful strength against their own local and insubordinate lords. To the south-east, castles at Evreux and Ivry kept watch on the borders of the royal Capetian domain: even against their own royal lords, the Normans defended a frontier. The process of binding men to their service cannot be followed in any detail. Both for their own official duties and in pursuit of their private vendettas, the counts relied on bodies of armed men and on subordinate officers, recruited from their relations, friends and tenants. In succeeding generations the lands attached to their office were divided amongst their children and distributed to their vigorous followers.[13] These men were on the make and, like the original counts themselves (sprung to a man from a morganatic union of Richard I), they rose in a single generation from ignominy to aristocracy. The leading feature of Normandy in the eleventh century was its great families: in every case, the family ancestor, who had no patronymic, could never be traced further back than the reign of Richard II. These men appear to have risen, as can easily be understood, with the help of the counts, including the duke himself.

The endowment of these families was not done by a controlled and judicious distribution of favours to loyal and trusted supporters. Although evidence is scanty it strongly suggests that the two monasteries of Fécamp and Bernay, founded by Richard II and his Breton wife Judith, were both deprived of lands by supporters of Robert 'the Magnificent'. The ancestor of the Montgomery family seized some of Fécamp's estates and the ancestor of the Beaumonts took what were to become the principal domains of his family, from Bernay.[14] If Robert the Magnificent connived at the Montgomery trespass on Fécamp's lands, it can only demonstrate his abject dependence on the favour of the Montgomeries, to the point where his own family pride and honour had to be sacrificed to their greed. Archbishop Robert of Rouen laid predatory hands on parts of duchess Judith's dower, when he became ruler of the duchy, and gave them to his cathedral. Within a few years they were obtained, undoubtedly by violence, for the Taissons.[15] This family made its fortune between 1025 and 1047 by which year their support in battle had become vital to the duke in Lower (that is western) Normandy. Those who found no friends or who lost their lands inevitably preferred to leave Normandy for lands of open opportunity so that the new lords consolidated their hold and became a new, powerful and ineradicable aristocracy. By the 1040s the new families were so certain of themselves that they began to surrender their more indigestible loot—churches and tithes—to monasteries which they founded in expiation of their crimes of violence. Here, their reputations were washed by the tears of the monks, whose piety was alone capable of softening the stony Norman heart. With their religious foundations they enter historical record as pious and upright benefactors. By whatever force

1 David and Goliath, eleventh century
Rouen, Bibliothèque Municipale MS 456, f. 1 *(see p. 299)*

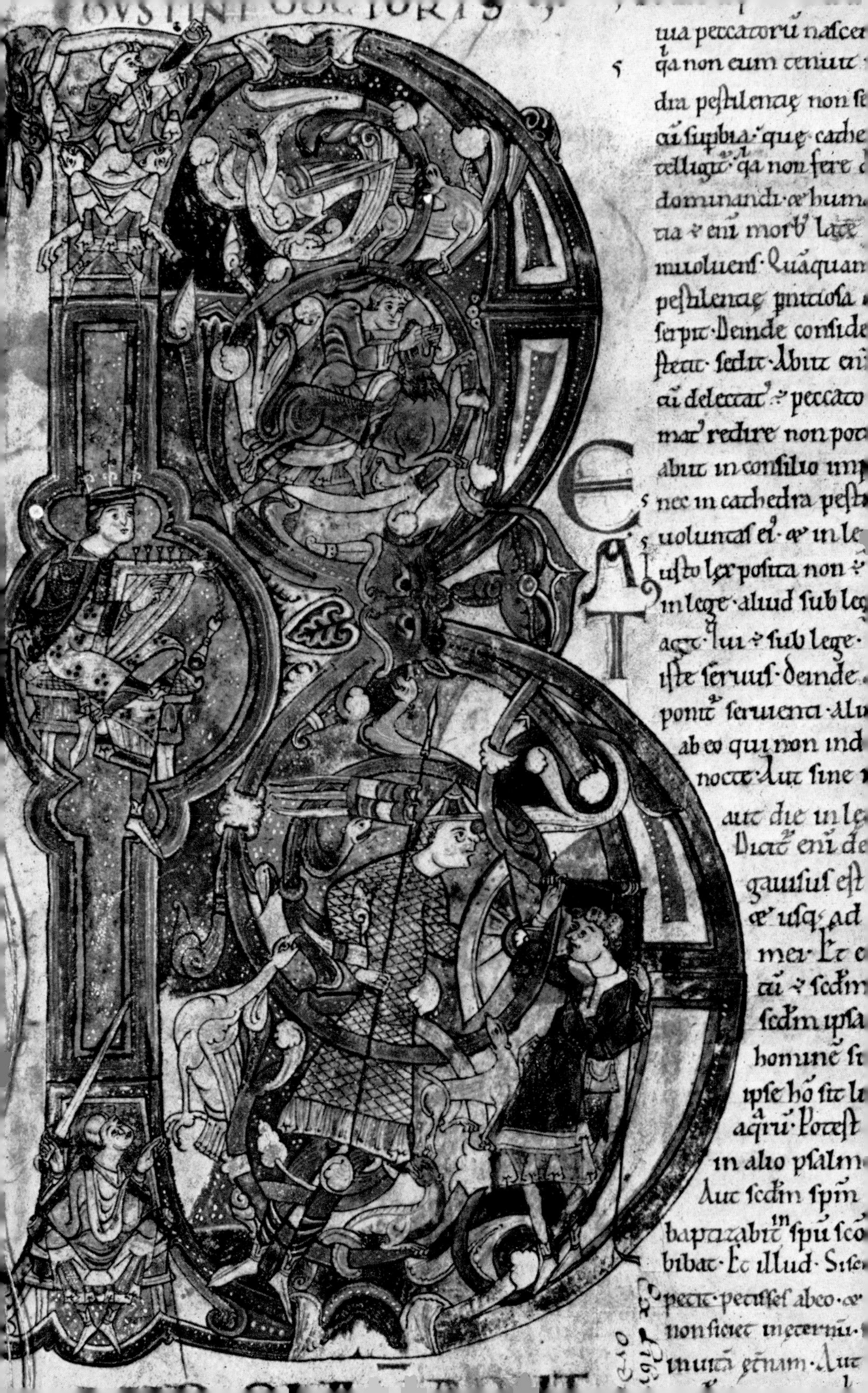

tia peccatorū nascer
qa non eum tenuit
dra pestilentię non se
cū supbia que cathe
telligit qa non fere
dominandi et huma
tia enī morbus late
inuoluens. Quaquam
pestilentię pniciosa
serpit. Deinde conside
stetit. sedit. Abiit enī
cū delectat peccato
mat redire non pot
abiit in consilio imp
nec in cathedra pesti
uoluntas ei. et in le
iusto lex posita non
in lege. aliud sub le
agit. Iui sub lege.
iste seruus. deinde
ponit seruienti. Alu
ab eo qui non ind
nocte. Aut sine
aut die in le
Dicit enī de
gauisus est
et usq; ad
mei. Et c
cū secdm
secdm ipsa
hominē si
ipse hō sit l
agri. Potest
in alio psalm
Aut secdm spin
baptizabit in spū sco
bibat. Et illud. Si se
pecit. pecisset ab eo. et
non fieret in eternū
inuita genam. Aut

or subterfuge they had established themselves, they had become men to be reckoned with. Their political support was not alienated by too close a legal scrutiny of their titles.

Norman Society

No problem of early Norman history is more important and more obscure than that of ducal authority. Yet to know exactly what William the Conqueror understood by the powers of his office, as distinct from his personal authority, could help to define his later part in the Norman government of England. Our sources of information about William's government in Normandy are, however, so few that it is doubtful enough what the powers of the duke were in 1087, so that to reconstruct them as they were before 1066 requires a great deal of ingenuity. This has not been wanting in Norman scholarship.[16]

In his hey-day, William undoubtedly led and disciplined his men, but in his minority and after his death Normandy was plunged into chaos and there were then no signs of ducal administration or ducal institutions to preserve continuity. It is altogether misleading to consider the Norman rulers as creators of institutions: they lived at a time when men owed their success or failure to their personal capacities and weak rulers could not make good their own deficiences by invoking traditional powers. The Conqueror, the most authoritarian of all Norman dukes, had no secular means of maintaining the peace of the duchy or punishing private war; not merely at the beginning of his personal government in 1047, but even in 1080 at the height of his power at the council of Lillebonne, he had to use the 'Truce of God' to restrict private war to certain seasons and could only invoke ecclesiastical censures against offenders.[17] This device, generally agreed to be a desperate remedy invented by churchmen, powerless in the ways of the world, had been introduced into France at the end of the tenth century, and its adoption by ecclesiastical synods in different provinces indicates that all 'public' authority had proved incapable of maintaining the peace. Significantly, it was unknown to England and the Empire before 1066, since the rulers there wielded secular swords of public order. The Conqueror's reliance on the church to reduce the sporadic fighting of his men is a marked proof of the limitations of secular authority and it is not reassuring to be told that his power is shown by the fact that the ban on fighting private wars at holy seasons and on holy days did not apply to the duke's own wars.[18] If anything, the duke's control of the church served partisan rather than public interests.

Until the very late tenth century there are no surviving deeds of the Norman dukes for Norman religious houses. If the practice of keeping written records developed gradually in the reign of Richard II, it grew with relative speed during William's Norman period. For his thirty-odd years (including twelve years of childhood) there are more than half as many charters again, as for all his predecessors put together.[19] No doubt his later reputation made monks eager to preserve what charters they had from him, and perhaps more careless of earlier ones. It is probable, however, that William was, more often than his ancestors, required to approve deeds and to draw his characteristic wavy cross at the foot of documents prepared by the monks themselves. For this increasing clerical work did not cause William to develop a writing office of his own. He had a court official called a chancellor, as his grandfather Richard II had, no doubt in imitation of his overlord the king of France,[20] but there is no sign that the duke even had a ducal seal. If the duke himself needed a scribe, such a person could be found, but in fact the use of written instruments was only occasional in Normandy before 1066.

The documents themselves show how little need there was for formal records. Transfers of land were made publicly by symbolic actions, like the offering of a sod on the altar of the church, so that every person present was a witness of the deed. Monasteries accumulated many gifts before a single record of them was put in writing, which therefore served more as aides-memoire than as legal deeds. The documents themselves were composed with little consideration for legal niceties. The language was imprecise, the phrases lacked formality and the structure was irregular and rambling. It is chiefly interesting to notice that, for all their evident lack of experience in such matters, the Normans were feeling their way towards literate government.

Later writers have often dwelt piously on William's amiable

disposition towards the church in Normandy. The churches and monasteries began to admire and respect him more as he proved able to defend their interests and to interfere effectively in their concerns. But there is no justification for believing that he enjoyed any formal power as protector or advocate of all the churches of Normandy. The churches and monasteries that were most closely connected with the duke were the cathedral churches of Rouen and Bayeux, the principal cities of the tenth-century counts, and the monasteries of Fécamp, Jumièges, Bernay, St Wandrille and St Ouen, all either founded by the duke's family or revived on the sites of Carolingian foundations with ducal approval. Most of the bishops of the eleventh century, even under William, were recruited from the great aristocratic families and their promotion was either due directly to family pressure or to recognition that their influence could not be gainsaid. If the bishops of Normandy did as he asked, they did so for the same reasons as their secular relations, not because the duke was director of the Norman church. Over monasteries the duke's power was equally personal. When William exiled the Grentmesnil family, he drove away from his monastery the abbot of St Evroul, Robert de Grentmesnil, and impatient of the monk's protests ordered the bishop of Lisieux, Hugh of Eu, to consecrate a new abbot. Robert was not formally judged by the bishops or the duke. The bishop and the monks submitted to William's wrath because they feared to do otherwise.[21] William enjoyed no formal rights over St Evroul, the monastery of the Grentmesnil family; if he disposed of it at his pleasure it was by force of his personality. This force was considerable. By virtue of his influence with the great lords, he was able to direct the churches and the monasteries, as if he disposed of them, but these powers were personal to himself and not dependent on his office. He invested new abbots and disposed of them as though they were secular vassals. These powers were important: they confirmed the duke's position as the source of authority in the duchy and they cost him nothing. William's only monastic foundations were at Caen, but he enjoyed a gratuitous patronage of the others. If he was politically powerful enough to dispose of the rights of his secular lords, it was obviously desirable that the monks should obtain some sort of ducal confirmation of their own property and privileges. It could be a guarantee that if their direct patrons were removed the duke would respect their holdings; it might secure ducal interference in judicial disputes if lesser men tried to take their goods. Very rare are indications that the duke would exact a penalty from those who transgressed his privilege; there are five such charters for Richard II, two for Robert the Magnificent and two for William. Considering the greater number of charters for William, this small number is even more striking. Moreover, the only religious houses of Normandy concerned—Fécamp, Jumièges, Bernay, St Ouen, St Wandrille and Bayeux cathedral—were direct beneficiaries of the ducal family. Such protection was not accorded to the monasteries of other lords. If anything these charters suggest that the dukes exercised progressively diminishing powers in this respect, Richard II's charters carrying the penalties for infraction of £100 gold, Robert's of £50 gold and William's of £10 and £3. These figures may be unfair, for, whereas the earliest are fanciful, the more realistic later ones could have been enforced. However, the great majority of the documents propose only spiritual sanctions against offenders. Ducal protection might be useful, but, if it did not deter offenders, the monks would do better to seek God's help.

The real question, and the most obscure, is the nature of ducal leadership of secular society, his power to command obedience, exact services and administer his own rights. In no respect is the total absence of eleventh-century charters for secular matters more deplorable than for elucidating the crucial question of political power. After William's death his sons established in writing the ducal customs of their father's time, which may represent only the achievements of the Conqueror's own reign, but which could be derived from practices older than 1035. Yet even after the Conqueror's great government, the duke's powers remained very limited. There are only four matters which so specifically concerned the duke that offenders fell into the duke's mercy, incurring fines at his discretion to recover his favour: attacks on men coming and going to the duke's court, or within eight days of an assembly of the army; interference with merchants and pilgrims; and offences against the duke's money: matters legal, military, charitable and financial.[22]

Apart from the duke's duty to protect all honest travellers in his dominions, the third matter, taken together with the fourth, is a reminder of the importance of commerce in eleventh-century

Normandy. It was William's financial resources and his credit that made him more powerful than his contemporaries. The extent of these resources cannot now be measured and speculation about the administration of ducal revenues is hampered by the paucity of texts. The duke's monopoly of coinage seems to be a valuable right, but there are few coins of this period, and coins from Le Mans, Angers and Tours were more generally used in Normandy, if charters are any guide. William also raised a tax known as moneyage for renouncing his right to alter the value of coins every three years, but it is doubtful whether such a custom existed before 1066. It has been argued that the duke taxed the Normans directly.[23] Special officials, the *gravaringii*, collected the graverie tax, though as the tax is elsewhere called a 'viscomital aid' it may have been previously administered by more ancient officials. The duchy was also divided into financial districts for the payment of a new tax called the *focagium*, levied on those who owed no military service; not only knights and sergeants but march lands were exempted. Possibly such a tax was also a post-Conquest phenomenon.[24] More certainly, the duke derived financial advantages from the commerce of Normandy. William himself developed Caen as a port, which argues that he wished to encourage trade;[25] Rouen was already a major trading city. William's connections in Flanders and England must have assisted trade with those countries. The relative value of his different sources of income cannot be assessed. The dukes, or at least Richard II and William, had considerable reserves of cash, which implies that there was both liquid wealth in Normandy and a relatively simple means of extracting it on the duke's account.

In spite of this conclusion, the duke had no important financial office. The ducal treasurer was a person without apparent distinction; and his chamberlain, who could have managed his household expenses, figures less prominently in the records than others. Nevertheless, the choice of Ranulf de Tancarville as chamberlain is interesting, if only because his residence was at a key place for crossing the lower Seine, which might suggest that the chamberlain's office and trade had something in common. The duke's revenues from the fines paid for offences against ducal customs were apparently collected by the vicomtes, the only local government officials in the duchy. These elusive persons first appear in the eleventh century and exercised what was left of the authority of the Carolingian counts in the original local government districts. They held castles for the duke, they acted in legal business and proclaimed the duke's judgments. They may have accounted for the revenues they collected; they could have paid a fixed farm for the privilege. In William's time, it is hard to allow that they were mere ducal officers, for they behaved more like confident aristocrats and the duke never challenged their power. Only one vicomte was banished for disloyal activity: Turstin Goz, of the Hiémois, was banished for his part in the revolt of 1047; his son later became vicomte. When the vicomte of Arques was replaced in 1054, on the fall of the count, his land was acquired by the vicomte of Rouen, whose daughter's husband got the land and the office. The vicomtes of the western part of the duchy remained hereditary officials. In these circumstances, ducal control over them was inevitably limited.[26] William's effective government and his authority over such men was more likely to be the result of personal influence than dependent on established procedures. The duke could become a master of the duchy if he obtained the consent of the aristocracy to his rule.

The limitations of the duke's legal powers are also demonstrated in the clauses of the declaration of 1091 which defined his legal responsibility for attacks on houses, arson and rape. This list of cases reserved for the duke looks similar to a list of royal pleas in England reserved by Canute and, as in England,[27] such pleas could be heard by others. Whereas in England such grants of jurisdiction were theoretically authorised by the king, who thereby maintained a judicial supremacy, in Normandy the barons with such rights held their courts 'in such places where they ought to have them'.[28] The privilege was not therefore a personal one granted to the baron as a favour, but seems to have been dependent on his particular estate. No ducal grants of jurisdiction to secular lords have survived, and it is doubtful whether any written instrument of privilege was ever in fact issued. The situation may be similar to that which later prevailed in the county palatine of Chester where the earl exercised royal privileges although he had no such powers over his numerous lands in other parts of England. The Norman lords with jurisdiction enjoyed their privileges in particular places only, not for all their property. Did these privileges come to them by specific ducal concession? It seems improbable that the duke either granted or retracted specific judicial privileges, which were inherent in certain lands and could only be lost by the forfeiture of the land itself. It looks therefore as though the legal privileges of barons depended on certain estates, rather than on ducal concession.

The significance of this conclusion is borne out by the scramble for lands in the eleventh century, over which the dukes also had so little control. William himself was no better placed than others to assert his rights over transactions in land. He was often to be found exiling his lords, or imprisoning them, and taking their property. But it did not then revert to his uncontested possession. Exiles remained convinced of their rights. One man who lost his lands offered one of his confiscated estates to a monastery outside Normandy, which even persuaded William to allow and confirm the donation. Exiles frequently returned to make their peace with the duke and were restored to their possessions. There was a deep-rooted sense of the right to inherit land and the duke's interference seemed arbitrary and unjust. Men might need to submit to the duke's power, but they harboured a sense of grievance and maintained a different theory of title. There was therefore no general sense in which William was the ultimate landlord of Normandy who had the right or power to confirm every man's estate.

A basic distinction can be drawn between allodial lands and others. Herluin, the poor knight who founded the abbey of Bec, was said to have done homage to no man for his land, because his estates were his patrimony, for which he was obliged to no lord, not even the duke.[29] By contrast, however, other lands could be obtained from a lord, in return for homage and for which 'faithful service' was expected and it is convenient to call such estates fees, held by 'feudal' tenure. Clearly it ought to have been easier for lords, the duke included, to declare such fees 'forfeit', without expecting to rouse the same anger of the holder or his heirs if they were deprived of such an estate. In practice this modern theoretical difference between allodial and feudal estates was very difficult to maintain because sons naturally expected to succeed to all their fathers' property, conditional estates included, so that in time these distinctions could be forgotten.

In William's reign there was both a popular tendency to insist that all estates, however temporary and conditional, would pass in normal circumstances to the holder's natural heirs, and a ducal insistence on taking homage from his vassals so that all their lands should appear to be held from him as lord. It is a nice point whether the duke who exacted such an oath from a returned exile was in a stronger position than the vassal who recovered a confiscated estate as its hereditary claimant. Both sides could interpret the agreement in their own favour and in practice the personal characters of lord and vassal would determine who was the real gainer: in different cases the duke or the vassal might appear to concede more.

The duke was able to operate only within a very narrowly defined field, and his acts of authority, when not utterly arbitrary, have to be interpreted in the light of custom. It is said that after William Fitz Osbern's death in 1071, the Conqueror divided his lands so that the first born son inherited in Normandy, and the second in England. On the same principle, the Conqueror left his patrimony, Normandy, to his oldest son Robert and gave his Conquest, England, to Rufus. This division was in fact contested by many barons. Their reasons may have been political, rather than legal, but it is certain that Norman custom did not allow landlords to dispose of their property by wills, as was the case, for example, in England before 1066. It seems more likely that the Conqueror's division of the Fitz Osbern estate was done in accordance with customary law, rather than by an arbitrary act of will.

Some years before 1066, the Taisson lands were divided in so meticulous and complex a manner as to suggest that the members of the family followed an archaic principle of division, allowing for the different devolution of certain estates and a degree of family bargaining that left little room for ducal initiative.[30] Later, when William had become much more powerful, Ralph Taisson died leaving an infant son. The tenants of the estate (the 'barons' of the 'honour') took advantage of the lack of government to commit trespasses and damage. When the Conqueror was asked to interfere he appointed two commissioners to preside over the assembled honorial barons, who chose four of themselves to declare on oath the dispositions of the child's father before his death.[31] The case is interesting in several respects. It concerned estates granted by Ralph to the monastery of Fontenay, and typically shows the prejudice against admitting that the head of the family had power to make alienations of property beyond his own lifetime. It was this principle which made it necessary for all grants to be approved at the time by the grantor's heirs, to as many generations then born, and to be reconfirmed in successive generations. Only later did the landlaw make this cumbersome procedure superfluous by recognising the validity of permanent alienations. The case is also important for showing that in disputes it was left to the barons of the estates in question to give evidence and to make sworn statements and that the duke's function, however important, was to convene the aristocratic assembly and to declare judgment. The duke's power of interfering in land settlements was clearly limited, though in exceptional cases of confiscation he might be powerful enough to set aside the 'rights' of heirs. For most of the time, the duke did not wish to rouse needless opposition. He protected existing claims in land and allowed his barons to exercise what powers they were entitled to on each separate estate.

The problem of what privileges resided in the land is related to the one concerned with what services were required by those who made grants. Those who held allodial land by heredity owed no service. Feudal tenure should have been different: a fee was property granted on condition of service and could be forfeited, as it would lapse, if the condition was broken. It is sometimes suggested that this feudal service or condition was to supply knights for the duke's army.

Although no ducal charter for monasteries makes any mention or reserve of the ducal service owed for land, many charters show that there were military tenants on the land so granted: these tenants were ordered by the duke to serve the monks in the future. The grants show first, that such tenants could perform useful services for the monks and second, that the duke displayed no anxiety about losing the service of military men. The grants did not apparently disturb the duke's military arrangements; the duke speaks only of the monks' advantage, not his own.

Likewise, when granting land and knights to monasteries that did later owe military service the duke never indicates whether these additional grants are made to enable the monastery to discharge its existing ducal obligations, or whether the additional estates increased the obligation of the whole. The monks of St Ouen later owed fourteen knights, but in the eleventh century there were as many as seven to be found on one of its estates. Military estates could be negotiated without reference to any obligation to the duke as though the parties to the transaction were the sole persons concerned. The abbot of Holy Trinity, Rouen, gave the knight Helgo de Maisnil and his service to one of his monastery's benefactors. Who then became 'responsible' for this knight's service: the knight himself, the abbot or the new lord? If the duke had had any interest in such matters it would be natural to expect some mention of it.

Short of an explicit declaration, unwritten tradition could have been sufficient at the time, though it would inevitably elude our understanding. But the vagueness of the words used in the charters adds another difficulty. *Milites*, knights, and *equites*, horsemen, do not appear to have specific meanings, but were they therefore used interchangeably? What of their land? Was it a 'fee' given for service? William granted to Fécamp one knight and his brothers with their allod but did not allow the grant of their *beneficium;* a knight might therefore hold two different types of land—an hereditable estate and land on condition; *beneficia*, at least, would seem like recognisable fees which the duke did not allow to pass to others. Yet, on the other hand, another of William's men, Gilbert Crespin, had received from the duke the *beneficium* of Hauville by his military service. If this confirms the view that the *beneficium* implies specific military obligations, it does nothing to support the theory that the duke supervised grants of fees, for Gilbert sold it to the monks of Jumièges for 200 pounds den., two ounces of gold and a horse worth £20: clearly a very valuable estate.[32] Did the monks then acquire responsibility for the service? If not, how is it that a military estate could be passed by its temporary holder to a religious corporation? Why did the monks pay such a price for a conditional estate? How is it that the temporary holder could get such a price for his holding, as though he had become outright owner? There are no answers to these questions, but the fact that they can be raised indicates that the obligations of tenure are by no means so simple as is often assumed. Knights themselves were not all created by grants of military fees, for they could possess allodial lands over which they had rights of alienation. At the same time the word knight is used to describe those who fought whether they had landed estates or not. To be a knight was to exercise a certain profession however remunerated or of whatever social standing, so that military service was not necessarily dependent merely on land tenure.

Arguments about the eleventh century military obligation are normally based upon a general inquest into the obligations of the duchy in 1172 and another more detailed enquiry about the obligations of the bishop of Bayeux made in 1133, which admittedly incorporates some older material.[33] In order to use these returns to understand the eleventh century, Haskins, in an influential and ingenious study, argued that since the only monasteries that owed service to the duke in 1172 were those founded before 1035, the obligations for military service must have been generally established before that date, probably by duke Robert the Magnificent.[34] These returns could therefore be used to indicate the general military obligations, at the time of the Norman Conquest itself.

Before criticising this argument it is interesting to see how little it could prove, even if it were true. The number of knights whose service was owed to the duke in 1172 was less than six hundred. It is unlikely that William conducted his military campaigns in France or in England in 1066 with an army of so few men, even allowing generously for contingents of knights from other provinces or the employment of mercenaries. If the feudal service owed was so small, its value to the duke in the eleventh century must have been very slight and it would therefore be unwise to draw any conclusions about the duke's military strength in the eleventh century on the basis of these feudal returns of 1172. However, a list of ships provided by leading Normans in 1066, which includes a few details about some knights supplied, makes it seem improbable that the Conqueror obtained 'feudal' contingents even from his own men.[35] Hugh de Montfort gave sixty knights; Remigius, monk of Fécamp, twenty; Nicholas, abbot of St Ouen (William's cousin) one hundred; and Walter Giffard, another hundred. The abbot of St Ouen's contribution of one hundred knights is far in excess both of the six he owed or of the fourteen he had enfeoffed by 1172; similarly the almoner of Fécamp's twenty was double the whole monastery's assessment in 1172. William's barons shared in his enterprise according to their capacities, not to discharge a duty to a much respected lord.

Haskin's whole argument can however be criticised radically. In the first place it seems very unwise to suppose that, even if the few monasteries owing service had contracted fixed obligations before 1035, the more numerous and important services rendered by secular lords had been fixed at the same time; for if monasteries, as undying corporations, were necessarily conservative and perhaps privileged, secular society was considerably changed by family and political disturbances between 1035 and 1172, and there is no reason to believe that secular obligations became petrified in the eleventh century.

If the returns of 1172 cannot be held to reproduce faithfully the service owed more than a century earlier and must allow for subsequent developments, it can however be argued that some of the obligations are even more ancient than quotas imposed about 1035. Using the same monastic obligations as Haskins, it is possible to provide an entirely different explanation of the service owed in 1172 that seems to imply a direct link with the Carolingian military system. The purpose of this argument is not simply destructive: it attempts to explain the growth of feudal tenures in the eleventh century.

Haskins was puzzled that only two of the many monasteries founded after 1035 ever owed service to the duke. The abbey of Caen, found in 1060, later acquired the fief of Taillebois and was expected to discharge its obligation to produce one knight. Similarly, St Evroul, founded in 1050, acquired at that time the vill of Cullei already the fee of one knight, and another fee called Bocquenée, which had been an estate of the count's archer. After 1050 St Evroul owed the service of two knights, for these two specific estates. This principle provides a rational explanation of why other monasteries, those founded before 1035, owed military service. They possessed estates which owed military obligations.

It might be asked why the later monasteries never acquired these obligations. The charters make it plain that concessions of land made after 1035 frequently (presumably where necessary) excluded grants of 'fees'. There are three possible explanations for this specific exclusion. First, the monks themselves, for religious reasons in an age of conscious ecclesiastical reform, might have refused estates involving burdensome obligations. Second, the new monasteries, unlike the older ones, were generally endowed by the new aristocracy, and not by the dukes. These aristocrats, who had in some cases acquired their estates with great difficulty, would naturally be more chary than the dukes about conceding military estates to monks and preferred to keep them in their own hands or for their own men. Further, they conserved their more limited estates and proved their religious generosity by meaner grants to their monks, particularly of such property as churches and tithes that were more appropriately and with less sense of loss granted to religious bodies. Third, it is possible that duke William discouraged or prevented the grant of military estates to monasteries. This explanation is the least likely because the duke appeared to take no interest in the dispersal of the military estates of the duchy. When the monks of Saumur (an Angevin monastery) petitioned for the restoration to them of an estate in the Côtentin, which they had been given originally several generations earlier and since lost, William gladly consented, remarking with some humour that 'even if we are Normans, we still know what it is right to do and we will do it with God's help'. The estate thus surrendered included several tenants, including five free knights. Saumur did not appear in any twelfth-century list of tenants owing military service to the duke. William apparently knew what he was doing and made no reservations about surrendering military potential to an 'alien' monastery. Charters to monasteries granting land with military tenants never refer to service owed to the duke, but imply only that the military tenants should for the future perform faithful service to their new lord, the monks. The duke himself appeared not to regret or to limit such concessions.

If it were possible to explain in this way why only two monasteries founded after 1035 acquired military holdings, is it possible to explain at what point the military obligations were imposed on land? In 1172 only one monastery outside Normandy, St Denis, owed military service, of one knight, for its fee of Berneval. This land had been restored to the monks by duke Richard I in 968, renewing a grant made by his two predecessors, Rollo and William. The only probable explanation for their grant is that St Denis, favoured monastery of Frankish kings, had enjoyed this Neustrian estate before the Norman settlement itself.

The Berneval charter grants the monks absolute rights of possession to the exclusion of all public authority by count, vicomte, vicar or hundredman or other officer of judicial power. In effect therefore the monks themselves acquired this public authority: for their 'fee' they acted as 'count'.

It is just possible that here we have an explanation of those subsequent military obligations. Could all 'fees' be traced to the original counts' lands? For the monasteries this seems easy. The only monasteries owing such service before 1035 were those founded by the dukes themselves on ducal estates, together with the monastery for Holy Trinity 'du Mont' at Rouen founded by the *vicomte* of Rouen. By granting public estates to monasteries, benefactors transferred those inherent obligations to the monks. Unfortunately for the more numerous secular estates no exhaustive survey is possible. It is however interesting to be able to trace five of the ten knights owed by the bishop of Avranches to the single honour of St Philibert, which had been given to the see by bishop John. After John's death, his nephew contested this gift and was allowed for life the commendation of the five knights of the honour. This example is extremely instructive. It shows that the obligation to owe five-knights service was derived not from an assessment of service owed for an estate of certain size but for five actual knights once settled on the land. It also shows that the honour was part of the family holding of bishop John and must therefore have come to him from his father count Ralph of Ivry, brother of duke Richard II. If all the service owed by 1172 could be traced to land once in the hands of counts, it would be possible to conclude that the obligations were derived from the original comital status of the land. The dispersal of these estates among their relations and their followers in the early eleventh century would explain how and why such fees came into so many hands, giving rise from that time to the secular aristocracy.[36]

The object of this argument is not to prove that Norman feudalism was Carolingian in origin but to explain why military fees were created in lands owing a military (if not 'feudal') service in Carolingian times, probably on the lands assigned to counts, particularly in border regions. It may be strengthened by two curious but more trivial pieces of evidence. First, in the return for the bishopric of Bayeux, there are statements about the small service of ten knights owed to the duke from Bayeux for 'the king of the Franks', which can have been of only ceremonial importance in 1133, and for the discharge of which it is incredible that military fees should have been created in such large numbers in the eleventh century. To introduce 'feudalism' for obligations that could be discharged by the knights of a single estate is to turn society upside down for nothing. But if the service due to the king of Franks was a mere 'vestigial' service, which survived perhaps two centuries or more, it would be easier to allow for its anomalous position.

The other argument in favour of a Carolingian origin for the military obligations of certain estates comes from the mention of vavassor service at Bayeux and Mont St Michel. The vavassors who held fifty or sixty acres of the bishop of Bayeux freely owed service to the duke in the army where they served with horses, lances, shields and swords. Some vavassors at Nulley owed castle-guard, duty and a special aid. Some vavassors' fees are listed as owing the service of half-a-knight, others of only a quarter. What appear to be three vavassories owe one knight. There can be little doubt that these equivalents in terms of fractions of knight service represent a recent means of trying to introduce system into a great variety of tenures. There was no general scale of equivalence. In 1172 the service of one knight at Lions could be performed exceptionally by three vavassors. Local custom and private negotiation established such rules—not a ducal mandate applicable to all Normandy.

The documents of Bayeux and Mont St Michel both specifically record the service owed by vavassors but no evidence of vavassors' fees can be found in secular lords' tenancies. However, fractions of knights' service, down to very small parts, are listed; and what would the difference in practice be between one of three or four vavassors who did service as one knight, and the man owing one third or one quarter of a knight's service?

Analysis of the service owed by vavassors to Mont St Michel suggested to Navel[37] that they were performing similar service to that owed by free men in the ninth century. What is most characteristic of them is their equipment: shield and lance, but not the knight's coat of mail (*lorica*). Some vavassors of Mont St Michel guarded the Mont, and went with sword and lance with the abbot when summoned to take *nammum* or on other business and returned to their houses the same day. In the estates of Bretteville and Verson, Navel detected an original ducal domain on which tenth-century dukes had tenants serving at their court as 'sergeants', and suggested that the vavassor service was derived from these sergeanties. When these estates passed to Mont St Michel in 1015 and 1024 they had already become burdened with duties which were never again modified, thus surviving till 1172 and later.

However, most of the military service owed in the twelfth century was knight service: vavassors were only the exceptions. It must remain a mere hypothesis that vavassories were petrified examples of an older type of service which generally evolved into knight service, because it is impossible to prove any such evolution. Its usefulness as a theory is that it would explain better than an unknown and improbable act of power by the duke, how military service could have been converted into knight service. Mont St Michel received the estate of Bretteville from duke Richard II in 1015. If the vavassors there had originally been ducal officials they must have existed at Bretteville before 1015, thus surviving as free tenants or sergeants of the duke at a time when many ducal estates were already being dispersed amongst the secular barons to the duke's general disadvantage.

The duke's brothers at the same time created estates for their relations and followers, men who would swear personal oaths to them and perform whatever services, military, legal, social or administrative, that were required by their lords. It may be assumed that the counts, and their vassals after them in their turn, had a particular interest in finding well-equipped and skilled men to engage in their local rivalries, to defend their new fortifications and to attack those of others. The twelfth-century knights were distinguished from vavassors above all by their superior equipment. To support a knight it is evident that an estate had to be more valuable than that of a vavassor or serving freeman. The counts who acquired lands owing the service of three or four vavassors could easily have commuted their service in order to equip one of themselves or another man altogether to serve as a knight. The knight's fee was essentially an estate that provided revenues for the knight's upkeep. The importance of the obligations inherent in the land was that those who contributed to the cost of the knight were strictly doing

only what they had always been doing, except that their personal service was no longer obligatory. Generally speaking, men prefer to pay taxes than to go to the wars: the creation of knight's fees could be seen as a welcome release from personal duties.

Admittedly the hypothesis is very fragile. The alternative explanation as propounded by Haskins appears to rest upon firmer documentary support, but is historically unconvincing. Twelfth-century documents cannot prove that service had been fixed in the eleventh century; on the contrary they suggest that some military obligation was older still. It can only be inherently probable to allow for considerable modifications of those duties in terms of the changes detectable in early eleventh-century society. Somewhere between the ninth and the twelfth century, knights' fees were created on lands with public burdens.

This new explanation allows much greater flexibility for the development of the military system in the eleventh century than Haskins' view, which postulated a scheme of service established and enforced by the dukes between 1025 and 1035 at a time when the duke was fighting for his very survival. Slight though the evidence for social evolution in Normandy may be, it is possible to look at the estates of the bishop of Bayeux at a number of different times before 1172, and the result is far from suggesting that the military tenures had been fixed early and continued unchanged: only the obligation to serve had become attached to specific estates.

The earliest record of them comes in a memorandum of 1035–37[38] of bishop Hugh, son of Count Ralph of Ivry, which states that owing to the influence of his uncle, archbishop Robert of Rouen and some others, he had been able to recover for his church estates that had been pillaged and appropriated in the chaos of the preceding years. The list of recovered lands is remarkably long and varied. It includes lands, churches, forests, mills, enclosures and services, but there is not the slightest reference to what military service was owed from any piece of land. Some of the estates there listed can be traced in later records as owing specific military service, but it would be unwise to argue that the service must therefore have been imposed at some time between the dates of the two documents. The record of 1035–37 was not intended only to list fees; allodial land is specifically included. Yet it is also interesting that in two cases, the lands of Herbert son of

2 David and Goliath, eleventh century
British Museum, Cotton MS Tiberius C VI, f. 8v. (*see p.* 299)

Burnege and of Raoul Fichet, they are said not to include their 'allod', which suggests that the land was a fee. If this point were certain, it would suggest that the entries under land of Manerbe, of Anquetil le Roux and so on, referred to the bishop's recovery of the 'fees' of more than twenty men and their families. These fees can occasionally be traced in twelfth-century records, but this is generally impossible because the descent of the eleventh-century tenants is unknown. The description of the lands in 1035–37 as land of Anquetil, of the sons of Esscerpene proves that the personal title to the land was still quite recent, as indeed might be expected in the Norman context. As elsewhere, the names of the tenants rarely include a place-name element, for they are not tenants with ancestry or locality. If their heirs did succeed in retaining the tenancies, thus creating hereditary fees, there is still not enough evidence to suggest that the Bayeux fees were created at any one time after 1035. Odo, bishop of Bayeux, added to the fees of his church by purchasing fees from others, and by obtaining concessions of forfeited fees from his brother William.[39] Thus the Bayeux fees were still being assembled in the late eleventh century and it is hard to believe that this was not generally still the practice. The position in the twelfth-century returns is certain. Many lords owed fixed service to the duke; one, two, three, ten or more knights. In some cases, the same lords are said to owe the duke so many and to have so many more for their own service. The bishop of Bayeux owed twenty knights and had one hundred and twenty for himself. But there are no fixed ratios between these two figures. The abbot of St Ouen owed six knights but had fourteen; Robert of Curcy owed five knights and had twenty-three and a third and another quarter for himself. In the Bayeux return of 1133 the local jury swore that the bishop of Bayeux owed to the duke ten knights for the service of the king of the Franks; that ten of the bishops' knights did this service through one knight for forty days; that the bishop also owed the service of twenty knights on the Norman border for forty days, wherever the king wished (it is not clear whether the French or the English king is intended) and that five knights did this service through one. The implications of this statement are elaborated in the declarations of various tenants of the bishopric, like that of Robert of Gloucester, who held ten fees in the honour of Evrecy and owed one knight for the French king's service and two knights to the duke for border service. This proportion was said to apply in all other cases of honours of ten and five knights, even, apparently, in one case, for an honour of eight. This representative, or proportional, service was not necessarily general: it was confined to the Bayeux barony. Nor can it be related to the actual number of fees at the bishop's disposal. If the bishop owed the duke twenty knights this did not oblige him to create six times as many fees on his own lands. It is not even clear that, if the bishop owed twenty knights to the duke in 1172, this was intended to be the same obligation as that of 1133, which was that twenty knights were owed on the borders. All that the Bayeux rule represents is a custom of that particular barony. The bishop owes twenty knights and, as a special concession allows his vassals (of whom he has a particularly large number) to send a representative for a group of five or ten. By this means the same twenty are not always obliged to serve. No general argument from the special customs of Bayeux could conclude that the duke was everywhere entitled to a fifth of the total military service of the duchy. The Bayeux evidence therefore suggests that Norman feudal services had not been fixed before the Conquest, but that 'honours' were still in the process of being assembled.

In pre-conquest Normandy there were two contrasting principles to be seen. On the one hand estates with specific burdens were passing rapidly from person to person, though their obligations to service remained constant; on the other, stability was maintained by the principle of homage. Before the Conquest, William made a determined effort to obtain the homage of his own Normans, and others, and to establish a personal bond between himself and them. On the morrow of the Conquest, he was to do the same in England. It was these personal commitments that William himself insisted upon and they express what he considered to be the effective means of obtaining allegiance. Not all Normans owed homage to the duke for their family lands. Only if they lost their lands by their conduct, as for example by going to Apulia without the king's permission,[40] or by falling into the king's mercy for certain crimes, could they sometimes be reinstated on their lands on condition that they did homage to the duke. Similarly, William could take homage from other men living outside the duchy, and not owning Norman land, who by the act of homage placed their goods at the duke's service, and who therefore homage placed their goods at the duke's service, and who therefore agreed to 'hold' their lands of the duke. When the count of Maine placed his hands in the duke's and became his man, he received back from the duke all his property. When the earl of Wessex became the duke's vassal, he too henceforward held his lands in England, which he had received from others, for the duke's service.[41] The duke did not impose new conditions on the land itself; he expected that all the services and advantages of the holdings would be put at his disposal; this was what vassalage implied, and this was its value to the duke. William was successful in obtaining the homage of many great men, but he did this by virtue of his personal power and this personal touch made his government of Normandy exceptionally strong. But of ducal institutions evolved over a long period the sources authorise us to think very little. The province is in a ferment; it is up to the individual ruler to make it serve authority.

3 The Conquest

William the Conqueror

The Conqueror emerged as leader of the Normans when at the age of twenty (up to which time he had shown no special aptitude for government) he desperately sought the help of King Henry I of France against his cousin, Guy of Burgundy, count of Brionne, and the two ducal vicomtes of the Côtentin and the Bessin who planned to make Guy duke. Henry intervened to save the weaker party and thereby keep Normandy weak, but the effect of the victory at Val ès Dunes (1047) was to show William the steep path to success. Its immediate effects simply prevented his complete eclipse, for it was followed by no striking improvement of the duke's position. But the unbridled anarchy of the duchy was now reined in by the new ruler, an excellent cavalier.

Guy of Burgundy was able to hold out for three years against William in his castle at Brionne on the Risle, the place of crossing from Rouen into Lower Normandy. Only one *vicomte* lost his office: William preferred to reconcile the others to himself and their offices passed to their sons.

Over the next twenty years William did not attempt to recover old ducal rights and property. At the most, his irreconcilable enemies, or those he refused for some reason to trust, were slowly eliminated. In particular, his uncles, William, count of Arques, and Mauger, archbishop of Rouen, who probably held Upper Normandy against him even after Val ès Dunes, were both driven out in 1055. William found a mild monk to become archbishop, thus breaking the see's long association with aristocratic families, and Arques was entrusted to a castellan. At the same time William used the old methods to encourage his own supporters: the Giffards and Warennes acquired the vacant lands and prospered in Upper Normandy. Similarly, in Lower Normandy, William drove his father's cousin out of the county of Mortain, but gave it to his own half-brother Robert, whose brother Odo became bishop of Bayeux, the most valuable domain of Lower Normandy. William did not try to organise a direct ducal administration: his vicomtes in the Bessin, the Côtentin and the Avranchin were members of local families whose position became stronger and more independent. The Taissons who had deserted to him at Val ès Dunes continued to enjoy lands they had acquired by dubious title.

The most striking change of William's government was his greater interest in Lower than in Upper Normandy, where his ancestors had been most at home. There are several reasons for this. It was in Lower Normandy that the aristocratic families had presumably enjoyed most independence: William's victory at Val ès Dunes, near Caen, was a demonstration of his power where it was most needed. William's capacity to dominate in Lower Normandy was one of the most striking reasons for his later success. It was not brought about by general redistribution of land or office; it was a personal power to command the loyalty of the powerful. William's residence in Lower Normandy was transferred from Falaise, his birthplace, to Caen, which he encouraged as a town and as a port.[1] In Caen, William built the two monasteries that were commanded by the papacy to cover the disobedience of his marriage, and the city was surrounded with a town wall about 1058. Rouen, the ducal capital, had older religious corporations and greater economic prosperity, but was less attractive to William. Maybe William already saw that Caen would supply the base that he needed for gathering the men and resources of Lower Normandy for the day when he would launch across the Channel.

The other reason why the lords of Lower Normandy were so important to William was the general situation of northern France in his reign.[2] In the tenth century, the alliance with the Capetians had naturally made the route between Rouen and Paris most important.

When king Robert II died in 1031 French royal power crumbled away, just as the ducal power was disintegrating in Normandy. Lesser lords were throwing up earthworks with timber defences to defend their 'castle' against their nominal rulers, who had found no answer to this military innovation. The king of France was defied in his own dominions and the little help given to William by Henry I in 1047 was noticeable only because the duke was himself in extreme need. In this age of disintegrating public authority only one ruler, the count of Anjou, notably improved his position. Castle-building was his speciality. When, after Val ès Dunes, Henry I perceived that William was becoming the effective ruler of Normandy, there was nothing the king could do himself to limit that power; but, by using the count of Anjou, Henry I hoped to keep William weak and in 1051 Angevins occupied Maine, the county between Caen and Angers. On the southern march of Normandy, the duke had little influence. The region was dominated by the family of Bellême, who had built their castle at a great crossroads and created their principality from land held of different lords. Bellême was a royal fief, Alençon was held from the duke of Normandy and Domfront came to them from the count of Maine. Members of the family held the bishoprics of Séez and Le Mans. When the Angevins occupied Maine, the Bellêmes were alarmed for their family interests. At this point William allowed, or encouraged, his supporter Roger de Montgomery to marry Mabel, the heiress of Bellême, and he himself occupied the castle at Domfront. The Normans' southern frontier became the major interest of ducal politics between 1051 and 1064: it was this that gave Lower Normandy its significance.

Henry I as king at Paris feared a powerful duke at Rouen. Increasing Angevin strength was less of a danger to the king at Paris, because another royal vassal, the count of Blois, lay between the king of France and the count of Anjou. The manoeuvrings of the 1050s involved the rulers of Normandy, Anjou, Blois and France in rivalries that outlived them, growing more intricate, until, under king Stephen, England itself became the ultimate goal of their ambitions. Anjou was the most active of Norman enemies, but it was Henry I who provided the incentive and the persistence. Having, till 1053, encouraged William, count of Arques, in his rebellion against William, in 1054 the king's army advanced towards Evreux, only to be beaten back at Mortemer. This defeat entailed the collapse of William of Arques. Henry joined an Angevin invasion of Normandy in 1057, but the aggressors were defeated at Varaville. The next year, William took the initiative and went to the Chartrain to fight Henry I. He began to intrigue in Maine itself, offering his heir, Robert, as a husband to the daughter and heiress of Geoffrey de Mayenne. Not until after the deaths of Henry and Geoffrey of Anjou in 1060 was William able to advance decisively into Maine where by 1064 he was master of Le Mans.

William's success made him the natural successor to Angevin military leadership in northern France, for the new Capetian king, Philip I, was a mere child in the care of his uncle Baldwin, William's own father-in-law. All lords and soldiers eager to accept the service of the most successful soldier of the decade naturally turned to William. No Norman duke had previously attained a great military reputation, and his own men, roused by his leadership as duke in a successful war, supported further campaigns against Brittany where the duke had family claims to enforce. William's military ambitions in Maine, Brittany or England sprang naturally out of his hold on the affections and the interest of the lords of Lower Normandy; his previous successes filled them with confidence in his leadership and made them eager to embark on his service. William's control over his men was the discipline of a successful general. In the 1050s he beat down his enemies; in the 1060s he conquered. As long as his success continued he remained master; but much later, when his son Robert contested his single authority, his barons wavered in their loyalty. Later dukes of Normandy also found that they could expect no loyalty unless they offered the continual rewards of new conquests.

William is aptly called the Conqueror, not for one isolated success but because the secret of his success lay in his conquests. William was also a statesman of exceptional ability because he knew how to wait until the time was ripe for action. His first moves towards England and Maine were both made in 1051; for thirteen or more years he did not try to force his policies. In an age when actions were often ill-considered, whimsical or petulant, those of William bear the stamp of a man who assessed his own capacities confidently but never underestimated his enemies.

William's greatest project was to acquire England. In 1051, he was recognised as the Confessor's heir; from then until 1066, when the Confessor finally died, William kept English hostages in Normandy as a stake in the future. He could do no more during most of this time than wait for the Confessor's death. As early as 1049 he was contemplating a marriage with the count of Flanders' daughter.[3] Leo IX, the pope, possibly acting to please the emperor Henry III against whom the count was fighting, condemned the proposed marriage, which took place only some years later. In 1049, Edward the Confessor himself was in alliance with the emperor and he too may have opposed the match, either to please himself or the Godwinsons. By 1051, when the king decided to recognise William as his heir, William had already offended the king of France by negotiating with the emperor on his own account, possibly in order to overcome imperial opposition to his marriage. It was at this time that the king began to use the count of Anjou against William, who enjoyed the favour of north European rulers, England, Flanders and the empire. The exact date of his Flemish marriage is, surprisingly, not known. It might have been celebrated by 1051 by which time he had the support of both the English and the German kings, and it was certainly before 1055, when the papacy first began to modify its attitude to the Normans. William's determination to push ahead with the marriage in spite of unreconciled papal opposition suggests that the most likely time was after the emperor's objections had been removed, but before he had persuaded Leo IX to withdraw his objections. Since Leo IX was a prisoner of the Normans in southern Italy between 1053 and 1054, he would have been either out of the emperor's diplomatic reach or not amenable to favouring Normans.

In spite of Mathilda of Flanders' relationship to the king of France, the marriage did nothing to close the breach between the king and the duke until after the death of Henry I, when her father Baldwin V, regent for Philip I, reconciled his nephew to his son-in-law. Whatever the virtue of the marriage for improving relations with France, its chief political value was that it offered additional facilities for a future descent on England itself. It was a marriage with a purpose, for William braved papal anathema to conclude it and had to engage in elaborate diplomacy until 1059 for release from papal censure. In 1055, the papacy had relented (under Victor II, another imperial pope), to the point of sending a legate to witness the deposition of archbishop Mauger. The full reconciliation was only achieved in 1059 when Lanfranc, the prior of Bec, went to Rome for the duke and negotiated a penance for his disobedience: the construction of two religious houses at Caen. In the same year, Nicholas II was reconciled to the papacy's former Norman enemies in southern Italy itself. William valued the new papal alliance. When Lanfranc's old pupil became pope Alexander II in 1061 the relationship acquired a personal warmth and it is not surprising that William appealed to Alexander for a blessing on his English project or that Alexander should grant a papal banner to the duke of his Norman allies.

William's own great lords had little interest in William's schemes or foreign policy. The most energetic and able were powerful in the marches and enjoyed their campaigning against Brittany, Anjou and the king of France more than hazardous prospects across the sea. William also engaged in these campaigns, either for their immediate value in keeping his enemies at bay, or because he realised that regular campaigns and steady successes were the best means of keeping his Normans happy at his bidding. William's political calculation may be exaggerated. Like Bismarck, his success created the legend that he foresaw the mistakes and stupidities of his enemies. To his chaplain, William of Poitiers, the duke appeared very different. William's uprightness is emphasised, as might be expected. His concern for religion may even be overdrawn: his respect for the pope did not prevent him marrying whom he chose. More precise indications of his moral attitude can be found in two matters to which the chaplain often returns. First, his respect for oaths. This was the general virtue of a man of honour, but William was particularly sensitive to the obligations of oaths. He even regretted the hostility of the king of France because it made it difficult for him to render his duty to the king. To his own advantage, however, were the oaths sworn to him by the ruler of Maine and Harold of Wessex, whose perjury was their chief offence. Second, his chaplain again and again admires his clemency. Rebels are pardoned; exiles restored to their lands; criminals mutilated rather than killed. To some, this may seem weakness; to others, self-confidence. It was a virtue in William that he could keep his dangerous enemies in exile or in prison without scruple, but knew how to afford magnanimity: this was a rare and clever political gift.

William was also a man of attractive character. The chaplain's account of his youthful rashness may seem like conventional praise of the brave soldier, but the instances he gives are too circumstantial. William engaged in personal battles and enjoyed slipping away with a few men to try his skill in skirmishes. His challenging Harold to a single duel, instead of battle, before Hastings is not mere bravado but characteristic. He was contrasted to the great general Julius Caesar, because as a knight he fought with his own sword in battle. William saved the day at Hastings by his personal interventions: taking off his helmet to persuade his fleeing cavalry that he was still alive and fighting excitedly himself, even on foot when his mounts were killed beneath him. His enthusiasm for warfare was no mere youthful trait. In his late thirties at Hastings he showed the same zest. William's other military skill was his inventiveness: he was not a mere sabre-rattler. The battle of Hastings presented unexpected difficulties for Norman campaigners trained for cavalry battles in the plain. Harold on the hill fighting on foot baffled the attack. Cavalry gave William no immediate success. It was William's tireless generalship that pushed his forces again and again back into the day-long battle. In Normandy, when his army came up against the more usual problem of how to take impregnable castles, William found engines of war or ruses for breaking resistance. Several times he is credited with finding a way to set fire to the castle and to take it by cunning. Lastly, William's good humour is his most attractive quality. On the great expedition, the duke's ship appeared, at dawn, to be all alone in the ocean, but William, by no means downcast, enjoyed a gay breakfast, washed down with spiced wine. When he donned his armour before Hastings it fell off on his left side, a bad omen;[4] William laughed it off and said he cared nothing for old wives' tales. His gaiety never deserted him. He pretended to stab the hand of the abbot of Holy Trinity, Rouen, when granting him a charter, so that by this memorable episode the gift should never be forgotten. On campaign, when he went out to explore the Sussex countryside, he was obliged to return on foot because the narrow and overgrown paths made the horses useless. The reconnaissance party got so hot that they took off their metal *lorica*. The duke carried not only his own but also that of his greatest companion, William Fitz Osbern, who was too tired. William enjoyed the escapade hugely and laughed about it. Of great physical size, William was in every way a man to impress both laymen and churchmen. Edward the Confessor chose as his heir, not merely a distant relation, but one of the most remarkable soldiers of the time.

The Great Gamble

The Godwinsons who offered hostages to William as a guarantee that they would respect his claims to the throne examined the future with some gloom. After Godwin's death, Harold seems to have decided to invite another of the Confessor's relations, this time on the father's side, to return to England from his exile in Hungary.[5] Son of Edmund Ironside, Edward, who had lived abroad for forty years without apparent contact with his native country, brought with him his three children, Edgar, Margaret and Christina, but died in England in mysterious circumstances before he could meet his kinsman. No formal promises could have been made to him, though it may be assumed that had he lived he would have been presented to the great lords as the Confessor's heir and received their oaths of acceptance. His young son, Edgar 'the Aetheling', was probably too young to succeed to his father's expectations. He had no following in England and his vague connections with the imperial German family, through his mother, were not sufficient to give him valuable continental friends. The whole episode is both romantic and sinister. Harold probably played the leading role in negotiating this return, and had Edward lived, Harold might have expected to manipulate him as a puppet as his father Godwin had managed previous kings. Harold made no move to secure the Confessor's formal recognition of the Aetheling as his heir, however young. Presumably Harold watched the situation abroad with some alarm, as he saw the pope reconciled to the Normans; William's chief enemies, the king of France and the count of Anjou, die; and William successfully occupy the county of Maine.

Though the Confessor appeared to lose interest in politics and in

William after 1052, Harold's power did not grow noticeably in the Confessor's last decade. Harold tried to expand the influence of his family by creating earldoms for his brothers in East Anglia and around London. The earls of Mercia were exiled, but they could not be kept out. The Welsh gave Harold the opportunity to make a brave campaign that proved his own military skill. But the family was not popular. Tostig who became earl of Northumbria provoked a rising against himself in the autumn of 1065 and the province may have been restless earlier. Probably in 1064, before either the Northumbrian or Welsh problems engaged his full attention, Harold went to Normandy to bargain with William. According to the Bayeux Tapestry and William of Poitiers, Harold set out on the Confessor's instructions and by going at all he put himself in William's power.[6] Possibly by a mishap he landed in Ponthieu and had to be rescued by William from the count of Ponthieu's prison; but his feelings of gratitude were complicated by further obligations, when he joined William's Breton campaign and accepted arms and armour from the duke. He took a solemn oath of fidelity to his lord, as was customary, but also promised to become William's advocate at the court of the Confessor and to do all he could by his counsel and his riches to obtain the English throne for the duke after the king's death. In the meantime he promised to the duke to surrender, and provision, the castle of Dover, which he himself had fortified, and other castles in England.[7] Harold then returned to England with his nephew Hakon, one of the hostages of 1052.

Harold must have decided to accept the succession of William as inevitable and intended to make his peace with him as a safeguard of his own future. William may have used unfair methods of persuasion, but if Harold did not put himself willingly at the duke's mercy he must have allowed himself to be put in a false position, for Harold was not so naïve as to have made an oath, not suspecting the presence of hidden relics, as later romancers have pretended. It is impossible to explain why Harold was in Normandy at all if he did not set out on the Channel deliberately.

If Harold, however, deliberately accepted some commitment to William in 1064, it remains to explain why, when Edward died in January 1066, Harold accepted the crown within twenty-four hours or so of the king's death. It is alleged that the Confessor advised this.

This was certainly the story that Harold put about and it was known and criticised in Normandy. The haste of Harold's coronation shows that he had doubts about whether he would have got the crown had he delayed. He apparently placated the Mercians by marrying the earl's sister and almost his first recorded action was to hasten north to treat with the Northumbrians. The other earls may have been very uneasy about his assumption of the crown, and Harold wanted no exhibition of indecisive consultations, such as in fact occurred after his own death. He took the crown in haste because he could not rely on getting it by other means. Had the Confessor's nomination been a sufficient justification for his kingship, Harold need not have been in such a hurry. Nor was Harold obliged to accept the nomination, if he preferred to accept the consequences of his oath to William. Harold simply went back on his word. We do not know whether this was because he discovered on his return that the English lords would not have William at any price and preferred to fight to the last man against him; we do not know whether his own Welsh campaign of 1065 had given him confidence enough to resist Norman troops which he had seen in battle and perhaps learned to despise; the most probable, and even creditable, motive that Harold had for taking the crown in January 1066, was that he could not resist the temptation when the time came. The throne was within his reach; caution and honour looked like cowardice. Hastily, unlike the Confessor, Harold hurried on the coronation before he could reflect again. He was defended, rather inconsequentially, against charges that he was precipitous and rash.[8] He always took decisions promptly and acted with vigour; he did not waste time with indecision. As soon as he heard of the arrival of his enemies, he marched against them with determination. He pursued glory and despised the safe, mediocre role.

When William heard of the usurpation he sent an embassy to remonstrate with Harold. It soon became clear that the crowned king would not cede without a fight: the coronation made him more formidable than he had been as earl of Wessex. William had to take counsel about how his campaign could be conducted across the sea. Perhaps in order to magnify the exploit, William of Poitiers represents many of the Normans as being opposed to such a risky enterprise. The attitude of the Normans is interesting. William had no power to command their services; what military forces they owed to him could not be transferred abroad by mere ducal whim, and they would anyway have been far too few for seizing England from Harold.[9] The duke needed so many men for this expedition that the Normans provided far fewer men than he needed. William's cause was therefore really dependent on his own reputation which caused men from Poitou, Burgundy, Brittany and Flanders, as well as further off, to swell the ranks of his army. Preparations for assembling all these men and negotiating with foreign rulers, the kings of Germany and Denmark and the count of Flanders, occupied many months. In the meantime William coaxed his great lords into sharing in the enterprise and it is clear from a list of naval contingents that the duke received generous support, not perhaps out of duty, but out of shrewd calculation that a bigger share in the investment would pay bigger dividends. The most difficult problem was certainly the provision of ships to transport the army and its supplies and its horses across the channel. Ships had to be specially constructed and the great lords who had maritime interests contributed considerable numbers of vessels.[10] The duke's special protection of the city of Caen and the development of its port was presumably rewarded by generous cooperation in the scheme; the shippers of Rouen with its long-standing commercial connections with England must also have helped.

The fleet originally assembled in the port of Dives, conveniently for the Normans of Lower Normandy. Harold expected the arrival of the fleet from that region and kept his own navy in the vicinity of the Isle of Wight from May to September. When was William's fleet ready to sail? It was certainly ready by August, if not earlier, but contrary winds confined it to port for a month. Harold's look-outs and defences, both at sea and on the south coast, dissuaded William from aiming at Southampton and Winchester, as the Confessor had done in 1035. When it sailed therefore it crept up the Norman coast, gathering contingents of men and ships from Upper Normandy to swell the numbers. William tarried at Fécamp at this time, and monks of Fécamp kept his force company. Somehow the great army was kept together and the cautious advance to St Valéry-sur-Somme in August and September created the illusion of activity and eased the problem of supplies. William then b cooped up again at St Valéry and had to organise a special religious procession to secure the wind he needed. Though William must have known that Harold had dispersed his naval force on 8 September, he could take no advantage of this until the night of the 28th–29th when the fleet finally set sail. By this time he would have known that Harold had gone north. So, although Harold had been expecting an attack from Normandy throughout the summer and had summoned his forces to oppose it, by the time the fleet arrived, the men were able to land without opposition.

The reasons for this defencelessness are obscure.[11] The *Anglo-Saxon Chronicle* says that Harold's force ran out of provisions on 8 September and had to be disbanded and that the ships were withdrawn to London. This may be the result of Harold's inferiority to William as a quartermaster, but it must be remembered that the force which was dispersed was a 'home-guard' for beating off landing parties and that by September its services were more important for the harvest. Harold's own army was still mobilised after 8 September, as William's was, and was indeed on its way north within a few days. It also seems likely that the withdrawal of the English fleet from the Channel to London was connected with Harold's fear of a Scandinavian attack in the Thames. This was a more serious threat than the belated arrival of William's force somewhere in Sussex, which by the beginning of September, had become its most obvious place of landing.

The Scandinavian force under the king of Norway, Harold Hardrada, arrived unexpectedly. Harold's preparations in the south show that it was the Normans not the Norwegians that he had been waiting for. Since May, his own brother Tostig had been trying to break into England, trying various points, the Isle of Wight, Sandwich and Yorkshire. Rebuffed, he had taken refuge in Scotland, where he had joined the Norwegians who had landed in Orkney. The news of this conjunction of his enemies must have reached Harold in early September and this news, had it come soon enough, would have been the best explanation for ordering new dispositions for the fleet. Hardrada's invasion was not expected in England, but had Tostig and William known of the Norwegians' preparations and planned accordingly? It was later alleged that Tostig, who like William, had the count of Flanders as a father-in-law, went from his

Flemish exile to Normandy in the spring of 1066 and urged the duke to attack his brother Harold. William was also in touch with the Danes, and could have learned of Norwegian preparations from them. Were the two invasions concerted? Did William know what was afoot and deliberately hold back his fleet until news came of the Norwegians' landing and Harold's departure to fight them? Such planning would be too perfect to be credible but, as things turned out, William's luck, if it was not planned, proved equally fantastic.

Harold must have decided by 8 September to dispose his picked army for dealing with the Norwegians wherever they arrived. The army of the northern earls, Edwin and Morcar, was also on the lookout for the force but Harold did not wait to see whether they would be able to hold the enemy before setting out himself as soon as the invasion in the Humber was reported. Though the earls would fight for their own earldoms against the exiled Tostig, Harold must have been doubtful both of their military strength and their willingness to remain loyal to his government. When Harold arrived in Yorkshire he found that the northern earls had been defeated and that they had negotiated with the victors, on whom he fell with fury and surprise at Stamford Bridge on 25 September. They were annihilated and a mere handful returned home. Four days later William landed at Pevensey; it must have been at least a week after the battle of Stamford Bridge that Harold heard of the new invasion and he was still in Yorkshire. For more than two weeks, therefore, William lived off the countryside waiting for Harold to arrive.

William's caution may seem surprising; why did he not take advantage of Harold's absence to advance on London, two days' march away, and seize the capital? If he feared to lose contact with his ships and his escape route to Normandy, Harold's 'carelessness' in allowing him to enter the country unopposed will seem less culpable. William could not risk anything dangerous to Harold's authority until Harold's disciplined army had been met and defeated, and it was obvious that both sides wanted and expected a pitched battle, to settle the dispute. During the summer Harold might have feared a forced coronation at Winchester, followed by a long campaign in southern England. As autumn approached, it was clear that, if William still risked a crossing, he would be committed to fighting once and for all. In one sense it was better for Harold to let him into the country where he could be dealt with decisively, rather than encourage him to dodge, like Tostig, from place to place.

In Harold's absence in the north, the local levies could not seriously be expected to prevent the landing of such a great force when the navy itself was in the Thames. Harold's watches were, however, obviously very efficient and as he was informed as rapidly as possible of the landing there is no reason to doubt that he had reliable information about the size and equipment of the force. William, on the other hand, may have had to wait longer to know which of the two Harolds from the north would descend to challenge his entry.

Harold has always been given credit for the speed and efficiency with which he marched against the Norwegians, defeated them and returned to deal with William. His speed has even been held against him. He reached London so quickly from York that he left troops behind him and with scarcely a pause dashed down to Sussex, before his army was ready, to surprise William. Harold, however, certainly waited several days in London before setting out again and, if his troops could travel north and fall immediately on the Norwegians and defeat them, there could have been nothing optimistic about calculating that, after a two days' journey south, they would be equally capable of defeating William.

The battle of Hastings has become a battle of such significance that its preliminaries and its course have been studied as exhaustively as its consequences.[12] Unfortunately there have been far too many people who think that they could have advised Harold better how to prepare and command his men, in circumstances of which they know infinitely less than Harold himself. All kinds of argument are used. Harold's cause was weaker because of his perjury and moral lapses; his soldiers were tired after their foot-slog from London; they spent the night carousing instead of in prayer; they were armed with mere bill-hooks or stones, desperately used against horsemen and archers; he should have waited for reinforcements; his impetuosity was caused by his concern to defend his own manors which the Conqueror had been devastating for over two weeks. His critics often convict him on mere speculation, by forced interpretations, by using legendary evidence—all in order to explain away the most famous English defeat in the most important battle ever fought on English soil. Harold must have been at fault in some tactical particular; hence the need to find it. Other writers believe that the enterprise is pointless. The inferior English military system was destroyed inevitably by the forces of cavalry from the 'advanced' continent. Few writers agree with William of Poiters that Harold's defeat was the consequence of his own pride. If he had never become king, he would never have been defeated and England would never have been conquered.

The controversy about the Hastings campaign might suggest that little is actually known about it. For a medieval battle, it is, however, exceptionally well recorded, on both sides. The positions of the two commanders have been traced; the course of the battle has been reconstructed by many writers with some plausibility; it is known that it was fought between 9 a.m. and dusk on Saturday 14 October. Every piece of evidence confirms that it was a truly heroic encounter between great captains, armies that were well-matched in size, skill and courage and that differences of equipment were not in themselves very significant. Harold had at least as many men, if not far more, than William. Edwin and Morcar's army was in no position to fight again that year and the commanders may have been unwilling to fight for Harold in the south. Harold could therefore expect to gain nothing by waiting longer. It is said that he should have waited and lured William into England or starved out his army or cut off his navy (for Harold's ships were redeployed in October). Such tactics are incredible. Harold was impetuous and his swiftness had been his great asset at Stamford Bridge. He was in his own country and his troops were more numerous than William's. He certainly knew the numbers of both armies better than we do. It was not honourable nor politically wise, nor in character, for the king to allow his avowed enemy to continue to occupy any part of England against him. He had dashed north to defend his reputation in Yorkshire; he did the same in Sussex for no better reason than that this was the duty of his office.

His plan was to arrive unexpectedly and attack William at Hastings and he summoned the shire levies to join his main army on Caldbec Hill ready to attack. When William learned of the troop movements, he advanced unexpectedly early in the morning, but he still did not catch Harold unprepared. Harold was put on the defensive but he took up a strong position on a hill so that William's chief arm, the cavalry, was at a disadvantage. Though the horses had nevertheless to charge up-hill for want of any other tactic, they were soon wearied and made little impression against the shield wall of Harold's finest soldiers, standing side by side and carving up their assailant with blows from their great axes. The cavalry that retired disheartened from the fray encouraged the shire levies to pursuit and only William's own intervention with his cavalry, presumably at the foot of the hill and on level ground, succeeded in restoring the courage of the van. Surrounding the English pursuers, the Normans cut them off from the main army. These tactics were repeated time and time again, not because the cavalry was disciplined enough to plan feigned retreat, as blushing campaigners might have claimed later, but because the English defence did not crumble as expected and succeeded in repelling the cavalry. Though the Norman archers were not particularly effective (for the English had few archers and the attack was held up for want of arrows) it was an arrow that killed Harold—at what stage in the fight is not certain. Dusk fell; the king was known to be dead, but the defence, though weakened, fought on and continued to skirmish into the night. As far as the personal contest was concerned the death of Harold gave William a clear victory and the retreat of the surviving English left the Normans in possession of the battlefield. The need for William's personal participation, the great length of the combat and the unfeigned admiration of Norman sources for their English enemies, leave no doubt that Hastings was no walk-over for the Normans, and no discredit to the English. It was a hard-fought battle, the Normans had won it and Harold was killed. What would happen next?

Keeping close to his fleet, William advanced round the coast from Hastings to Romney, Dover and Canterbury before striking towards London. His army fell sick with dysentery and he himself was affected. The English hardly resisted his advance: their leaders were uncertain what to do. William's object had been to become king. He had killed Harold. If he was not to be recognised as the Confessor's successor, he had a right to expect another candidate to step forward with an army to challenge him. Some Englishmen favoured the choice of Edgar the Atheling; Edwin and Morcar were in favour of themselves. For more than two months, their irresolution left William without a definite goal and enemy. He made a great circuit and took Winchester, but it was at London that the decision to accept William had to be made and William had to bide his time. He could see that no one seemed capable like Harold or the Godwinsons of rallying the English. There was no man of the royal kin to lead soldiers into battle or unite the divided earls. It is doubtful if any effective English army could be put into the field to dispute William's claim: the victorious army of Stamford Bridge had fought to the death at Hastings. Only a force drawn from a range of sources comparable to William's mixed continental army could be a match for it. Harold's isolation from the continent left England without allies. The English leaders faced the stark consequences of their own position and they treated with the Conqueror.

Part Two

The Normans in England

4 The Norman Settlement

The King

Archbishop Eldred of York crowned the Conqueror in Westminster Abbey on Christmas Day 1066, with a ritual of great splendour and meaning.[1] The King was led to the altar, where he prostrated himself while the *Te Deum* was sung; then he rose to be chosen king by the bishops and people present, and made three promises in a clear voice.[2] He took God to witness that he would give peace to the church and people; forbid all rapacity and iniquity; give equity and mercy to his people. At this point the archbishop poured over his head the chrism that 'flowed into his inner being and penetrated his inmost heart'. This anointing was the most important and ancient part of the ceremony; it impressed upon him as a layman an indelible mark of his consecration as a saint: to mediate between God and man. No ceremony of comparable dignity was known in the church; nearest to it for solemnity was the consecration of a bishop. Contemporaries, convinced of the sacred trust conferred, often compared the role of the king and the bishop, but had no doubt about the king's superiority, for legends grew up that the oil used in the ceremony had a heavenly origin. Only once anointed did the king receive in turn a ring for his finger, a sword at his side, a crown on his head and sceptre and rod into both hands. Resplendent with royal insignia, the king was led to the throne where he was acclaimed by his people and mass was celebrated. The English king, by a privilege otherwise reserved for Eastern and Western emperors, stepped into the sanctuary, where only God's chosen Ministers might stand, to offer bread and wine for his own communion.

At the end of the coronation ceremony, the bishop normally recited an admonition which referred to the fact that the king's father had recommended him as his successor. William, likewise, could claim the nomination of his kinsman, the Confessor. The office was also said to be transmittable to his heirs: the crowned king had the disposal of the crown. Harold had claimed it by virtue of the Confessor's authority to bequeath it, even to one not of royal kin. What difference was there in William's kingship? Was he a king in the old tradition or not? In the ceremony of Christmas 1066, at least one new element was added to the ceremony. The question to the people had to be put twice, once to the English and once to the French: 'Do you consent that he be crowned as your Lord?' The religious ceremony assigned a place for the royal election, but in England this had become a mere formality; by the time the king came to church, the recognition of his claim had already been made. Possibly the emphasis on the public acclamation of William came from its importance in the Frankish ceremony, used for Philip I in 1059, though the Frankish coronation rite had been borrowed from England. The double question established the real difference in William's kingship: he was king not only of the English but of the Normans as well.

As king of the English, William had been recognised at Berkhamsted by the chief Englishmen and had promised, as in the coronation, to give peace, and justice and repress wickedness. According to William of Poitiers, the king was not immediately anxious to be crowned. The coronation ceremony did not need to take place immediately. The Confessor had waited several months and Harold had only been in a hurry, in order to present men with an anointed king rather than a perjured usurper. William offered three reasons for delaying the ceremony: the confused situation of the country where rebels still lurked to disturb the tranquillity of the kingdom; his wish to be crowned at the same time as his wife, Mathilda, who was then still in Normandy; the need to tread warily as he neared the summit of his ambitions. This passage in William of Poitiers is remarkable: did William disclaim his anxiety to become a king to see what his Normans thought of it all? His decision was made for him by the army. William of Poitiers may not have seen into the inner workings of the king's mind, but, if the Normans were as eager as William to make him king, it is odd that no Norman should have stepped forward to urge the desirability of immediate coronation. It was left to Aimeri, vicomte of Thouars from Aquitaine, to dispel William's doubts. He denied that knights were normally drawn into such decision-making and claimed that all William's men wanted him to be crowned without more palaver. The wisest and the best men, however, the chaplain comments, by no means would have desired his elevation as monarch, had they not seen his suitability and expected to gain for themselves greater advantage and honours. The two groups of his subjects could not be more contrasted: the English submissive to his power, requiring solemn promises before God as guarantee; the French consenting proudly to their leader's elevation in the expectation of what they would get out of it.

From the beginning William tried to be faithful to the English trust in him. He took the allegiance of Englishmen, and with his Norman understanding of homage he granted back their lands to be held of him; he promised that the men of London should have all the privileges and rights of their fathers; he issued orders for his soldiers to prevent brigandage and tried to keep his knights out of taverns and brothels: Normans, to their surprise, got no better terms than other, despised, Frenchmen like Bretons. Throughout his reign William tried to be loyal to his promises. The impartial Englishman who summed up his career and set down both the good and the evil about him,[3] recognised that he stood comparison with his English predecessors. He was a man of great wisdom and power who surpassed in honour and in strength all those who had gone before him. He kept good order in the land for 'he was so stern and relentless a man that no one dared to do aught against his will'. He was kind to those who loved God. He even tried to learn the English language to deal directly with his subjects but in his late thirties he was too old and too busy.[4] In other ways too, the habits of a lifetime could not simply be given up by an act of will. Considering his disturbed boyhood, his military training, his experience of government in Normandy and his position in England as Conqueror, William did wonders in preserving his English inheritance and persuading the Frenchmen to be absorbed by English institutions.

The Norman kingship was symbolised in the crown. The Conqueror developed the English custom of wearing his crown in leading cities of southern England on the greatest feast days of the church.[5] As Christ's vicar he shone before his subjects as the representative of the Incarnation, Resurrection and Descent of the Holy Spirit. For these occasions William wore an arched crown of imperial type, hung with twelve pearls, which a Greek craftsman made for him. His predecessor's great building at Westminster became the special seat of kingly majesty, and the king had to make extra provision so that the monks could entertain the great retinues which descended on them for these state occasions.[6] His kingship was unrivalled anywhere nearer than Constantinople. The kings of France and Germany were children at his accession. Before he died, the German king had split Germany and Italy by his quarrel with the pope; even at Constantinople, the Roman empire in the east had been buffeted, by both the Turks in Asia Minor and the Normans in the Balkans. But it was of Constantinople that William and his people thought when he boasted in Normandy in 1067: now I have become *basileus*.[7]

Did William keep up his intention of ruling in the English tradition? He had every motive to do so. His success would depend on the degree to which he could gain English loyalty in order to become less dependent on his French military forces. His immediate policy was not to antagonise the irresolute Englishmen who accepted him at Berkhamsted. He had all the lands of the Godwinsons and the men slain, in exile or condemned for standing against him in battle, to distribute to his followers. He had no need to be vindictive to reward the faithful. Twenty years after his coronation, William could have learned from Domesday book that there were only two major landowners left in England of original English descent. How had his policy failed? The English did not continue to acquiesce in William's Norman rule. In the early 1070s William of Poitiers referred to their constant negotiations with the Danes and their spirit of sullen rebellion. The risings against the Normans, which began in 1067 and reached their peak in 1069 without dying away completely until the 1080s, meant that, as they were suppressed, a greater number of men were slain or exiled than had suffered in the three major battles of 1066.[8] Great stretches of the countryside were mercilessly ravaged; streams of refugees swarmed out of Yorkshire into the Scottish Lowlands and into the south Midlands where they fell sick. Exiles and political misfits were swept to the shores of Ireland, Flanders and Denmark. Soldiers killed more people than they could remember and did not always wait for war-time to plunder or rape. Strongly though William might disapprove of his soldiers' disorderliness, he could have condoned the chastising of faithless men who did not accept him at his face-value: other conquerors have become cruel, impatient, and suspicious with less justification than he had.

The English leaders had better means than we have of knowing whether the Conqueror's fair words meant much. But we can judge that, however justified they thought themselves, their conduct was politically immature. They had admitted the Conqueror to England without a further fight after Hastings. If they had no worthwhile army in 1066, they do not appear to have put a better army into the field later. The fyrd fought for the king in Normandy in 1068 and resisted the attempted invasion of Harold's sons in Somerset. Sporadic risings and rebellions had no political coherence for want of a leader. No English or Danish rival to William considered, as William had considered in 1066, what was needed to take England. A single command and foreign allies were essential. Since Normandy could not be used as an ally, Flanders had to be won over, if the southern cities of government and commerce were to be liberated from the Normans. We cannot blame the English leaders for failure, because the king was not only ruthless but clever, but we do not need to sympathise unduly with them: they did not calculate what rebellion would cost. They were wilful and particularist, and the leaders, by their rebellions, drew their followers into a morass in which all perished.

Edric the Wild kept up guerilla warfare in the West Midlands; Hereward skirmished and ravaged till the last in the Isle of Ely; Harold's sons plundered in the south-west from their Irish retreat; the more responsible Edwin and Morcar, who had prevented the mistake of a general rally to the desperate cause of Edgar the Aetheling in 1066,[9] madly surrendered to the great risk of open defiance of William before their Danish allies had proved themselves in 1069; the unfortunate earl Waltheof, who may have been as blameless as later legend believed, at least permitted himself to be implicated in a plot that could have brought the English no possible benefit. Edgar the Aetheling was no match for William. Treated to gilded captivity by the Conqueror, he escaped to Scotland where he married his sister to the uncouth, but impressionable, king Malcolm. The English lords who followed the Aetheling established important settlements in the Lowlands, anglicised the Scottish court and supported the queen's campaign for intensive religious reform. But this haven for English refugees was no post from which military adventurers could strike at the heart of William's government: instead they indulged their taste for fatuous Border raids with the prospect of small, but immediate returns. In all cases the natural English leaders displayed no sense of their responsibility to the English cause, only devotion to their personal or family fortunes. They played as mercilessly as the Normans with the well-being of England, developed no leaders or policies and found themselves mastered by a king who knew exactly what he wanted and what it cost to have.

Considering the provocation, the Conqueror's restraint seems admirable. There is no evidence that he ever deviated from his principle of not disturbing any man's right until that man had personally stood against him. Domesday book is full of examples that show it was possible for Englishmen to survive after the Conquest. The stark contrast between the 2,000-odd royal English tenants of 1066 against two in 1086 only proves that it was the principal men in the kingdom who suffered most. The Englishmen who believed the Conqueror's promises and remained loyal to him continued to enjoy their father's rights, as the Conqueror promised. The leading men on the Canterbury estates in London were of English families; at St Paul's, old names remained in common use amongst the canons for the next two generations:[10] a heavy preponderance of English personal names proves survival of families, particularly at a time when Norman personal names had become popular. It is difficult in reverse to tell from a Norman name whether a Norman or an Englishman by birth is involved. The Latimer (meaning interpreter) family had two brothers: Robert Latimier and Aelfwine, bailiff of Cetham.[11] Englishmen with Norman names possibly had one Norman parent. Intermarriage was common. The bishop of Worcester married the daughter of a tenant to a Norman knight who got his father-in-law's lands. Even tenants-in-chief, like the d'Oilly and de Wirce families could acquire lands this way. The English element did not obtrude and in the long run slipped out of sight. Those common English names, Tom, Dick and Harry, are Norman, and the taste for them quickly pushed the Alfreds, Harolds and Wulfstans into obscurity. But the Englishmen who donned Norman names and pass as Normans in our documents prove not Norman ruthlessness but Norman popularity.

The degree of William's own combined commitment to his English policy even after 1069 can be shown at three different levels of society. First, at the level in which treason was most to be feared, William had confidence enough in Waltheof as late as 1072 to marry him to Judith his own niece and to grant him the earldom of Northumbria. Waltheof was a reputed nobleman, son of a former earl of Northumbria. Edgar the Aetheling, who had abandoned the estate given him by William and slipped away to Scotland, returned to fight with the Normans, first in Apulia, where he went with the king's blessing and a crowd of soldiers, and later in Normandy, for the Conqueror's son Robert against Rufus. Second, the king used the ambitious English abbot of Evesham, Aethelwig, as his justiciar over many shires and kept him in office till his death in 1077. Aethelwig used his position to enrich his monastery and the monks admired the way both Normans and Englishmen feared and respected him. This single example of special authority created, maintained and enjoyed must dispose of the idea that the king chose not to rely on capable Englishmen. His regret must have been that there were not more men like Aethelwig. Third, it is well known that skilled professional men of the English state, in 1086 as in 1066, were Englishmen. The royal scribe, Regenbald, did the same work for William as he had for the Confessor; the king's huntsmen were, if possible, more used by the Conqueror than by the Confessor. The king's goldsmiths, Odo of Winchester[12] and his brother Eldred (possibly others too), the chamberlain, Humphrey, whose brother Aiulf was sheriff of Dorset—all these men provided the essential continuity in government and administration. If the language of the royal writ was more commonly Latin than English, a local official record like the Northampton Geld Roll of 1075 could still be written in the English language.

The king's wish to keep the English loyal was a need of his government. The degree of complexity achieved by the English state demanded skills that Normans could not always supply. The king's regret for his failure to keep the loyalty of the greatest Englishmen could have been genuine, but the continuity which was maintained at the technical level was sufficient to preserve the old order. And it was this that William needed if he was to be a king and not a mere leader (*dux*) as he had been in Normandy. How would the Normans react to him now?

The Normans had no great respect for kings as such and few Normans ever needed to consider their duty to a king. Even William's chaplain found his respect for the king of France rather puzzling. They were glad to receive lands in England, but it is unlikely that they welcomed the obligations they acquired in the English state: attendance in law-courts, royal tax-paying, keeping the public peace. What William expected to gain from the monarchy in the way of authority and heavenly mission, meant nothing to the Normans. It was therefore not only the English, but the Normans too, who rebelled against royal authority.

As early as 1067 the king's ally, count Eustace of Boulogne, was in arms against him. A little later the leading Bretons, count Brien and earl Ralph, lost their English lands by rebellion. Earl Roger, son and successor of the king's right-hand man William Fitz Osbern, did not scruple to plot with earl Ralph, a Breton, and earl Waltheof, an Englishman, against the Conqueror, in 1075. The earls planned to divide England into three, seeing no further advantage for themselves in the king's government. Norman loyalty cannot be pressed too far when even the king's own brother, Odo of Bayeux, had no shame in resisting his authority and had to be kept in prison. The Normans had no feeling even of uniting against English enemies. Faithful to their own traditions they fought for themselves, not the king. As time passed and the English and Norman leaders were reduced by rebellion, William found himself relying more and more on his oldest friends. Some he could not afford to alienate: count Eustace was reconciled after 1067. With others, the king broke completely: many of his Breton allies left England and there were

3 Emperor Gratian, eleventh century
Alençon, Bibliothèque Municipale MS 11, *f.* 1 (*see p.* 299)

relatively few Frenchmen from other provinces who clung to estates by 1086. The Normans of Domesday book were a far more considerable element in the country than they had been in the great army assembled in 1066.[13] In 1075, when the earls' rebellion had been suppressed, the king could not afford to alienate their good will by executing the rebellious earl Roger. The less guilty Waltheof paid with his life for his prevarication: but then, William did not need to fear an English outcry against him. Indeed, the English characteristically expressed their feeling for the earl by cultivating his memory as a wonder-working martyr. The Normans were more dangerous. Successive confiscations of land from the English had meant that the king distributed ever more valuable estates to the few. By 1086 the broadly distributed lands of the English lords of 1066 had been largely concentrated into the hands of less than two hundred, mainly Norman, lords, of whom less than twenty held perhaps a quarter of the country's resources. These twenty included Robert of Mortain the king's brother, Roger de Montgomery, earl of Shrewsbury and Hugh, earl of Chester. In each case the Conqueror had been obliged to rely on these men more than he had intended after his original policy had broken down. Robert of Mortain had obtained the Cornish and other estates first granted to count Brien; Roger had been sent to the Welsh marches to replace the English Edwin of Mercia who died after 1071; Hugh had been sent to Chester when the Fleming, Gerbod, had relinquished his post. The Conqueror's original plans for a 'multi-racial' settlement had disintegrated. By the end of the reign he was more than ever dependent on a few loyal Norman lords who ruled with him over the leaderless majority of passive Englishmen.

The Norman Barons

The stages whereby the conquering Normans of 1066 acquired the estates they held twenty years later have been omitted in Domesday book, which also generally passes over the temporary estates enjoyed for a few years by men who died without heirs or who forfeited their lands for rebellion before 1086. Not a single royal document exists to grant the king's rewards to his followers and probably the transfers were never recorded in charters at all. The lands of the men in the soke of Bury St Edmund, who had stood against the king in battle, were surrendered to the king by the abbot; the king assigned new tenants to them, whom he sent to the abbot to become his men, as the previous holders had been.[14] This summarises the procedure, adopted no doubt in general, for ensuring that rebels lost their lands, that the deserving got their reward and that lords were not cheated of their due. From the moment of his coronation, when his faithful English subjects submitted and received back their lands from him, William had all the lands of the dead, exiled and rebellious English to distribute to the followers, and successive rebellions kept his capacity to reward men with forfeited lands high for several more years. He probably promised his immediate captains and vassals a large share of the conquest, either in the number of estates or in aggregate value.[15] Count Eustace of Boulogne had a hundred manors, at a rough calculation; perhaps he had been promised a hundred as a fine round figure. Hugh of Avranches was given some very valuable estates near London, picked out as plums by the Conqueror to please this powerful man. As the king lost the loyalty of the great Englishmen who had originally accepted him, their estates too came on to the market and the surviving Normans tended to gain even more. By 1080, there were only four earls left in the kingdom: the king's two half-brothers, Robert of Mortain and Odo of Bayeux (who was in prison by 1086), and the two most important Normans, Hugh of Avranches and Roger de Montgomery.

The battle of Hastings was in the first place an obvious defeat of the Godwinson family which suffered by death and confiscation. Their great lands in southern England and those of their supporters became available for the Normans immediately and leading Normans were promptly invested with authority in Kent, Sussex and Hampshire, particularly in view of the importance of the Channel ports for communications with Normandy. Probably by 1067 Roger of Montgomery[16] had already become the principal tenant in Sussex. He invited his Norman monks at Séez and Troarn and the nuns of Almenèches to share his good fortune there, but rather surprisingly none of his secular followers from Normandy benefited by sub-tenancies. One of his leading tenants, even in 1086, was an Englishman, who had probably inherited his holding, and accepted Roger as his lord; other English survivors may have dropped out before 1086. Roger's other leading Sussex tenants were all men of importance in their own right: Reinald de Bailleul, who was married to Roger's niece, held other lands directly from the king; Robert Fitz Tebald, whose holdings were worth £190, was a more substantial man than many small tenants of the king.

Not so long after Roger had been given his position in Sussex, he was granted an earldom at Shrewsbury and given responsibilities on the Welsh border. He was already a 'marcher' baron in Normandy on the Maine border and he was well aware of what this involved. Warfare was endemic; this meant an active life, general military responsibilities, need for good army captains and technical experts for castle-building and siege warfare. Great opportunities of plunder, land, excitement and responsibility demanded active service of marcher lords, service which they were generally pleased to give. The original marcher earls at Chester, Shrewsbury and Hereford all had considerable estates in other parts of the country. These estates were given to compensate them for the expenses for their commands or the poverty of their border holdings, or possibly to supply them with the resources that they needed in the marches. When Roger considered his new earldom he apparently found it was not so easy to find the tenants he needed there, as it had been in Sussex. There were no previous English tenants left and their forfeited lands were entirely at his disposal. Roger offered some small estates in the hundreds of the county that bordered on the Welsh to tenants from his distant Norman march: those of his lieutenants whom he had kept in active service in England, until he had found them a quarter suitable for the display of their talents. Their estates were smaller than those of his Sussex tenants: either he did not value their services highly or he thought that their border service would give them ample opportunities to enrich themselves. When he had also made tenancies for his niece's successive husbands and the Corbet and de Say families, Roger created other Shropshire estates for eleven of the king's great tenants-in-chief. Roger's interest in finding tenants-in-chief for himself may be connected with the need to arouse their interest and secure their cooperation in his marcher campaigns. The assignment of lands proves, however, that the division of England amongst William's followers was not intended to chop the country into distinct regions such as the earldoms of Canute. Not only were the earls confined to smaller regions in border zones; they invited other royal vassals to participate in their areas.

It also shows that the number of leading Normans was very small. The few there were became more enmeshed in one another's affairs as the reign advanced. For, if leading men dropped out, there was no one to take their place. William Fitz Osbern, like Roger de Montgomery, had first been given responsibilities on the south coast and then transferred to Hereford. After his death in Flanders, his second son Roger succeeded him as earl of Hereford, but, when he forfeited his estates by rebellion in 1075, they passed to the king who found no one else to take them on. The shortage of prospective tenants also helps to explain why the Conqueror was not vindictive to the English. Provided that they did not provoke his anger, they remained useful tenants; had there been eager numbers of Normans pressing for estates, the king and his barons might have been tempted to look for excuses to dispossess Englishmen. All the evidence suggests on the contrary that the Normans were few and became fewer.

The redistribution of land after the Conquest was never a tidy operation of taking the king's 200 chief supporters, assigning them a given area and sending them away to make their own sub-divisions amongst their own vassals. The case of Roger de Montgomery shows something of the way he set out to divide up his estates as they came to him, but it does not do justice to the extent that the old English pattern of land-holding survived intact for a time. Roger was not simply given Sussex; he got those lands, or some of them, forfeited by the Godwinsons. Similarly at Bury St Edmund's, the king claimed to redistribute the lands, not of all the abbot of Bury's men, but only of such of them as had fought against him. The surprising consequence of this approach was that the king obviously proceeded on a personal basis. He made a list of the men who opposed him; for each man he acquired a list of his total properties in whatever county, all the estates of a single man were then assigned to a new tenant. How did the king obtain this information? He may have had access to some lists of exiles' lands composed in his predecessor's reign.

The priest Spirites had been exiled by the Confessor and his lands were forfeited to the king; but they were reunited when granted to Nigel, the Conqueror's physician. Similarly it looks as though estates of Edric of Laxfield, also exiled by the Confessor, had been redistributed to others in the meantime, but that William Malet had managed to reassemble them in his own hands by 1086.[17] It is important to notice that the Conqueror did not organise any surveys of forfeited lands, county by county, and send down his vassals to each county for a share in the available land. The whole process of granting lands was so continuous that it was unthinkable until 1086 that a survey should precede redistribution. The real reason for the king's approach was that his system disturbed the pattern of existing society least, and did most to preserve the illusion that he was not really upsetting any man's right. For each man who was dead, who had opposed him or who had fled, the king would find another to do the old services, to hold of the previous lord and to become the Norman successor to an Englishman. This is true even of ecclesiastical estates. The king's chaplain, Guncard, obtained four churches held by a single man under the Confessor and his tenure was so secure that he was able to give them to the abbey of St Wandrille when he became a monk there.[18] Thus Domesday book as late as 1086 implied that every landed man was obliged to discharge those services which his predecessor had performed for the same land in 1066. There was only one general flaw in William's reasoning. He did not find one Norman for every Englishman who forfeited, not presumably because there were insufficient men, but because men of the standing or quality required could not be had. There was after all no major objection in principle to granting one Norman the estates of several different Englishmen wherever they were. This system of apportionment meant that the tenants-in-chief sometimes found that subtenancies were already occupied by grants previously made. The system could not be made to work rigorously; it led to law-suits and hardship, but as a principle it suited the king's need, for it meant an easy way of rewarding his own men, each time a new rebel and his lands fell in.

By 1086 the process of redistribution was arrested and its results described in Domesday book. In place of 2,000 Englishmen, there were less than 200 Normans. It is true that the king's share of the land had doubled and that many free English tenants' lands had been absorbed in the royal domain. The role these Norman barons had to play in England in 1086 was nevertheless obviously far more prominent than that of the two thousand Englishmen they replaced. At the same time, the very small numbers of Normans involved, however highly placed, could clearly have a very limited effect on English society in general. These men had no interest to disturb the natural economy and the organisation of labour. They were lords whose interests did not extend beyond collecting their revenues or governing their own social group. The mass of the population was not dispossessed, for they did not fight in battle, or, if they did, held land by no tenures that could be forfeited to the lord. They worked the land and held by customary rights and duties to the lord. It made little or no difference to them if their lord's estate passed by forfeiture to another. What change that occurred affected the upper ranks of society only.

How little the great change-over could disturb the obligations of land-law may be seen from the case of the king's thegn, Edwin, who had promised before the Conquest to bequeath his estate of Little Melton to the monks of St Benet of Hulme,[19] but who was still living in 1066. Sometime in the next twenty years, his estate had come into the possession of the Norman, Godric, but Edwin's promise or the monks' claims had still some legal force. Godric agreed to honour his predecessor's concession, only stipulating as a condition that his own son should become the monks' rent-paying tenant. Had he known of this example, the Conqueror would have regarded it as an ideal fulfilment of his wish to disturb no man's right, even to the point of honouring 'future' estates of the Englishmen of 1066.

The Services from Land

When the Norman lords entered into possession of their properties they found that the land itself was burdened not merely with tenancies in expectancy, but with more definite obligations. Whatever the land owed, the new lords, by the king's decree, had to pay. If, in the twelfth century, Fulk de Lisures went in person before the king when hunting, with his horses and arms and a horn hanging at his neck, it was because this was the service Aelfwine the Huntsman had owed, before Fulk's predecessor, Richard Engaine, the tenant in 1086.[20] But services were not always described with such particularity, that their servile, or sergeanty, character is made plain. Land was burdened in normal circumstances with public obligations, of which a remarkably long list survives in a charter of Henry I. The customs of earthly servitude, or public duty, are declared to be: paying geld, paying scot (a church due), working on bridges and castles and parks, 'hidage', attendance at law courts in shires and hundreds, paying the murder fine, 'war-penny' and danegeld and performing host-service and all other customs, works, aids and essarts.[21] Some of these dues are obscure, some are trivial; others are very important. In order to remove any doubts as to who was particularly responsible for doing or paying what was owed, the obligations had been divided and attached to particular estates, and it is likely that the Normans continued this practice. As a result, the duties had become extremely precise and confined to quite specific estates, sometimes very small. The Evesham cartulary, for example, indicates how some of these customs had become the special responsibility of the particular tenant of the land. In a list of knights and free tenants enfeoffed unjustly (as the monk compiling the cartulary believed), it is noted that they do no service to the church for their lands (as they should, is implied) but only the service of the king, and that they do half-heartedly (*tepide*). In a survey of Wickwane, a tenant called Walter Frussel held one hide of land, paying geld for half of it and for the other half going to the shire (-court) and in the royal service, and this man ploughed in summer for the abbey. Another tenant, John, held only one virgate and he did royal service and had to carry the monks' cloth (*pannos cuiuslibet monachi*) round England at the abbot's expense. Elsewhere, two tenants, Reginald and Bernard, held one hide of land free of all service except the king's service. The church in the same place held one hide of land which owed royal service and had to send a man to the army with his sack and bow (*et debet servitium regis et debet ire in exercitibus cum sacco et cum trubla*). In Tetlesthorp, Edgar held two virgates of land and went to the shire and hundred courts for his holding and for one virgate only owed royal service. These strange examples of men holding small pieces of land for which they pay geld, or do court service and go into the army, and still owe separate royal service, not defined, show how difficult it is even to pin down what contemporaries understood by the latter term. It could mean the labour services, the repair of town defences and bridges, which the king had obliged his people to perform from ancient times. These obligations would have become tied to particular holdings and the tenants had to discharge this service along with other services owed either to the immediate lord, like court service, or to the 'state', like the geld. But these could hardly be the services the knights and freemen of Evesham performed unenthusiastically for the king. But in 1166 the abbot of Evesham told the king that one of his knights, Ranulf of Coctone, did the full service of a knight with horses and arms and that, as long as he was in the king's service, the abbot found the knight's expenses.[22] This suggests that the knight was sent off for an indefinite period to do what the king required, and this could be the service which the Evesham knights performed half-heartedly. Earlier such general services seem to be implied by Rufus's writ releasing the abbey of Ramsey from the burden of supplying ten knights at feast-times for the king, and limiting the obligation in the future to that of the abbot's predecessor to produce three knights north of the Thames.[23]

The most universal obligation on the land was to pay the king's geld. This right to taxation was the sole duty on the land which Henry I did not revoke in his charter for the house of canons at Kenilworth,[24] though the king could choose to waive his rights if he wished. Geld-paying was very ancient and its long, unchronicled history probably would explain the anomalies and inequalities that are first apparent only in 1086. In some places the assessment for taxation antedated the Danish invasions. Some counties were more heavily assessed than others: Wiltshire for example owed more than the other counties of Wessex, though they had all been governed together by the house of Cerdic for more than three hundred years. Counties were not even uniformly rated. Lindsey paid less than other parts of Lincolnshire.[25] Individual exemptions granted to churches and others had added their own confusions.[26] In 1086 there were still estates which had never been assessed for taxation at all. Most of these had been held by the Confessor and often they had paid a fixed sum, called the farm of one knight or a fraction of a knight, apparently to commute an ancient burden of supporting the king's suite. Such estates are found almost exclusively in Dorset, Somerset, Wiltshire and Hampshire,[27] which may indicate that the West Saxon kings had never converted the old tax on their own ancient demesne into the geld, a tax introduced into the rest of England by their conquest of the tenth century. There are however exceptions to this. In general, lands which secured exemption were not later reconverted to paying it and, as a result, the geldable possibilities were constantly eroded. By the time of the Conqueror, the tax was levied on particular estates and was a fixed obligation on most, if not all lands. The Conqueror earned a rebuke from the monk of Canterbury for his love of red gold and his heavy demands in taxation, but there is other evidence that makes it doubtful whether William was more grasping than his predecessors, unless he be compared only with the Confessor, who had abrogated the geld in 1051. William, like earlier kings, allowed exemptions and modifications. In Northamptonshire, he approved two general reductions of the whole county's liability, first by increasing the extent of tax-free demesne land, second by arbitrarily reducing the assessments on the hundreds of the shire.[28] He appears to have allowed his tenants-in-chief to hold their demesne lands as exempt, and his concessions may go further still. Roger de Montgomery assigned to his own sub-tenants the estates with the heaviest burden of geld.[29] His motive for doing this could hardly have been to avoid paying geld himself, if as a tenant-in-chief he was exempt for his demesne anyway.[30] But if he had the privilege (accorded by the Confessor to the abbot of Bury) of collecting geld from his own men, when others paid it to the king, Roger would have had a particularly sensible reason for granting heavily geldable lands to his followers. However extensive this practice may have been, it is doubtful whether William seriously worried about the revenues he lost by concessions, for ultimately it was in his better interest to keep his great men loyal to himself. He was also able to raise the rate of taxation on what lands did pay geld, from the normal one shilling on the geldable hide, to six shillings. This sextupled tax seems very stiff, but set beside the steady diminution of the number of hides liable for tax at all, it may rather indicate that the country was in a better position to pay taxes than is often thought, even though the incidence was unprecedented and, therefore, unjust. It is obvious why Domesday book so meticulously records what geld is due from each parcel of land, for an estate of many hides could be assessed for few and it was necessary to know what the liabilities of each estate were, simply because there were no general ones known to all.

Domesday book is a record of the lands of England and the duties and the burdens attached to each estate. Of all the services expected in Norman times, knight service is perhaps the best known. An entry apparently connected with such service may be quoted for Bishampton in Worcestershire, where the four free men who held it in 1066 had been bound to render 'sake and soke' church-scot and burial fees, 'expeditions', 'sailings' and hundred-pleas, to the bishop of Worcester. Later evidence, however, suggests that knight service was much more widely demanded than the rare entries of Domesday book would suggest, but whereas it has been possible to regard Domesday book as a geld-book, no one could describe it as a record of knight service or knights' fees. Arguments about knight service in Norman England tend to be so involved because the most remarkably full record of landed obligations is effectively silent about it.[31]

As with the geld, it was possible to be exempt from all public burdens of a military character. The monks of Evesham who had sixty-five hides of land in the hundred of Fishborough free of all burdens[32] claimed this. They implied that this privilege annulled the abbot's right to make thegnland or create heritable estates there. This apparently did not diminish his power to make grants that would automatically expire at his own death, and the monks could lease such land at will, because it could be promptly recovered. This was what happened at Knightwick, which was given to the monks of Worcester for their own use, but which they temporarily leased to the nun Edith, because the community was too small to need it; they had recovered it from her without difficulty when the community became large enough to find a use for it.[33] Lands granted as thegnland or in heritable tenures were not so easily recovered, because they served to discharge public burdens.

The first problem is to define the differences between these two tenures. The theoretical distinction is between a temporary lease, however long, in thegnland, and a freehold estate in heritable tenure and although, by the twelfth century, concepts of Norman land-law had already modified the English tenures, these differences may be substantially found in pre-Conquest tenures as well. Although Domesday book itself frequently refers to thegnland, it appears to have been the more exceptional of the two. What can be discovered about it?

After the Conquest, the abbot of Westminster conceded an estate in thegnland and declared that the holder should enjoy it for life, but he had no right to sell it, mortgage it, or diminish the abbey's interest in it; after his death, the abbey would recover possession. This same estate had been held by a thegn, Wulfric Bordewayte, and his successor, William Baynard, owed in return for the land the service of one knight. He also had to pay the usual aids and tithes from his land.[34] In this case, the monks allowed the creation of a temporary estate for the purpose of obtaining thegn or knight service. It is easy to see how once such a tenancy had been created for a thegn, there would be a strong incentive to replace the tenant when he died with another man who would perform the same services. A particular association between the land and the services would therefore arise. The abbot of Abingdon naturally gave the thegnlands of those who had been killed in battle to his knights and the bishops of Worcester and Hereford gave thegnlands to their knights.[35] In return for these holdings, the new tenants performed services. On the Conqueror's assumptions, the old lands were obliged to discharge all the old services.

Although these tenancies were for life, there was an inevitable tendency to turn them into heritable tenures, provided that the rights of the lord were reserved. An example of such a renewal may be found in the bishop of Hereford's charter for Roger de Lacy.[36] Roger's father, Walter, had held six hides of land belonging to the canons of Hereford (which might therefore have been assigned to their own needs and have been exempt from public burdens). When Walter died, the land should have reverted to the canons, but Roger offered to pay a 'relief' to the bishop, in order to renew the tenancy. The bishop had no reason to refuse this request and may even have welcomed the chance of keeping a tenant like Roger. The canons' rights were safeguarded by making it clear that the tenancy was only temporary and that it would need to be renewed in each generation. For this estate, Roger owed the bishop the service of two knights. In fact, the bishop in this case allowed the creation of thegnland, in the sense of the Evesham cartulary. For even if Roger had taken up his father's tenancy, it is specified in the charter that he had no right to do so.

The Hereford charter is particularly interesting because it shows that the performance of knight service was not itself what distinguished temporary tenures of this kind. In the charter, Roger himself is styled *miles*, though he was in fact the greatest tenant-in-chief of Herefordshire, after the bishop; he is also called the bishop's knight when he took the tenancy; and the two men he promised to send to do the bishop's service were also called 'milites', though it is probable that he would have sent two men from his own household to do what was required. At all events, the two men would not have been the bishop's own tenants. In Domesday book, the bishop's knights there entered as occupiers of thegnland held very small estates of one or two hides on his own episcopal manors. Socially these knights came, perhaps, midway between Roger himself and the knights of his household who did the bishop's service. Doing knight service was open to men of very different social standing and even to men without land at all. It is for these reasons that it is not possible to distinguish between thegnland and heritable land by the differences of service performed. It is a difference of security in tenure.

These differences may be found in the records of some ecclesiastical estates. (The secular records are not available for this period.) In the 1090s, a list of sixty-five men owing a total of ninety-seven and a quarter knights to the archbishop of Canterbury was drawn up.[37] Most of these men, or their predecessors, can be traced in nearly contemporary records as tenants of the archbishop in Kent, though a few held lands of him in Sussex, Surrey and Oxfordshire. The strange thing is that only ten of them can actually be found in that section of Domesday book entirely devoted to the archbishop's knights. Why are these ten singled out as knights, while the knightly service of most of the sub-tenants is blandly ignored in Domesday?

The Domesday list is actually composed of thirteen names. The three missing from the later list had probably lost their tenancies in the meantime, for they had been more prominent tenants of the bishop of Bayeux, who forfeited his lands in 1088, bringing down some of his clients in the process. Of the ten survivors, seven actually held lands belonging not to the archbishop, but to the monks, and if the monks' lands at Canterbury were as exempt from burdens as those of Evesham, the creation of knightly tenures on them could only have been temporary. This appears to have been the case, for the monks of Canterbury told Henry II at the end of his reign that there were no knights on the monks' lands, but only on the archbishop's.[38] The literal inaccuracy of this statement could be excused if the monks were correctly stating that knights would not be permanently enfeoffed with their land. Temporary tenures were not commitments of that order.

There are however two discrepancies to consider. In the first place, can all men enfeoffed on the monks' lands be found in this list of the archbishop's temporary knights? From other lists five tenants of the monks can be found, who later owed knight service; three of them held land of the archbishop, and it could have been for those lands that the service was owed. This leaves two anomalous cases. William Fitz Hermenfrid, who held half a sulung at Pett 'in the fee of the archbishop' and owed one knight's service, appears therefore to have been overlooked in the list of knights. Dirman, who owed half a knight's service for his half sulung at Keston, remains the solitary exception to this rule. The archbishop's knights are grouped together in Domesday book, not because they are the only tenants to owe knight service, but because they hold by temporary tenures, as the separately listed thegns of the bishops of Worcester and Hereford held their lands.

If this could be accepted, we would have an explanation to hand as to why, in the second place, three of the archbishop's tenants are found on this list of his knights and not simply entered in the normal way as sub-tenants. The archbishop wished to emphasise that they too held precariously, and not with security. Sheriff Hamo's estate had been formerly leased to abbot Alnod and the count of Eu's estate had been held by Alfer of the archbishop: both obviously special tenancies. There is another factor which may be considered in connection with these two anomalous cases. For their holdings, the services expected of them were burdensome. The sheriff owed six knights for one sulung and a half; the count owed four knights for two sulungs at Ulcombe: obligations well above average. This leaves the estate of Ralph Fitz Turold, which later owed seven knights and a half for six sulungs at Eynsford, which cannot be fitted into any scheme. However, there is enough evidence to suggest that the list of archbishop's knights in Domesday book is an account of the holdings of those regarded for one reason or another as temporary leaseholders.

A different type of division between tenants may be derived from the evidence of a record composed under abbot Baldwin (1087–98) of Bury.[39] The lands of the enfeoffed men of Bury are there grouped under their holders, but not apparently in any particular order and certainly not divided into those who held thegnlands and heritable tenures. The services that they performed are not specified, as they are at Canterbury, but the variation was presumably as great, for the tenants are by no means of comparable importance. Some of them, Frodo, Arnulph, Adelo, Berengar, Roger Bigod, Richard Burchard and Gozelin, had estates of five carucates or more; others, like Falco, Henry, Norman, Durand and Robert held less than half a carucate. The larger estates normally included the lands of many sokemen and freemen, whereas the smallest estates did not carry such tenants, and these distinctions are only blurred by a few exceptional cases. The Bury enfeoffed men were two quite distinct classes. At one end of the scale, there were smallholders with only agricultural workers on the land; at the other end, there were substantial fee-holders with legal rights over other freemen. Between them, the twenty men of the second group had over two hundred and fifty free tenants, quite apart from labourers. The existence of differences amongst the enfeoffed men raises the problem of what services could be demanded from them. The sources normally refer to these services as knight service, without specifying further, and by the twelfth century any distinction between the services expected of thegns and those demanded from sub-tenants had been lost. It is nevertheless interesting to consider whether the greater and lesser knights might not originally perform have different functions.

Thegnlands had existed certainly since the tenth century, when the meaning of the term thegn was minister or servant. Bishop Oswald of Worcester was granting to thegns at that time estates in Worcestershire of less than five hides on leases intended to run for only three lives; in return he expected the thegns to perform various services for the church of Worcester, particularly in attendance on the bishop and in all such duties where military men could be useful. On thirteen of his seventeen Gloucestershire thegnlands, the bishop of Worcester in 1086 could still call upon the services of the descendants of such English thegns.[40] Hemming, the monk of Worcester, refers to one of the services that such men could have performed. Having described the long suit between the bishop and the abbot of Evesham over Bengeworth, he says that if ever any man, particularly the abbot's brother, should attempt to overthrow the judgment in Worcester's favour, the priests and deacons of the church of Worcester would go to the ordeal, and the knights of the church swear and offer battle in the courts against all comers.[41] The household knights or thegns performed a variety of functions of this kind and could have continued to serve in this way for the moderate-sized estates they are found enjoying in Domesday book. The English lords were as noted before the conquest for keeping great retinues of knights around them as the Normans became afterwards.[42] The English bishop of Worcester tolerated them at meal-times and even Anselm did no more than advise that their presence in the monasteries should be regulated by the provision of separate dormitory accommodation, wherever possible. Knights were not necessarily noisy, crude soldiers, unfit for clerical company, whom monks were anxious to turn out of monasteries on to country estates. They were laymen necessary to the running of any great man's household. When the bishop of Durham needed a proctor for his bishopric (*procuratorem sui episcopatus*), he appointed the knight Boso, and told him to be present at his pleas (*hic ad placitum meum adesse deberet*).[43] The knights are the lord's men, who serve on his business where he needs them: they defend estates, arrest evil-doers, guard treasure, carry messages to the king and other great men, serve in retinues, grace his feasts and assemblies, swear oaths of knightly value and challenge enemies in law-courts. These services are those owed by any knight to his lord and he does not always discharge them in return for land; but it would be natural for the lord to assign land already burdened with such obligations, and not of any great value or extent, if he wanted to reward a knight for faithful service.

That such estates of limited attractiveness came to others in course of time may be shown in several parts of England. The enfeoffed knights of Worcester may have had only modest holdings, but the champion, or knight, of the abbot of Evesham was his own brother, Ralph. Even so, the abbot gave him no fine manor of the abbey but a number of small estates for which his sons, in the reign of Henry I, owed two knights. There were three hides of land in Weethley (Warwickshire), three hides at Kinwarton and two hides and a half at Stow-on-the-Wold (Gloucestershire) and in the Worcestershire hundred of Fishborough, two hides and a half at Littleton and one virgate at Bretforton. To make two knights' fees out of such fragments of estates is unexpected enough, but it is even more odd to find that not only the abbot's brother, but other tenants, Hugh de Bretforton and Hugh Travers, also held lands in Littleton, that Hugh de Bretforton, like Ralph, also held lands in Bretforton and that Hugh Travers, like Ralph, held land at Stow. Thus whereas two radmen held Bretforton in 1086 and owed appropriate riding services, two men with estates in the same place were classed as knights in 1166.[44] Can it be that the land burdened with duties before 1066 was made to render the same type of services later, even if the small holdings were augmented, out of favour to the new tenants?

The same pattern is suggested by evidence from East Anglia. Before the death of Henry I, Robert Fitz Corbuchon had created a fief of fifteen knights. In 1086, Robert's estates in Essex, Suffolk and Norfolk were held by himself, twelve named tenants and four 'knights'.[45] There is no proof that these men all owed one knight service each, but the actual numbers involved are not so different. The tenants, as on other lands, were however of unequal wealth. Humphrey held four estates in Norfolk; Nigel had three in Norfolk and two in Essex; Brant had only one estate in Norfolk. The later total of fifteen could have been reached by a great variety of combinations of knights. Did the total service then owed bear no relation to pre-Conquest obligations? At Brom, Humphrey had been preceded by a thegn called Anant, and at Stratton by a 'thegn': perhaps Anant himself, on the well-established principle of one Norman for one Englishman. Gerard's predecessor at Wenham had been a thegn called Anti, who had jurisdiction there. At Tolleshunt Major in Essex, the eight freemen who could take their four hides to what lord they pleased in 1066 had been succeeded by four knights holding of Robert Fitz Corbuchon. But the land was still in service. There

are no regular equations for turning so many English freemen into Norman knights, but the fact that certain lands that had supported thegns later supported knights cannot be denied.

In Kent, too, the Canterbury records show that specific lands had been set aside for the purpose of providing knights. At Westgate, there were as many as six knights holding lands; at Wingham another six; and at Lyminge, four. Some of the tenants held in more than one of these places, as well as elsewhere, and their quotas of service could have been assessed in relation to their total estates. But the evidence does not support the view that service was ever proportional to the size of the holding. Thirty-three and a half knights (more than a third of the total) were owed by fourteen men (nearly one fifth of the men owing service) who held land on only three of the archbishop's manors in Kent. Five of the tenants at Wingham, who had no lands elsewhere, obviously owed the service of one knight each for their holdings at Wingham itself. Three of them held one sulung each; two of them held one sulung and a half; the Domesday values of these small holdings, of approximately equal size, ranged from £6 to £2. Vitalis, the other Wingham tenant, also held one sulung and it is reasonable to suppose that he owed one knight for that estate. He also owed two other knights but he had many estates in Westgate, Northwood, Mallinbrooke, Swalecliffe and elsewhere from which such an obligation could be derived. If it could be accepted that particular estates were burdened with the duties of providing service, it could be easily explained how these manifest inequalities could exist.[46]

If such military burdens were attached to specific estates in several parts of the country when the Normans acquired them, what was their reaction to these duties? The Normans were quite hard-headed about their property. They found thegnlands, as estates with specific burdens, suitable for granting to such persons who could do the services required. That the Normans still desired the old services may be seen from the case of the abbot of Evesham. He lost four thegnland estates to the sheriff of Worcester's men, who would not do the services expected; the abbot had therefore to create new tenancies. Not surprisingly, he thought he could rely on his brother for whom he made an estate out of many small pieces of land. (The abbot also saw fit to grant four whole hides of land to the sheriff himself, and

4 St Edmund crowned by Angels, *c.* 1125
New York, Pierpont Morgan Library, MS 736, f. 22v. *(see p. 300)*

this estate, at least later, owed the service of one half a knight. The abbot apparently believed that it was worth trying to secure such a powerful man as a tenant by offering him a big estate on generous conditions, though the chapter did not give its consent to the transaction.)

Thegnlands, like other lands owing services, could therefore be granted even to powerful men. Sometimes the holdings had to be amalgamated or supplemented to create a holding the great man would consider worth taking.[47] The new lords would not, however, have accepted these lands if the burdens attached to them had been in any way heavy or dishonourable. The sources show that abbots commonly gave such lands to their relations as a favour. When abbot Baldwin of Bury received an estate from the king, with instructions to give it to whom he pleased, he gave it to his own brother. The archbishop of York told Henry II in 1166 that his predecessors had created estates to provide for their relations and officials, even where no service was owed.[48] Yet lords did not lease their lands, even to relations, without some expectations of service, not perhaps in specific terms, but generally. This question may be raised in connection with the grant made by the bishop of Hereford to Roger de Lacy, the great tenant-in-chief of Herefordshire. If all the service that the bishop wanted was two knights, which could have been performed by men from his own household or by the knights he had enfeoffed with small episcopal manors, why did he grant six hides of the canons' lands to Roger? It is of course possible that the bishop was not so free an agent in this grant as he appears in the charter, and that Roger's father had come into possession by dubious claims which the bishop had not been strong enough to defeat. But it is also worth considering that the bishop could have gained by the transaction in invisible ways. Maybe Roger found it easier than the bishop to find two knights from his household at short notice; and Roger, as a tenant or vassal, would be a person of consequence in the bishop's clientele. There are a number of indications that great lords went out of their way to obtain vassals of consequence by granting them valuable estates. At Bury, the abbot secured the services of the king's own knight, Peter, by granting him an estate, for which Peter undertook to provide a knight, within or without the kingdom, whenever the abbot needed the company of one. If the abbot took

Peter himself on a journey, the abbot had to pay his expenses, but if he was employed on legal business, he had to pay his own. A later abbot of Bury secured a tenant who would go to the abbot's pleas with the abbot and his steward, with his own horses, near or far, and to the shire and hundred courts. To obtain this tenant, the abbot offered him not a life tenancy, but a grant in fee and heredity.[49] This must indicate that tenants could not be had on the old terms, and that landlords had to offer more favourable ones. The grant of the bishop to Roger also shows that lords were far from desiring exclusive disposal of services. There were real advantages from taking vassals amongst persons with good connections with the king or other great tenants-in-chief. Haimo Dapifer took an estate from the abbot of St Augustine's Canterbury, promising to give 'counsel, aid and succour to the church, to the abbot and his successors, concerning all pleas in the shire or in the king's court, against all barons, except those whose vassals he will have become by the giving of hands'.[50] This exception is an honourable one. No man can become the faithful vassal of one lord and contemplate disloyalty to another; no lord would value the services of a vassal who entertained such a thought. For the same reason, Nigel d'Oilly who got an estate from Abingdon abbey agreed to take the abbot's part in any pleas in the king's court, unless the king himself was pleading against the abbot: Nigel was the king's own vassal. This limitation to the services which could be expected of royal tenants-in-chief who took sub-tenancies from others, was more than compensated for by their great social importance. They could advise the king on their lord's behalf, would be his spokesmen or his friends at court, even if they did not oppose the king directly, and their presence in the honorial court of the lord would give weight and dignity to the assembly.

The functioning of this system may be glimpsed in an example from Abingdon. A royal miller used his control of the water courses alternately to submerge the nearby fields of the abbey and to cut off water from the abbey mill further down stream. The abbot found that he could get no redress against the miller. Finally, a number of men, of whom Hugh de Buckland was the principal, went to the king to protest. The king agreed to give the mill to the abbey and the miller was thereby put at the abbot's mercy and subject to his commands. Hugh de Buckland, the prime mover, was probably the royal sheriff of this name but it was as the abbot's tenant that he owed service, counsel and aid to his lord, which he did by using his influence as a man of social prominence.[51]

In the feudal hierarchy, services were not rendered exclusively from the lower to the upper strata. It was a mutual dependence of lords and vassals, offering each other service, counsel and aid according to their capacity, to which they were pledged as men of honour by the oath and the giving of hands. These obligations are quite different from the render of fixed services, for a man of honour did not measure his service in such terms: he placed his life and holding at his lord's disposal. The feudal network was a social, rather than a military, one which held the upper ranks of society together: lords and vassals mutually sustained one another in all the legal problems that brought them into the courts of the king and of the barons. Lords cheerfully became the vassals of others giving permanency to the personal association by holding lands of some men, though they were themselves lords. The relationships resemble most the mesh of capitalist management. The chairman of one company is not diminished by being a director of another company or a shareholder in many more. The intricacy of landholding in England is often commented upon, and the interdependence of lordship was a certain factor in the development of collective action at a political level. Even if the basic principle was known to the English before the Conquest, the smaller number of Norman lords made it inevitable that the tenurial relationships between them should become even more intimate.

When the Norman lords entered England and accepted the estates of the vanquished, they acquired public responsibilities as well as private investments. For the lands with obligations in thegnage, they generally found humbler vassals to carry on the services. The other lands they distributed to sub-tenants in return for unspecified loyal service. This service was not an empty formula and it was valuable.[52] Had they not found it so, they would have granted all their lands to farmers, like Hugh de Port who supplemented his sub-tenancies by taking estates for money rents. The practice was not universal, but it was common. Even knights could take life-tenures in return, not for service, but for annual cash payments.[53] Money was not the principal consideration for Normans. They wanted to build up clients of vassals, or honours, peopled with men of distinction, and they used their estates for this purpose.

The distribution of lands to the tenants-in-chief has been made to seem like a folly. If the king only gave away lands in order to get service of military men, as has been believed, he would have committed the mistake of giving land to soldiers he intended to summon to arms at short notice. But if the landed settlement was to establish social ties sanctioned by land ownership, the Conqueror pleased his Normans as much as he pleased the English, by making every Norman responsible for his English predecessor's dues.

Royal Knight Service

This discussion of landholding and the services owed by tenants has so far ignored the relationship of these tenures to the performance of public burdens, because it is possible to present a picture of land tenure that is perfectly intelligible and consistent without referring to public burdens. Had the system not been useful to the landlords themselves, they would never have perpetuated it. Yet once the interests of the lords themselves in securing services is admitted, the arguments for ascribing this system solely to royal initiative alone are undermined. In the light of this discussion it is altogether incredible that the Conqueror introduced an entirely novel military obligation. The theory that he did was elaborated to explain the alleged existence of quotas of service (*servitia debita*) in the reign of Henry II. Since it is obvious that these quotas are totally unrelated to the wealth of the tenants-in-chief and appeared to be explicable only as the whim of a tyrant, historians have agreed to assign this role to the Conqueror at whose feet England lay defenceless in 1066.[54] Not only would this make nonsense of the king's claim that his men should hold on the old terms, it would have saddled them with new burdens as well binding them to discharge the old.

One of the strongest arguments in favour of this theory comes from a writ of 1072, addressed by the Conqueror to abbot Aethelwig of Evesham, in which the king refers to the service of five knights owed to him from the abbey. Since this is the same number of knights enfeoffed by Evesham in the survey of the king's knight service made in 1166, it has been concluded that, if Evesham owed the same five knights about 1072 as it did in 1166, the Conqueror had introduced a quota system of knights by that year, substantially as it still existed a hundred years later.

The importance of this writ to the belief that the Conqueror introduced 'feudalism' into England justifies a close examination of this document, which is the only contemporary evidence for the existence of a quota system. It may be divided into two parts. In the first, the abbot is told to order men under his authority (*sub ballia et justitia tua*) to have all the soldiers they owe the king at Clarendon for the octave of Whitsun (3 June 1072). In the second part, the abbot is told to bring with him the five soldiers he owes to the king from his abbey. In both cases the soldiers should be prepared (*paratos*). This double part is important. Who were the men under Aethelwig's authority? This great abbot was so powerful till his death in 1077 that after the Conquest Normans and Englishmen were drawn into his service and took him as lord. Such men seem to be the persons the king has in mind. He does not know how many they are, nor in what counties they are, nor does he know how many soldiers Aethelwig's vassals owe him. But, if the Conqueror had just imposed fixed quotas, how could he be so ignorant and why did he have to rely on Aethelwig to produce as many men as were owed? Yet the Conqueror knows that Evesham abbey owes five men. How could the Conqueror know this? The abbey's estates were probably more or less constant between 1066 and 1072, for the vassals, whom Aethelwig began to receive, brought their lands not to the abbey but to the abbot, by the English system of commendation, still flourishing within six years of the Conquest. If the service of the abbey of Evesham was already owed from its own estates, the Conqueror could easily discover this, and would expect the old service on the old terms.

Admittedly it is not possible to prove that Evesham owed five soldiers to the king before 1066. Nevertheless, there is evidence of at least four 'thegns' connected with Evesham estates. Aethelwig had granted the manor of Witton to his own uncle who was killed at the battle of Stamford Bridge. Assuming that the Conqueror granted the land of the Evesham tenants who had fallen in 1066, as he did at Bury, this estate would have been liable to sustain another fighting man in the dead uncle's place. In fact, Witton passed into the hands of soldiers of Urso d'Abbetot, the sheriff, though whether they were in occupation by 1072 cannot be proved. Another estate, Hampton, had been held by a thegn who had the right to take his land to whom he pleased: he sold it to Aethelwig before the conquest. By 1086, Urso's soldiers had got this manor as well. About 1071, the abbey acquired an estate of two hides at Sheriff Lench; before 1066 two thegns had held it.[55] Now, if the Conqueror's demand of five knights from Evesham abbey was not an arbitrary imposition, but a demand for the service owed by soldiers for specific estates which were held by the abbey by 1072, and for which the abbot had become responsible, there would be a perfectly comprehensible explanation for the number of soldiers involved. Moreover, the king's constant repetition that he asked for the old services, could be accepted as true. The new element that is obvious in the king's government also becomes clear. Whatever may have been the case in the past, William insists that the services owed from land should be rendered through the lord. The services remain the same, but the way of rendering them is feudalised. The Conqueror did not want thegns to retain the liberty of taking their land where they liked, by changing their lords. He insisted that lordship was permanent and that service would henceforth be rendered along fixed lines. It is true that, by this rule, the king caused some men to lose their freedom to do service how they liked, but at least the services that they owed were traditional, and their sense of grievance was not acute. Such a privilege had probably been exceptional even in 1066. The Normans ironed out this anomaly. Services were stabilised.[56] Far from suggesting that the process was complete by 1072, the writ by its two parts shows that the king had to use both territorial and personal obligations to reach all men.

The Conqueror's writ to Evesham cannot be used as a categoric proof that the king had introduced arbitrary quotas to replace an earlier territorial obligation in land. There is room for allowing that the new way of paying the service owed was related to older obligations. But the writ cannot possibly crystallise doctrine on the king's military resources, because it has nothing to say about his infantry or his archers or his stipendiary soldiers. If, however, the writ is studied carefully, it can be seen not to give specific military information at all. It says that soldiers should be brought 'prepared' to Clarendon, the king's hunting lodge in Wiltshire, for the octave of Whitsun (3 June 1072). Historians have interpreted this to mean 'prepared' for war, and have suggested preparations for the campaigns in Scotland in the autumn of 1072, and even in Normandy in 1073. These same historians also believe that the feudal service owed was limited to forty days, or two months at the most. If this were the case, lords would have done better to take or send their contingents nearer to the site of the campaign and nearer the date of the first encounter. But this interpretation is forced, because the writ requires soldiers to come 'prepared' but never declares that they were to be prepared for war. Soldiers (*milites*) could be prepared for other things.

In 1086, the Conqueror summoned all the landholders who were of any account throughout England to swear oaths to him on Salisbury plain. Had the conqueror wished to take oaths of this sort in 1072, would not this writ be the form used to assemble men, and would the phrases have been different? The lords produce their men, 'ready' to take their oaths, no doubt in their full equipment. On the broad plains around Clarendon, the great host could be encamped for a civil ceremony, possibly including the knighting of young men new to arms. The Conqueror's writ is therefore evidence that the king was entitled to the service of knights, possibly from those holding lands liable to service from very ancient times. As in the case of the feudal returns for Normandy in 1172, the English returns of 1166 can be most fruitfully examined for the ecclesiastical estates because there are enough other records for them to make comparisons with other periods possible. It is notable that in 1166, the only monasteries to owe military service were ancient ones: twenty-two monasteries and two nunneries, all south-east of a line from the Wash to the Bristol Channel, the area of the English kingdom in the tenth century.[57] Does this mean that the public burdens had been imposed then?

There was in England an ancient public obligation on every five hides of land (six carucates in the Danelaw) to provide one soldier, and a law of Canute states that the man who discharged the military burden on the land was entitled to possess it, that is acquire a bookright in it.[58] This would explain why a man who possessed five hides was considered to be a thegn, the representative English soldier of the eleventh century. It is however obvious that not all thegns held five hides. Bishop Oswald of Worcester gave smaller estates for three lives to thegns, who agreed to do the due service in return for the privilege of being able to hand their estates to whom they liked for two generations. Domesday shows that some thegns had estates which made them liable to support military expeditions. When the abbot of Evesham was obliged to admit that he held Bengeworth only from the bishop of Worcester, he undertook to do the necessary services like the other 'feudatories' of Worcester—paying various dues to the bishop, as well as the king's tax (*censum*), supporting expeditions and doing other royal services.[59]

The bishop of Worcester had a liberty of three hundreds called the Oswaldlaw,[60] over which by an ancient constitution the bishop had the right to all payments by custom or for jurisdiction, including those owed to the king. If this position gave the bishop responsibility for organising the military resources of his three hundreds, which does seem to have been the case, the bishop was liable for sixty men. By 1166, the number of knights owed by the bishop was disputed, but sixty is the figure given in at least one place. Even more interesting, however, is the evidence that most of the knights the bishop had enfeoffed were settled in the Oswaldlaw itself.

The Oswaldlaw had not descended entire to successive bishops since Oswald's day. Hemming gives a long list of properties in the bishop's soke that had been taken from him unjustly in the course of the eleventh century. Bishop Wulfstan had had only modest success in recovering Bengeworth and Hampton and had been obliged to take the abbot of Evesham as vassal. Yet the loss of his holdings in the Oswaldlaw did not reduce the bishop's obligation to the king to find sixty knights as before, because he was still responsible for three hundreds to the king. The desperation of the bishops may therefore be easily imagined. To make good their losses they pressed their lands in other counties into service and the conversion of the lands to new purposes was stoutly resisted.

Thus in 1166, the bishop claimed fifteen knights from the earl of Gloucester and from Humphrey de Bohun, apparently for lands in

Gloucestershire. These two admitted only to owing five knights. The succession of their lands from 1086 to 1166 is so confused that it is not possible to identify who was holding their lands in 1086; but it is worth remarking that, in Gloucestershire Domesday, six radmen were settled on the bishop's manor of Westbury and the services they owed in Gloucestershire may lie behind the five knights offered by the great feudatories. The other Gloucestershire estates also rendered unusual services. Only Hugh de Barville in 1208 owed one knight for an estate of five hides of land, held by Schelin in 1086. At Stoke Orchard, there were seven hides of land, of which five were held by two brothers, Bernard and Reginald Archer in 1086, but they did not at that time do the services expected. Their descendant, John Archer, was in 1166 described as the king's sergeant and, surprisingly enough, he did the service he owed directly to the king, and it was the king who performed what service was owed to the bishop. The remaining fragment of two hides was apparently converted into the quarter knight's fee held by Robert the Frenchman for his land at Stoke. At Henbury, where six radknights held in Domesday book, three men later owed the service of one knight; and of four hides at Bibury (where three radknights had served in 1086) a mere half a hide held by John de Bibury later owed service. Quite apart from the obscurities surrounding the Gloucester-Bohun lands, the Gloucestershire evidence suggest that the bishop was having great difficulties in wringing knight service from his lands there. In Warwickshire there was a mere half knight's fee at Flecknoe. In 1066, Turkil held two hides and a half-virgate (almost the size of half a military unit) and his son, Lewis, was in possession in 1086. At that time the bishop claimed Lewis as a tenant, but the bishop then lost his case and it is therefore something of a surprise to find Aestrop Masteng owing half a knight for this estate in 1166. Somehow a later bishop had recovered ownership. This small fee remained anomalous amongst the bishop's estates in that county, and its liability for service seems to have begun with Turkil, who had perhaps been a thegn.

By contrast to his shaky position in other counties, the bishop's hold of what he retained in the Oswaldlaw was much more firm. Some of the individual knights' fiefs there must have been very ancient. The first and very unusual proof of this comes from the bishop's claim, which was not disputed, to be the lord of three fees held by the king himself. The royal obligation to the bishop was derived from the king's possession of four separate pieces of land, all in the Oswaldlaw: Bushey, Bisley, Queenhill and Broc, which the king had already obtained, apparently by forfeiture, in 1086. Bisley had been previously held by Brictric son of Algar, who had one hide of land there 'at farm' perpetually from bishop Leofric, and had rendered to the bishop whatever he owed to the king: *ad servitium regis*. The Conqueror owed to the bishop the service that the bishop owed to the king, an obligation that was older than 1044 but was still being demanded in 1166.[61] At Queenhill, the king had succeeded a Norman, Ralph de Bernai, who had replaced an Englishman, Ailric. Probably the duties of that land also went back earlier than 1066. Similarly, the fee of Croome was originally held by Siward and passed with his daughter to the knight enfeoffed by bishop Wulfstan; the fee of John d'Abbetot at Mindlip and Alcrinton had been Edric the Steersman's before the Conquest.

In other instances from the Oswaldlaw, the case is not so clear, but many of the fifteen fees held by William de Beauchamp of the bishop in 1166 can be linked directly with the Domesday tenants, so that if the obligations of 1166 had been determined by the Conqueror, as is commonly alleged, and if the services performed in 1086 were those demanded in 1066, as Domesday itself implies, there must have been a continuity of service from the Confessor to Henry II. Moreover, if those obligations were related to the special status of the Oswaldlaw, it would be easy to show why Beauchamp's own sub-tenants, Roger de Lench and Osbert d'Abbetot, were liable for service. It was because their holding had originally been part of the Oswaldlaw, that they had become liable for service, and remained so even after their estates were added to other hundreds. There are few exceptions to the rule that all the traceable holdings of the bishop's knights in Worcestershire were made in the Oswaldlaw. It is startling to find that the only two sub-tenants of Beauchamp who held in other hundreds than the Oswaldlaw were the only two men whose holdings from the bishop himself were also in other hundreds. The exceptions are doubly exceptional, which surely confirms the general rule. The evidence of the Oswaldlaw therefore proves that it was most commonly on land owing public service that the bishop endeavoured to settle the knights who came to be responsible for discharging military service. The Conqueror naturally expected the performance of the services owed from the land, just as he demanded the payment of other taxes.

The argument that it was the Conqueror who imposed quotas of service is also supplemented by the evidence of the king's interest in making individual enfeoffments. At Peterborough, the king twice interfered personally with the process of creating estates. He gave a piece of the monks' land to Ferron and insisted that one-and-a-half hides of land belonging to the monks' soldier Ansketil be ceded to Eudo Dapifer, so that Ansketil had to be compensated elsewhere. In the first case, the king effectively cancelled the monastic exemption of the estate; in the second, he intervened on behalf of a powerful tenant-in-chief.[62] The king also acted personally to make a knight out of the nephew of a previous bishop of Salisbury on the bishop's manor of Poterne, but the exact implications of this are in doubt.[63] In none of these examples, however, is there any hint that the enfeoffment of these men was made in order to obtain service for the king. They are favours to the individual, and once established they entered into normal relationships with the lords of their land.

What happened when the king's knight took an estate from a tenant-in-chief may be gauged from the case of Peter, who was given land by the abbot of Bury. It is possible that Peter's obligations to the king had not been previously specified, but once enfeoffed as the abbot's tenant, he was obliged, or anxious, to define his service to both lords. Peter therefore undertook to provide three or four knights for the king's military requirements, when properly warned, but this does not mean that the abbey lands merely subsidised the king's service, for the abbot also obtained services of value; it was this that made it worth while to find an estate for the king's knight. The uncertainty about the number of men Peter had to send when the king wanted them shows that written agreements by no means defined due service very precisely. If written obligations were imprecise, it is even more likely that oral commands would be general rather than specific. Bury is not an isolated example. The abbots of Abingdon and Glastonbury also disputed with their tenants as to how many knights were owed.[64]

The king's interference on behalf of his friends or supporters does not need to be interpreted in a sinister way. The real beneficiary of all enfeoffments was intended to be the local landlord, who had formally to authorise all the grants. The abbot of Evesham gave four hides of land at Church Lench to the sheriff of Worcester, without consulting the chapter. After the abbot's death, the king gave them to the abbot's brother, Ralph. Ralph later surrendered the four hides to the abbey and admitted that he had come by them illegally.[65] The king's will was not in itself sufficient authority for enfeoffments, as it surely would have been if they had been made for his benefit. At Peterborough, the king forced the monks to do his will but the grants were made by the lord, not by the king.

The king's interest was not for that reason a negligible one. Just as other lords wished to obtain more influential men for their service, so too the king came to be more interested in finding knights for his own service and securing all that was owed to him. Knights became more valuable both politically and militarily, and the reason seems to be connected with their expense. As the knight became more heavily equipped and kings could afford to hire fewer of them, so it became desirable to stipulate the services to be obtained from the tenant-in-chief and their vassals.

The emergence of the knight can be seen at both ends of the scale. At the upper end, those holding heritable tenures are described in terms of the number of knights' fees they hold. To be a knight was no longer to be a mere soldier, but a person of social distinction. The ceremony of knighthood acquired a religious solemnity quite undesired in the eleventh-century act of giving arms. Churchmen justified the use of weapons in righteous causes, where before the Crusades, they had regularly denounced brutal soldiery. Knighthood was a distinction great men were proud to receive because it had become something more than a mere coming of age. At the nether end, the simple knight or fighting man of the eleventh century must also have lost his common qualities. He had become a person in great demand and was raised to a level in society previously reserved to others.

Behind these changes may be discerned not only a development of military techniques but also the new ethics of chivalry.[66] As social and political problems came to depend for their resolution on the attitude of a small group of heavily armed knights, all those who pondered how to secure their loyalty in peace and war inevitably hoped to establish permanent ties confirmed by land-holdings of sufficient value to sustain the cost. The first hint of this changing royal attitude, if it is not the much discussed oath of Salisbury in 1086, is certainly the clause in Henry I's charter of 1100, where knights doing military service *per loricas* in person were exempted from geld-paying. The knights were thereafter assimilated to tenants-in-chief which explains how it is that kings could come to treat all these land-owners alike as fee-holders. This transformation was accomplished slowly. When the king raised an aid for the marriage of his daughter in 1110, the unit of assessment was still the hide,[67] as though this feudal due was a geld, but later feudal dues were collected from knights' fees, which therefore acquired a different status from other lands.

What this represented as a scheme of land-holding may be gathered by contrasting it with the assumptions of Domesday book. In 1086, the king was dealing directly with the tenants-in-chief. He was not concerned to obtain information that would bring the sub-tenants into prominence. The estates of sub-tenants are scattered amongst their lord's holdings, which are arranged in the geographical order of hundreds, not the personal order of tenants. Domesday book is not a book of fees. Forty years later, Orderic Vitalis, who may never have seen the Exchequer volumes, naturally assumed that Domesday book was a record of the 60,000 fees the Conqueror had created.[68] (This figure was shown by Round to represent Orderic's expression for a large number, as we might say, trillions.) Orderic's mistake is instructive. By his day, the knight's fee was the natural unit of society and Orderic assumed, as many others later, that the Conqueror must have been responsible. Domesday book shows that he had not then introduced them, but Domesday book itself suggests how the change could have come about.

The Conqueror's military system was to expect his great tenants-in-chief to support his campaigns by supplying as many and as good soldiers as they could. After the Conqueror's death, many of the great tenants-in-chief lost their lands. Only one earldom of the Conqueror's reign, Chester, remained twenty years after William's death. It became a palatinate earldom, where the earl was the real viceroy, and it is probable that the other earldoms of the Conqueror's reign would have developed similarly, had they survived.[69] They did not. The Conqueror himself, and his sons to a greater extent, found that they had begun to deal directly with the sub-tenants of their greatest feudatories. It was at that point that kings needed to take an interest in the holdings of these lesser men. Rufus was particularly interested in dealing with the knights of the kingdom, even where tenants-in-chief survived. He complained, as he did to Anselm in 1097, if contingents were not up to standard. He could be persuaded, as he was at Ramsey, to modify and define exactly the services knights should be made to perform. Henry I also made individual pacts to define service. To the abbot of Evesham he conceded that the abbot's service when the king was on campaigns in person would be to provide four knights and a half, and it was this service, not that of five knights as in the writ of 1072, that the abbot still owed in 1166. It was also Henry I who revalued the geld and hide obligations of the see of Worcester and reduced the scutage liability of the see of Ely. If the barony of Shelford was divided into two parts, for each of which the descendants of two families continued to be liable collectively for half the service, it was because Henry I had divided the barony and the obligation could never be further sub-divided. When William Pantulf of Wem later claimed to hold directly from the king, it was because the king had acquired the Montgomery lands by Robert of Belesme's forfeiture in 1102.[70] In all these examples, the events of the reigns of the Conqueror's sons seem to have been responsible for establishing the obligations of service that were rarely modified later. The alleged quotas of 1166 could as easily be explained by decisions taken under Henry I, as by an imperious mandate of the Conqueror. But there is no likelihood in either case that the king imposed services arbitrarily or at one fell swoop. Those services which were owed were in part derived from much more ancient obligations, discharged in a new way, through the feudal hierarchy, and the definitions of service were negotiated piece-meal. It is not even certain that the definitions had all been agreed by 1166. Few of the letters sent by tenants-in-chief to the king refer to fixed service and several great barons had to consult the men of their honour to know what their service was. This must mean that in practice due service was determined by precedent rather than by a royal decision given once and for all after the Conquest. Henry II never professed to be interested in due service. He wanted to know (a) how many knights had been enfeoffed and (b) how many were enfeoffed but still lived with the baron on his demesne, so that they could be summoned to swear allegiance to the king in person: for he was determined to bind even landless knights to him by personal oaths. It was the idea of J. H. Round that, by adding these two figures together, it would be possible to arrive at the quotas of service due to the king, as if tenants-in-chief would have knights about them or give them lands solely to be able to do service to the king. This is equivalent to the paradox that men only make money in order to pay taxes to the government. The king obviously wanted his share of the services, but it has not yet been proved that knight service grew up entirely for the public advantage.

5 Changes under the Conqueror

Military Matters

The contrast between Normans and Englishmen has been most emphasised in military matters. The Normans became an epitome of the warrior race and the English shrank to decadent weaklings. Within a generation of the Conquest, the Normans could complacently despise the English for allowing themselves to be beaten. Once spoken, the slander could not be silenced. Modern efforts to prove that the English were stronger in government or the arts of peace do not salve hurt pride or answer the charge.

Few contemporary sources contrast the English and the Normans as fighting men. In his vision, the Durham knight, Boso, saw a great field where all the native-born men of his province were sitting on their fine horses carrying long spears, as they usually did, making a great noise by striking them against one another; they were succeeded in his vision by Frenchmen, charging up on their snorting horses and equipped with all manner of arms, who also made a great tumult with the clash of their arms and the noise of their horses. Both groups fought mounted with equal fury. The differences could seem as slight, or as important, as the differences between modern regiments.[1]

For virtue and courage, there was little to distinguish the English from the Normans. For centuries the English had been brave warriors fighting to the death for their lords, commemorating their valour in poetry. Noblemen expected to become illustrious by their martial deeds. The English army was effective enough to win battles against powerful enemies. Under Edmund Ironside they snatched victory from the Danes and Canute had to share possession of England with Edmund and forgo the kingship until Edmund's death. At Stamford Bridge, under Harold II, the army had shown that it could throw back the victorious Norsemen. The defeat at Hastings was not dishonourable. Yet this one battle has discredited the English military system.

The victorious army at Hastings was not exclusively Norman. The first cavalry charges were made by Bretons and the thousands of troops William had gathered from different parts of France must also have played their unlauded part in final victory. If the duke could assemble a great host in the prospect of being able to reward them if successful, could the king of England not offer more substantial inducements for soldiers to serve in his armies? In 1066, he had used a contingent of Flemish knights, obtained through his good relations with his father-in-law, Baldwin V. After 1071, William lost the friendship of the new count, whose forcible entry into the country he had tried to prevent by sending his ablest lieutenant, William Fitz Osbern. When Rufus made peace with the count in 1095, his first concern was to negotiate for the right of hiring Flemish knights and Henry I made two treaties with count Robert at the beginning of his reign.[2] The Flemish knights remained an important part of the Norman king's armies until after the death of Stephen in 1154. Norman armies were not therefore necessarily superior for racial reasons.

The contrast between the English and the Norman armies has sometimes been expressed as a contrast between infantry and cavalry, to the latter's advantage. This seems very unfair and even surprising. If the contrast were so important how is it that Harold's inferior infantry should be able to hold up the thundering cavalry in a battle that lasted about eight hours? William of Poitiers never suggests that the infantry, armed with their double axes, were the least bit contemptible. The cavalry, of the Bretons at least, though they were entrusted with the van as crack troops, fled from the defence. But the emphasis on cavalry may be misplaced. We are told that the Conqueror deployed his troops at Hastings in three ranks. The first two were made up of infantry, the front rank of archers and ballistics men, the second, of men equipped with a military tunic who probably wielded swords. Only in third place came the knights, trained to throw lances as they dashed forward. Effectively the sources concentrate on the, not always glorious, exploits of the cavalry, in which the leaders themselves fought. The Normans were proud of their cavalry, and those who wrote about campaigns for noble patrons mentioned only the force they were interested in. The Americans are similarly proud of their Marines. It does not follow from what we hear about the favourite troops that the other forces served merely to cheer on the stars. But we must confess that we know next to nothing about the two front ranks of infantry, even if it was an arrow which killed Harold—the most important single event of the whole battle. The Norman infantry could have been hired men, or non-noble Normans. How numerous were they, and what was their real function in battle? That they were there at all argues that they served an essential purpose, for William had had to bring all the men he needed with him; he had not scoured the countryside, as some writers like to believe that Harold did, to find his infantry.

If the composition of the Norman army has not been adequately analysed, the English forces have been studied from the fragments of information about how they were recruited that inevitably give the impression of a medley of soldiers as futile in battle as Falstaff's men, as indeed they would have been in an age of soldiers raised on Swedish drill and Prussian discipline. English armies did have victories with such troops and the system of recruitment was therefore adequate for the needs of the time. Canute and his successors, including Harold II, had household troops, professional soldiers who accompanied the king in battle. How numerous were they? Were they adequate to fight a battle? The Rochester text calculates that an army was made up of thirty-five men[3]: in this sense, the household troops were certainly an army in their own right. We do not know if these men were retained by salaries, by the promise of lands, or were sworn vassals maintained at their lord's expense, as in heroic times. They could certainly be supplemented by thegns, royal and otherwise, whose equipment, armour, helmet, lance and sword in no way distinguished them from the later knights. In Canute's reign, thegns could be classified in three ranks.[4] If the earl owed eight horses, lances and shields, four helmets, tunics and swords together with 200 mancuses of gold, to be allowed to succeed to his father's estate, the royal thegn owed exactly half as much, except that he gave only one helmet and tunic and fifty mancuses. A middling thegn was much poorer, owing as his relief one man's equipment and two pounds. In the Danelaw, the royal thegn, unless he were known to the king personally, gave only four pounds all together. These thegns were certainly horsemen, though they appear to have fought dismounted. Later the Normans themselves fought on foot as at Tinchebrai in 1106, and it has been argued that they could have learned to do this from the English. At all events, if knights dismounted to fight, the fact that thegns did so cannot be used as evidence of inferiority. However, the Norman leaders' interest in cavalry would have encouraged them to fight on horseback where possible, and several battles, like Val ès Dunes and Varaville, were apparently cavalry engagements. But the use of horses at Hastings was not so strikingly decisive and was necessary only because the Normans, without them, would have had to fight while moving up the hill on foot, a serious disadvantage. The use of horses in Normandy would likewise have been most necessary for enabling troops to charge up to fortified points during sieges, in order to make a rapid withdrawal.

When the Conqueror considered how to raise his armies after the Conquest, he had no reason on military grounds to recruit only Normans. Judging from Hastings he required infantrymen, archers and knights. How did he find them? It is easiest to answer this question with regard to knights. The knight needed a horse, a shield, a lance for throwing, a sword for use when dismounted and a military tunic, or *lorica*. When the count of Anjou desired to meet William of Normandy at Domfront, both rulers described what horse they would mount, what shield they would carry and what they would wear. This probably represents the respective order of priorities.[5] A knight's special pride was his horse, which gave him his French name, *chevalier*. The Conqueror's fame as a horseman made it natural for distant friends to send him pedigree horses as a valued present. When two knights intended to meet, the first thing they would want to know would be what kind of horse to expect. The shield was the second characteristic. It did not at this time carry symbols to be detected by observant heralds or gentlemen with a memory for genealogies and heraldry, but only devices, that were at most personal and perhaps merely decorative. The particular shield carried by the Conqueror had therefore to be described. The tunic is variously depicted in the sources. Sometimes it appears knee-length and skirted; in the Bayeux tapestry the Normans seem to be wearing a combination tunic and breeches, which was presumably more comfortable for riding. The infantry are also said to have worn tunics, so it is difficult to decide how distinctive the knight's tunic was.

The Norman knight was therefore a man equipped to fight on horseback and the cost of horses meant that he had himself to be a man of substance or else obtain his equipment from his commander. But he did not need to be a man of landed estate or social distinction, and the regular use of the word 'knight', rather than the French chevalier or the English thegn shows that, when the Normans came over, the English did not regard them as distinctive because they were mounted or because they were socially important; as knights they were serving men, retainers of others: *cnihts*.

These knights were not necessarily even vassals of their captains. In the Penitentials of 1070, fighting men were analysed into four groups: (i) men armed by the king or (ii) by his captains; (iii) men owing service, that is vassals; (iv) others hired for wages.[6] These distinctions did not imply social differences, for hired men might be of the same social class as their fellow soldiers and observed the same moral conventions of loyalty to their captain, even if they were not of his household or if they did not hold land of him as vassals.

Mercenaries may have been very numerous and of great military importance in battles. The count of Flanders allowed Henry I to recruit five hundred men regularly and this single corps of soldiers in continuous service must have been the most important single contingent of the army, and one that was expensive to maintain.[7] Yet it would be easy to exaggerate their general importance, by assuming the priority of military over political considerations. The Norman kings were not coping chiefly with military problems like that of permanently providing for the defence of their own territories or planning offensive wars. They were really trying to solve the political problems posed by their relationships with other great men, especially with their vassals. They extended their political influence by receiving their enemies into personal subjection, rather than by the conquest of their lands. In this way, William I attracted the count of Maine and the earl of Wessex into his service. William's conquest of England, his most sustained military effort, was not, in theory, anything more than a vindication of his rights. Even when his territories were threatened by other rulers the king's major concern was to prevent his local vassals going over to the enemy and taking their forces with them. The attitudes and the strength of the king's vassals were therefore more important in politics than the mercenaries themselves, who only assume the dominant role when they monopolise military resources. This being so, the king's first political concern was to make certain of the loyalty of his own men, and one of the best means to this end was to obtain their regular participation in his wars, thus committing them to his own schemes and promising them the rewards of service that they demanded: success in fighting, excitement, commands, opportunities of patronage and personal distinction.

In his armies, therefore, he expected to find his own faithful vassals, who brought with them their own men, and the king would be gratified by the distinction of their contingents. His gratitude for their services could overflow into all ranks of the army; lukewarm service would be tepidly rewarded; generous investment would yield substantial profit. The king's vassals, like the king himself, faced similar problems, militarily and politically.[8] If they needed a large force, they could hire mercenaries. Anselm provided them for Rufus's Welsh campaign in 1097; William Fitz Osbern spent excessive sums of money on them and was rebuked by the Conqueror for this.[9] Lords were expected to provide opportunities for their vassals and dependents to gain the rewards of military service, so that lords who preferred to pay hired men for what they wanted would have found themselves without vassals at all, to the loss of their own social standing. Therefore, though at any one time mercenaries might have formed the larger part of a feudal contingent, they could never have taken first place in military calculations; their services were temporary and could be terminated without rancour, whereas tenurial relationships bound society together and mutual interests of this importance could not be sacrificed to naked military power.

Of the other branches of the army, much less can be said. Some of the Conqueror's archers held lands in sergeanty, to use later terminology,[10] but most of them could have been hired men. Skill with the bow was not confined to sturdy freemen, like those encouraged to shoot with the long bow in the fourteenth century, for the king and his friends used a small bow in the chase. Mounted bowmen would, however, have been unnecessary in fighting where the enemy was immobile, as was the case in siege warfare or, as at Hastings, where men fought on foot in hand-to-hand encounters. Whether the king found many archers in England is in doubt. Apart from the exploits of knights, the sources confine themselves to such comments as indicate that the cavalry was supported in battles by hosts of other men.

Where did the king find his infantrymen? Some must have come from Normandy and no doubt others were drawn from England, but we know very little about them. All freemen were obliged to bear arms. The Assize of Arms (1181) specifies the arms to be borne by men according to their wealth and since the Conquest had made little appreciable difference to the character of the weapons used, it is easy to believe that the obligation to bear arms under Henry II was only a continuation of the pre-Conquest duty of freemen.[11]

Of course, the fact that all freemen bore arms does not mean that they were all liable for service, as 'territorials' in the king's army. Their duties to arrest malefactors and the protection of their own dependents would have made weapons necessary. Even small units of armed men united to put down disturbances or challenge invaders were still naturally acting to protect their own peace and possessions and did not have to be roused by public officials to defend their lands and houses. But the king's interest in their arms indicates that the king was not indifferent to this reserve of military strength, and local shire contingents were certainly brought into service under the sheriff, the king's official.[12] Yet even the use of shire levies in particular campaigns is not the same as trying to add 'territorial' units to the regular army.[13] When English forces are alleged to have assisted Rufus and Henry I, against the supporters of their brother Robert,[14] it is not difficult to imagine that local levies were referred to, such as seem to have been involved at Worcester in 1088. The chroniclers also state that English soldiers were used by the Conqueror on the continent in 1068 but it is a big jump to conclude from these vague phrases that an army of Englishmen was raised by traditional or by formal obligations,[15] for the words used imply no more than the personal services of many Englishmen in battle, as Harold had fought for William, probably with his own followers, in 1064. Had the Norman kings inherited or created a valuable force from shire levies, as part of their regular military forces, it is hard to see why such forces should have been allowed to fall into neglect later on. The obligation of all freemen to bear arms is not therefore a sufficient foundation for believing that all freemen served, or were liable for service, on more than a local scale. All that may be concluded is that freemen, bearing arms and swearing personal loyalty to the king when they came of age, were expected to put themselves at his service when required, which could at best have been most useful when the king was campaigning in their area, for only on a limited scale could they be summoned, equipped and assembled effectively, and in time.

These personal obligations are to be distinguished from ones arising out of possession of land. For example, freemen on small estates within any given five-hide unit might in fact discharge the land obligation by paying a thegn or soldier in proportion to their holding, but their personal duty to the king could not be performed vicariously. These different duties might be thought to represent the difference between a cavalry service discharged by land and an infantry service performed in person, except that the texts are so few and vague that they cannot support a theory, propounded as inherently probable. The Conqueror and his sons used infantry troops and they must have raised them from their own people, but we do not know how this was done. Possibly the king recruited a paid army of freemen, as he hired cavalry soldiers, by attracting men to his service. Our ignorance about the recruitment to his armies is as great as it is for recruitment to service in his peaceful concerns. Were all his menials, foresters, messengers, and guards drawn only from his own estates, or did he find his servants where he could, or simply attract men to his service by the glamour of royalty or in the hope of advancement? Perhaps his infantry were 'pressed' men, vagabonds, criminals, or runaway peasants, and men who simply joined the army, like English armies of other periods in their history, which were no more contemptible then than later. We frankly do not know. Neither the monastic chroniclers nor estate records can be made to state more than the fact that after 1066 the king of England used Englishmen as well as Normans in his armies. It is consistent with the interpretation here advanced, that Englishmen, far from being held down by forces of oppressive Normans, participated in all aspects of Norman government: civil and military.

The castle and the knight stand popularly as symbols of the new Norman military government. The Norman castle, however, no more resembled the great stone castles of Edward I than the Norman knight resembled the chivalrous nobleman, though it is of these features of the thirteenth century that men tend to think first when castles and knights are mentioned. Only five stone keeps of Norman castles now survive in England: Bramber, Pevensey, Colchester, Rochester and London's 'White Tower'. Stone castles took longer to build and they were expensive. Bishop Gundulph of Rochester, the architect of Rochester castle and the 'Tower', estimated that the cost of building Rochester castle would be £60.[16] However desirable such an impregnable stone castle might be, kings were not always prepared to pay the price. Henry I, like his father, built most of his castles by causing a great circular ditch to be dug and a central mound of earth to be raised on which a wooden stockade was erected.[17] They were built quickly: one at York was built in eight days in 1069 and the first Norman castle at Hastings was probably built even more rapidly. They were cheap. Wooden towers could be added: a late authority asserts that such towers were transported in ready-made sections from Normandy for the Hastings campaign. They were apparently effective, for the type was not much modified and they are found all over the country, in different sizes.

It is sometimes assumed that England had no castles before 1066. In fact the Confessor's Normans had built at least three such castles in the Welsh marches, and Robert Fitz Wimarc, a kinsman of the Conqueror, who lived in England before the Conquest, had a small castle at Clavering in Essex. Certainly the Normans did not consider that England was castle-less. William of Poitiers, the Conqueror's campaigning chaplain, thought that Dover had had a castle before 1066 and he describes both its natural position and the artificial defences which rendered it impregnable to arrows. The Conqueror's troops, faced by this obstacle, considered that it could only be taken by setting fire to it. The chaplain evidently believed that the English could have defended it longer, had they a mind to do so, and their terrified submission to the Conqueror is described a little scornfully. But the admiration for the castle glows in the same way as his description of the marvellously situated castles in France.[18] It suggests that Harold could have rivalled even continental castle-builders of his day. London and Exeter, of English cities at this time, also had stout defences for resisting sieges. The Conqueror was held up in both places because the citizens, presumably utilizing the original Roman city walls, could maintain their own defence. At London they even ventured out to attack besiegers. Whether such defences can be called castles may be doubted; they show, however, that the English knew how to defend themselves and it is doubtful whether London was worse defended than Rouen. The Norman motte-and-bailey castle was admittedly less well known, but it must be remembered that such castles had been evolved on the continent only since the end of the tenth century and that their chief function was to provide protection for small groups of soldiers exposed in enemy or marcher country. The shape of the castle, an enclosure and an inner keep, also made it valuable to lords who wanted a place of defence should the mercenary troops of the outer stockade become rebellious in sieges or for want of food or pay. Such outposts enabled commanders to place and protect troops where they could more easily invade, destroy and ravage enemy lands, like the castle put up by the Conqueror at Ambrières on the route from Domfront to Mayenne. England had been a country without border warfare of this sort, except in the Welsh marches, and a small start had in fact been made there, with Norman help, towards the construction of such defences.

Small castles of motte-and-bailey type were put up by the Normans in their first months of campaigning in England. The one at Hastings had covered the Conqueror's first camp. When he moved north in 1067, he rapidly built a castle at Nottingham to cover the passage of the Trent, as he moved into territory of doubtful loyalty. At York itself, the fickle city was overlooked by two castles built in 1068 and 1069. On the northern journeys of these years, castles were put up at Huntingdon, Cambridge and Lincoln. Returning from the north in 1069, he planned a castle at Chester and others on the

Welsh border, beginning at Stafford and Tutbury. The chief ports on the south coast—Hastings, Arundel, Bramber, Chichester, Lewes and Pevensey—were overlooked by castles. The Pool of London lay beneath the Tower and other fortifications in the city had been prepared before the king's coronation. Royal fortresses in such places as Cambridge, Warwick, Shrewsbury and Lincoln were erected on sites from which houses had to be cleared away. The whole country was sown with castles, not simply on the borders but in the centres of population. Do they represent a policy of terrorising the people or providing cover for frightened, because offensive, troops? Apparently, castle-building on this scale extends the habits of the marches into regions totally unsuited to it, unless the whole country had become liable to the terrors of frontier wars.

How many castles were there in England by 1100, or by 1135? Estimates vary enormously. Archaeological evidence is not very helpful, because the hundreds of motte-and-bailey sites known could have been occupied at any period between 1066 and 1200 for short or long periods. Some sites may have served for only one campaign, others may not have been constructed before Stephen's reign, when the king had least control over castle-building. Yet with 200 major barons in the country by 1086, as well as marcher castles and royal strongholds, it is not difficult to believe that there were 400 or more castles by 1100. The Conqueror kept some control over castle-building and Henry I destroyed the castles of his enemies. Henry's dependence on the loyalty of his castellans in Normandy was so great that in one case he was obliged to blind his own granddaughters to appease a castellan, whose son had been blinded by the king's son-in-law.[19] Castles were important in warfare and the Normans knew where to place fortifications. The example of Normandy is not, however, so useful when considering the case of England, because the Norman castles were in border regions and the English ones were not. It has been shown that there were unexpected concentrations of castles in bands around London and Coventry, and the suggestion has been made that the Conqueror planned castle-building on a national scale as part of his military strategy.[20] Castles would guard not only sea-ports and estuaries against invaders from overseas, but also present a hostile army with a series of obstacles impeding any advance on London and Coventry.

Allowing for the construction of castles as look-out points on the coast and as hunting-lodges near forests, most castles were built along rivers or roads, particularly overlooking bridges or fords. Some castles in towns occupied sites where houses had had to be destroyed, but more often the castles in Domesday book had been built just outside the town and a new burg had grown up at the foot. The growth of suburbs increased the prosperity of the town and shows that the castle did not inhibit urban life, even if it inspired awe in the local inhabitants. One use of the castle in the town was to provide a place of refuge to non-combatants in times of trouble. When the rebels of 1088 threatened Worcester, the bishop's knights went out to meet the enemy beyond the Severn and insisted that the bishop should take refuge in the castle, until the result of the battle was known.[21] The chief value of the castle was to defend a small body of men from attack, and the obstacle they presented to an invading hostile force was only to hold up a general advance by obliging a detachment of invaders to besiege it. The defenders of the castle had no cannon with which to attack the enemy and had to rely on arrows or cruder missiles like stones, and they themselves were extremely vulnerable to fire. Nevertheless, castles were strong points in which soldiers normally lived and which could sustain sieges, like the siege of Tonbridge in 1088, where the rebels defied Rufus.

The residence of a Norman baron was also a castle. At Bayeux, in the eleventh century, even the citizens built towers for themselves, as in fourteenth-century Italy, and this appears to be the practice forbidden by the king before 1100.[22] In London, the king had his residence at the Tower, but there were also baronial castles at Montfichet and Baynard Castle. At Winchester, the king and the bishop had one castle each. A castle was built as headquarters near the forest, at Windsor or Rockingham, and the royal castles witnessed some stirring public debates with churchmen. They were places not only for war, but for discussions and legal affairs. Though hardship may have been caused to the local population by insisting on unwonted labour services in their construction, castles were not imposed on the country without respect for existing obligations. When Windsor castle was built, the tax assessment was modified to allow for the half hide of land the king had taken away. If the king insisted that the abbot of Abingdon provide a castle guard from the abbey's knights, the abbot simply enfeoffed the knights with vacant thegnlands. The abbey lost little by the new service demanded. If we ask why there were so many castles along the roads, rivers and at bridges, the answer is not simply a military one. It was in such places that population gathered. If towns are situated where roads cross rivers, or at the head of navigable streams, it is not simply for military reasons, but because these sites have advantages for travellers and commerce. Castles are built at such points, either to keep watch for possible enemies, bands of pirates or robbers as well as political rebels, or to provide places in which the local population may seek refuge against such enemies; in normal circumstances the castle will house the local lord and his men, who guard the town as their own valuable estate.

The existence of castles in great numbers in the hands of local lords transformed the problem of conquering England after 1086, but not merely for the kind of obstacle that they presented to invaders. The Norman lord in his castle was an individual to be reckoned with in politics as in war. He did not fight for his region but for his lord. Unlike his neighbours he might be committed to a lord in trouble with the king and he could hold his castle against the rest of the countryside. It is true that within his castle he could more safely defy authority, for a time, but it was his political attitude, and that of his contemporaries, that made him potentially dangerous. At the same time, the Norman kings had the advantages of the system. By relying on their castellans to keep loyal, the kings did not fear regional risings. The area was sown with castles which had to be committed individually to a rebellious enterprise. There was no regional chief as he had existed before 1066.

Changes in the Law

In the legal sphere, the king set out with the intention of allowing the customs of Edward the Confessor, but a place had to be found for his Frenchmen in the courts, so that they could join issue there on equal terms with the English; their own French customs had also to be accommodated, if the Frenchmen were not to lose their law. The two different systems did not exist side by side, they coalesced as men worked out the implications of different rules of law for each case. The problem was not new. In a similar form it had existed under Canute and, significantly, the Normans used Canute's two great law codes as a guide to English law, without seeing any need to refurbish it in a new digest.[23] The oldest surviving manuscript of Canute's laws was made just after the Conquest, but translations had to be made before the end of the century, to enable the new generation of French-speaking lawyers to gain knowledge of them. By 1100, Canute's declaration of his wish to codify the law appeared in Latin in the chronicle of Florence of Worcester. The Latin versions of the codes, the *Institutio* and the *Consiliatio*, were produced by a Frenchman before 1117.[24]

With the law books, the old rules of law naturally retained their force. In the *Articles* of William I, which appeared under Henry I as the statement of his father's law, the opening clause, with its stress on the unity of religion and faith as the basis of the common polity of English and Normans, takes up the phrases of Canute's first code in the new context. The second clause, whereby all freemen are obliged to swear fidelity to William, both in and out of England, faithfully to defend his lands, and honour and to serve with him and before him against his enemies, was inspired by a law of Edmund. The laws were to be enforced in the traditional shire and hundred courts and all freemen were expected to be in surety groups, as in the past. The English tariffs of payment for crimes, mutilations and homicides were still observed under Henry I, who promised to enforce them, as they had been before the Conquest. Basically the old law stood.

Changes were also inevitable, though some were planned and others grew up without legislation. First, Norman custom had to be admitted into English law. Both the English and the Normans at this period normally settled legal disputes by an appeal to God: the ordeal.[25] Preliminary hearings established whether an accused man could find enough neighbours or friends to swear his innocence, or whether he was of such ill repute as not to deserve such procedure. If the hearing found against his legal reliability, the priests presided over a ceremony in which the accused, after religious preparation, was flung into a pool of water or obliged to carry a hot iron. The form of judgment not known in England was the trial by battle in which the accuser fought the accused until victory showed who upheld the truth. This was one form of the ordeal as it existed in Normandy and William allowed Frenchmen to use this method in the English courts. What, however, if a Frenchman willing to do battle challenged an Englishman? Obviously one side or the other would have to surrender customary procedure. An Englishman was allowed in these circumstances to refuse battle and appeal to divine judgment by fire or water. Englishmen, however, had the option of adopting trial by battle, thus extending their range of judicial procedure. Trial by battle survived surprisingly late, but there is little reliable evidence of its frequency. Since it was possible for one of the parties to decline battle and opt for a different judgment, cases tended to be resolved by compromise in the courts.[26] Even a Frenchman who was accused and boldly offered to defend himself by battle could not force his accuser to fight: in this case, the Frenchman had to find oath-helpers and recite the holy formulae, like the English, without the slips of the tongue that betrayed a guilty conscience.

William also had to defend his Frenchmen against unpunished assassination. When an Englishman was killed, his family, not the king, was normally responsible for finding and accusing the murderer. Most English killings were obviously done in public as a result of quarrels, brawls or fights and the killer was therefore known. William must have soon discovered that Normans were attacked and killed furtively, and without families to pursue the criminal, their murder went unavenged. It was with the Normans that the crime of 'murder' (in which the criminal was unknown) entered English law. In order to secure some punishment for this crime and prevent local conspiracies against Frenchmen, the king ordered the lord of the victim to trace the murderer within five days and obtain from him the blood-price, or compensation, according to the victim's rank, as English law required. If the lord was not successful in finding the murderer, he would himself become liable to the king to pay forty-six marks: a very high sum. The king foresaw that some lords might have difficulty in paying from their small estates: in that case, a collective fine on the hundred in which the murder had been committed would make good what the lord still owed. In Henry I's time the murder fine was still being paid, though not at the rate of forty-six marks, but at sums varying from thirty marks to one mark, usually ten or fifteen marks.[27] The king did not get even all these sums, for the great lords of a hundred were allowed to keep the sums due from their manors. The object of the law even in William's time was primarily to persuade his Frenchmen's lords not to shrug off murders as unpunishable. It was also intended as a temporary measure to cover the Frenchmen introduced for the campaign, men who had lords, but no families. The application of the principle for detecting murder in a case where it could not be proved that the victim was English (and so entitled to the old procedure), established a new crime at law.

William's law on murder is a good illustration of the way temporary devices served a permanent need, or, at least, effected profounder consequences than were intended. The changes introduced by the Normans into English law were not confined to these two matters, though it was these two laws that William consciously introduced as novelties. The so-called *Articles* of William exemplify William's claim to uphold the laws of the Confessor, modified where necessary. The most important changes are not in the laws, so much as in the punishments. He commuted the death penalty to blinding or castration, though under Henry I many criminals were hanged. More lasting was the condemnation to forfeiture for offences like selling men as slaves out of the country or selling beasts anywhere other than in cities before three witnesses. Canute had legislated for both matters in similar terms, but before William the penalty had consisted of fines, usual in English law. Did William impose stiffer penalties because he had more of a problem to control illicit trading or piracy than Canute had had? It seems more likely that he introduced into England the penalties he had known in Normandy: forfeiture of property, land or life for specific offences.

If the king could impose forfeiture, he became more interested in securing convictions, particularly of dealers in slaves and cattle. It seems unjust to suppose that the king by his heavy murder fine and forfeitures was interested primarily in raking in the profits of justice. The records of murder fines suggests that the avaricious Henry I did not mind sharing the profits with others; the reason why these punishments were introduced to replace old ones probably reflects a changed economic situation as well as a new approach to law.

If the old fines of 120 shillings to the king could more easily be met by offenders and so failed to deter, forfeiture was a real deterrent. Heavy fines dissuaded men from illegalities as well as enriched the king. Undoubtedly more important, however, was the initiative which the king showed in securing enforcement of justice. Without introducing any new royal court, except for his own immediate followers, the king became much more interested in punishing offenders. Forfeiture came into Normandy from Carolingian law: the survival of the practice in the eleventh century is remarkable proof of the survival of that law to the duke's advantage. By Henry I's reign, if not sooner, the Norman rule was adopted that a man who failed at the ordeal was declared 'infamous' and lost his inheritance. In the Norman view, a man who was outlaw automatically fell into the king's mercy and his property was declared forfeit. Outlawry had been introduced into England by Canute: an outlaw was a man put beyond the protection of the law and his 'bocland' was naturally lost because it was land alienable by legal instruments. The Normans, who did not admit the alienability of land, nevertheless allowed that forfeiture for attacking an enemy under the duke's protection could destroy the family claims to the land.[28]

When the Normans arrived in England in 1066 they had their own conceptions of land-law. On the one hand, they understood that an 'allod' was family property for which the holder did no homage to a lord, but which he could not alienate without the whole family's consent; the present occupier had the slenderest right to prejudice the expectations of his heirs. On the other hand, the Normans apparently knew how to make temporary leases. These were called 'fees'; services were performed regularly in return for them and the tenure was known as 'feudal'. It is not clear whether feudal leases could be granted by any possessor of an allod, or whether they were created only on specific estates, such as land formerly in the domain of the dukes and counts of Normandy at the time of Richard II. These leases were never put in writing, and by the nature of Norman custom were well understood to be temporary concessions. It is assumed that, to renew them from one generation to another, the heir of a feudal tenure was expected to pay a relief in order to be accepted by the lord of the fee on the same terms as his father had been, but the Normans cannot be shown to have used the word relief before 1066. The very idea that temporary leases could be inherited was no more generally admitted than the idea that the head of a family had authority to make a permanent alienation. How common the practice of enfeoffment had become in Normandy by 1066 cannot be demonstrated, but inalienability of family property was such a tenacious idea that it seems likely that allodial lands were still the most common type of tenure. It is also certain, however, that a son's right to succeed to all his father's possessions was so generally admitted that from the first there was a strong pressure on lords to allow sons to succeed to the father's fee, once the concession of fees had become at all common.

These ideas of tenure were so well understood that they were not put into writing, and the conservation of customary tenures was so strong that there was no place for written instruments for transfers of land in Normandy. Confirmations of such gifts were sometimes obtained by ducal charters but in Norman law it was the actual physical ceremony in which grants were made that effected the transfer. Written documents were clearly not at all necessary and could not by themselves be considered binding. This attitude explains why the Normans did not make wills and did not admit death-bed wishes. All their legal transactions were binding only during the lifetime of the persons involved, who were personally bound in honour by their temporary leases, but who could not prejudice the rights of others after their death by written instruments. In a society thus living literally from one generation to another, personal commitments and honour were the sole guarantee of order.

The English had evolved their principles of land law at an earlier date than the Normans. In England all men held by custom, which differed from place to place and according to status. Since the conversion of the English to Christianity, however, the king had made grants of land by charter, that is written instruments modelled on those of the late Roman empire. They had been originally made for the benefit of the Roman missionaries, but they had subsequently been granted to laymen. By receiving such a charter, the beneficiary enjoyed the special privilege of holding by book-land. Essentially, such written instruments were held to define the legal obligations of the land-holder; they would specify on what terms or by what privileges the estate might be enjoyed and the most coveted privilege was the right of holders by book-land to dispose of their land freely on whatever terms they wished. In the course of the tenth century, at least, written instruments were introduced for the specific purpose of creating short tenures with some of the advantages of book-land for the period of their effectiveness. Unlike Norman feudal tenures, the leases conceded by the bishop of Worcester to his tenants for life and the lives of two heirs were made by written instruments.[29] It was the advantage of such a lease that it was more flexible than grants made by custom, and it offered the tenant the temporary assurance that his immediate heirs would be provided for and the lord was promised defined services for longer than one life. There was also a possibility that it could be renewed.

At the Conquest therefore the Normans were introduced to a system of land-holding altogether unfamiliar, yet by the terms of their settlement the king had imposed on them the obligations of their predecessors in the estates. Did this give the Normans the right to will their lands or create leases for three lives? It seems not. How soon the king became aware of the discrepancy between the two systems of land-holding is not known. In 1071, when William Fitz Osbern died, it was the king who divided his lands between his two sons.[30] Whatever advantage the Normans might have discovered for themselves in the English system, they were so familiar with their own and so little dissatisfied with it, that it was essentially the Norman system that prevailed for their tenures. The great mass of the English population went on holding by customary, or folk, law. It was book-land that disappeared as a legal concept.

With the exceptions of those few who certainly married English heiresses, the Normans owed their English estates to the king's gift.[31] Though they might have become allods, they certainly were not allods in any recognisable way when distributed. They had been granted by the king to his personal followers, without charters. When a lord died he had no right to dispose of his estate, but had his heir any right to succeed him? Certainly his first son had a strong claim to his father's Norman lands, whether they were allods or fees. The Conqueror did not refuse William Fitz Osbern's son his patrimony in Normandy. If he gave Roger, the second son, the estates of his father in England, it was a concession made in his lifetime and in Norman manner the tenure was binding as long as the parties both lived. No written instruments were necessary or desirable, no conditions or services had to be, or could be, specified, because custom admitted of no arbitrary power to impose services. These tenures could also be created at many levels. The king conceded lands to his tenants-in-chief, who made grants to sub-tenants, who could themselves assign fractions of the estate to others. In the reign of Henry I, not only the king and his tenant-in-chief the king of Scotland, but also the lord of the fee had to approve a grant of land made by the Foliot brothers to Ramsey abbey. Feudal tenure extended to four levels and all four lords were concerned for the land and one another and had power to refuse consent. This was what feudal tenure could mean: a hierarchy of relationships that bound all the feudal class together.

These personal relationships rooted in the land were new to England. Before the Conquest, short leases to thegns had been made on church lands and perhaps elsewhere, but the lease itself established only the church's right to the reversion. It is possible that the lease-holders, as was not uncommon in other parts of the country, had the right to seek their personal lord where they liked. This commendation of a vassal to his lord lacked the permanency of the Norman system. The commended man could withdraw from his obligations and take himself and his lands to another lord, whose protection at law or service in battle was more attractive to him. This practice was still known in the Conqueror's reign, but the Normans clearly disliked it and attempted to curtail it, so that for the future a vassal found that, having committed himself to one lord, the lord's heir considered himself entitled to the same services as his father: a natural extension of the Normans' belief in hereditary right. As late as 1077, when abbot Aethelwig of Evesham died, the men who had commended themselves to him personally withdrew from the abbey's service and took themselves to Odo of Bayeux, and the new abbot did not succeed in recovering his predecessor's rights.[32] Possibly the fact that churchmen were involved explains the anomaly; at all events by 1086, the practice was clearly unusual and it disappeared entirely within another generation.

The Normans in England found that they were obliged to work within the English system, except in cases of special privilege. For matters that concerned their own tenants the lords expected to provide judgments in their own courts and wished to attend public courts as little as possible, and then only to answer for their landed vassals.[33] This restrictive conception of lordship played its part in transforming the character of English justice. Before the Conquest, if a man was accused of a crime, and failed to appear to answer in the court, his family, lord or personal warrantor was obliged to step into his place. In practice, the family had ceased to bear the chief responsibility for producing the accused, and lords preferred to opt out of their obligations for the vassals, except where the vassal had property on which the lord could distrain, to cover himself. The personal surety system was most essential in the case of men who had no land and who could be persuaded only by their neighbours and friends to stand trial in the public interest. All men had therefore to find a warrantor for this purpose, and if a man had been convicted of one crime, or was often accused, he had to find not one but several sureties of his good behaviour.

The Conqueror assumed that all freemen, not only those of doubtful reputation, would have several sureties, and by Henry I's reign the so-called frankpledge system was in operation.[34] The term implies an association freely entered into by neighbours but it was later enforced by the sheriff who toured the hundred courts twice a year to compel landless freemen to complete groups of ten men, mutually bound on oath to answer for one another's good behaviour. These groups of ten, or tithings, are first noticed under Canute, when all men were obliged to join one for the specific purpose of pursuing cattle thieves. They swore on oath that they would not connive with rustlers. At some stage in the century between Canute and Henry I tithings came to be used not only for police work but also as associations for collective security. Did this come about gradually, or did the Normans accelerate the process?

The strongest argument against a theory of natural evolution is that the previous system itself had been produced by royal orders. A union of the surety and police systems suggests such a command, though there is no trace of one in the texts. The development of frankpledge has been associated with the murder fine levied on the hundred; this may have been the case in the twelfth century, but there is nothing in the murder law to make it likely. There, the lord himself was responsible for finding the murderer and paying the fine; only if he did not do so or could not afford to pay, did the hundred become involved. Hundreds obliged to pay heavy fines by the negligence or poverty of lords would have had an incentive to produce the criminal themselves, because the lords with property in the hundred were not liable to pay and had no interest in organising a search for the culprit. It would not be surprising if the hundred man set the groups already existing for the purpose of pursuing cattle to trace other fugitive criminals. But this cannot possibly explain why the tithing also became responsible for the good behaviour of each member of it. This must represent the fact that these police groups of neighbours found themselves without the traditional support in the courts previously supplied by lords and had to adopt a system of mutual help. The lords had no conception of responsibility to vassals except where land was involved. The old system of personal lordship disappeared. The landless freemen with public responsibility in the courts entered into their own free associations. The distribution of the system throughout England, but not in the marches, suggests that the Conqueror's reign was the time at which the new system was introduced, by a royal order, that did not apply in the border earldoms. The tithings, perhaps in view of the importance of cattle theft in the Conqueror's reign, became the basic unit of order in the country: an old institution, that received a new boost after 1066.

The King and the Law

William could not help introducing French concepts into English law, because his Frenchmen were entitled to their own customs; likewise the duke had his own conceptions of public responsibility. In fact, though they were different from English ones they were compatible. There are two matters in which the duke's existing attitude to law affected the English.

The first concerned the forest. The king was said 'to love the red deer as their father', a striking if rather unexpected metaphor, since the king's intention was to chase and kill. Canute himself had warned men to keep clear of his forests, and allowed men their own hunting; the Confessor was addicted to the chase. What changes did William introduce? He was responsible for the definition of 'forest land', as land removed from ordinary legal jurisdiction and put under special stringent rules which the king alone enforced. This type of forest law had been devised by the Carolingians and the count's enforcement of the law in the ninth century had devolved on the duke in his own interest by the tenth. Louis the Pious had forbidden counts to have unauthorised forests of their own, but it is doubtful whether the duke was really able to make this an effective ban in Normandy. Eleventh-century Norman counts kept their own forests. The chief purpose of the regulations was to control the hunting of the great animals of the chase—the red deer, the fallow deer, the roe, and the boar—and to limit the destruction of great trees and the overfishing of rivers. The duke's enforcement of these rights of protection provoked a peasant rebellion in the early eleventh century, which was put down with great ferocity. The amount of land under forest in Normandy cannot be calculated. For England, Domesday book is more help. The forest continued to grow under the Conqueror's successors, though there were frequent protests about it. But apart from the eviction of tenants in the New Forest to make way for William's forest, the real hardship was caused only to those who hunted without permission, rich and poor.[35]

The measure has been regarded with general distaste. But it has its justification. Men had hunted these animals from the earliest times. If hunting became limited, it was because the area available for it was constantly diminished by the spread of agriculture. In these circumstances, the limited resources available had to be priced out of general range and hunting became an aristocratic, even royal, privilege. The Carolingian empire itself had provided the conditions for an extension of cultivated land, by assuring peace and order. But with plans for clearing new lands, the natural reserves of game and timber were threatened. The value of these woodlands for technical trades, like leather-making and glass manufacture, their contributions of rare natural products, for food, for fuel, for charcoal, need no emphasis. Agriculture and prosperity, no less than amenities, were involved. By modern standards, the dangers may seem exaggerated, but to rulers like the Carolingians they were real. No one supposes that their massive capitularies were capricious devices for extending their personal sport and privileges. The Conqueror was familiar with the problems, and when he arrived in England he must have been surprised that there was no adequate protection of these resources of the whole community, particularly in view of the extent to which woodland had already been cut and put under the plough. That his methods were drastic may be the case; that their efficacy depended on a determination to enforce the law, reinforced by personal motives, is certain. However, it is easy to overdo his love of the chase; in Normandy his youthful recreation was falconry. The bishop Geoffrey of Coutances stocked his Norman deer park from England. It was probably in England that the Conqueror became a devotee of the chase. More than personal tyranny made well-meaning kings from his time resist the pressure on them to surrender forest land. Governments are often unpopular because only by their arbitrary methods can they overcome noisy oppositions that defend their own interests. It is by no means more obvious that kings were more selfish than huntsmen, poachers and squatters.

At the great council of Lillebonne in 1080, the king defined his forest jurisdiction and proposed to conduct enquiries into trespass and to fine offenders by means of the inquest. The use of this inquest procedure is another direct link with Carolingian government. No pre-Conquest example of the inquest procedure is known from Normandy and claims for an English origin of the procedure have been made on the strength of the Wantage oath of 1012.[36] This argument seems misleading. A lot is known about English procedures before 1066 and the place for royal initiative in justice was minimal. The inquest as used by the Conqueror has the stamp of authority: the king orders an enquiry, he summons the parties and compels witnesses to give evidence. All that is English about the process is the use of the royal writ to initiate it. The abundant evidence for inquests after 1066 never suggests that comparable enquiries had been made under the Confessor. The Conqueror's powers to make enquiries of this kind in Normandy may have been in abeyance before 1066, but there can be little doubt that, given the existing authority of the English monarchy, he enhanced its power by Carolingian traditions.[37]

The English king promised at his coronation to forbid all rapacity and iniquity and to show equity and mercy to his subjects. The Conqueror promised to do this at Berkhamsted before he became king and again at the coronation ceremony. He took these responsibilities seriously. How the kings before him executed their promise, the sources do not say. Law-courts were public and presided over by the king's official, but there was no *curia regis* as it came to exist by the twelfth century in which later kings reckoned to fulfil their coronation promises. The Conqueror's *curia regis* was properly a court of his tenants-in-chief, secular and ecclesiastical: a feudal court of honour for his vassals, and as such it would have been used in 1075 when the king decided to settle the dispute between the earl of Hereford and the sheriffs himself.[38] For ordinary legal matters the Conqueror expected the old public courts in the shires and hundreds to function as before. He had, however, as has been seen, one valuable contribution to make to the legal advantages of his subjects: the inquest procedure. Used by Carolingian emperors through their courts, its survival in Normandy, like that of other Carolingian laws, forest law, monetary privilege, even military obligation, is a matter of conjecture rather than proof. In this case the top of the iceberg as seen in England after 1066 implies a deep and broad base beneath the waters of early Norman history.

England was ready for a profound enquiry into landownership and a clear recognition of right; it may also have been in need of tying social relationships to land. Domesday book shows that the monks' long memories could extend the tale of disputed titles and usurped right well beyond the Confessor's reign. With the bishop of Bayeux in gaol, the monks of Ely boldly pressed their claims to Snailwell, occupied by Hugh de Port as the bishop's tenant. On investigation, it seemed that Odo had got Stigand's lands and that Stigand had been lent the manor by abbot Leofsige before 1044.[39] The bishops of Chester and Winchester revived memories of usurpations going back to Canute's reign at the great inquest of 1086[40] and Worcester's losses were traced by Hemming back beyond William Fitz Osbern and Edwin and Morcar to unjust stewards, royal tax-collectors and the Danish pagan raiders under king Sweyn at the beginning of the eleventh century. England had been troubled by a succession of oppressors. The Normans did not simply continue the tradition for another generation adding their illegalities to the pathetic record of abuses. The king offered to give justice, reverse illegal possession and investigate alleged wrongs. Order would be drawn out of chaos by royal enquiry.

Some litigants never admitted defeat. The monks of Ely are an example of this.[41] If written evidence was to hand this could have settled disputes about ownership,[42] but it obviously could not help in such a general enquiry as the king ordered into thefts of church property.[43] Witnesses had to be assembled on a large scale. At Bury, the monks carried one dispute before a court with representatives of nine counties.[44]

Over twenty years the king and queen, leading Norman bishops and sheriffs heard innumerable law-suits about rights of property and jurisdiction of which most records have vanished.[45] If some surviving documents give the impression that wrongs had still not been put right and that injustices flourished like weeds in waste-land, the impression is false. In Domesday book, the commissioners gathered together a special collection of unresolved disputes or unsatisfied complaints for the counties of the South-West, East Anglia, Hampshire, Huntingdon, Lincoln and York. Admittedly there is no sign that these were resolved by judgment, but they had been set aside for special treatment and easier disputes had been resolved in the work of investigation. It was not the king's fault, if he died too soon to find solutions for the abuses brought to light or if his successors were less conscientious. A writer like Hemming at Worcester, who made out that the church was still being defrauded of its property after Domesday book, is a partial witness. The king's judges had looked into Worcester's claims and had heard and believed Worcester's opponents; from the Worcester evidence alone we are in no position to judge in Worcester's favour. Hemming thought that William Fitz Osbern's violent death in 1071 was divine vengeance on him for his share in seizing the lands of the monks, and allowing his sheriff and his officials to do the same. The earl's death, the forfeiture of his son Roger, the king's own favour to the bishop had all availed nothing to reverse usurpations of Fitz Osbern's brief two years in the west country. If Worcester had not succeeded in making good its claims, when no particularly powerful earl stood between the monks and the king, perhaps the claims were not well founded anyway.

The inquest procedure was initiated by a royal writ ordering named men to open an enquiry into a complaint. On one occasion, the bishop of Worcester gave the king a silver chalice of great value to obtain the writ he required.[46] This was not a flagrant sale of justice, for the king did not sell a favourable judgment, but allowed his bishop to benefit by a procedure of enquiry normally reserved for the king's own purposes. Moreover the writ-process is still new in the Conqueror's reign and no set fees have been agreed for issuing writs *de cursu*. The use of writs in this way is new. He is taking an English type of document (used before the Conquest as evidence of landed title) and making it serve a different purpose. The bishop is therefore prepared to obtain such a writ: he thinks it will be worth it.

In his great suit with the abbot of Evesham, the bishop of Worcester obtained from the king a writ directed to the bishop of Coutances, Geoffrey Mowbray, the sheriff of Worcester, Urso d'Abbetot (tenant and usurper of the Worcester lands) and Osbern Fitz Scrob, tenant-in-chief.[47] Bishops, sheriffs and tenants-in-chief were the men usually deputed by the king to assemble the court, compelling lawful men to appear at the royal command to answer the questions. The Conqueror's writ was sent from Normandy and bishop Geoffrey presided at the court in Worcester. The bishop claimed Bengeworth on the grounds that his tenant Aerngrim had commended himself to Aethelwig, abbot of Evesham, who had thereupon invested Aerngrim with the land as a fief, as though the bishop's rights did not exist. The bishop claimed that he had witnesses who would swear to the situation as it was in the Confessor's time. Abbot Walter, Aethelwig's successor, defended his rights. The barons of the court agreed that there was a case to answer, and they, or Geoffrey, decided that, since the abbot could not produce any witnesses of the Confessor's reign to dispute with the bishop's, he should be allowed to swear to the truth of what he claimed on the relics of the abbey. Since this procedure was accepted on both sides, Geoffrey ordered a trial. From a letter of bishop Geoffrey written in 1086,[48] it appears that the trial took place at Hillborough before the men of four counties. Abbot Walter brought his relics; the bishop lined up Edric, his steersman under the Confessor, Kineward, a former sheriff, Siward, a rich man of Shropshire, Osbern Fitz Richard, and others as his witnesses. The abbot's friends, impressed by this array of living witnesses, persuaded him to recognise the bishop's claims to Bengeworth, and to take the estate as a tenancy from the bishop, in return for service.

For such a dispute about the lands of Ely,[49] the king ordered Lanfranc to inquire from the bishops of Coutances and Winchester and the others who had obtained a sworn description of the lands of the church of St Etheldreda, how the swearing had been done, who had sworn, who heard the swearing, the extent and the names of the lands, how many there were, how much they rendered, who held them, all noted and recorded separately. 'Do this, so that I shall know the truth about it by your writ and let the abbot's messenger bring it to me'. The terms of this order are so much like those of the more famous questions asked by the king at the time of Domesday book, that it has been supposed that this letter was connected with that enquiry. Though this is not in fact the case, the similarity is revealing. The kind of enquiries the king had been ordering throughout his reign were very similar to the ones he ordered over the whole of England in 1086. There are two obvious differences. At special request in particular circumstances, the king had allowed his writ to be issued and had collected a fee for his favour. In 1086, the king himself, of his will, used the inquest procedure to get the facts about his land and how it was governed. Had he been concerned merely to tidy up legal niceties for litigants with long memories, he need not have planned anything so extensive, however general usurpation was. Domesday book gives a general impression not of confusion and usurpation, but of orderliness, each estate set out under the names of leading tenants. This order may have been introduced by the inquest itself or it may be the specious orderliness of written records. But it does not suggest that the landed settlement remained generally contentious. Had it been so, the king would have been better advised to wait and receive silver chalices and the like from every man who desperately wanted to recover his claims. By ordering such an enquiry himself, the king forfeited those desirable extra gifts and embarked on a huge undertaking, unparalleled in medieval Europe.

Though the scale of the enquiry suggests a carefully considered plan carried through with deliberation, the final redaction bears the marks of hasty execution, if only in the final stage.[50] This raises a problem about how far the Domesday enquiry was planned to serve an immediate need in the winter of 1085–86. Whatever haste may then have seemed necessary with a view to later action, the king adopted a regular and orderly procedure, first by consulting his great men at the Christmas assembly of 1085 and then by sending commissioners into the country, to satisfy his desire to know all he could about England, its peoples and its society. If he had intended to use the digest of the information that was prepared for his treasury to introduce changes or reforms in his government, his violent death in September 1087 prevented him from doing so, though it is extremely likely that his son showed what the king had intended the record for, by tightening the crown's grip over its tenants-in-chief. For although pressing dangers faced William in 1085, it was not to meet any temporary difficulties that Domesday book was designed. It recorded the customs of England in each place, establishing their legality by age and their unjustness by innovation and offering therefore as definitive a picture of English society as could have been expected in the eleventh century. It was not the Conqueror's fault if society changed more rapidly than he expected. It is often a disadvantage that codifiers overlook.

The questions asked by the commissioners have been preserved in a later record, but the Domesday volumes themselves prove that there was no consistent use of the same questionnaire in all counties; a lot of the information collected locally was also discarded or compressed in the volume composed and kept in the royal treasury at Winchester. This Exchequer volume is what the government ultimately obtained from the enquiry and presumably best represents the essence of what the government wanted to know.

It is divided into counties in each of which the king's lands and those of his tenants-in-chief are listed in order. Disputes about possession were brought to light and settled or, in some counties, listed as an appendix to be dealt with later. When each estate was assigned to a tenant in the hierarchy of land ownership, a summary of its resources, liabilities and value completed the entry.

An enquiry of these proportions was obviously not undertaken principally to put an end to legal disputes, but it was important that the experience of the reign had shown how the facts of ownership could be obtained and settlements imposed. The king used the shire courts to collect the information required. The commissioners sat in the court and summoned representatives of every hundred to them; possibly, as in Cambridgeshire, the priest, reeve and six townsmen (*villani*) of each village attended, though in some parts of England the hundred's part in the proceedings was minimal. Taking the king and his tenants-in-chief in order of status, bishops and abbots before secular lords, the commissioners apparently required each hundred in turn to declare what the great lords held in their hundred, and to give what information they could about the estate, its previous tenants and its customs. The manorial bailiff could have supplied the more trivial information, either by oral testimony or in the form of a written statement: his information was not controversial and needed no publicity.

The information gathered was somehow reduced to the proportions of the Domesday book. The larger of the two tomes comprises the record for thirty-two counties; the smaller contains the material for East Anglia, in much greater detail and in much more leisurely format. The Exeter Domesday book for the five south-western counties is a similiar volume, but whereas it was heavily abbreviated and incorporated in the first tome of Domesday, the East Anglian volume was never reduced to the proportions allowed for other counties. It is therefore reasonable to assume that this regional summary was not completed in time for the Exchequer clerk of Domesday I to incorporate and condense it into the normal proportions, particularly as the special social character of East Anglia made uniformity of nomenclature particularly difficult.

However, in view of the existence of regional tomes like these, it is possible that there were formerly others, from which Domesday I was composed. For there are regional variations in the composition of Domesday book, which may be explained, either as the result of assembling the materials in regional centres, or by the fact that the commissioners themselves visited more than one county and developed their own ways of acquiring and recording information. There may be an element of truth in both these alternatives. From that time to now it has been difficult to decide whether the work of collecting these vital statistics of the Conqueror's England is more remarkable than the volumes in which the records survives. The

Conqueror has left no greater monument than Domesday book and it has survived, parchment and ink, as a more lasting memorial of the Conqueror's idea of government and his conservation of preceding English administration, than his abbey at Caen or his Tower at London. The Normans wrote little of their business affairs in the Conqueror's time, and the English comparatively much. It needed a Norman king to make the English encompass the wealth of England in a few hundred folios.

Royal Administration

When the king promised to repress iniquity and do justice to his people he summarised the function of his government; but in order to make it possible for kings to carry out their duties fully, specific offences had been reserved for royal judgment and great estates assigned to maintain the king and his officers. The kingship may therefore be considered from two rather different stand-points. The theory and duty of the office could inspire princes to dedicate their life to their people; the opportunities and privileges of their position could make them particularly selfish exploiters of those powers. The Conqueror was certainly not one of these; nevertheless he developed a system of administration of the royal rights that served his selfish sons after him.

The most remarkable of the Conqueror's innovations in administration was the development of the royal writ, the minute scrap of parchment that conveyed the king's will to all his people.[51] In form, the writ was a letter addressed by the king to named individuals, and those that survive from before the Conquest show that the statement of the king's will had come to be regarded as sufficient evidence of title to land or privileges and had therefore ousted the solemn charter with its imposing phrases and curses as the expression of the king's favour. The use of these slight, terse letters in English law is the most remarkable proof of the sophistication of pre-Conquest government and the Conqueror best proved his capacity to govern like his predecessors by using, not neglecting, the full resources at his disposal.

It is probable that the king's writ had been used before the Conquest for more ephemeral purposes than confirming ownership, but no examples of the administrative writ earlier than 1072 have survived and there can be no doubt that William and his successors enormously extended the scope of the writ in royal business. In view of the apparent absence of the writ from Normandy, they showed exceptional percipience in adapting written instruments of government for themselves. After 1070 the language of the writs was normally Latin rather than English; the Norman kings added to the writ clauses that emphasised its authority—under the Conqueror, giving the name of the witness who had been present when it was written, and, at the end of the reign, giving the place of issue. It bore no date, but it was a personal command witnessed by one of the king's court. Its short crisp authority was further enhanced by the fact that William's chancery, unlike Edward's, wasted no time or effort writing names or words that could be abbreviated, so that the sense of urgency and peremptory command are conveyed in the very letter itself. The use of these letters in administration would have grown naturally with the kind of government for which the Conqueror had become responsible. If his possessions in land were twice those of the Confessor, he had twice as much estate administration. His personal association with all the tenants-in-chief of England and their relationship to him was of a kind unknown in the previous reign. The disturbances and injustices of the Conquest itself involved constant legal disputes, which the king agreed to have settled by his own inquest procedure, and the writ was used extensively in these matters alone, to set the inquest commission to work. The writ could be used for commands and prohibitions of all sorts, and few enough of them survive; but few as they are they indicate how under the Conqueror the royal writ had become an instrument of government, proving the king capable of sharp rebuke and energetic action over the whole country.

England was governed at three different levels in the eleventh century. Most public business, the law courts and geld-paying were conducted in the hundred, a very ancient unit of local government. When disputes could not be settled in court, or justice could not be had there, the shire court was available. Shires had also a long history in West Saxon government, but the shire system had been introduced into other parts of England only after the English absorption of the Danelaw in the tenth century, and the process of shiring England was still not complete in 1066. But it was to the shire court that the king normally sent his instructions and it was for this reason that the language of the writ was in English, so that it could be read out to the assembled company. The Conqueror must have changed the language to suit both the English and the Norman members of the court. Those who could not understand either could nevertheless see the great double-faced seal that was attached to the writ and accept that as evidence of the royal mandate. The Norman kings concentrated their energies on dealing with the shire courts and left supervision of the hundreds to their chief representative in each shire, the sheriff.

Before the Conquest, the king's will had been transmitted to the country not only by his written commands but by the great earls over whole regions, whom Canute had first appointed as viceroys. After the Conquest the king appointed no more earls of this sort, and by 1075, the last of the old ones was in exile. The king therefore dealt directly with the shires, without using earls as intermediaries, except in a few marcher counties. The chief royal official in each shire was now the sheriff.[52]

The Anglo-Saxon sheriff had been overshadowed by the earl. Originally as reeve of the shire he had been responsible for the administration of royal property in each shire and had acquired as the royal representative a leading part in proceedings at the shire court. Edward the Confessor did not have so much royal property as William and in some shires he had so little that his sheriffs would have anyway been much less significant figures. They are so obscure in some places that a list of the Confessor's sheriffs cannot be completed. All this was changed under the Conqueror. He possessed by 1086 twice as much property as the Confessor and had a stake in every county except Sussex, and the three marcher earldoms. In these circumstances the king's bailiff in the county became a person of major importance and it is interesting that some Englishmen succeeded their fathers in office to carry out the royal administration: they were not necessarily disqualified. Most of the king's sheriffs were, however, Normans, and considerable landowners in their counties by 1086. The king was not obliged to give the office to their sons; the shrievalty did not in most cases become hereditary. The men chosen as sheriffs had not been very prominent in Normandy and they made their way up from the lower or middling ranks of the Norman landed classes. About twenty of them were great tenants-in-chief in 1086 but only four left heirs who subsequently became earls. A few counties were managed together by one sheriff in the Conqueror's reign for convenience, but essentially each county was a separate unit of government and the sheriff was its all-powerful governor.

The fear with which the shire regarded its sheriff emerges as the deepest moral of a story told about the monks of Rochester and the sheriff of Cambridge, Picot. The monks accused the sheriff of taking some of their property and granting it to a sergeant of the king. The case was heard in the Cambridge shire court over which Odo, bishop of Bayeux, presided as the king's representative. Twelve legal men, chosen in court to swear on oath the true judgment, found in favour of the sheriff and Odo had no alternative but to pronounce accordingly. Within a year, a monk, who had been bailiff of the estate in question, went to the bishop of Rochester and declared that at least one of the twelve men had perjured himself. The bishop told Odo, who examined the man and accepted his confession of false-witness. Picot was then instructed to send up to London the other eleven men, together with another panel of twelve men from the shire. In a great assembly of barons, the monks recovered their estate. The second panel of twelve men were not allowed to escape easily. They were asked why they had wilfully consented to the first false judgment, and when they pleaded ignorance, they were sent to the ordeal by hot-iron. They failed and the whole county incurred a fine of £300 to the king.[53] Picot terrified his shire; twenty-four lawful men preferred not to cross his path. Justice against him could only be obtained in a special assembly presided over by the king (or in this case his regent); for less persistent suitors, or those with no powerful friends, the sheriff,'s word would not be challenged. As Hemming of Worcester said of the sheriff, 'he could favour or harm the monks as he chose'. Urso of Worcester usually chose to trespass on Worcester property, according to Hemming, but he was not a mere tyrant. He also observed the forms, got tenancies unscrupulously but on legal terms, or became a vassal, in return for what he wanted. The sheriff could afford to use the forms of law.

The sheriff's family and friends were shielded by his power. Urso's brother, who was also the king's dispenser, trespassed on an estate of the bishop of Worcester, but persuaded the queen herself not to listen to complaints. The sheriff's officials were made to work in his interest. Since the sheriff usually paid a fixed sum, or 'farm', to the king, and then collected the revenues of the royal estates in the county by his own efforts, he had a monetary interest in collecting more than he paid. Sheriffs therefore valued the services of rack-renting bailiffs. Robert Malet, sheriff of Suffolk, farmed the county for £60 weight and £8 tale. Roger Bigod offered the king an extra £2 tale and one gold mark (£6) for the shrievalty. Roger's reeve, Aluric, showed how Roger could afford the increase by pushing up the contributions of the freemen on royal manors: twelve freemen at Ringsfield, who had paid nothing in 1066, paid £15 twenty years later; eight freemen at Barnby contributed £30 instead of 13s. 6d.; at Herringfleet, the farm jumped from 20s to £5. No wonder that Roger could afford so much, when the rate had been £33 in 1066.[54] Aluric himself took on the shrievalty at £60 weight, but alleged he made no profit. If so, he must already have milked the udders dry.

Because of the legend of Robin Hood, the medieval English sheriff has donned the guise of a bogey man.[55] His estates, his power and his responsibilities could make him a terror. In an imperfect world, the sheriff nevertheless represented the power to get things done, and his good will was worth having at a price. Sheriffs presided over courts in which men had their own business to transact and they saw that it was better to do what they could for themselves with the king's representative, rather than to stick their necks out on behalf of someone else.

The sheriff was appointed to look after the king's interests and it was to him that those with grievances appealed. When the bishop of Norwich found that his park had been broken into and his deer stolen, he cursed the offender till his flesh should rot with Herod's, but it was the sheriff he expected to seek information and to obtain redress on his behalf.[56] The sheriff made it his business to investigate all trouble and this meant dealing with the hundreds in the king's name. It was there, twice a year, that he enrolled young men into the frankpledge system; it was there that murders were declared and paid for. When the king raised a geld, the sheriff supervised the collection of it in each hundred, where four men collected the amounts due.[57]

Sheriffs were the key figures in Norman government because they were the only officials who dealt regularly not only with the least unit, the hundred, but also with the royal government at Winchester. When the geld was levied, the sheriff had to amass all the sums due from his shire and arrange for the tenants-in-chief to transport it to Winchester, where the king's treasury was still resident. Unfortunately it is not easy to see how much control the central government could exercise over the sheriffs either for accounting or for legal purposes. The oppressions of sheriffs are manifest in Domesday book, and if the king's ear could be gained, justice could be done.[58] But many of the abuses of the sheriffs were due to their determination to make a profit out of their office. They appear generally to have farmed their shire, namely to have paid a fixed sum to the treasury, and to have reckoned to make good their investment by raising more money from the king's rights than they offered to the king himself. Their financial dealings with the treasury would therefore involve annual payments of the farm, with allowances made for whatever expenses they had incurred at the king's command. Until these annual accounts took the form of a special exchequer enquiry, the regularity of the procedure is in doubt, though the competence displayed by the treasury clerks in compiling Domesday book does not suggest that they had much to learn about orderly account keeping.

Domesday book reveals that, even if the sheriff was the man normally responsible for the royal revenues in each shire, some of the royal estates were in the hands of others, not necessarily men selected by the sheriff himself. In practice therefore the royal administration was much more complex than the shrieval system would suggest. Sheriffs were busy men with many royal duties, and they had themselves to find subordinates, or farmers in their turn, to manage the royal manors directly, and the king was inevitably approached by individuals willing to assume responsibility for certain estates. Though normal procedures may be asserted, room must be found for considerable variation in detail, to allow for the particular history of each estate, anomalies due to forfeiture or to such matters as the queen's dowry, which created a new county in Rutland, and for the nature of the royal property itself.

The most remarkable part of the royal demesne was the towns, most of which remained in royal hands after the Conquest.[59] The Norman period seems to have been a period of growth in the towns. At Bury, an important town had grown up around the shrine of St Edmund since the reign of the Confessor. The Domesday figures of town revenues show that only in two cases was the assessment not raised between 1066 and 1086, and in some places the rise was steep: five times in Colchester, three times in Hereford, Lincoln and Norwich. Even towns which had lost houses for castle-building under the Conqueror could have prospered and certainly gained in size. The Normans encouraged towns and markets, either to collect tolls and sales taxes, or because from their Norman experience they knew the value of commerce for general prosperity. The Norman lords who adapted the customs of Breteuil for the use of the border towns in the Welsh march appear to have imported local practices in the spirit of colonists, and it is likely that these towns were settled in part by Norman townsmen. The importance of the towns is borne out by Domesday book, which for each county gives first a description of the chief town, while later entries often give detailed accounts of other local town customs. Unfortunately the two chief towns, London and Winchester, are not described, though the complexity of their structure may be gathered from other sources and may explain the difficulties experienced by the commissioners in gathering or digesting information.

The customs of the towns which are described reveal that the communities were highly organised, with their own legal and judicial rights, that local tenants-in-chief and village communities maintained their own town houses, for marketing or legal business,[60] that the townsmen themselves were privileged as holders of town property and conscious of the status conferred by such tenures. At Northampton, at least, the burgesses had sense enough to arrange to farm the town from the sheriff. In other towns, the town-reeve, appointed by the king, secured a special position for the town within the sheriff's jurisdiction, for it was the town-reeve who presided over the town law-courts and markets, defending the customs of each place, so that the sheriff's responsibility could have been confined to collecting the king's dues from the port-reeve in order to pay them in at Winchester. At Dover and Hereford, the royal town-reeve dealt with the treasury himself.

The townsmen, even on the royal demesne, were not enclaves of unusual activity. The burgesses of Cambridge lent their plough teams three times a year to the sheriff; those of Hereford owed reaping services in summer on adjacent royal manors. The burgesses of the principal towns did military service, or owed it, and those on the Welsh border were certainly involved personally in campaigning. Townsmen were therefore fully integrated into the pattern of eleventh-century society. They had agricultural property of their own, they owed services, both menial and national, like country estates. What special status they enjoyed was due chiefly to the protection of the king. They were the first parts of the royal demesne to claim privileged customs in the boroughs, that gave them a special standing at law; not till the thirteenth century did the dwellers on royal demesne in the country also claim to be privileged. The social standing of burgesses is difficult to assess, but if the burgesses of Shrewsbury paid a relief for taking their inheritance and those of Hereford gave horses and arms to the king as other country freemen, there can have been little social discrimination as yet. The burgesses of Huntingdon in the reign of Henry I were comfortable, hard-drinking, high-spirited people with pursuits and religious habits similar to those of the Norman lords, though they seem to have been very English by ancestry.[61] Even if townsmen formed less than one tenth of the population of England, they were a higher proportion on the king's own directly managed property and the Norman kings showed themselves to be aware of the value of the towns in their government.

6 The Church

In 1066 reports circulated that before he died, the Confessor had had a vision of two former Norman monks he had known, prophesying that devils would be admitted to the kingdom to burn, slaughter and play havoc with the king's people. Although the monks accused the earls, as well as the bishops, abbots and others in holy orders of being servants of the devil, they attributed the chief blame for this imminent disaster to the sins of the clergy: if the kingdom was ravaged, 'history' showed that this was the fault of the priests, who had failed to chain up the devil by their prayers. Too many clergy had been attracted to holy orders by love of riches and worldly glory and though the pope had sent legates and the king and queen had criticised abuses, the clergy had neglected to amend their ways.[1] On the Norman side, abbot Walter of Evesham believed with some smugness after the Conquest that the Norman victory had also demonstrated the inadequacy of prayers addressed through the old English saints: God had heard only the prayers of his faithful Normans.[2] How did the Normans change the English church?

The King, the Pope and the Archbishop

The Norman Conquest took place at a time when the traditional pattern of relations between the king and the clergy was already being disturbed in Italy and Germany by new applications of the belief in the primacy of the apostolic see in Rome; but few changes of lasting significance had been made by 1066 and William was able to make himself master of the English kingdom before pope Gregory VII (1073–1085) began to challenge the exercise of royal rights over the church. The image of the Christian prince as protector of the clergy, benefactor of churches and just governor of his people derived from Constantine, the Roman emperor who had presided at the council of Nicaea before his own baptism, and it had been refurbished by Charlemagne, the first barbarian Western emperor. In England the tradition of Christian kingship was well established. The pages of Bede recorded the piety of the earliest Christian kings, of whom Oswald was the prototype; the martyr-kings Edward and Edmund received wide public veneration in the mid-eleventh century. Edward the Confessor himself was no sooner in the tomb than he began to inspire the respect due to saintliness in the popular way that had brought acknowledged sanctity to his predecessors. His life had not been remarkable. He had an easily earned reputation for continence; he had been respectful of religious virtues. His coronation had made him a special kind of layman and the fact that he was the last of the royal line of Cerdic gave additional reason to consider his death-bed vision like a prophecy of heavenly inspiration.

Edward the Confessor had, like some of his predecessors, at some stage contemplated going to Rome, but instead his devotion to St Peter was expressed by the reconstruction of a great church dedicated to the apostle at Westminster. In other respects Edward's relations with the Roman see were as courteous and dutiful as they had normally been since Gregory I's mission. Peter's pence were paid to help the papacy and the English colony in Rome. Formal consent was obtained at Rome for the transfer of the see of Crediton to Exeter in 1051. The monasteries of Ely and Chertsey obtained from pope Victor II papal privileges confirming their possessions, which threatened the anathemas of St Peter on violators of their property. Nicholas II intervened in England and summoned archbishop Eldred of York to Rome for the synod of 1061 to explain why he had moved from the see of Worcester to that of York without papal authority. When it was discovered that the king had ordered him to do so, all the bishops of the synod persuaded the pope to approve this, on condition that Eldred at least consecrated another bishop to his former see.[3] The king himself was represented at the council by bishops who could have obtained papal confirmations of the property of the see of Dorchester and of the king's own abbey at Westminster. The king's chaplain Giso was consecrated by the pope himself as bishop of Wells and the queen's chaplain Walter was consecrated as bishop of Hereford.

Nicholas II had every opportunity in 1061 to scrutinise the condition of the English church and did not hesitate to interfere. If he was disturbed by what he heard, there is no evidence that he reproved royal influence in the church. Generally speaking, the pious character of Edward allowed the practice of sound religion and the appointment of clergy of weight. The exception was Stigand, archbishop of Canterbury. Stigand's position as archbishop had been condemned by a succession of popes. He had occupied the see of Canterbury when the archbishop, Robert of Jumièges, was driven into exile by the triumphant Godwinsons in 1052; Stigand had used Robert's pallium until he had prevailed upon pope Benedict X (commonly regarded as an intruder himself) to grant him another; Stigand had also kept his see of Winchester after occupying Canterbury and he held some monastic property. It was a long indictment. His later years are full of contradiction. After Benedict X's expulsion from Rome and the failure of Stigand's efforts to obtain permanent papal recognition, the English bishops respected papal wishes and did not seek consecration at his hands. Harold refused to be crowned by him[4] and used Eldred of York even to consecrate his collegiate foundation at Waltham. But Stigand was not deposed and Nicholas II does not appear to have forced Edward the Confessor into a more decisive mood, though Eldred got short shrift when he tried to emulate Stigand in pluralism. The visit of a papal legate in 1062 did nothing to improve matters.

Before setting out to challenge Harold in 1066, William diplomatically solicited help or neutrality from the princes of Europe, including pope Alexander II. According to Orderic Vitalis, this embassy to the pope went to get advice once it became clear that the great secular barons of Normandy were not eager to support the duke's hazardous enterprise. Alexander is there said to have encouraged the duke on the grounds that Harold was a perjurer, and certainly gave William a banner as a sign of the protection of St

Peter. William later sent Harold's war banner, woven with gold thread, a great sum of money and some valuable ornaments to the pope in gratitude for his help. Later writers[5] went further and asserted that the pope wished William to conquer England in order to introduce reform into the irregular English church, and in particular to depose Stigand. But Stigand was not immediately deposed after the Conquest. The king was crowned by Eldred of York, but he treated Stigand ceremoniously by taking him to Normandy in 1067 and allowed him to consecrate Remigius of Fécamp to the see of Dorchester,[6] though Stigand had not consecrated a bishop in England since 1058. The Conqueror's own chaplain, William of Poitiers, was uneasy about the king's attitude to the archbishop and tried to explain this on the grounds that Stigand had too much influence with the English to be treated summarily.[7] Stigand had obtained William's promise to respect his position, as part of the terms agreed at Berkhamsted in 1066. The decision to depose him obviously still rested with the king, not the pope, and the king did nothing till 1070.

By 1070, the Conqueror had lost Eldred of York by death; several other English sees were also vacant. To consecrate a new archbishop of York would require the cooperation of the episcopate of the province of Canterbury, for York's single suffragan, Durham, could not act alone. William probably decided that the time had come to deal with Stigand. Stigand's personal offence by 1070 appears to have been political. The prior of Canterbury, Aelsi, went to Denmark on a mission in 1069, and may have been implicated in the Danish invasion of that year. He was sufficiently dubious about the warmth of his reception on his return to stay in Denmark until 1080.[8] Stigand's part in the invasion is circumstantial, but it could have been sufficient to stir the king to reprisals. The same Hermenfrid, who had attended the council in Normandy which had deposed Mauger of Rouen (also for political offences), was one of three legates who approved the removal of Stigand and his brother, Ethelmar, bishop of East Anglia, and Ethelric,[9] bishop of Sussex (who went on protesting about this injustice until 1076) and several abbots. No more than Nicholas II's legates in 1062, did the legates hold a council to reform the church. Walkelin, the king's clerk, was consecrated to the see of Winchester, the king was solemnly crowned and then they hastened back to the continent to persuade the abbot of Caen, Lanfranc, to accede to the pope's wish that he become archbishop of Canterbury.[10]

In 1070 eight bishops appointed by the Confessor were still living. Five of these were from the Rhineland, so that only three, the bishops of Durham, Worcester and Exeter (who died in 1072) continued to represent the native English episcopate. The blame for this obviously lies with the Confessor himself. William had already chosen one bishop, Remigius of Fécamp, who was rewarded for his contribution of twenty knights and one ship to the Hastings campaign. In 1070 the king's chancellor, Herfast, was appointed to East Anglia, his chaplain Stigand to Sussex and the king's brother Odo, bishop of Bayeux, secured the see of York for the treasurer of Bayeux, Thomas. These men, selected by the Conqueror as his bishops, were by no means old friends or supporters of the abbot of Caen and Lanfranc can have had no illusions about the extent to which they would cooperate with him in his ecclesiastical policy. Herfast had been an enemy of Lanfranc's at the ducal court in Normandy; Remigius he accused of buying his see from the king; against Thomas he argued that as the son of a priest he was unworthy of his dignity; as a monk himself, Lanfranc was inevitably opposed to Walkelin's radical plan to introduce secular cathedral chapters into Winchester and Canterbury in the place of the traditional monastic ones.

After Lanfranc was introduced at Canterbury, the king could have consulted him about new appointments to the bench of bishops, but the king's chaplains were still promoted: Osmund (Salisbury), Maurice (London), Peter and Robert (Lichfield-Chester), William (East Anglia) and Osbern, an Anglicised Norman (Exeter). The king presumably chose Hugh for London and two other Rhinelanders: Walcher (Durham) and Robert Losinga (Hereford). Two bishops of Chichester are of unknown origin. In Lanfranc's time only three monks, apart from himself, became bishops. William, a former clerk at Bayeux who was abbot at Le Mans before being appointed to Durham, proved his intransigence by defying Lanfranc in a political quarrel in 1088 and counselling Rufus against Anselm in 1095. The two others, Arnost and Gundulph, were bishops at Rochester, a see traditionally entirely submissive to its great neighbour, Canterbury. Whatever influence he had with the king over appointments, Lanfranc cannot be held clearly responsible for the choice of a major bishop. None of them but Gundulph had been trained in his school at Bec or his abbey at Caen and this lack of sympathy prejudiced the prospects of gaining general cooperation in the work of his primacy.

If this is so, it might be worth considering why Lanfranc was chosen as archbishop. Strangely enough, after the political deposition at Rouen in 1055, William had covered this act of authority by the appointment of a respected and unobtrusive monk; in 1070 he had another reason for choosing a monk at Canterbury, because the chapter there was monastic. William clearly did not favour Walkelin's views about root and branch reform. Conservative as ever, he did not propose to raise a hornet's nest about his ears by suppressing the monastic chapter. If the powerful Stigand had not been able to destroy the monastic communities of Canterbury and Winchester in nearly twenty years, the king would be wiser to leave them be. William must have found after four years that the monks of Canterbury were too formidable a group to drive into opposition; to obtain their cooperation he needed a monk he could trust to rule over the cathedral. Monks suitable for promotion to episcopal office were uncommon. Looking around, the king probably found no real rival to Lanfranc, who had to be forced by the pope to leave the cloister.

Lanfranc was the pope's former teacher and had been a frequent visitor at Rome,[11] where he had led the mission in 1059 to obtain papal forgiveness for the duke's marriage. Since then he had obstinately refused to accept the archbishopric of Rouen, but had become abbot of Caen at the pope's special request. The legate now presented Alexander II's wish for Lanfranc to go to England. William's own good relations with the papacy (at least from 1059, if not from 1055) he probably owed to Lanfranc's position with the pope. As long as Alexander lived, Lanfranc reckoned to enjoy papal support and did not hesitate to elicit it. He complained to the pope about the king's choice of Remigius of Dorchester and Thomas of York, because of infringements of canon law involved. These stories are told by Eadmer, the biographer of Anselm, and may represent no more than preliminaries to the important point for Eadmer: that the guilty pair surrendered their pastoral staffs to the pope, who handed them to Lanfranc, who himself restored them to their owners.[12] This symbolised their dependence on him, by an analogy easily perceived in a world of lords and vassals. But the quarrel with York was no mere preliminary manœuvring. At least until 1073 Lanfranc made it his first aim to secure the submission of the archbishop of York to the authority of Canterbury and to obtain a papal confirmation of that submission. He soon discovered how necessary he was at this juncture to the see of Canterbury. The monks of Canterbury under the long intrusion of Stigand had seen their see suffer in dignity. The diocese of Worcester and part of Dorchester had been occupied by the archbishop of York, who as a crowning indignity had usurped the place of Canterbury at the coronation ceremonies of Harold and William. Under Lanfranc the see recovered its power to challenge these innovations. York did not have enough suffragans to consecrate him: Thomas had to wait until Lanfranc had been consecrated by the bishops of his province before he could receive consecration himself. Lanfranc was unashamedly opportunist: as consecrating bishop he had the right to demand a profession of submission from Thomas.

When Lanfranc and Thomas went to Rome for the pallium, Alexander, instead of confirming Lanfranc's success, authorised him to assemble a great concourse of prelates to establish their rights. At Easter and again at Whitsun 1072, the king presided over the heated exchange of precedents and documents and finally made peace between the archbishops on the basis of Lanfranc's primacy. York took second place, though styled 'metropolitan' of York. Lanfranc within his 'island parish' (as he called it)[13] had authority to direct the bishops of all Britain.

Alexander II, who died in 1073, did no more than recognise Canterbury as the metropolitan see of all Britain without pronouncing on the question of primacy or precedence; Gregory VII, his successor, who held pronounced views about the duty of all metropolitans to Rome, thought that Roman authority could bypass metropolitans altogether and deal directly with the bishops. Lanfranc's relations with Gregory could not fail to become cool. In 1076 the council that he summoned rejected the rigorous condemnation of clerical marriage pronounced by the pope in 1075 and which even the archbishop of Rouen held to be necessary, and introduced a modified version of his own

In 1075 various harmless transfers of sees to country towns were justified by the authority of the canons,[14] though the earlier transfer of the Devonshire see to Exeter had been specifically authorised by the pope and Gregory VII attached importance to such formal acts of Roman authority. The pope instructed Lanfranc to prevent the bishop of East Anglia from interfering in the monastery of Bury, which was under the special protection of the Holy See. Lanfranc had never been on good terms with Herfast and may have smarted at the pope's implication that he did not know his duty. A few years later Gregory admonished Lanfranc for not visiting Rome since his election (though as Hildebrand he had been serviceable to the archbishop and may even have enjoyed his friendship). In 1082, the pope sent a peremptory summons for him to go to Rome without delay. Lanfranc did not soften. He did not go to Rome and by Gregory's death in 1085, if not sooner, England had become neutral in the conflict between the Roman popes and the imperial pope, Clement III. Lanfranc reproved an over-zealous supporter of Clement for his abuse of Gregory, but he indicated his position by saying that the king would decide which pope to support.[15] By 1085 therefore the king was not committed to supporting the papacy and this royal independence persisted till 1096, when by Anselm's insistence England was restored to the Roman obedience. Lanfranc, however, did nothing to secure royal adherence to a Roman see that had betrayed his expectations. Though Lanfranc came in as a friend of the pope, he died tolerating a breach in England's relations with Rome incomparably more serious than all the irregularities of Stigand's time.[16]

Gregory VII's pontificate focused the attention of Europe on an aspect of papal policy that had loomed ever larger in the previous generation: the degree of obedience owed to Rome, the only apostolic see in the Latin church. Popes Leo IX, Nicholas II and Alexander II had all asserted the universal jurisdiction of Rome and repudiated the notion that metropolitans had exclusive rights over their own bishops. Lanfranc's defence of the Canterbury case on the 'primacy' of Britain was therefore flatly opposed to general papal policy and his pursuit of this ideal, in conflict with the declared will of Gregory VII expresses one of his decisive characteristics. It is also the best explanation for his increasing reliance on William after his failure to obtain recognition of Canterbury's primacy. This development has been described solely in terms of what appears like Gregory's own aggressive interference, but this is to neglect the extent to which Lanfranc was trying to work out on his own account the implications of the theory of a British primacy.

The idea of the ecclesiastical unity of Britain had been nurtured at Canterbury before Lanfranc's arrival, but the new archbishop brought with him a theory of metropolitan power which he had personally developed while still at Bec, with all the resources of his legal training. He had there made his own abridgment of the False Decretals,[17] underlining the passages that emphasised the respect due to metropolitans (although this was not even the dominant interest of the unabridged work). Once installed as metropolitan at Canterbury, he invited the English bishops to read and digest the canons he had assembled; copies of his legal handbook were made for use all over England: Salisbury, Exeter, Gloucester, Worcester, Hereford, Lincoln and Durham. Lanfranc annotated his own copy where he found useful precedents. 'In the decretals, it is written "the ordering of all things belongs to the metropolitan in each province"; in the council of Nicaea "the decision on all provincial matters should be made by the metropolitan bishop"; in the council of Antioch "the bishops of each province should know that it is for the metropolitan bishop to be concerned for the whole province—for this reason let everyone with business to do, take it to the metropolitan, and it is right that he should be honoured accordingly"; in the councils of Toledo "it is proper that everyone should be corrected by him from whom he has received consecration: by most decrees, the see which confers the dignity should pronounce ecclesiastical judgment".' Lanfranc's authorities were in themselves sufficiently crushing, but in the letter to bishop Herfast, he concludes with his own reflections that 'there are many other excellent things about the powers of primates and archbishops in these writings and in other authentic books of orthodox fathers, which, if you read diligently and committed to memory, would prevent you from conceiving anything against your mother the church, and would cause you to reprove others from saying what you said about presuming to interfere in someone else's parish'.

The functions of the metropolitan that he emphasises here are judicial and administrative. He does not refer specifically to powers of selecting bishops, nor to the need to consult them in regular synods, nor to their obligations to carry out any agreed plan of reform. He is himself much more concerned with the dignity and privileges of his position than with his own duties. At his first synod in 1075, his overriding concern was to have Thomas of York sit in second place to himself and to demonstrate the primacy of Canterbury at a time when he was still smarting from the rebuff given to him by the popes in refusing to confirm the privileges of his see. Compared to the seating arrangements of the bishops in council, reform was a subsidiary matter.

Within these limits of protocol, it is probable that Herfast was not the only bishop to be unimpressed by Lanfranc's lectures. Amongst his letters, the only one that assumes a tone of authority was the one directed to the bishop of Chichester, typically complaining that the bishop's archdeacons were meddling with the priests on the estates of Canterbury in Sussex, which was a matter that touched the privileges of his own church directly. Lanfranc had no coercive powers over the bishops and normally relied on his moral influence. His letters prove that his colleagues consulted him about general and particular issues, without suggesting that he claimed or exercised any rights to interfere directly in their dioceses. Thomas of York asked his advice about how to treat married clerks genuinely devoted to their wives; Maurice of London asked a difficult question about the penance to be imposed for murdering a captive, and was encouraged to undertake the reform of the nunnery of Barking; Robert of Chester earned a rebuke for attacking the monks of Coventry. Lanfranc may have had an exalted view of the rights of metropolitans, but in practice his bishops were expected to concede him formal respect only.[18]

Had Lanfranc been allowed more influence in episcopal appointments his authority over the bishops might have been greater. But it was the king who disposed of the churches, advancing those who served him personally. The experience that the English bishops had in common was therefore in the king's entourage where their loyalty and obedience were taken for granted. Lanfranc's direction of the episcopate could only be effective if the archbishop had the king's support. Later generations of Anglican apologists have tended to see in him the model of the wise prelate working with the king to promote the unity and the sanity of church-state relations. After Lanfranc's time, the revival of the cult of St Dunstan could have put men in mind of an earlier period of happy cooperation between king and archbishop, but while Lanfranc lived, talk of harmony or alliance would have seemed ignorant. Lanfranc was William's archbishop, not prime minister. His pretensions as primate were derived from the traditions of his own see at Canterbury, not from political considerations. It was subtle of the monks at Canterbury to advance their own interests as national ones.

William's own favourable attitude to Lanfranc's position in the church has been assumed rather than demonstrated. There are two principal strands in William's ecclesiastical policy. At the time of his coronation, William promised to defend all the churches of England and their pastors. This responsibility would have been quite sufficient to make him support Canterbury against York, both in 1070 and in 1072. There is no escaping the conclusion that the king's decision was really the essential one, and it was in order to secure the king's favour that the monks of Canterbury argued that if the see of York was not subordinate to Canterbury, the archbishop of York might be forced by Danes, Norwegians or Scots capturing York to crown their leader and thus split the kingdom. In 1070, after York had twice fallen to the Scandinavians within the year, the monks had a strong case.

William must have seen how specious it was. Granting Canterbury the primacy did not eradicate the archbishop of York's episcopal powers. William himself had, after all, been crowned by archbishop Eldred. Crowning a king at York might be serious, but no invader was so simple as to believe that such a coronation would make him master of England. The practical realities of eleventh-century kingship made a coronation at Westminster or Winchester necessary; there, the coronation would be effective whichever bishop officiated.

At Canterbury, the particular privilege of the archbishop to crown the king was more important than any abstract claim to primacy. The monks still smarted from the insult to their see given by Stigand's exclusion from the ceremonies of 1066. They argued against York in these terms not simply as an excuse, but because the archbishop's rights at the ceremony were an important part of their tradition. Such an argument was also a mute rebuke to the king for his own insult to Canterbury. But however essential the political argument was at Canterbury, there is no reason to believe that it was this that swayed the Conqueror in Lanfranc's favour. William had gone to great pains to secure Lanfranc's service. It would have been reasonable to please him where possible. William had to choose between the niceties of ecclesiastical law, presented on the one hand by the monks of Canterbury claiming ancient precedents and on the other by Thomas of York with no powerful college of clergy behind him. It would be typical of William, in these circumstances, to give a decision in favour of what appeared to be traditional English custom, for it was an article of his policy to maintain and defend the ancient rights of his people. So William threatened to send Thomas and all his noble Norman relations into exile if he did not submit. Thomas, weeping for the insult to his see and pleading the laws of his church, made a profession of submission for his own life and reserved the rights of his successors to raise the case in Rome.[19] If William's promise to defend all the churches of England is the first certain strand of his ecclesiastical policy, the second was not so much to exclude all papal interference by upholding the primacy of Canterbury, as a royal determination to exercise all the rights of his royal predecessors. When Gregory VII wrote directly to the king in 1080, referring to his own personal services to the king and enlarging on the superiority of the papal office compared to the royal, William wrote back firmly and respectfully: 'I do not wish to do fealty, nor do I wish to do it now, because I have neither promised it myself, nor found that my predecessors did it to yours'.[20] Gregory's claim to fealty was based, at least in part, on the assumption that the traditional payment of Peter's pence was 'tribute money'. When the king heard, however, that payments had been discontinued during his long absence in Normandy, he did not think it would be simpler to cease payments altogether if the pope was going to misinterpret their character: instead he promised to pay the arrears. If, as seems probable, Lanfranc had been responsible while the king was away for the collection of Peter's pence, the king's complaisant answer is in marked contrast to Lanfranc's own intransigence.

William was a traditional ruler in the Christian church, respectful of the rights of churchmen, but conscious of his own great responsibilities as crowned ruler. He was no longer a mere leader, but a king, made by a ceremony that emphasised God's consecration of him to holy office. And, as God's vicar, William ruled as surely over the church as over his barons. The coronation ceremony was of vital significance to William precisely because it gave him a spiritual authority more aweful than all his military and political power. Ritually cleansed before submitting his head to the holy oil, he rose from the unction purified by a kind of second baptism and consecrated to mediate between God and men. He was his people's intercessor before God for the salvation of both their bodies and their souls. His dedication was there manifested, as Christ had shown himself to the Gentiles at his Epiphany. The king was the representative of Christ, the Heavenly Spouse of the church and the king's coronation therefore symbolised Christ's union to the church in marriage. The ceremony of anointing expressed a wealth of meaning to those able to ponder these mysteries. The king's bishops never doubted that he had been raised to an unscalable pinnacle of dignity. Naturally he had undisputed power to appoint and direct bishops and abbots. He was also bound by his office to expel unbelievers from the church, condemn heretics and eradicate their damnable teaching within its breast. Such a king reigned with Christ and dispensed Christian justice in His kingdom. At the coronation, he was girt with a real sword, with which to correct offenders; but at the same time, by the gift of the Holy Spirit, this sword was as capable of imparting inner virtue as it was of giving justice. His sword wounded sinners and avenged injuries to the Lord of Sabaoth; it excised all scandal from the kingdom and smote the enemies of God like a lion. By his sword, the just king proclaimed himself: in word and deed, in speech and example, by threats and blandishments, by laws and edicts, by empire and judgment. In Almighty God's government, both in holy church and in this world, he held the seat of highest rule, the seat of glory and beauty, of justice and strength, of judgment and equity, of kingdom and empire, of mercy and pity, of grace and loveliness, of modesty and love, of propitiation and reconciliation, of David and his pacific son Solomon, the seat of Christ and of God, the seat which had no equal or comparison in the positions of this world. This position of the king in the church, which was defended in such terms by an early twelfth-century Norman priest,[21] was expressed by the English coronation rite used in 1066 and it still went unchallenged in the Conqueror's time. Rufus, in a memorable phrase, condemned all infringements of his rights as an attempt to take his crown. It was churchmen who turned the military leader into a crowned king; in Norman times, it was to the king that they looked as their real head and defender.

The Bishops

In one striking particular the position of the English episcopate was very different from the Norman. In Normandy, the bishops of whom anything is known were members of the great families, including the duke's own; in England, the king consistently promoted chaplains from his service, as the German kings had done for a century and as had become frequent in England since the time of Canute. This suggests that the king was much more free to make appointments in England than he was in Normandy. Some of the bishop's chaplains may have been well connected, but significantly, it is their previous service rather than their families that are known, and when the family looms into view it is usually a clerical family of great ramifications, not an aristocratic one.

Apart from their previous service in the king's chapel most bishops shared no common outlook. They passionately defended the rights of their new churches even against one another, and never needed to show even that degree of solidarity common to secular barons for limited political goals. Their sense of the privilege of their churches often brought them up against the monasteries of their dioceses: this gives them one further common trait. The debate between the secular and the regular clergy, however petty it now seems, occupied important men to the exclusion of other business. It was not all petty because, to their mind, it was part of the defence of their church.

The first function of the Norman bishop was to defend the accumulated rights and traditions of the see itself. When Lanfranc died and the monks wrote his obituary notice,[22] he was praised for defending his church at Canterbury rather than his responsibilities as British primate, except in so far as this was considered part of Canterbury's tradition. He had first built a new church at Canterbury, from the foundations up (it had been destroyed by fire in 1067); he had filled it with many monks and given it ornaments; he had built new houses for the monks and given them many fine books; he had recovered lands of the church which had been lost for many years; he had built a house for the poor and feeble outside the city and revived the hospital-church of St Gregory; on his archiepiscopal manors he had built fine churches; for Rochester, Canterbury's dependent see, he had begun a new cathedral, furnished it and recovered some of its property; he had above all placed the sees of York and others in subjection. Only one matter of no special concern to Canterbury was mentioned: the foundation of the church of St Albans (where his nephew Paul became abbot) and over which Canterbury might have hoped to prove some rights.

William bishop of Durham, who dared to defy Lanfranc in 1088, was essentially a man of the same qualities and outlook. He favoured monasticism to the point of driving secular canons out of the chapter and introducing in their place monks to look after the uncorrupted body of the monk-bishop, St Cuthbert, which had been the chief treasure of the diocese since Bede's day; over the body he began to raise the magnificent cathedral that still stands as the saint's mausoleum. To the monks he assigned a definite portion of the see's property. To remind the chapter of his care for their interest and to ensure their daily commemoration of him in their prayers, he declined the honour of being buried beside St Cuthbert, on the grounds that it was impious to bring what would decay into the presence of the incorruptible, and preferred to be laid in the chapter-house itself.[23]

It is a great pity that the cathedral canons have not left the same intimate picture of one of their bishops for William of Malmesbury wrote little more than a hundred words about the diocesan of his monastery, Osmund bishop of Salisbury.[24] Unlike his successor Roger, Osmund respected the rights of abbeys in his diocese and dedicated himself to improving the standard of his own cathedral canons. His own charter of foundation and endowment are not very informative; his famous liturgy comes down to us only in a modified thirteenth-century form. He is known to have finished his cathedral church at Old Sarum and to have attracted distinguished canons to the cathedral, which became celebrated for its liturgy and learning. He wrote manuscripts for the library himself, was chaste, virtuous and humble, suffering patiently from a painful disease. Osmund emerges as a character only in the pages of his monastic biographer, who believed that he cherished the memory of the Old English saints, not in his own cathedral, but at Malmesbury itself. For when abbot Warin, a former monk of Lire, found it expedient to overcome his original antipathy to the former saints of his monastery, the relics of St Aldhelm were translated there under Osmund's auspices. Warin gave the bishop Aldhelm's left arm-bone which he kept in a silver reliquary and with which he cured two of his archdeacons. Once again it is the saints of England's monastic past who steal the limelight from the Norman bishop.

Monastic records do not always distort the truth about late eleventh-century bishops. At Worcester, Wulfstan inspired accounts which are rich in details about matters that were central to the concerns of all prelates. Brought up as a monk in the monasteries of Evesham and Peterborough, Wulfstan was prior of Worcester when Eldred was obliged by Nicholas II to surrender that see in 1062. Wulfstan was consecrated in his place, the last bishop to be appointed in the Confessor's reign. He survived, on good terms with the Normans, till his death in 1095.[25] Esteemed by the Conqueror, sent by Lanfranc to visit the see of Chester and consecrate the bishop of the Orkneys, consulted by Anselm about the rights of the see of Canterbury, befriended by Geoffrey Mowbray, bishop of Coutances and Robert Losinga, bishop of Hereford, Wulfstan had numerous opportunities to influence important decisions and while representing ancient traditions was to be moulded in his turn by new pressures. Three times a year he made his way to the Conqueror's court for the great crown-wearing ceremonies and once cured a Frenchman of belly-ache on his way to Winchester. Wulfstan's sanctity and his care for worldly responsibilities went together. Although Eldred had been obliged to surrender the see of Worcester in 1062, he retained his influence over his former prior, and his successor at York, Thomas of Bayeux, had no intention of abandoning even shadowy claims at Worcester. Wulfstan was responsible for wresting the diocese of Worcester from its long subordination to York and restoring it to the province of Canterbury. This success was achieved in a royal council and Wulfstan carried to that meeting a book containing the lives of the great tenth-century saints, thus firmly trusting to their intervention on his behalf.

One of those saints, Oswald, had been the bishop of Worcester who first retained the see in plurality when he became archbishop of York. Yet Oswald was Wulfstan's model. Wulfstan was obliged by the examples of his contemporaries to tear down the old church which Oswald had built and erect another, much larger one, though he protested that only proud men could think the new one superior. All the same, he spared no expense so that the body of Oswald might be translated to the new church and placed in a magnificent shrine adorned with 72 marks of silver. Wulfstan stood sobbing in the church-yard, regretting the change, but for all his traditional upbringing he accepted the new magnificence: the time for small Anglo-Saxon churches was over.

When at Worcester, Wulfstan accepted his role in the monastic community, taking his turn with the offices and the celebration of mass and not exalting himself amongst the brothers. He sat with them often, talking of their concerns and urging them to look after their interests, particularly by committing their memories to writing, so that those who came after them should not be the poorer because the past was forgotten. Wulfstan was not thinking simply of cultural poverty. He had the contents of the monks' muniments chest spread out, so that he could scrutinise all the old privileges and wills, and he ordered his monk, Hemming, to compose a volume in two parts, so that all the monks' possessions and the bishop's should be separately accounted for, and their title deeds copied for greater safety.[26] As a result of this encouragement, it is possible to follow the fortunes of at least one post-Conquest bishopric in some detail, at least from the monks' point of view.

Of the many despoilers of the monastery in the eleventh century, Hemming seems to select the neighbouring abbot of Evesham for particularly odious mention. Aethelwig was said to have seized Acton by the great strength of his iniquity and he had similarly used his power to take the bishop's lands in Warwickshire. His intelligence and his knowledge of secular laws (which alone he studied) put him into great favour with the Conqueror who made him a provincial judge of very wide power. His influence made him so feared that most of the men of the region, including the rich and the bishop's own men and knights, took him as lord, because he promised them protection against the Normans, who also feared him. When Wulfstan tried to recover his possession of Bengeworth, the abbot promised to pay certain dues, but as he was wily he did not keep the agreement and the meek and candid Wulfstan was no match for his clever neighbour. When Aethelwig finally died of gout, Wulfstan prayed like a Christian for his soul, but was himself struck down by that disease; his life was despaired of, until he learned in a vision that he had brought this divine punishment on himself by causing special prayers to be offered for the impious abbot. When the prayers were stopped, Wulfstan recovered. The community of Worcester so hated the late abbot of Evesham that, whatever Wulfstan thought about it, the monks preserved their hostility beyond the grave.

At Evesham, Aethelwig left a very different impression. A later writer, using the evidence of ancient charters, oral testimony and very little personal observation, in general confirms the impression of Aethelwig's great influence with the Conqueror.[27] His preeminence in secular wisdom explained why the king made him governor of the counties of Worcester, Gloucester, Oxford, Warwick, Hereford, Stafford and Shropshire. Wherever he went in England, the French and the English accepted his word as the best law to be had; the earls, the sheriffs and all the barons venerated him. He was the father of the poor, the judge of widows, children, orphans, and pilgrims; he consoled all the unhappy; he looked after the refugees, old and young, women and children who fled from the Conqueror's devastation of Yorkshire, Cheshire, Shropshire, Staffordshire and Derbyshire and he nursed them in the great plague that followed. The glowing account of his justice is illustrated by only two examples. At Canterbury, he was at least commemorated for helping Lanfranc to recover lands belonging to his church; for Wulfstan, his simple holy neighbour, he acted as a wise counsellor and a generous banker: did he not lend the bishop two marks of gold to help him defeat the claims of York to the see of Worcester?

These two monastic accounts both display the intense local feeling even of churchmen at this time. Hemming is aware of no common sentiment that should bind two Englishmen or two monks together. This spiteful parochialism also had undoubted advantages for the communities. As Wulfstan himself pointed out, the monks had a duty to their future brethren to become determined fighters for their monastery. Even if the community was not immediately successful, it continued to keep its old records and revived disputes after a few years with undiminished enthusiasm. This spirit was nurtured in English monasteries and proved to be a factor of unexpected importance.

The growth of monastic life in the tenth century had had a serious effect upon the dioceses of England. Wessex was rich in monastic foundations, so rich, that most houses seemed relatively modest. The bishoprics, except that of Winchester, were even poorer. From the beginning of the eleventh century, a new effort seems to have been made to stimulate the religious life of the bishoprics. Monastic cathedrals that had been common in the tenth century gradually reverted to the more normal status of secular chapters. By 1066, only three of the fifteen bishoprics of England were served by monks, though little enough is known about the strictness of discipline at Canterbury, Winchester or Worcester. This effort to keep monks out of the episcopate had necessarily to be sustained by a programme of recruiting secular clergy from abroad, for there were no places in England comparable to monasteries, where superior clergy could be trained. Both the Confessor and the Conqueror drew many bishops from the Rhineland, which had long since developed a tradition of cathedral schools. Harold had encouraged the idea by founding a house for secular canons at Waltham and tentative experiments in reviving collegiate, or minster, churches showed that with patience, England could have integrated the new clergy into its ancient parochial structure. This was the system that the Normans also understood and leading churchmen naturally advocated an extension of the system in England after 1066. Walkelin was keen to replace his monks of Winchester with secular canons; Remigius of Lincoln actually founded a secular chapter there and built a house for monks at Stow.[28] At Salisbury, Hereford, Durham, Chester and York, the new Norman prelates set to work.

The results were disappointing. At Durham the canons were soon evicted and the revived communities of Monkwearmouth and Jarrow forcibly amalgamated and installed at Durham itself; the bishop of Chester abandoned his see for Coventry where a monastic community served the cathedral. The reasons are not hard to find. Giso, bishop of Wells, wrote a brief memoir about his see, in order to instruct his successors how to look after its interests.[29] At his own consecration, he had found the bishopric depleted, the canons scattered, the common buildings in ruins. He had had to recover its possessions from despoilers as highly placed as earl Harold and archbishop Stigand. He had wormed gifts out of the Conqueror and had persuaded others to give or sell land to the church. The canons had been reassembled and he had built for them a cloister, a refectory and a dormitory, as they were known in Brabant, his place of origin. He intended to set down exactly what revenues belonged to the bishop and what to the canons, in order to prevent disputes arising in the future. Giso's principal concern was with the endowment of his church. He advised his successors to augment the property 'so that they might possess in glory the benefits of Christ's ultimate recompense, when they pass from this present life'. The bishop's concern for the material well-being of his see recurs in all these individual stories. Giso's successor took his advice, but took the easy way out: he acquired from Rufus the city of Bath with its former monastery of St Peter, and thither he transferred the seat of the bishopric. The monks of Bath became the chapter whilst the canons of Wells fell into neglect for two generations. The material worries of bishops were so great at this time that they needed loyal communities of devoted monks to defend the sees and could not support the burden of secular chapters. Canons were individually responsible for the estates of their own canonries, and as they were often married men, they considered their holdings as family possessions and cared little for the problems of the see as a whole. After the Conquest the new bishops at Thetford (East Anglia), Selsey (Sussex), Ramsbury (Wiltshire), Sherborne (Dorset), Wells (Somerset), Lichfield and Dorchester (on Thames) found that the sees themselves were in mean villages, with no famous saints, no powerful traditions, and with poor churches.[30] And some of them looked around their dioceses and saw that there were rich, proud monasteries in their midst. Not surprisingly they considered whether they could not put down such rivals and improve their own position by annexing those monastic fortunes.

The most determined effort of this sort was made by Herfast of East Anglia. When he was appointed in 1070 the see was at Elmham. In 1086 the see was worth £420 but the monastery of Bury St Edmund, the fourth richest monastery of England, was considerably richer and was worth £655. Herfast and his successors had made and continued to make every effort to transfer their see to Bury and abbot Baldwin, former monk of St Denis, whom the Confessor had raised to the abbacy for his medical services, worked hard and ably to prevent this from happening. Bury was not a particularly ancient monastery, having been established by Canute to look after the miraculously preserved body of St Edmund, king of East Anglia martyred by the Danes in the ninth century. Until Canute's reign the body had been in the care of secular priests and the monastery had been erected through the influence of the bishop for the original place of martyrdom, Hoxne, was connected with the see of Suffolk. The independent monastery was lucky in being built at Bury. There a large wooden church had been put up in the tenth century. This pre-history of the monastery is obscure, but its vague connection with the bishop was sufficient to give Herfast a claim worth pursuing. What could Baldwin do?

The monastery had received valuable privileges from Canute, who appears to have regarded these favours as expiation for the sins of his Danish ancestors. Baldwin also took his case to Rome and secured a bill of exemption, placing the monastery under the special protection of the Holy See, a privilege still rare at this time, at least in England. Alexander ordained Baldwin as a priest, while Lanfranc and Thomas of York were in Rome. Baldwin's preparedness to give his life for his sheep, as his admirers claimed, had secured a valuable ally for the monastery. Gregory VII interfered on its behalf and even bishop Herbert Losinga's dramatic submission to Urban II in 1094 did not cause the papacy to waver in its support of abbot Baldwin. The abbot also used his healing powers as a doctor to cure bishop Herfast of an eye injury on condition that the bishop abandoned his claims to Bury. He was not so easily put off and renewed it several times before his death. So abbot Baldwin went from strength to strength until he completed a great new basilica, where the body of St Edmund was laid with great pomp in 1095.[31] But the see of East Anglia was moved from Elmham to Thetford, before it finally came to rest at Norwich, where bishop Herbert, former monk of Fécamp and abbot of Ramsey, established a monastic chapter.

The contest was the most acrimonious here because by its exceptional papal privilege, the abbey became independent of the bishop and the bishop's control of his diocese was considerably weakened. This great, wealthy and privileged house within the diocese was a prejudice to his authority, an incitement to others and a snub to his own dignity. The bishop of Lichfield who had experimented with a college of canons at Chester ultimately succeeded in his cherished aim of acquiring the monastery of Coventry, because the monks there did not have the kind of papal support or royal protection which saved Bury. Little by little the Norman bishops fortified their sees with monastic chapters. When the great church of St Etheldreda at Ely, the second richest monastery of England, became the seat of an entirely new diocese in 1109, there were only seven of the sixteen sees that did not have at least one monastic chapter. By 1109, however, the high-water mark of monastic influence had already been reached. In the succeeding generation monasticism was heavily attacked by the new bishops. How can we explain this fluctuation?

The movement for monastic chapters was a device for keeping the loyalty to the see bright and constant. It was not a belief in the virtues of monasticism for the church. The bishops who introduced monastic chapters into their cathedrals were rarely monks themselves, and they soon learned to appreciate the difficulties of having monastic chapters with the right to elect new bishops and responsibilities for running the diocese. Few monks were promoted by royal favour to bishoprics. Monks could not be found. After Lanfranc's death, there was a vacancy of five years before Anselm, abbot of Bec, was installed in his place. After Anselm's death, another five years elapsed before the former abbot of Séez was translated from Rochester to Canterbury. When he died, the bishops insisted that the archbishop should not be another monk. A secular canon, William of Corbeil, was elected. He was the first of many, and the monks of Canterbury did not gladly consent to this diminution of their influence in elections. Similarly, at Worcester, the line of monk-bishops inaugurated by Oswald came to an end on Wulfstan's death. At Durham, the appointment of Flambard did not continue the precedent of William of St Carilef. Only at Winchester, with the election of the abbot of Glastonbury, Henry of Blois, in 1129, did a monk gain an important bishopric in Henry I's reign. Even this is misleading: the abbot was the king's own nephew.

The dearth of monk-bishops under Henry I only perpetuated the tradition of the Conqueror's reign. How then is it that the new bishops were less favourable to the monks than the old ones? It is not simply that the Conqueror's sons appointed unworthy prelates. Complaints have been raised against Rufus's appointments, but they were not all bad. He accepted Anselm as archbishop of Canterbury. He chose John of Tours, an excellent physician as bishop of Wells; John was a patron of learning, who gave books to his monks and hospitality to scholars. Herbert Losinga, abbot of Ramsey, bought his see of East Anglia from the king, but made his peace with Rome on his own initiative and lived to be a credit to the church. He was learned and eloquent, attentive to the needs of his diocese, a scholar and a writer of prayers for Henry I's consort. Gerard, Rufus's ambassador at Rome, whom he promoted to the see of Hereford, was described by Anselm as one of the most erudite men in England. Even Ralph Flambard, notorious bishop of Durham, had his conduct examined by Anselm, and somehow survived the test, though modern detectives with less charity and less knowledge suppose the worst.[32] There were some undistinguished men among Rufus's nine nominations, but no more than might have been expected in any period.[33]

Henry I was not conspicuous for improving on his brother. There were several long vacancies before sees were filled: five years at Canterbury and Durham, four at Hereford, and two years each at Salisbury, Norwich, Coventry, Worcester, Chichester and Ely. His appointments, when they came, were of practical men. His first, that of William Giffard, a distinguished canon of Rouen who had been Rufus's chancellor to Winchester, was apparently made to conciliate political interests. Roger who went to Salisbury in 1102 was reputed to be the most rapid singer of mass Henry knew and he raised his own relations in the royal service. William Warelwast, another ambassador to Rome, received the see of Exeter in 1104. Henry established the type of devoted servant who got a bishopric as his reward and continued to serve the king's government. These appointments might seem to show that the king was more concerned to promote his officials than to pick suitable diocesan bishops. But the episcopate was not as colourless or as scandalous as it might seem. These bishops display two remarkable and interrelated characteristics, neither of which was calculated to impress the monks, who have left the most detailed accounts of them.

Their first achievement was to revive the secular cathedral chapters. The most outstanding examples of this were at Salisbury and at Lincoln, under two very different bishops: Osmund, formerly royal chaplain, and Remigius, former monk of Fécamp. In both cases, the model of the chapter was provided by Rouen, where the archbishop, John of Avranches, was a noted writer on liturgy and much interested in introducing the customs of his own cathedral into other places.[34] The strength of the Norman ecclesiastical tradition at this period was what sustained the Norman bishops who grappled with the peculiarly English problem of powerful monasteries in their dioceses. Inevitably, the creation of new sees at Lincoln and Salisbury, places formerly without any ecclesiastical prominence, considerably retarded the revival of those dioceses by comparison with the more spectacular achievements of Canterbury under Lanfranc, or Durham under William of St Carilef. But by Rufus's reign, the cities of York, Lincoln and Exeter, amongst the principal communities of the realm, were resplendent with the new cathedral dignitaries.

It was Rufus's reign that really set the seal on the revival of secular chapters. The most famous of the reforming bishops, Osmund of Salisbury, built up his chapter by attracting distinguished canons until his cathedral won a reputation for learning and liturgy that began to rival the established superiority of the monks. About the same time, Maurice of London had completed the arrangements of his see, with a hierarchy of cathedral officials and prebends and plans for a new St Paul's. There was a remarkable survival of English family canons with children to succeed them and many prominent men in royal service or local landowners were found in their company. In spite of this and the extension of the system in the early part of the twelfth century, Maurice had clearly succeeded in giving new life to the cathedral.[35] At York, Thomas of Bayeux had to work hard to hold on to the accumulated benefits of his predecessors. The several collegiate churches of his see, York, Beverley, Hexham, Ripon and Southwell, inevitably dissipated his interests. The devastation in the north added exceptional difficulties. He had to reassemble the canons, provide for their common needs, persuade them to improve their own holdings and to participate in common concerns. By the time of his death in 1102, the see was well on the way to recovery and the new spirit was exemplified in Thomas II's defiance of Anselm in 1108 which stirred the collective passions of the whole chapter of York, as the chronicle of Hugh the Cantor demonstrates.

The new Norman bishops had earned royal promotion by their administrative abilities. It was these gifts that were needed in the dioceses, where ecclesiastical law and order foundered for want of them. William of Malmesbury, with typical monastic prejudice, denounced the bishops for not setting an example of godly living;[36] the bishops themselves concentrated their energies on what they could do, by slowly organising and staffing the diocese.

The divisions between the dioceses were more than geographical. A man from Salisbury who prayed for a miracle of healing in the Exeter diocese might have been ignorant of spiritual boundaries but was ridiculed for expecting to have his prayers answered in such circumstances.[37] The bishop was the unrivalled pastor of his diocese. Other bishops had no powers there except by his leave. Bishops who were lazy or corrupt were not easily corrected and apart from those dealt with in 1070 no bishops were deposed in the Norman period. The bishop's duty was to preserve the good order of the whole Christian society, lay, monastic and clerical. He defended the moral order, protected ecclesiastical property and attended to the needs of all the clergy. Bishops did not regard these duties as very different from the ones they had performed for the king. Anselm's council at London in 1102 had to remind bishops that they should behave like religious persons and surrender their secular offices; in 1125, the legatine council reproved bishops for threatening violence if they were not paid fees for blessing abbots, consecrating churches and ordaining clergy.[38] Bishops were certainly not faultless, and society did not help them to live up to their own best examples, by obliging them to assume general responsibilities for a host of matters that no longer seemed of equal seriousness.

Since the bishop was specially responsible to God for the Christian behaviour of his diocese, the king recognised that attacks on church property, irreligious conduct by clergy and moral lapses of the laity were offences against the whole community for which the bishop was entitled to compensation.

The social matter in which the church took most interest was marriage, over which the bishops were only at this period claiming exclusive jurisdiction. As late as 1076, Lanfranc had to remind laymen that they ought to obtain ecclesiastical blessings on their marriages. In 1102, Anselm objected to the celebration of marriages in private. Laymen had many reasons for resisting episcopal supervision of marriage. They often contracted alliances for political purposes or to unite fortunes. For some reason the match might be broken off in a hurry and it was easier to dissolve a marriage not celebrated in church. The church also insisted on the free consent of the parties, which created additional difficulties when young children were involved. Probably even more irritating was the insistence by churchmen that marriage within seven degrees of kinship was unlawful. Such a rule frustrated the wishes of many relatives to make their ties of kinship even closer and placed real obstacles in the way of finding a partner in the small, closely interrelated, communities of western Europe. Laymen did not easily accept the idea that the church had exclusive rights over marriage. Pagan fertility customs, however attenuated, persisted, and it was natural for the less well-instructed to think that the fecundity of the wife was a more important consideration than the free consent of the parties. The Conqueror himself, for all his churchmanship, had married in defiance of papal censure. Laymen went on grumbling, even using the tiresome regulations about kinship to try to secure dishonest annulments.[39] But the bishops continued to press their claims, in this as in other respects. The effectiveness of these regulations depended on the bishops being able to find persons who would track down offences and secure the regular cooperation of the secular authorities in prosecuting offenders.

The bishop's right-hand man in the diocese was the archdeacon. This was a post almost unknown in England before the Conquest.

As early as 1072 Lanfranc ruled that bishops should appoint such an official, already known in Normandy; by 1100, every diocese had one and in the twelfth century each shire of the diocese had its own archdeacon. In a special way, the archdeacon became a kind of bishop's sheriff, particularly in attending to legal business and defending the bishop's rights. Archdeacons were very powerful persons locally and the effectiveness of decisions of the bishop, even of the primate, would ultimately depend upon their zeal. Throughout the reign of the Conqueror and his sons, complaints were made that archdeacons were married and turned a blind eye to married clerks,[40] or were 'farmers' holding more than one archdeaconry who condoned other clerks dealing in clerical benefices: archdeacons were at first not particularly more holy in their way of living than their inferiors.

One of the archdeacons' principal functions was to make certain that all offenders against the bishop's laws were punished. Such offences had, in primitive society, to be paid for, not only by fasts, pilgrimages and mortifications, but often in fines as well. These dues were the bishop's right. A variety of other customs also fell to the bishops: the iron used in the ordeal for example, was normally in the bishop's care, unless it was specially conceded to others.[41] The bishop's rights were therefore brought into frequent consideration in the courts. It was the archdeacon who acted for the bishop in these matters.

The bishop also had spiritual courts of his own, but little is known about their functioning in the eleventh century. In England, matters that concerned the bishop were often if not always brought up in the ordinary hundred courts like other offences. After the Conquest, the king directed that bishops should no longer hold their pleas in the hundred courts, but only in places they should choose.[42] The meaning of this order is not as clear as is sometimes said. It did not necessarily mean that the bishop set up separate courts of spiritual jurisdiction as they existed later in the twelfth century. In the reign of Henry I, from which the earliest additional evidence comes, those who offended the bishop, for example by fighting or killing clergy or in churches, by ignoring fast days or marrying widows with indecent and unlawful haste, were tried in the shire court, not the hundred court.[43] The archdeacon called the presiding officer's attention to these spiritual pleas, and by preferential treatment, they were then tried first, even before royal pleas. This royal privilege for ecclesiastical cases was justified on the grounds that, if the king did not secure their enforcement, they would never be respected. In return, the king received a fine from offenders. The procedure could have changed since the Conqueror's time, but it would then be necessary to explain why ecclesiastical reformers of Henry's reign, of whom there were many, never complained of the system or demanded a real separation of courts. Moreover, if the practice of Henry's reign is not what might be expected to result from the Conqueror's order, it is not incompatible with it.

The function of the order may now be seen in its proper perspective. It intended to restore the bishop's privileges over his pleas and also over the ordeal, and it opens by saying that the bishops' customs had not been observed as they should be in England, for in Normandy, the bishops had certainly not allowed their privileges to be lost. The matters in which the bishop is concerned to obtain his fine are nowhere defined in English law, but a comprehensive list of 'episcopal laws', drawn up in Normandy at the Council of Lillebonne in 1080, presumably indicates their nature: desecration of churches and churchyards; offences by the clergy of all kinds, from duelling to neglecting synods; injuries to religious persons; offences by laymen including adultery, incest and desertion of the spouse, consulting the spirits of the dead, resisting justice till excommunication was pronounced. The bishop was entitled to take any goods over which there was any dispute in the houses of clergy, and goods left behind and found in churchyards. No question of principle is really involved though three types of offence connected with ecclesiastical property, with clerical persons and with supervision of the married state may be distinguished. A good instance of the limitation of this list is shown in the last instance, where a layman condemned for rape paid a fine to the bishop if the offence was committed within the churchyard, but not if committed elsewhere. No provisions were made for setting up courts to hear such matters. The last case clearly implies a secular judgment, even if the bishop got the fine as a result of disclosures in the course of proceedings. Laymen could hear ecclesiastical pleas, though priests could appeal against their judgment to the bishop's court. These were the types of case heard in the shire court in England.

The specific purpose of William's ordinance was to remove cases from the hundred courts where the bishop had difficulty in obtaining his due; in practice they were probably heard in the shire court, where the bishop himself frequently sat with the sheriff. But in some English dioceses there were many shires and the bishop could not have attended all the shire courts in his diocese. The archdeacon therefore became the bishop's special representative at those courts, which explains why archdeaconries were normally defined by the boundaries of one shire and were not new areas cut conveniently for the diocese. It is a curious fact that the Conqueror's writ now survives only in two late copies of the thirteenth century, in similar forms but addressed in the first place to all the sheriffs where the bishop of Lincoln had land, and in the second to the three sheriffs of the three shires of the diocese of London. Though these two were not the only dioceses that extended over more than one county they were two of the most important ones, and it is obvious that the two bishops simply could not cope with all the hundred courts involved and would even have needed to decide in which shire court matters concerning them should be heard, simply because there were also too many shires in their diocese. In the Conqueror's reign, when bishops had only one archdeacon, he too would have had his work cut out to scamper round wherever required. Hence the ordinance emphasises the bishop's right to choose to have his pleas where he liked. Such a regulation was not necessarily general and in practice the smaller dioceses had no difficulty in allowing the bishop to take his dues from the shire court itself. Even if the bishop's motives for enforcing Christian discipline were ascribed to financial advantage, society would not have been shocked by such acquisitiveness. It was considered normal to pay for crimes, even assassination, and it would be a mistake to think that the money payments in any way diminished respect for a bishop's sanctity or for Christian laws. On the contrary, society gave the same serious sanctions for ecclesiastical as for secular offences.

Jealous defence of episcopal rights was also fully compatible with the regular exercise of episcopal duties, though naturally the sources do not enlarge upon routine matters. The author of the life of Gundulph stated that the bishop, then as now, had certain personal and undelegatable duties: preaching to the people, confirming children, ordaining priests and consecrating churches, and Gundulph had to act not only in his own diocese, but often as Lanfranc's deputy in both royal and episcopal business. Bishop Wulfstan was fond of preaching on his regular visits in the diocese. His special theme was peace. There was nothing sweeter to be heard, nothing more desirable and nothing more worth finding than peace, which was the condition and the goal of human happiness. It had been announced by the angels at the beginning of the Saviour's life, it had been given by Him to His disciples from the cross and He had left His peace with them at His resurrection. Peace was not just a condition of political existence. Wulfstan not only preached it, he made it, between neighbours and litigants. The fine words he used had daily applications. The Norman Gundulph preached no less eloquently to the people. His favourite theme was penitence. His command of the English language was inadequate to move congregations, but his own copious tears which choked his utterance so affected them that they wept and wailed in harmony with his sobs, as he recounted the stories of the Magdalen.[44]

Confirmations were great occasions for such public addresses, but they were rarely recorded. Anselm's confirmation of many children at St Omer in 1097 was exceptional only because the local bishop had been unable to take them himself for several years.[45] One of Wulfstan's confirmation ceremonies aroused comment simply because his tireless confirmation of two or three hundred children on one day seemed like a miracle to the eight assistant clergy who trembled with fatigue at his side. On that occasion, Wulfstan had also consecrated a new church and the great number of new churches needing consecration at this time was itself a considerable burden for all bishops.

Local parish churches were often provided by laymen, the lords of the manor or other parishioners who were anxious to spare themselves distant journeys in winter and wet weather.[46] Bishops had far more to do than bless their handiwork. They had to define the areas of the new parishes and make certain that there was an adequate endowment for the priest.[47] They had to gauge nice divisions of lands, revenues and tithes, so that the former priests, of the local minster, or mother church, would be compensated for the loss of income, tithes and casual offerings, like burial fees. Arrangements had to be made about defining financial liabilities for the upkeep of the fabric. The bishop's duty to consecrate churches created peripheral problems that took more time and roused jealousies needing legal skill as well as moral acumen to resolve. Bishop Herbert of Norwich refused to consecrate a new churchyard until the king's permission had been obtained, in case disputes should arise later about the old one and the king blame the bishop for acting too hastily.[48] These duties required not merely the display of sacral power, but intelligence and experience of public affairs. It has rarely been found possible since to combine in their due proportions all the diverse qualities bishops require.

Bishops normally consecrated the churches of their own diocese, but they were also asked by their friends in other dioceses to bless a new church. Bishop Remigius of Lincoln raised no objections when Wulfstan of Worcester was invited to such a ceremony in his diocese, but when Anselm attempted to consecrate a church on his own archiepiscopal manor of Harrow in 1095, the canons of St Paul's vigorously challenged his rights to consecrate in the London diocese.[49] If Anselm was only doing what seemed normal to him, the rights of diocesans must have been much impaired after the Conquest, when it is remembered that all the bishops of Normandy had their own estates in England and could have consecrated their own churches.

The problem became much more acrimonious when the consecration of monastic churches was involved. Monks who feared their local diocesan and his claims to fees and visitations attempted to elude his jurisdiction and those monasteries that obtained exemptions, like Bury, ostentatiously excluded the local bishop and invited a distant one to do honour to the new building. Bishop Gundulph of Rochester, the smallest and the weakest see, was much in demand in the 1090s as a consecrator of great new churches. As became a saintly monk, Gundulph did not expect too much as a consideration for his services; but in 1102, when he examined the body of the Confessor (he was also a veteran inspector of relics) he tried to pluck a hair of the Confessor's beard as a relic and had to be rebuked by his old colleague at Bec, abbot Gilbert of Westminster for such shocking abuse of hospitality.[50]

The bishops who were thus active about their dioceses have nevertheless gained a bad reputation, by the posthumous influence of monastic writers. Monks rarely found the bishops of Henry I's generation attractive, unless they were monks themselves.[51] Bishops who pressed their rights on the monasteries of the diocese could expect little sympathy. Bishops with monastic chapters often found that the monks normally regarded them as oppressive and luxury loving. Bishops did not care very much for the monk's opinion and would have been surprised at the courteous attention accorded to the more lurid scandal, that William of Malmesbury himself had second thoughts about including in his 'Deeds of the Prelates'. In part this antipathy between bishops and monks may be explained by the existence of a great social gulf. Bishops were concerned with the most serious business of their community; monks had nominally renounced society and were dedicated to the world beyond the grave. Bishops mingled with the great lords of the realm; monks were absorbed in their microcosmos. The monks and the bishops were not aware, as we try to insist they should have been, of some bond between them as religious persons. Laymen were also Christians, and particular ecclesiastical loyalties could unite laymen and monks in the defence of their own church sooner than create sympathy between rival ecclesiastical orders.

Perhaps the most stark example of the mutual repulsion comes in Eadmer's report of the way Henry I's ambassadors, the bishops of York, Coventry and Norwich, gave an account of their conversations with pope Paschal II, from which Anselm's ambassadors, two monks of Canterbury, had been excluded. The monks had obtained a written reply to their questions. The bishops maintained that what they said was more worthy of consideration. Their word as bishops was more weighty than scraps of parchment, with leaden *bulla*, scribbled over in the hand of little monks who had renounced all dealings in this world, and so forfeited their rights to testify in business matters. This Norman contempt for writing ill becomes a bishop but Eadmer's version of events may not be trusted too literally. It is only the type of argument used that is revealing. According to him, the monks protested that, since the problem was not a secular one, they had the right not only to speak but also to produce the parchment as evidence. But the bishops persisted in their objection: 'We know that you are a sensible and honest man; but our clerical order itself requires us to believe that the words of one archbishop and two bishops are more telling evidence than those of a monk'. When the monk, Baldwin, asked what they thought of the papal letters, the bishops quite unabashed insisted as before: 'If we do not prefer the evidence of monks to that of a bishop, how can we prefer the evidence of a sheep's skin?' Eadmer was shocked and left the last word with Baldwin, who triumphantly retorted 'Aren't the Gospels written on sheepskin too?'[52] The whole episode is so remarkable a statement of prejudice that it must be taken as a typical exposition of the bishops' confirmed belief in their own superiority, in both secular and clerical matters.

As their administrative system began to take shape and the bishop's officials began to bustle about the diocese and the cathedral, bishops became less involved in upholding monasticism than they had been under the Conqueror. They were really planning for a new type of parochial clergy and this meant a deeper awareness of the needs of parishes. Monasteries did not always concur in what the bishops planned at the parish level. In the past the monasteries with lands had built small churches on them and appointed clergy to serve them and the bishops had not interfered in the relationship between patron and priest. The monastery itself had been the real focal point of religious devotion. It was there that the patron saint was buried and the celibate monks had venerated his memory. The parish-priest was on the other hand, a married man, of no great education or sanctity: a singer of the mass. Nor as a priest was he always accorded great respect for his ordination. Even cardinals had argued that his moral lapses invalidated his performance of the sacraments. But things were changing. Gregory VII had insisted that the orders conferred by the laying on of hands gave the humblest priest a status superior to any layman's. All bishops did not go so far, but they were all concerned about improving the position of the clergy and arguing how it could be done. Monks found themselves going over on to the defensive. The values that they represented were being questioned. As monks they were no longer automatically considered to represent the highest realisation of the clerical ideal. Disputes between the bishops and the monks which arose over petty and local conflicts could be raised to a level of more serious discussion when two different ideals for the religious society were being canvassed. The two different approaches were not irreconcilable, but in Henry I's reign they were still novel enough to excite very partial sympathies. Abbot Richard of Ely pressed his old friend the former abbot of Ramsey to add his contribution to the controversy by writing a treatise on the virtues of monasticism. Herbert Losinga refused. Though he was a bishop, he remained a monk and had given his cathedral a monastic chapter; but he told Richard that it was not for the clergy to quarrel amongst themselves. They would do better to concentrate on making laymen respect all the clergy who were ministers of the altar.[53] Herbert was a scholar and able to see ahead to the ultimate solution. He arrived there the more easily because, as a Cluniac monk, he saw the virtue of monasticism in the fact that monks had become priests themselves. But the specific virtues of monasticism perished when monks acquired the status of priests. The heroic days of monasticism were numbered.

The Monasteries

The monks had great advantages; they were a corporate body which never died and never faltered in their admiration of their wonder-working patrons. Popular sympathy assured them of a support that was not given to local married priests. They fostered a belief in the superhuman virtue imparted by sexual abstinence, as in the legends of Edward the Confessor and Edmund of Bury. The case of Bury is an admirable illustration of how the uncorrupted body of the martyr king could assist the monks to become incredibly wealthy in a brief period of time and to build up an enclave of authority that the bishop could not penetrate. The monks maintained that incorruption of the flesh was a divine favour accorded only to those who had never succumbed to the temptations of the flesh. This was a rare virtue much admired by those unable to master the desires of the body; and the monks, as dedicated celibates, aroused a good deal of popular respect. Visitors and sick men drawn by the saint's reputation flocked to his shrine in admiration and hope. They offered gifts and prayers. The monks recorded and publicised the cures and miracles and converted the offerings into adornments for the church, or optimistically set about the construction of a large new building that became famous for its size and beauty, attracting more admiring crowds.

English religious life in the eleventh century was traditionally monastic, and was exceptional in Europe for this.[54] Monks had been the first Roman missionaries; the Irish monks had instilled the ascetic, scholarly and pastoral virtues into houses of Italian Benedictine discipline; the earliest bishops had been monks and in the tenth-century reform monks easily dominated both the monastic and the diocesan revival. Though they had been supplanted in the bishoprics by the Confessor's reign the new type of bishop drawn from the secular clergy had put down no roots in ecclesiastical life. There was no ideal of the city-bishop as he had existed in Italy and Gaul; there were no bishop saints, except those like Cuthbert and Augustine, firmly appropriated by the monks. It was the monks who remembered the past, recorded the present and prayed for the future. Monks breathed their own particular spirit into the English religion of this period. The communities were rich and were held to preserve the essential qualities expected of religious men: power to subdue the natural order by miracles. Their riches did not excite censure, but expressed men's faith in the monks' value to the community. Most of the houses had grown up around the shrine of the original founder and the monks cultivated the memory of their own patron to the exclusion of any other loyalty. Though, technically, they were all Benedictine and had adopted the customs of the tenth-century reformers, the common characteristics of the customs did not give the monks a common way of life as adherence to the rule gave common purpose to all Cistercian monks a century later.

Norman monasticism hardly affected English monasteries, except to accentuate its traditional virtues. Lanfranc admittedly drew up his own monastic constitutions (modelled on the customs of Cluny and Bec) for his chapter at Christ Church. Copies of the manuscript existed in other libraries, at Dover priory, Battle abbey, Durham, Worcester and Hereford cathedrals, and the customs were probably adopted at Rochester too.[55] Lanfranc was said to have written a copy for the use of his nephew Paul, abbot of St Albans, and the influence of abbot Gilbert Crispin, former monk of Bec, could have caused their adoption at Westminster. Useful as the customs were, they had to be adaptable to the communities' existing traditions. It is doubtful to what extent Lanfranc expected them to be more than a general guide to monastic discipline, for strict interpretation of rules was still exceptional; as the name implies, they were intended as 'customs'. This matter of monastic uniformity, which has seemed of great importance to modern observers, was not emphasised by those with living experience of the monastic community. At St Albans,[56] Paul was said to have founded a school of religion and devotion for the whole kingdom, which, however vague, does not amount to introducing Norman observance. It was more important to his monks that he had personally contributed to their welfare and reputation; he had given twenty-eight manuscripts (including service books) to the community, with relics and vestments; he had founded a priory at Wallingford and acquired the priory at Tynemouth, where the sainted king Oswald was said to be buried; he had spent one thousand marks on rebuilding the monastery. His only shortcomings were to destroy the tombs of former abbots and not to look after the property well.

Each house was highly individual and considered its own special interests. Very small changes could seem extremely tyrannical in such communities. The monks of Glastonbury refused to exchange their own tradition of Gregorian chant for that of the Dijon school used in Normandy, to the point where three monks were killed and eighteen wounded by the abbot's knights in an attempt to impose the abbot's will.[57] It is unlikely therefore that new customs could be introduced without active groups of Norman monks as leaven in the lump to adapt existing customs to the old. In the process of adaptation, the new Norman influence was diluted. The sources indicate that much more typical of what happened to English monasteries under the Norman abbots was the story told at Evesham about abbot Walter, formerly monk of Caen under Lanfranc. He had new ideas of his own when he arrived at Evesham and had no veneration for the local saints Egwin and Wistan, of whom he knew nothing. He used Lanfranc's authority for putting their miraculous powers to the test. The monks were required to fast and pray before the ordeal; then the relics of the Evesham saints were subjected to the judgment by fire and Walter was duly impressed when the sacred bones did not even change colour.[58] The Norman monks and abbots had to adopt the traditions of their new monasteries, if they were to command any respect or obedience. Even more important, sceptical Normans risked losing the benefits of the monks' prayers for their ultimate salvation, unless they convinced the communities of their devotion to the communal traditions. A monk of Jumièges, Ethelelm, who became abbot of Abingdon, aroused anger there for stopping all ceremonies in honour of saints Ethelwold, bishop of Winchester, and Edward, king and martyr, though the abbey had amongst its prized relics the bishop's arm, finger and hair and the king's blood-stained shirt. One day at table he sat with his friends and relations (whom he had enfeoffed with the monk's lands) mocking Ethelwold and his works, saying that the church of these rustic Englishmen should be destroyed. His impiety was promptly punished in the most humiliating way: after the meal he was found dead in the privy.[59]

One of the reasons why the Normans did so little to alter the strong individuality of the monasteries was that they too defended the particular rights of each house. There is a curious correspondence between the Conqueror and abbot John of Fécamp through which preliminaries to one abbatial appointment by the king may be glimpsed.[60] William chose Vitalis, abbot of Bernay, as abbot of Westminster. Lanfranc's advice was given, but this did not suffice. Vitalis was reluctant to give up his position at Bernay. In order to persuade him, William proposed to appoint Vitalis' own brother Osbern as abbot of Bernay. Abbot John of Fécamp had however to give his approval because Bernay had been a house founded from Fécamp. Since Osbern had not been a monk of Fécamp at all arrangements had to be made so that Osbern's own monastic superior should first cede him to Fécamp before John could authorise his promotion to Bernay. The complexity of this little case reveals just what was involved by royal nominations. The king had several monastic corporations to consult and placate before he had his own way, and Lanfranc's position is only that of general adviser. Within limits the same may be expected of the heads of other Norman monasteries who provided monks for English monasteries. Lanfranc's influence over the new monastic heads in England could only come from the promotion of monks from the houses he knew: Bec and Caen. There is no need to minimise the effect of such appointments in the houses where they were made, but it is helpful to remember that the Norman monks were true to the Benedictine spirit: they were members of the house they were raised in, and much less aware than modern historians are of what Norman monks appeared to have in common.

The most intimate picture of a monastic community in this period outside the pages of Eadmer's *Life of Anselm* is drawn by the bishop of Norwich, Herbert Losinga, in his frequent and nagging letters to his chapter. He found the monks were not sufficiently enthusiastic for the cathedral building programme; they were thieving, gossiping, over-familiar with the serving brothers; they wandered about, copied documents for money, scribbled literary trifles, harboured immodest desires, bathed and let blood too often. It lacks the forced and fervent view of monasticism that Eadmer tried to uphold, but it rings only too true of what a real community of comfortable, good-natured bachelors, without real worries, would be.[61] All the same, English monasticism breathed an indomitable spirit, before which the most daring Norman abbot and bishop might quail. This spirit enabled the monks to improve their hold on the church by reviving many monastic cathedrals, as they had existed in the tenth century under Dunstan. And its power was further demonstrated by the revival of old English cults within a generation of the Norman's arrival. Norman sceptics, who had begun to doubt the virtues of the Anglo-Saxon saints, were themselves confounded by the zeal they had provoked. Had they allowed the old cults to moulder on undisturbed, they might have rotted away within a generation. As it was, the Normans themselves quickly appreciated the value of these legendary saints, where every village had its own. The saint's protection of his church inspired holy fear in thieves and despoilers, veneration of his memory and thanks for his miracles stimulated bequests and offerings; around the personal cult the monastic community could develop the legends and the history of its house and beyond the common obedience to the abbot, establish a common devotion to the patron saint. Amid all the disturbances of landed interest and usurpations of rights, the Norman prelates who defended their individual churches with typical Norman enthusiasm found that the English saints were powerful allies. Abbot Walter of Evesham who opposed the claims of the

English bishop of Worcester had to rely on his saints' relics in a law-suit. Admittedly, he did not win the suit, but the abbot did not discard the sacred bones. When he ran out of money for re-building his church, he sent monks round England with the bones working miracles and found that the saint's old power to attract money had not diminished.[62]

The Secular Clergy

The most serious of all the bishops' many responsibilities was to supervise the life and work of the parish priests. As parish churches were built ever deeper into the countryside, for the convenience of local communities and lords, so the parish priest became more isolated from his clerical brethren in minster or collegiate churches, more exposed to the influence of the laymen in his parish and more vulnerable to the pressures of the patrons of his church. It is unlikely that many parish priests were well instructed. The bishop of Norwich had to explain even to his own chaplain that the latter's sister could not marry another while her husband was still alive. He also admonished a priest who was ashamed to wear the clerical tonsure (the only visible sign of clerical status) and to chant the mass and kindly advised him how to perform secular duties without staining his priestly character.[63] The clergy were a special order in the community but they had little collective spirit comparable to what made the monks so conscious of their own value. Priests of this kind were the ones most exposed to the practices of ancient religion, divinations and auguries that were condemned again in 1126.[64]

The parish clergy probably differed little in outlook, education or dress from their parishioners. Their essential function was to celebrate the sacraments, conceived of as holy rituals of great meaning. The symbolism still did not need explanations of the kind devised only in the twelfth century by the learned theologians of St Victor and their successors. Priests did not need to be able to give instruction beyond the basic prayers and catechism; communities were small and held together by so many ties of work, kin or lordship that they naturally expressed their unity in religion. Modern problems of priests were quite undreamed of. When the Normans considered what kind of priest would be desirable, they pictured him as a local worthy,[65] respected and distinct from his fellow-laymen who could suppress the worst of popular superstitions and behave decently in the parish. Priests had to avoid being in lawsuits which involved the shedding of blood: a fear of blood pollution. All magical practices, veneration of the dead, unauthorised rites at springs of water, divination, warding off diseases by hanging up dead animals, pagan marriage rites, drinking contests—all were matters that parish priests would need to guard against. They would have to find respectable stone altars, not use wood-chalices or give beer at the communion. To emphasise their difference from laymen, they should wear respectable clothes and a tonsure, but this was the only sign of their clerical status; there was no clerical dress except in the monasteries of Norman England.[66]

These disadvantages make it unlikely that the local parish priest received or merited very great respect from his parishioners, though they probably accepted the effectiveness of his spiritual commission. Those men who wished to give themselves up to the service of God would normally enter the monasteries, where the community would help a man to renounce the temptations of the world, the flesh and the devil. Resisting the temptations of the flesh often seems to have been the virtue most esteemed in eleventh-century religion. Not surprisingly perhaps the monks themselves fostered a belief in the superhuman virtue required for sexual abstinence and the special divine grace conferred on those who remained pure. The incorruption of the flesh after death in the cases of Edward the Confessor and Edmund of Bury was ascribed to their continence, and the monks naturally scorned clerks who did not even try to emulate these chaste examples. It is probable that the monks received more popular veneration, for this reason, than the local parish priests, who must have been generally married men. The monk of Durham declared what future torments lay in store for the miserable wives of the clergy and their husbands, who had been consecrated to God for making things holy,[67] but the monks of Rochester tolerated married clergy in their parishes and allowed sons to succeed their fathers.[68] The monks could have drawn some satisfaction, as well as compensations, from maintaining a parish clergy that could not rival their own holiness.

Not surprisingly, the clergy themselves made a virtue of their condition and could not understand reformers who thought that they should renounce marriage, as if they were monks. They went on defending clerical marriage, as it might be defended now, by pointing to the great number of clergymen who had been born into clerical families. This was, however, considered by their critics as more of an abuse than an advantage. Many sons intended to succeed their fathers in their benefices, thus threatening to destroy the powers of both patrons and bishops. But the fundamental reason for the campaign against clerical marriage was that reformers desired to obtain more respect for the sacraments. They emphasised the priest's special dedication to God and they wanted to establish visible and social differences between laymen and clergy, to help the clergy succeed in a higher vocation.

The movement was still recent at the time of the Conquest. Clerical marriage had been condemned in papal councils in 1049 and in 1051; in 1072, this canon was reissued at Rouen for the Norman clergy. After Gregory VII had called for a massive onslaught against the abuse in 1075, Lanfranc published a decree which obliged cathedral clergy to discard their wives immediately but allowed urban and rural priests to keep them. For the future, deacons and priests were required to swear to remain celibate before they were ordained. Lanfranc's compromise has been interpreted variously as defiance of Rome, moderation and slackness. It was certainly not effective. Married canons at London were still common after his death, and it is hard to believe that all ordinands made this profession or kept it. Clerical marriage survived almost unscathed and his successor had to repeat the more stringent papal measures before anything was done. The compromise may be realistic in another sense. England had probably a high proportion of clergy in the countryside, by comparison with the continental clergy living in recognisably urban centres. Lanfranc may have accepted that little could be done to coerce such men and, familiar as he was with Italy, he might have thought that the pope was more concerned about the situations in the collegiate churches. The first generation of Norman bishops largely achieved the desired result by a subterfuge. By introducing monastic chapters, cathedrals automatically lost their married canons. At Rochester, the canons and their wives were pensioned off with country livings and the monks took over; but Lanfranc had to face criticisms of his policy, even from Normandy, which, however ill-informed, prove that any sign of tolerance was deeply suspect to more determined reformers. The bishop of Worcester did not allow such concessions in his own diocese, so that individual bishops were left, inevitably, to adapt Lanfranc's proposals for themselves. In 1080, at the great council of Lillebonne, the Norman episcopate had reiterated its condemnation of clerical marriage and this excited some opposition. In the next two or three decades, an unidentified Norman priest[69] wrote several pamphlets about ecclesiastical innovations that he could not approve of. He defended the view that clergy, once ordained, could not be deprived of their sacral power, even for clerical marriage; he argued for the marriage of the clergy and defended the sons of the clergy from the slurs cast on their birth by reformers. In less than two thousand words, he protested that to impose celibacy on the clergy was a human decree in contradiction to the freedom offered in the Gospels and with the nonchalant inconsistency of the controversialist cited Paul to the effect that it was better to marry than to burn.

But for the existence of the single manuscript of Corpus College Cambridge (415) in which these pamphlets were later copied, these sentiments would be quite unknown. Arguments about the representative character of the author's views leave the impression that the author held very individual opinions. But the manuscript is not an autograph, and several different hands copied his works in the twelfth century, long after the battles he had fought were apparently lost. The manuscript was brought to England at an unknown date. The situations of the clergy in England and Normandy at the time of composition were sufficiently alike to have roused similar views in both lands. Whether all the married clergy could have found such scriptural and ingenious defences for their position or not, the author enlarges upon a theme that must have been dear to many clergymen of his time. The single survival of only one text cannot be an argument against the popularity of such teaching at the time. The fact that the defence of the married clergy was made in Normandy is a reminder that the Norman church was less impregnated with the monastic, celibate ideal than England was. It was in Nor-

5 Ansbert and St Wandrille, eleventh century
Le Havre, Bibliothèque Municipale MS 332, *p.* 78 (*see p.* 300)

mandy that the cathedral churches were in the hands of secular canons and where strong clerical families had good connections with leading churchmen. The prominence given to Norman monasticism in modern writers has tended to obscure the important role played in the church by such families. Odo of Bayeux kept a nursery of talent in his cathedral. His treasurer, Thomas, was the son of a priest: he became archbishop of York; Thomas's brother, Samson, became bishop of Worcester, and Samson's own son succeeded his uncle at York. Odo's own predecessor at Bayeux, Hugh, was the son of count Ralph of Ivry, and his brother John was both bishop of Avranches and archbishop of Rouen. Their nephew, Robert Bloet, was made bishop of Lincoln by Rufus, and Robert made his son, Simon, dean in his cathedral. The sons of bishop Herfast obtained his church at Thetford after his death.[70] These children were not necessarily born after their father's ordination, but the family affections of the clergy naturally enabled members of clerical families to rise more highly in the hierarchy. Even under Henry I, Richard of Belmeis, bishop of London, went on strengthening these family connections in his diocese, by providing for his relations in the cathedral.

Bishops did not necessarily sabotage plans for reform deliberately, but if clerical marriage was to be eradicated and clerical families weakened, bishops had after all to think ahead to the next stage of the problem: how to find priests who fulfilled their requirements. This problem became apparent in Henry I's reign, when Anselm took up the challenge of clerical marriage in earnest. In 1102, clerks, from the order of sub-deacon up, were told to renounce their wives and to profess chastity; sons of priests were debarred from inheriting churches;[71] laymen were instructed to shun masses sung by unchaste priests. The canons were not immediately published. When Henry I tried to secure enforcement by fining the clergy, Anselm protested that the king was exceeding his powers and taking bribes to keep his eyes closed. He wanted to leave enforcement to the archdeacons and sentences of excommunication. In 1108, at a new council, steps were taken to meet objections of Gerard of York, that the canons were too vague to be enforceable. Negligent archdeacons would have to be punished and offending clergy condemned to forfeit their goods to the bishop. Where could devout and conscientious archdeacons be found? The regulations show that some of these officials had been combining their offices, had not taken the order of deacon themselves, and had winked at offences. Until the bishops' control of their officials was tighter, who would implement the decisions of the bishops in council? In the legatine councils of 1125 and 1127 canons designed to remove the clergy from their feminine companions imply that the abuse was still glaring.

The revival of church councils after the Norman Conquest is sometimes used as an argument for the view that the Normans intended to introduce general reforms into the church. The measure of their aims and achievements over clerical marriage shows the limitations of legislation without the machinery to enforce it. Nevertheless, the canons of such councils as survive are the best evidence for assessing what the bishops took to be desirable changes. By excerpting from the canons it is easy to give the impression that the bishops were totally scandalised by the existence in England of practices that were common all over Europe at the time. Lanfranc's first council in 1075 issued many canons as a reminder, including a provision against the buying and selling of sacred orders of ecclesiastical office with a cure of souls, an instruction to employ clerks and monks from outside the diocese only if they brought letters of recommendation with them, and a brief repetition of the clause from the rule of St Benedict that forbade monks to own private property.

In 1076, the council at Winchester considered the problems of the parochial clergy more carefully. Apart from clerical marriage, the bishops condemned men who seized church property on the grounds that no written evidence of title could be produced and those who tried to exact from the clergy money payments in excess of those paid in the previous reign. Monks were warned not to perform parochial duties. These clauses emphasise the bishops' concern for what may be called the parson's freehold. In Anselm's council of 1102 the same basic concern to obtain an unmarried ministry with adequate legal endowment emerges from the clauses. Once again, bishops had to make sure that churches were adequately endowed, that monks should not cheat parish priests or evict them without the bishop's approval or undertake parish ministries themselves except with their abbot's authority. Laymen were told to pay their dues to their parish priest and to use the local cemetery, so that the priest should not lose his burial fees. These are all genuine problems, but they do not imply that the English church needed or was thought to need a drastic reform. Yet that is in fact what was required and the bishops came to see that it was no use complaining about clerical marriage unless they considered how to find a different type of priest.

Essentially, the problem was to obtain a more worthy parish ministry. In the past men had not thought married priests unsuitable and it took a long time for different ideas to receive general acceptance. The same might be said about the outcry against selling spiritual benefits. If the bishops themselves exacted fees or customs for ordinations and consecrations, it was not surprising that the clergy demanded fees for holy oil, baptism, penances, visiting the sick, extreme unction, burials, even for the communion. They might themselves be money-lenders or farmers of estates and offices and they might have to pay laymen for their church.[72] Such practices were regarded as normal and represent a naïve belief that spiritualities could be dealt with like any other object. Spiritual rituals were sources of power and some people could not see that it was blasphemous to sell them or trade them, as they bargained over other powers and rights. Reformers came to see these practices as terrible abuses. Behind the church or oil sold they saw the spiritual value which it symbolised and trembled to see the holy things of God dealt with like merchandise. What had happened? The abuses were not new, but they seemed reprehensible instead of part of the natural order. No doubt the church facing the harsh realities of the economic world could no longer afford to buy favours from laymen, but the economic factor would not explain why they scrupled to sell what they could have sold at high prices. Men's ideas of the holy were changing and the new spiritual values had to be emphatically distinguished from corrupt and material ones. To this end, the whole church had to be shaken free of its entanglements in the natural order of society.[73] Priests had to be different from laymen; they had to understand the spiritual commitments they had taken up at ordination; their spiritual and intellectual understandings needed to be transformed. An entirely new type of clergy had to be found. The legislation of diocesan synods could not do this. If we consider the real diocesan difficulties of Henry I's bishops, it becomes clearer why it is necessary to judge them in the light of their foundations of collegiate churches rather than for their failure to eliminate deep-rooted evils.[74] They could not hope to influence parish clergy until they had at their disposal many well-educated, celibate and devoted priests, not only in their own cathedrals, but in the leading centres of their dioceses. From them would ultimately come an example of holiness of life that would show how the priesthood could become worthy of respect. So, the worldly, well-connected bishops founded houses of canons. Giffard of Winchester founded St Mary Overy, Southwark; Warelwast of Exeter, founded Plympton; Richard of London, St Osyth's, Essex; Thomas II and Thurstan of York introduced canons into the minster churches of their see: Hexham, Ripon, Southwell, Beverley, St Oswald's Gloucester, and encouraged canons in the cities of the north: Bridlington, Nostell, Carlisle, Guisborough, Kirkham and Grimsby. Henry I's chamberlain, Geoffrey de Clinton founded a house at Kenilworth. More than sixty houses appear to have been founded under Henry I and no part of the country was without them.

There was still great variety about the conditions under which canonries and collegiate churches were founded. This period of experiment naturally put them at a disadvantage in a contest with the monastic order, still solidly loyal to the single rule of St Benedict. The variety of rules and customs eventually proved the more vital character of the reform and allowed greater freedom for different inspirations to work in the church. The old English church was itself well organised to profit from these reforming tendencies, because its collegiate old Minsters could be easily adapted either for a community of canons or for canons who lived separately under certain rules. These collegiate churches were strong in the north: both Durham and Beverley are good examples of this, but even in London, there had been an early house at St Martin-le-Grand.

Tentative experiments depended on private initiative until Urban II in particular stimulated a movement for standardising the rules of the communities.[75] Only by the death of Henry I was there a clear distinction drawn between the regular canons, living the life of monks under the rule of Augustine, and the secular canons, for whom endowments were provided but who accepted no other rule of common life than the obligations of the clerical order. Before then it would be difficult to determine what the canonical life always involved and it would be unrealistic to expect contemporaries to have attached importance to distinctions which became significant only later. Urban II declared that there was a special virtue in a community of canons who helped the weak and redeemed their own sins with tears and alms by working in the world. Monasticism, he explained, was reserved for those who could climb to the heights of spiritual perfection by leaving all secular cares behind them and clamouring daily in their prayers for the Divine Mercy. For the canons who had no Benedict as their father, Urban II proposed patrons like his namesake Urban I, St Augustine whose rule was the earliest source of their inspiration, St Jerome who had written about the duties of the clergy, and Gregory the Great who had advised Augustine to found a hospital at Canterbury, recently revived by Lanfranc, of which Urban must have heard. These were very ancient and respectable antecedents indeed.

The eastern regions of England seem to have developed houses of canons earlier than elsewhere. Monasteries were fewer and were concentrated in the least accessible places. Eastern England had the big towns and lay nearest to the influences of the Lower Rhine valley. Aiulph, a priest of Colchester, who won Anselm's support for his plan to build a house of canons there, actually went to Mont St Eloi with two companions to learn to live by the rule of St Augustine. In Rufus's reign, Pagan Peverel founded a house for thirty canons at St Giles, Cambridge, on a site near Cambridge castle where only six canons had lived before. These canons were to 'lead his soul to eternal life'. There was also a house of canons at this time in Huntingdon. The house at Colchester which boasted of being the first Augustinian house in England founded a priory at Aldgate which received royal patronage. This and another house, Merton priory, also in the vicinity of London, became influential sources of later foundations.[76]

The progress made by such foundations had its proper effect on parochial life only at a later date, when learning, and eventually education, had provided the instruments to be used there. Before that time was reached, many of the houses of canons had become privileged communities of learned clerks, little interested in evangelism or parishes and devoted to learning and the religious life. Yet the effect of the new movement cannot be measured solely in terms of the direct influence they had locally. In the first place, their growth in the towns certainly indicates that there was a special type of work to be done there and a confidence that these foundations would help, through charitable, educational and pastoral work. For the first time since the erosion of ancient civilisation, the Christian church was measuring itself against the urban communities, and setting to rights the busiest and the most prosperous parts of the community. Secondly, even if the canons could not do more than set good examples, to start with, they had for the first time demonstrated that a life dedicated to God could be lived with dignity by ministering to the needy at the parish level and thereby raised up an alternative ideal to monasticism, which required utter renunciation of the world.

England only shared in a revival that convulsed the intellectual and moral outlook of Europe, taking and giving what the Latin church offered and needed. The canons were less committed to a narrow range of loyalties and sympathies than the monks and they responded with enthusiasm to the new types of order and discipline in their lives and thought, breaking down the rigid conceptions of rule and privilege with logic and principle. The passions and torments of the monastic saints cede in interest to struggle between the intellect and the emotions and the superhuman wrestling match is replaced by a civilised debate between protagonists as the image of the means to salvation.

By 1135, the religious life of England was very different from what it had been in 1066, but the changes had not come about through the determination of the original Norman invaders to reform a corrupt English church. If any one aspect of policy must be stressed, the bishop's own pursuit of the interests of his see and his office deserve special attention. A period of close association with monasteries was succeeded by one of barely veiled hostility in which the bishops began to introduce an entirely new religious element into the English church. As against these signs of a consistent policy that would lead ultimately to the well-disciplined dioceses of the thirteenth century, the power of individual churches to resist assimilation continued to give older and prouder houses a privileged position in the community. To put these houses into sharp focus is to realise that there could be no single plan for the English church. The bishops struggled for their dioceses, and the abbots no less valiantly for their houses; the monks often fought for the community against the abbot. Other Christians, kings, laymen, royal officials and local landowners often had their own interests to consider. The English church acquired from this Norman period a spirit of local patriotism that remained of lasting importance. Jurisdictions overlapped and clashed. The creation of enclaves of territory in the diocese indicated a weakness that remained permanent.

Looking back over the years of Norman rule, William of Malmesbury implied that the corrupt condition of the English church in 1066 had been corrected by the Normans. But he is inconsistent. He thought that the English bishops had been unscholarly and secular-minded. From his particular accounts his Norman contemporaries hardly seem better. He asserted that they did not enforce their own rules, and that instead of setting a good example by preaching they oppressed the poor and became the yes-men of the rich. He denounced the monks of Canterbury for their addiction to blood-sports (apparently a rhetorical amplification of a few innocent remarks of Eadmer) and implies that monasticism had improved by his own day. But the abbot of Chertsey could not have been the only abbot with permission to hunt hares, wild-cats and pheasants with his own hounds on his own lands in Malmesbury's time. The clerk Thurstan had a personal licence from Henry I to keep greyhounds for chasing hares and foxes. In this respect it is unlikely that the habits of the clergy had changed so much.

Changes came slowly and were only beginning to show their true face in the 1120s. When they came they were not particularly Norman by inspiration; they came as part of the English response to the great revival of western Europe. By that time the Normans had themselves become absorbed into their adopted country. They had raised new buildings, which for all their magnificence, perhaps because of it, celebrated sanctities of the past. The Normans were vigorous, they got things done; they recovered property, obtained privileges and charters: they were pompous and worldly-wise and they put all their energies to the service of their churches. What they wanted was to make the most of the accumulated blessings of their English predecessors.

Part Three

Norman England

7 A Generation of Difficulties

The New Context of Norman Society

The Conqueror had held the government of England and Normandy and of church and state firmly in his own hands. Whether he had pursued a deliberate policy of concentrating authority is doubtful. He was a conservative who enjoyed his rights, but he never tried to deny the rights of others. If the pope had a claim to Peter's Pence it was paid; if his son Robert had a right to succeed him in Normandy, the Anglo-Norman realm would be divided equitably. William did not cling, as his successors clung, to an idea of what his authority should be. Nor did he attempt to rule the future from the grave. He could have had little doubt that his sons would quarrel, but he left them to work out their own solutions.

The reasons for the assignment of Normandy to Robert, the oldest son, England to Rufus and a cash payment to Henry the youngest may seem like a pathetic attempt to provide for each son, as in a fairy story. The scheme was not so fanciful. By 1086 England and Normandy were still very different countries united only by the prominence in both of a few hundred landowners. The Conqueror could see that it was possible to govern England separately from Normandy and offered it to Rufus, his energetic, able son. It is true that the Conqueror's division of lands was apparently only a last-minute decision on his deathbed where he forgave Robert and granted him the duchy. He accepted as a matter of course that each of his sons ought to be provided for and that his single authority would disappear with him. It was his sons who would not agree to share his power amongst themselves; their rivalries tore William's scheme of government to shreds.

Robert had been first recognised as the Conqueror's Norman successor in 1066. As the first son he could anyway claim the patrimony, but who was to say that his younger brother was entitled to England? The position of the king-duke could not easily be assimilated to that of other barons who allowed the divisions of their estates on that principle. Robert's supporters in Normandy thought it right that he should succeed in England as well. By 1088, Odo of Bayeux, Geoffrey of Coutances and Roger de Montgomery had risen in his favour. Their support for Robert may seem self-interested: as he was easy-going they expected to be allowed a free hand in government. If the presence of Odo of Bayeux does make the cause seem suspect, both Geoffrey and Roger had been loyal servants of the Conqueror: they found the division of England from Normandy unacceptable. As duke of Normandy, Robert was their natural lord; inevitably they preferred his claims to Rufus's. As the oldest son, Robert commanded more respect than Rufus, who had only his coronation at the hands of Lanfranc to commend him. The Normans had never been much impressed by kingship. However, when Rufus rallied English support, captured the rebel stronghold at Tonbridge, exiled his troublesome uncles, Odo and Robert, and showed that he was real master of the land, he stood out as a lord able to attract vassals. He bought parts of Normandy from the impoverished lords of St Valéry, Aumâle and Eu in 1090; by 1091 he forced Robert to admit him into the duchy as part-ruler, offering English lands to Robert's friends, help with the recovery of Maine to Robert and recognition of Robert as his heir in return for key places and castles in Normandy. However attractive Robert could have been to Norman lords who wanted a light yoke, Rufus, with his hard cash, his energetic conduct of war, his projects and his firm government, attracted a far more substantial following. By the winter of 1093–94 Robert realised that Normandy was slipping through his fingers. He denounced his agreements with Rufus and for two desultory years campaigned in Normandy. At last he opted out of his inheritance; as always short of money, he borrowed

10,000 marks from Rufus, giving Normandy as surety, and went on Crusade at Easter 1096.

Rufus's advantages over Robert were twofold: he offered rich lands in England to Robert's supporters and opportunities of successful campaigns elsewhere, in Celtic Britain and in the Norman marches. Rufus in fact had understood the real secret of his father's success: expansion. Robert had only Normandy. (The Vexin and Maine had been acquired, and lost, by the Conqueror.) He had little to offer his vassals for their loyalty.[1] His position is perhaps pitiable, but with the same determination as his brothers, he could have turned his undoubted courage to his own advantage. His vassals certainly grew to prefer Rufus to Robert, even if his yoke was heavier; nor did they perceive now they might divide their loyalty somehow between the two brothers.

Nevertheless, when Robert returned from Crusade in 1101 with a wealthy Sicilian bride, he had no difficulty in rallying his vassals against his younger brother Henry who had seized Rufus's crown after his death. Once again the Normans were prepared to support the legitimate heir in his claims to England. It was Robert who accepted the deceptive terms of Henry I in 1102 which once more cheated him of England. He was soon on the defensive again in Normandy while Henry I prepared for a final show-down. At Tinchebrai, in 1106, Henry captured his brother and kept him in wonted idleness, as a prisoner, till he died in 1134. Thereafter Henry governed Normandy but his legal title to do so was precarious. When Henry's own son William was drowned in 1120, leaving Henry with only a married daughter to succeed him, many Normans naturally considered that William the Clito had the better claim to the succession. Henry did not allow himself to be defeated by the Clito (who died in 1128) but the spirit of opposition was itself disturbing. Henry's last years were dominated by his efforts to secure the acceptance of his daughter's (second) husband as ruler after him; he had still not found a legal way to guarantee the unity of his dominions. The lord who offered leadership in war and united lordship across the channel would be the natural favourite.

The competition amongst the Conqueror's sons for his inheritance would have caused enough difficulty, but the princes and their supporters found that the world they lived in also seemed to resist their demands more than it had the Conqueror's. In two respects, the Conqueror's capacity to command total obedience was contested by forces over which the new kings had little influence: political and ecclesiastical. By 1086, when England was surveyed, the limits of conquest and appropriation of other men's rights had been set; thereafter, the barons had either to devote themselves to the unfamiliar arts of estate-management or they had to seek less valuable conquests on the fringe of the realm: the days of heroic conquest were over. The development of new ideas of church government at Rome also undermined the kind of power that the Conqueror had exercised in England. Neither Rufus nor Henry I would accept the consequences of this and tried desperately to retain their father's customs. But what their father had had without much of a fight and without troubled conscience, his sons could only enjoy at the cost of rousing determined opposition. The difficulties of the Conqueror's legacy were not all of the old king's making.

It is sometimes wondered why the Conqueror's sons did not concentrate on conquering Britain and uniting it, if they were looking for fields of military endeavour. Seen from the English point of view, nothing could seem more natural, but the Normans preferred to expand in France and leave Celtic Britain to marcher campaigners. They were not only partial to France; they were wise. No king of England before Edward I could find the resources and the skills in castle-building and government for the successful conquest of Wales. It cost Edward years of effort and no Norman king could have drawn upon such resources as Edward had. Scotland has never yet been conquered from England, and attempts to conquer it have always proved costly and results illusory. The Normans never considered the effort worth it. As for Ireland, all English advances there have been made in the haphazard individual way that the Normans themselves pioneered. It is unlikely that the Normans gave the conquest of Britain serious thought as a policy. Had they done so, it would have been sufficient to take stock of the border regions, for them to realise that the kings would be unwise to aim at more than a vague recognition of their overlordship, such as previous English kings had enjoyed and leave individual barons to make such personal conquests as they could. The main political problem for England in the eleventh century was not to pacify and unite the British Isles but to bestride the Channel. The southern frontier was so much more important that the best energies of England's kings until the fifteenth century were expended in France.

The Conqueror did obtain the homage of native princes in both Wales and Scotland.[2] Rhys ap Tudor, prince of Deheubarth who relied on Norman support to retain his dominance in Wales, paid tribute to William and received a visit from him at St David's in 1081. Barons established themselves in the march, but apart from the advance point at Cardiff hardly penetrated into Wales. In Scotland, the king, Malcolm Canmore, despite his marriage to the Aetheling's sister (or because of it) did homage to the Conqueror in 1070. His court was full of his wife's English relations and friends, who introduced not only English but Norman influence.[3] Scotland could be regarded as a client state. The northern region of England was very unsettled. Durham and Newcastle were marcher lands where the king relied on the loyalty of vassals, like the bishop of Durham, to rule in his name.

After the Conqueror's death, much greater determination was shown on both sides to define authority. The marcher earls, Shrewsbury and Chester in the west and Northumberland in the north, became aggressive on their own account, but they were less successful than they must have hoped. Their opponents had both realised their danger and how to repulse it. Though issue was joined on the border, the two sides were locked like wrestlers in an embrace of ambiguous intimacy, which lasted for centuries. The explanation for the violent activity under Rufus cannot be a simple one. In part, the marcher barons had become surer of their own strength by 1086 but they also began to realise that their personal field of expansion had become narrowed to what could be done in the strange territories beyond the region surveyed and evaluated in 1086. Rufus personally, by his fitful displays of vigour, by the foundation of Carlisle castle in 1092 and by his expedition to Snowdonia in 1095, stimulated an awareness of the importance of the march regions. More difficult to assess are the forces that enabled the Welsh prince Gruffydd ap Cynan and the Celtic Donaldbane to put heart into resistance and challenge what the 'English' had already achieved. Gruffydd had been striking at the Normans in Wales since 1075, using the Danish kingdom of Dublin as a retreat. His Irish men were not popular with his Welsh tribesmen in Gwynned, but it was his Irish and Danish army that gave him a first striking victory at Mynydd Carn, though he did not himself reap the benefit of it. Gruffydd's use of Ireland is something of an enigma; but his use of it as a base, the intervention of king Magnus of Norway (who was lord of the Isle of Man) in 1095, and the fact that the Norman invasion of Ireland was later launched from south Wales, all suggest that the western seas enabled the peoples of western Britain to maintain regular contacts that largely elude detection. Whether the Scottish Celts also obtained help or comfort from the same quarter cannot be proved: the Latinising influence of Margaret of Scotland reached to Iona, an old centre of Celtic Christendom, and could have excited equal resentment of alien interference. The situation in the marcher regions had changed, and the Normans, abandoning their casual approach, prepared for a great attack.

Just as the Welsh joined the marcher barons against Rufus in 1088 as an excuse to raid England, so Malcolm Canmore was drawn into England by the party of Robert of Normandy, probably through his brother-in-law, the Aetheling. Malcolm pretended that he had done homage to the Conqueror and would therefore do homage to his elder son, and only after Robert's reconciliation to Rufus did Robert himself persuade Malcolm to accept Rufus as king. Malcolm subsequently went as far as Gloucester to obtain an interview with Rufus, who refused to receive him. The earl of Northumberland prepared an ambush for Malcolm on his return, in which the king of Scots was killed. Northumberland's action, no doubt intended to facilitate his own advance into the Lowlands, in fact precipitated a Celtic reaction at Dunfermline, which forced all Malcolm's sons to go into exile. The oldest, Duncan, Malcolm's son by his first wife, was, rather oddly, the candidate imposed in Scotland by Rufus. He survived two years and was then murdered. The Celtic reaction managed to hold its own until 1097, when Rufus and the Aetheling finally succeeded in restoring Margaret's sons to Scotland. They reigned in turn, Edgar, Alexander and David. The new kings appear to have learned the lesson of the revolts. Anglo-Norman influence in Scotland did not decline culturally, but politically: the new kings were no catspaws of Norman policy. Henry I's marriage to their sister may show his desire for brotherly relationships with the

Scottish kings, who had shown their importance in the north. The greatest of the kings, David I, was an English earl by his marriage to Waltheof's niece; as earl of Huntingdon he was one of Henry I's natural counsellors. He was also Henry's brother-in-law and as uncle of the 'empress' Mathilda he played a major role in English politics after 1124. David did not allow his English associations to weaken Scottish pretensions in the north. He occupied Lancashire as far South as the Ribble; in 1138 his armies marched to North Allerton before the English stood against him. He could not maintain his supremacy, but he had counter-attacked and Scotland had shown that it was not to be seized whole or penetrated piecemeal.

In Wales, there was no king to give the Welsh the same rallying-point, against enemies who were more numerous and nearer to the centres of English power. In their own ways, however, the reissue of Hywel Dda's code of law and the revival of Welsh poetry in the Gwynned kingdom of Gruffydd ap Cynan symbolise the cultural resistance of the Welsh that has ever since challenged English political superiority. But at this time there was still occasion to fly to arms. However, the Welsh revolt of 1088, which had overwhelmed the earl of Chester's cousin, Robert of Rhuddlan, provoked a strong reaction in the earl, who swept across north Wales building castles as far as Carnavon and setting up a Norman bishopric at Bangor by 1092. The next year, when Rhys ap Tudor died, the Norman marcher lords, led by the aged earl of Shrewsbury, descended on south Wales. The earl's son, Arnulf, was set up in Pembroke castle and a castle was built at Cardigan. The Normans had therefore cut right through Wales and threatened to divide it into pieces. It was the escape of Gruffydd ap Cynan from the earl of Chester's prison in 1095 that inspired a great Welsh revolt in the south as well as in the north. The Normans were attacked and driven out of their forts, only Pembroke and Carmarthen holding out. The failure to take Pembroke, whose castellan, Gerald of Windsor, was the ancestor of the famous Geraldines, proved the inferiority of the Welsh and enabled the Normans to recover their fortunes. But it was not a complete recovery. In north Wales, the death of the earl of Shrewsbury, in 1098, obliged the earl of Chester to withdraw the frontier he could defend to the Conway; Gruffydd was left as the Welsh leader in his peninsular kingdom: Anglesey and Snowdonia. Henry I led an

6 From a manuscript of *The City of God*, *c.* 1100
Florence, Biblioteca Laurenziana MS Plutarch 12: 17, *f.* 2*a* (*see p.* 300)

expedition against Gruffydd in 1114, but Gruffydd retreated out of range into the mountains and Henry I gave up the attempt to deal with him. Gruffydd himself went to Normandy with the king in 1115. The king and the prince agreed to respect one another's power.

Likewise in south Wales, the Norman advance and the Welsh revolt had created a confusion of lordships, rivalries, claims by descent and marriage. The southern Welsh lordships—Pembroke, Cardigan, Carmarthen, Builth, Brecon and Glamorgan—and the Norman sees—St David's and Llandaff with numerous other settlements, secular and ecclesiastic—proved that the Normans had come to stay; the power of Cadwgan in Powys enabled him to dominate the Welsh lords for a few years, that augured well for the capacity of the Welsh to resist complete absorption. In the regions thus divided between rival groups, yet living in constant contact, not always settling quarrels within their own camps, but borrowing support where they could find it temporarily, the stimulus it gave to both sides was the most remarkable achievement of these seemingly futile border wars. The Welsh put their cultural heritage into the oldest manuscripts now surviving. The Mabinogion collection of tales could have delighted the Norman as well as the Welsh courts; at all events, it was in this region that were told the tales of Arthur that spread into French romance. These incidental results of warfare were quite undesired benefits. The great attack had been blunted by a strange kind of opposition. The Normans had met their match and incidentally brought a world of fairy tale into the reality of western Europe.

Henry I, like Rufus, never allowed his activity in Britain to distract his attention from the major interests of politics. For his first six years as king, he had plotted the conquest of Normandy, and after 1106 he spent not less, but more time there. Normandy and its problems preoccupied him. Unlike his brothers, Henry had been born as a king's son (for this reason he probably bore the imperial name, Henry) and could have been expected to take more interest in the richest part of his dominions. In his own way, Henry may have done so. After 1106, he emerged as the most powerful ruler of western Europe, with the one possible exception of the emperor, Henry V, whom he accepted as a son-in-law in 1111. Had Henry wished he could have left Robert as a puppet in Normandy, or at least have allowed Robert's son, William the Clito, to take it as his vassal. Henry did not choose to do this. He wanted his father's dominions to remain united, and he devoted his life to adding Anjou to the realm, and trying to secure that the whole empire would pass intact to his heir. His motives are difficult to understand, but essential to the understanding of his monarchy. It was Henry who enlarged the dominions of the English king in France beyond the Norman border, which committed generations of his successors to the defence of the Plantagenet empire.

Rufus himself had contemplated the acquisition of Poitou in 1100, which could only have been held with control of the cities of the Loire valley. Rufus's scheme was not long prepared: it was the spontaneous response of the soldier to the possibilities of the moment, namely, the count of Poitou's imminent departure on crusade. Rufus had done his best to recover the Vexin, that strip of territory between Normandy and Paris, which would give greater security from attack by the king of France. He only recaptured Gisors. Rather than pour great effort into the capture of a vital, but minute, scrap of land, Rufus turned equably to capture Le Mans and easier prey elsewhere. His attitude inspires legitimate doubts about whether Rufus would have understood modern ideas of strategy or frontier defence. He was an opportunist and he wanted to keep his troops occupied in successful conquests. Henry I was not necessarily so naïve, but he also knew how to respond to the occasion. Unable to conquer Le Mans himself he was politically strong enough to persuade the count of Anjou to accept the county from him, as overlord, and attempted to capitalise on his hold over Anjou politically by negotiating marriages there for his children. William was married to Mathilda of Anjou in 1119, a match that had been agreed in 1114 when she was sole heiress to her father. After William was drowned in 1120, Henry had to drop the project, but, after his daughter Mathilda was widowed in 1125, he forced her to marry the new count of Anjou, Geoffrey, very much her junior in age. The marriage was not popular with Mathilda or with the Norman barons, who traditionally detested the Angevins and dreaded that Geoffrey would become their duke; whether the English or the Angevin barons earnestly desired it we do not know, but it seems unlikely. The idea was Henry's.

The original approach to Anjou had been made incidentally in connection with Maine.[4] The Conqueror and Rufus had taken Le Mans, but Norman occupation of the county remained unpopular both with the inhabitants and with the Angevins. Henry had to settle Maine, for his authority over the Norman barons of the southern march depended on his capacity to defend their interests there and to prevent them taking their loyalty to other princes. Henry thus became involved in warfare in the southern march in 1111–14, as a result of which, without taking Le Mans himself, he obtained political recognition of his overlordship from Fulk V of Anjou, who had married the heiress of Maine. In fact, the terms of peace went further still: Henry was acknowledged as suzerain of Brittany as well as of Bellême and Maine. The king of France thus lost his nominal rights over these counties and found that Henry had effectively usurped royal authority in north-west France. Henry took advantage of Fulk's attitude to secure the hand of his heiress for Henry's own son. This too was opportunist.

The project of alliance with Anjou, however casually entered into in the first place, must have obsessed Henry by the 1120s, when the scheme of marriage was revived, not this time with the prospect of Norman dominance in Anjou, but the much less desirable prospect of Angevin dominance in Normandy and England too. Was Henry's idea a simple expression of his determination to give his daughter an 'empire' after all?

Mathilda had been married to Henry V at a time when her father was deeply disgruntled by the failure of his ecclesiastical policy and impressed by the way the German king held his own against the papacy.[5] Until Henry V's death, relations between the courts were friendly. Henry I followed his son-in-law's Italian campaigns closely and found him a prompt ally in a great war against the king of France in 1124. Henry V, on his side, admired Henry I's wealth and threatened to introduce his taxation system into Germany. Mathilda acquired very haughty ideas by her marriage to such a powerful prince. Though crowned empress only by an anti-pope and correctly styled queen in Germany, when she became a widow, she returned to her father as an 'empress', a pretension that her father appears to have flattered. To unite her against her will to Geoffrey in order to provide her with an empire adequate to her pride would have been an ironic compliment, but would make Mathilda's own indifference to her glorious prospects inexplicable in the light of what is known of her character.

By the 1120s Henry seems to have become firmly convinced of the desirability of uniting the lands of northern France west of Chartres in single hands, and holding them together with the rich English monarchy. The king of France, Louis VI, was committed throughout his reign to minor campaigns against the disorderly barons of the Paris region and had no power to challenge Henry. At the most he could muster a heterogeneous force of vassals to irritate Henry; even the old alliance with Anjou failed of its effects. Louis's strong card was his support of Robert of Normandy's son, William, to whom Henry would not be reconciled, either in 1120, when his son died and his nephew became his obvious heir, or in 1124, when another important rising in his favour took place in Normandy. Louis did not discard the Clito, but, by making him count of Flanders, Louis directed his attention to the better prospects he had in England, just across the water, than in Normandy. Till 1128, the Clito was Henry's most dangerous enemy, because his probable successor.

Henry's projected empire did not include Flanders or Denmark, England's maritime neighbours, but it did extend the southern border of the Anglo-Norman realm well beyond the territories of the Norman lords with possessions in England and Normandy, so that their loyalty, on which the king needed to rely, was not shaken by temptations in northern France. It enabled Henry to ignore Louis VI's authority in his own sphere of influence, though his son William did in fact do homage to Louis VI for Normandy, when the Clito had just shown his strength after the Norman rising of 1118. Louis lost his power to intervene through Anjou, once the alliance was confirmed. In addition to these tangible advantages, Henry's empire gave him the satisfaction of adding to his dominions and passing them to his children, without much campaigning, and the prestige of becoming the most considerable prince of Europe after 1125.

Henry's horizon as a politician seems much broader than his father's, possibly to the Conqueror's disadvantage. The Conqueror too had his vision, though his achievement in England has outshone his other exploits. His sons realised, correctly, that they could not simply retain his conquests: they had to go on, to show what they could do. Henry I was not able to command the same brilliant, and perhaps ephemeral, victories as Rufus, but, in his way, he also set out to dominate a greater whole than his father's heritage and he discovered, by diplomacy and calculation, how he could emulate his father in a society where easy conquest was no longer enough.

It was in ecclesiastical matters that the Conqueror's sons faced the greatest opposition to their policy of maintaining their father's rights intact. Without any special effort on his part, the Conqueror had found himself at the end of the reign with the power to choose whether he would recognise the imperial pope, Clement III, or the Roman pope. Rufus was determined to retain this initiative, whatever it cost him, and he and Henry I had to defy opposition even in England to maintain their authority over the church. Whether the Conqueror would have carried defiance of Rome to the degree they did seems unlikely. Their father had insisted on custom, but never refused the pope his due. In fact, Henry I lost face by trying to maintain customs that had come to seem like abuses, and which he had to forgo. The difference between the situation in 1087 and in 1135 may be shown from the case of Henry's favourite, Hugh, whom the king had made abbot of his own Cluniac foundation at Reading. Hugh was summoned to Rome by pope Honorius II, as Lanfranc had been by Gregory VII. The king, the convent and the abbot himself, all protested against the papal command, but the pope was unmoved and Hugh went. He returned as the pope's special agent for the prompt collection of Peter's Pence, and, when Henry I promoted him to the see of Rouen in 1130, Hugh revealed himself as a faithful exponent of the new papal policy. As a condition of reform in the whole diocese he exacted oaths of obedience from the clergy. The abbot of St Wandrille flatly refused to profess obedience to the archbishop and took his complaints against Hugh to Henry I in England. Henry like his father believed it was right to protect the individual privileges of each church. In this case he could do no better than write to the pope, Innocent II, knowing that it was the pope who directed the church and not himself. Bitterly, Henry had been made to realise that his father's customs counted for little against the papacy.

> More particularly therefore I humbly beseech you as a father to correct these and other matters, which seem contrary to the honour, customs and dignities of my kingdom and duchy . . . lest you compel me to depart from my love, fidelity and service to you and yours, by these unfamiliar novelties and similar burdens, because I cannot continue to hold this land without its familiar and lawful honours nor will I be allowed by my barons and men (whose counsel and help I cannot do without) to enjoy this land any longer in such ignominy and despite. They vigorously and frequently taunt and insult me as one who will allow the former honours and rights of the kingdom, hitherto maintained intact, to be torn away from me in my time by negligence and carelessness. The barons of my land will in no wise consent to let the archbishop remain in peace and amity unless you and he take thought how to mend these and similar matters. . . . Because I am ready and always was ready to obey you in those matters that concern God, the Holy Roman church and the dignity of your person, I demand that my due honour, as formerly accorded in full, be preserved by you and that I be reinvested with those things of which I have spoken.[6]

Innocent II was suitably impressed by Henry's tone. He also feared that if pushed Henry might go over to his rival, pope Anacletus II, who had visited England as legate in 1121 and who was befriended by the Normans of Sicily. In fact, Henry I could not exploit the papal schism of 1130, as his father had that of 1082. His churchmen were in no doubts, even if the king was. But Innocent had to be circumspect. He advised Hugh to submit for the time being and to prefer charity to justice, for Henry would be generous if he were humoured. Announcing his work of mediation to the king, Innocent nevertheless saw fit to treat him to a lecture on his duties in the kingdom and duchy, to which God had assigned him. His distinctions in honour, wisdom and riches should convince him of his duties as a ruler to prune bad customs and cut them to the roots of their vicious origin and to plant good new ones in their place. Abbots and other clergy who do not submit to their bishops are leaderless and cannot please God or save their souls, if they live without authority and become proud of their own dignities; in this way their souls are in danger and the king might be held responsible for it at the Day of Judgment.[7] Innocent II's conception of a submissive hierarchy in the church left little place for Henry's rights and honours, and Henry's support of clerical pretensions could seem dangerous to papal government. The pope might defer to Henry for the time being, but there is no doubt that he is really master of the church in Henry's dominions and that the clergy will normally obey him rather than the king. The contrast with the Conqueror's reign is complete.

How had this change come about? The transformation of the Roman see itself between 1085, when Gregory VII died in exile, and 1131, when Innocent II, also in exile, could preside over a great church council at Reims, occurred irrespectively of the wills of the kings of England. Rufus and Henry I both tried to keep out papal influence and pretend that nothing had happened over the years to affect either the papacy or the monarchy but the pretensions of kings could not sap papal growth. It might seem that Henry had had success in this policy. In 1115, Paschal II reproved him for denying St Peter (that is the Roman see) his proper respect in England. The king decided which papal messenger and letters might be admitted; the king restrained appeal to the Roman court against unlawful ordinations; unlike his Anglo-Saxon predecessors, the king did not visit the Holy See or welcome Roman pastors. The pope threatened that St Peter would take away Henry's benefice if he went on in this way, particularly by refusing to pay Peter's Pence. As pope, he claimed the right to examine the lives and learning of Henry's bishops, to judge their disputes and to authorise the translations of bishops from one see to another. Henry had no right to move Ralph d'Escures from Rochester to Canterbury without papal permission.[8] Henry was apparently still exercising all his father's powers. In fact, Henry could only do this by manifest illegalities, whereas the Conqueror had upheld his own rights without trespassing on the rights of others. The one man who did more than any other to change all this was Anselm, the abbot of Bec, who became archbishop of Canterbury very much against his will in 1094.[9] Rufus is supposed to have appointed him as a gesture of repentance on his bed of sickness, to atone for the long vacancy at Canterbury. Even more than Lanfranc, Anselm was out of sympathy with his fellow-bishops. Eadmer expressed his effect on them in the following words that he put in the mouths of Walkelin of Winchester and Robert Bloet of Lincoln, but which sum up the situation psychologically[10]:

> We know, Lord Father, that thou art a religious and holy man, and that your conversation is in heaven. We, however, are weighted down with the cares of our relations, whom we are responsible for, and for the numerous things of this world that we love; we cannot raise ourselves to the sublimity of your life nor escape with you from this world, But if you would only come down to our level and walk in our ways, we will advise you as best we can and look after your affairs, when neccessary, as if they were our own. If, however, you wish, alone, to cling to God, as you have begun to, you will continue to remain alone, as long as our interests too are at stake. We do not go beyond our fidelity to the king,

Even at Canterbury, Anselm did not get whole-hearted approval. He had been consecrated by Thomas of York, eager to avenge the ignominy Lanfranc had heaped upon him; Thomas had been the centre of a stormy scene at the ceremony, had refused to acknowledge Anselm as primate of all Britain, calling him only metropolitan of Canterbury. Anselm had sat meekly and did not interfere in the dispute between his supporters and Thomas. Yet his last year of life was distorted by his belated and vehement defence of the rights of Canterbury to the obedience of the new archbishop of York. Though he came in with compromise, he went out with anathema.

His mildness did not represent weakness. He stood up for the causes he was persuaded of. The position of the Roman see was such a case. It was not the popes themselves who cajoled him to revive the papal case. Popes consistently preferred to obtain royal favour and did not altogether welcome Anselm's stand on their behalf. When Rufus admitted the legate of Urban II to England, it was not to Anselm at Canterbury, but to the king at Windsor that he first hurried to pay his respects. At the end of Anselm's life, Paschal II similarly submitted to Henry I's pressure and sent a legate to judge between Anselm and Thomas II of York, though Anselm happily died before papal duplicity became manifest.

Anselm was not at the centre of the intellectual activity of the age and he was out of sympathy with the leading members of the clergy. He was older than most of the other leaders; his peculiar intellectual gifts set him at a distance from the other learned men of his day. Yet in his own way Anselm summed up in his thinking the aspirations of others: to establish truth and certainty on foundations that could not be eroded, as the values of previous generations had been in the conflicts of their own time. For Anselm, the see of Peter did represent a rock of certainty and he clung to it with quiet persistence. So, he sat at Rockingham amongst his noisy, querulous and frightened bishops, trusting to his own innocence and God's mercy, defending what seemed to him the natural order of things, yet turning the world upside down round about him.

Before Anselm came to England as archbishop on 1094, while Rufus still pretended to recognise no pope, William, bishop of Durham, attempted to appeal to the pope, as if he, at any rate, knew who the pope was, and Herbert, bishop of Norwich, having bought his see from Rufus, sought forgiveness from Urban II. Rufus's bishops could have been in little doubt about the legitimacy of the Roman pope, however discreetly they kept it from Rufus. Anselm went further. He had already accepted Urban II as pope, while still abbot of Bec. When he became archbishop of Canterbury in 1094, he wished to obtain the *pallium* from Rome as a sign that his appointment was recognised as valid. Rufus at first refused to allow recognition of Urban, but when he became convinced that, out of gratitude for the royal recognition, Urban would please him by removing the now tiresome Anselm from office, he conceded Anselm's point. Rufus was soon undeceived, but he could not go back. English ties with Rome had been renewed by Anselm's persistence and the king's wish to preserve his neutrality could not resist the pressure from below.

A second phase in the growth of papal authority began with Anselm's return from his first exile in 1100. Henry I invited him back to play 'Lanfranc' to his Conqueror. For a few months, Anselm allowed himself to do what Lanfranc would have done in supporting the king. He dissuaded the barons from turning to Henry's brother, Robert of Normandy; he investigated the circumstances in which Mathilda of Scotland had entered Wilton nunnery, and, satisfying himself that there was no impediment, duly married her to Henry and crowned her as queen. When pressed by Henry to go further along this road, he replied that he had never at baptism or in any other sacrament promised to serve the laws and customs of the Conqueror or of Lanfranc, great and religious men though they had been, but only the law of God.[11] The particular desire of Henry that he could not satisfy was that he himself and the other bishops should do homage to the king. True, he had done homage to Rufus in 1094, as was the old custom, but since then he had heard at the council of Melfi in 1098 that this custom was inacceptable in the sight of God and he would not do it again or consecrate any bishop-elect who did homage to the king.

Anselm did not categorically state that the pope's decision was binding as such on the whole English church, but it was binding on him personally and his position as archbishop committed the whole English hierarchy with him. The archbishop of York, Gerard, was debarred from raising the pretensions of his own see in rivalry to Canterbury, by the oath that he had sworn to Anselm at the time of his consecration as bishop of Hereford. Anselm made sure that when Gerard went to York, this personal submission was perpetuated. Anselm's personal loyalty to Roman decisions was quite sufficient to put the English church at the pope's disposal. His obedience was something of an embarrassment to the pope, Paschal II, for Anselm carried submission to the point of frustrating Henry's wishes, which was further than the pope wished to go. Though he still refused to do homage to Henry, Anselm was quite willing to write to the pope and accept any honest solution that he proposed, so both the king and the archbishop therefore submitted their case to Rome. This was in itself a significant admission of the papacy's position: it could arbitrate between them. To the king, Paschal wrote explaining and justifying the decrees against lay-investiture. This appeared totally discouraging, but it ended with an enigmatic remark that the pope would allow to Henry's honour whatever he demanded that was in accordance with the will of God. Henry interpreted this to mean that Anselm should consecrate the newly invested bishops-elect. Anselm could only escape by a discreet withdrawal to Canterbury. Another joint embassy had to be sent to elucidate Paschal's meaning.

Paschal was an unhappy pope, full of the best intentions for agreement and concord, but exposed to violent determined men who gave him no peace. His reception of the joint embassy was reported differently by Henry's and Anselm's ambassadors. What did he really say? He sent a long letter to the king:

> There are some men of perverse mind who try to incite the hearts of kings to anger God by investing bishops and abbots; their counsels are to be evaded like the plague lest you offend Him, through Whom kings reign. If you propitiate Him, you will reign happily and obtain full power and riches; if you offend Him, all the counsels of the well-born, the help of knights, arms and riches cannot avail when He attacks. Do not believe that anyone can dispel our friendship for you, if you abstain from investiture and preserve the due honour and liberty ordered by God for his church. Therefore by the judgment of the Holy Spirit, we have forbidden all kings, princes and layment to grant the investiture of the churches.[12]

The letter had, however, again generally commended Henry's ecclesiastical policy and, though Paschal had declared his unchanged opinion on investiture, he had not mentioned homage at all or threatened anything more than divine vengeance on offenders. Henry's ambassadors, the three bishops, Gerard of York, Herbert of Norwich and Robert of Coventry, men of learning and integrity, reported further that the pope had told them in private audience that Henry would not be excommunicated, if he invested only religious persons with the pastoral staff, provided in other respects Henry led the life of a good prince. The pope regretted that he could give Henry no written authority for this concession, because it might encourage less scrupulous kings to usurp the same privilege. The cautious Paschal may have attempted to try some subterfuge of this kind, but Anselm wanted a clear, frank solution and the case went back to Rome.

Anselm had not been left without an answer to his embassy. Since he had specifically asked the pope to modify the terms of the decision on lay-investiture, if it were at all possible, he received a straight answer to his plea when Paschal announced that he had just renewed the decrees in the latest Lateran synod. Anselm could not understand the reports of the bishops, finding nothing in his own letters to bear them out. Paschal had, however, promised Anselm not to send a papal legate to England over his head; that Anselm should have the same authority as Lanfranc; and that Anselm was to have complete freedom to do and say what he thought fit. These instructions could have been interpreted to give Anselm discretionary powers in treating with Henry, with the assurance that he would not be accused or arraigned before any court short of Rome itself. But Anselm did not want this type of responsibility; he wanted the decisions to be made in Rome, and, by insisting on this, he carried the English church further than ever from the customs of the Conqueror and of Lanfranc.

Over several years his obstinacy made it necessary for frequent embassies to go to and fro between England and Rome. He went himself to secure an acceptable decision and, when Paschal finally declared investiture to be inadmissible, Anselm withdrew into a second exile, which was long drawn out by extraneous events like Henry's conquest of Normandy, Paschal's exile from Rome and his own illness. At last, a compromise was agreed at Bec, which the pope accepted, though only as a concession for Henry's lifetime. The solution was ingenious and specious. Henry was allowed to take the homage of his bishops; Anselm agreed not to refuse consecration to a bishop who had done homage. The ceremony of investiture was given up, to Henry's great chagrin, because it implied that the kingship was not the source of ecclesiastical honour and thus diminished respect for him. Nothing at all was said about the procedures for episcopal elections. It might seem that with homage Henry had kept the substance of his father's hold on the church. This is not how Henry saw it. Anselm had obliged him to part with his father's rights as king, and to make do with a ceremony of lordship; the papacy had been admitted as a party to the king's dealings with the bishops and the king had been obliged to seek papal approval of what seemed his natural, unquestionable rights.

These admissions once made, it was not easy to go back on them. In the succeeding years, after Anselm's death in 1109, Henry attempted to rule the church as imperiously as his father had done. It was of his conduct during these years that Paschal II complained in 1115. Henry was so furious with the pope, and his legate, Anselm, abbot of St Saba and nephew of archbishop Anselm, that, when he was sent a second time as legate, Henry detained him four years in Normandy refusing him permission to cross to England. The papacy's attitude was, however, also equivocal. When Henry had become exasperated by Anselm's wish to humiliate the new archbishop of York in his last months of life, Henry had obtained from the pope a docile legate, Ulric, who should have judged between the two archbishops, had not

Anselm's death spared him this *volte-face* at Rome. The pope had no wish to go against Henry altogether and preferred his own temperate attitude to Anselm's. Paschal II appears to have wished to tolerate Henry's customs: he gave Anselm luke-warm support, allowed the compromise of Bec, sent the legate to please Henry in 1109. The pope went on hoping that Henry would make concessions, if he were sufficiently accommodating.

Anselm's work was not, however, all in vain. The papacy had come to be a source of law and authority, and Henry could only keep it out by violence. He obliged Thomas of York to submit to Canterbury, after Anselm's death, and then prevented any further quarrel between archbishops by leaving Canterbury vacant for five years until Thomas died. Then he transferred the timid Ralph from Rochester to Canterbury and nominated his chaplain Thurstan as archbishop of York. Henry was quite clearly unprepared for Thurstan to refuse submission to Canterbury. Thurstan, however, made out that, as metropolitan of York, he owed obedience only to Rome and would swear no second oath to Canterbury. Henry appealed to Thurstan to give up his pretensions in order to prevent further disturbance in the kingdom and scandal in the church. When Thurstan said he would rather surrender the see than diminish its dignity, the bold chapter at York complimented him and assured him that he need have no fear that they would elect another in his place. Henry was justifiably outraged. Anselm's individual respect for Rome had been bad enough. Now Rome was invoked to protect other privileges and a chapter of canons was presuming to dictate to the king. What Anselm had done on his own, by virtue of his personal association with Rome, had become available to all clerks with grievances.

Henry could not overcome Thurstan's objections to Canterbury. Only after four years did Thurstan eventually manage to escape from England without the king's permission, and go to France, where he was received and duly consecrated by the pope in spite of Henry's wishes. The pope defied the king and set aside Canterbury's claims to receive an oath of obedience from York.

The result of the pope's show of authority was felt immediately.[13] Not only Thurstan, but also the archbishop of Canterbury's old enemy, the abbot of St Augustine's, Canterbury, obtained bulls of confirmation from the pope. Papal privileges were worth having if the pope had power to enforce them. Other monasteries and cathedrals sued at Rome for papal bulls; papal legates came to England in 1121 and 1125, in the latter year holding an important legatine council while Henry was in Normandy and publishing the decrees of the latest papal synods. The archbishops went to the Lateran Council of 1123. Only the influence of the German king prevented Calixtus II from challenging the election of William of Corbeil as archbishop of Canterbury on the grounds of its irregularity. The king of England had no right to summon the chapter monks of Canterbury to Gloucester and oblige them to elect a secular canon nominated by the bishops. The privilege of elections in the royal presence had however been reserved to Henry V in 1122 and to please Henry V[14] Calixtus allowed the same privilege to Henry I: but Henry I did not pretend that this had been the custom under the Conqueror. When William of Corbeil showed the documents proving Canterbury's superiority over York, they were pronounced to be forgeries at Rome. Canterbury sank ever deeper in the mire.[15] There was now no return possible to Lanfranc's reliance on the king against the pope. The Conqueror's government of the church, however well justified at the time, could not be repeated by Henry. His bishops went to Rome for their needs, just as his Norman barons began to turn towards other princes, whose prospects seemed brighter than the king's.

Yet, in fact, the king only shared his power; he did not lose everything, by papal interference. There was no doubt that the new ways were more complicated: Henry could not simply please himself. In ecclesiastical as in secular matters, Henry had to compromise. The days of the Conqueror's effortless superiority had passed. The king had to match his will against others of similar strength.

Lordship

The uncertainties about who was real master of the Anglo-Norman realm after 1087 caused genuine difficulties in the whole of society.

The disputes with the papacy had also cast doubt on the validity of accepting old customs uncritically. If lordship and custom were both challenged there was no stable principle in society left to trust: inevitably the less scrupulous tried to seize what they could from others without invoking any legal right. The immorality of this generation has received generous attention. They were disloyal and avaricious; homosexuality,[16] which started in the army, spread to all classes; affectations of dress and hair styles shocked the chroniclers; bishop Serlo of Séez denounced men who indulged the feminine preference for silky beards to bristly, shaven chins. All the vices seemed to have been cultivated at the same time. These men were not simply more wicked than their fathers. They grappled with unusual problems without being sure of the old principles; they thought that where the old rules no longer applied, they could simply please themselves. In society as a whole it became necessary to re-establish notions of loyalty and law, capable of commanding acceptance.

Loyalty was the major problem. It would be easy to ascribe the rebellion in favour of Robert against Rufus in 1088, or Waleran of Meulan's support of the Clito in 1124, to factiousness. Modern critics believe that such treason should have been punished by death. The kings themselves were surprisingly tolerant and did not allow themselves to become vindictive. They knew that loyalty could not be enforced by the apparatus of the state. It was up to them to inspire their vassals with respect. Where rival lords disputed leadership of the same family, vassals had no fixed principle to help them choose which lord to support. The extent to which secular princes were confused may be seen from the way even the conflict between church and state (now so easily debated in abstract terms) could seem like a problem of lordship to Anselm.

Anselm's quarrel with Rufus about the recognition of pope Urban II in England was based on his personal commitment to Urban before he became archbishop of Canterbury. In spite of his new office, he refused to deny his old obligations and abandon his lord. He never argued that the other English bishops owed any obedience to Rome, for they had made no previous, personal submission as he had. His case was never a political advocacy of the claims of the Roman see to universal jurisdiction. What he defended was the conception of honour, by which he faithfully discharged his obligations as a vassal. Rufus also saw it in this way. To Anselm's monotonous plea to be allowed to go to Rome for his *pallium* in 1095, Rufus retorted in exasperation that Urban had done nothing for Anselm, who should therefore throw off his yoke and behave like a free man, as his dignity required, and await the royal will and orders in all things. Rufus was not being cynical. He did not object to Anselm having a Roman lord but thought that the lord had done him little good: Anselm would be justified in renouncing such a lord; there would then be no impediment to his doing his duty to the king. Rufus did not regard himself simply as another lord or even as a superior lord; he was king, God's vice-regent. Service to the king was free; the service of a vassal was servile.

Whatever view of kingship Anselm had, he certainly believed that Rufus had authority over him. When he became archbishop, he was eager to convene a church council, but he never doubted that it was the king's right to summon it, though he had expected the king to act on his advice. What answer did he have, when Rufus retorted, 'When it seems fit to me, I will do it because I wish it, not because you do'? None. He was not always lost for an answer. When he complained that Rufus left abbeys vacant and Rufus replied, 'Aren't they my abbeys? You do what you like with your vills and I do what I like with my abbeys', Anselm did not object to Rufus's proprietary claim. He made a distinction: 'They are your abbeys, but only so that you may defend them and keep them as their advocate, not to invade them and lay them waste'. This is the pure milk of feudal doctrine. Lords and vassals are bound by mutual ties and the lord has no right to abuse his power over his vassals to their detriment. All the same, vassals were expected to submit meekly to their lord's high-handed actions. Anselm spoke of Rufus as one to whom 'I owe faith and honour and I should do these becomingly'.

Anselm therefore had two lords: how did he attempt to resolve the problem of his duty towards them? At the meeting with Rufus in Rockingham Castle between 25 and 28 February 1095, Anselm put this dilemma to the bishops: how could he obey the pope and not break faith to the king? In a sense, both were religious duties. According to God it was a grave matter to despise the vicar of St Peter, and no less grave to violate the faith he had promised to the king. Anselm however had found a way of driving a wedge between them. Quoting 'render unto Caesar, the things that are Caesar's, and to God, the things that are God's', Anselm concluded that he owed obedience for the things that were of God to the vicar of St Peter; to the king he owed faithful counsel and aid, according to his capacity for the things of the world, for matters of worldly concern pertained to the royal dignity. The vicar of St Peter had a further crucial advantage: Peter, with the power of binding and loosing, was the natural judge of Anselm's dilemma of obligation. Anselm's doubts were lifted off his shoulders; he would appeal to the pope as Peter's vicar.

It may seem odd that Anselm should appeal for advice to one of the two parties involved but it was a typical feudal solution to a problem of conflicting lordship. A man with several lords had to decide who was his liege lord, and his liege lord was not necessarily the lord of greatest social prominence. When he had decided who his liege lord was to be, the vassal was expected to keep residence on the fief he held of that lord, however small.[17]

Similarly, Anselm had to decide where he really belonged; he had to put his obligations in order of priorities. He decided that, because the vicar of St Peter was God's special governor of God's things, it was to St Peter that he owed submission. From Peter could even come, if necessary, the annulment of oaths he had sworn in conscience to the king. This conclusion was outrageous.

Anselm's position, however shocking, was rooted in law. The king, the bishops and the barons all argued the problem in terms of law. The bishops refused to sit in judgment on the archbishop because no vassal might judge his lord. All they could do in obedience to the king's command was to renounce their obligations to him. The barons, invited by Rufus to do likewise, promptly refused: they could not renounce one to whom they had never sworn fidelity. They went on to remark that they could not refuse obedience to Anselm as archbishop, for he had the governing of Christianity in England, and no fault could be found in him as such. Thus the law was proving useful in two particular ways. It made distinctions for judging men in different legal capacities and it prescribed forms for judgment that prevented the king simply having his own way.[18]

Law did not, generally speaking, work to the king's disadvantage, because the king was too useful to men hoping to turn law to their own account. Abbot Rainald of Abingdon gave his own nephew Robert an abbey estate at Dumbleton. When the abbot discovered, as the monks said, that his predecessor Alfric (later archbishop of Canterbury) had cursed those who alienated church lands, Rainald tried to recover his nephew's holding, but Robert, not surprisingly, was unimpressed by the archbishop's posthumous curses. The abbot found that there was nothing he could do except appeal to the king, for an 'imperial' order for the land to be restored to the abbey. It is not clear that Rufus could have found any legal justification for interfering. But the abbot attributed his inaction to more obvious causes. To his tears, he added gifts: £50 and two royal horses. Robert quickly bettered this, offering £60. The price mounted and still Rufus had done nothing. The abbot advanced to £70 and Robert was only prevented by a sudden, miraculous, paralysis from continuing to bid. The king's authority to provide solutions for intractable problems made him a key person in a society without fixed rules of law. Kings would have needed superhuman virtues if they were not to take advantage of this.

Before considering how Rufus and Henry I did exploit their kingship, it is necessary to consider the two main and inter-related problems that perplexed landowners of this period. Basically, all men wished to be able to bequeath their lands to their children. At the same time, as lords themselves they wished to retain their freedom to take back lands, or fees, which they had temporarily conceded to others. There was therefore a conflict between a lord's interest and claims by hereditary right. The strength of feeling for family rights to land is shown by a case from Abingdon. One of the abbey's knights, Anskill, was tortured by Rufus, and after his death the king gave the estate to his dispenser, Turstin. Turstin's son duly succeeded to the estate. In the meantime, Anskill's son, William, had not accepted the loss of his father's land as permanent; he finally recovered it by marrying Turstin's daughter, the abbot's niece. It is doubtful if he managed to get legal recognition of his claim to the estate.[19] Psychologically, it is, however, very revealing that William left no stone unturned for the recovery of the forfeited patrimony. Likewise, his mother was so anxious to get back her marriage portion which Rufus had taken with the rest, that she took her suit and her favours to Rufus's brother Henry, to whom she bore a son, and from whom she eventually recovered her due.

The fact that Anskill was a knight is particularly significant because it seems to be in this period that the knights won recognition of the claims of their heirs to temporary estates. The emergence of knights as a social group under Rufus may be seen by comparing Domesday Book with Henry I's charter of 1100.[20] Henry stated that knights had become so essential to defence of the land, that to those who held '*per loricas*' he granted exemption from tax to their demesne lands, a privilege previously reserved for tenants-in-chief. An important distinction between knights and other landowners has been abolished. Thereafter, a landed tenant owing service is normally called a knight. This is not the normal usage of Domesday Book. Knights as such appear rather rarely in Domesday and if Domesday Book were consulted, it would not be possible to trace all the estates held by one man, because Domesday Book does not group information about sub-tenants together: it is focused on tenants-in-chief. Rufus, however, either for his military needs, or as a result of baronial rebellions, had come to take a direct interest in the sub-tenants. The knight was not a mere victim of royal tyranny. He was becoming a person of importance. Henry I in his charter claims that his services are indispensable. Rufus and Henry both insisted on getting all the knight service they could. At all events, the most obvious concession that lords could make to their knights in order to keep them in their service was permission to allow their sons to succeed to the holding. In this way the hereditability of knights' lands at this time obliterated the distinction of tenures that is recognisable in Domesday Book.

This concession to the wishes of those in occupation of land, who pressed for the rights of their children, may seem like a severe defeat for the lord's right to dispose of his fees. In fact, the lord made no difficulties about this concession, provided that the heir admitted that he owed his fee to his lord's favour and not to hereditary right. What the lord required was the vassal's recognition of his lordship and his right to service. When Gilbert Latimer, tenant of the monks of Abingdon, died leaving three married daughters (of whom the oldest was a widow), the abbot found that the family claimed to be holding parts of the estate, by dispositions which Gilbert had made for each of them at marriage. The abbot said he knew nothing of all this. Gilbert had certainly made no written record of this settlement, did not obtain his lord's consent, and presumably had no legal right to do so. Nevertheless, the abbot thought it wise to let it pass, provided that the elder surviving husband did homage to him for the entire estate and discharged the service of one knight.[21] By compromises of this sort between lords and families, both sides could be satisfied that they got what they most needed.

There were no established rules for determining the rights of lords and families; indulgent lords might please families by exacting only moderate conditions; but there was nothing like a fixed custom to prevent others from abusing their rights of lordship. Before criticising such lords for their illegalities, it is fair to insist that they were only exploiting the equally 'illegal' claims of their vassals to enjoy their estates as a family inheritance. The most notorious of all wicked lords was, of course, Rufus himself. In fairness to Rufus, however, it is necessary to ask in what way exactly the king defied recognised custom. As an example, take the king's famous demand for relief from the tenants of the see of Worcester when the bishop died in 1095.[22] Three of the most important tenants were the sheriff of Worcester and his brother, Roger Dispenser, and Roger Fitz Durand, who became sheriff of Gloucester; these were excused from paying the relief that the king demanded. The other tenants were asked to pay sums ranging from £1 to the £40, owed by the bishops' steward. Oddly enough the figures add up to £250, exactly £5 for 50 fees, but this sum was not of course equitably apportioned amongst the fees of the bishopric; some leading tenants were excused altogether; the abbot of Evesham who (later) owed no knight service to the bishop was nevertheless asked to pay as a tenant. These arrangements would seem very irregular by later standards but it is not clear that Rufus was trying to defy established custom except in one respect. Henry I in his charter of 1100 was prepared to give up Rufus's habit of taking money from the church domain and from tenants during episcopal vacancies, promising that he himself for the future would take such relief only after the new bishop or abbot had been installed. The objection to Rufus's practices was not his arbitrary impositions but his collection of them when the vassals' natural lord was not there to stand between them and the king.

Rufus left a bad name as one who imposed on his barons' heirs the obligation of buying back their father's lands instead of simply paying the relief. When earl Hugh of Shrewsbury was killed in 1098, Rufus allowed his elder brother, Robert de Bellême, to pay a fine of 10,000 marks to have the lands. If the barons and Henry I agreed that this practice was unlawful in 1100, what did they understand by a 'lawful and just' relief? Contemporary law-books suggest that the traditional payments were, as before the Conquest, the gift of horses and equipment according to rank made by the vassal's heir. Rufus's practice of asking for sums of money was, however, normal custom in the twelfth century. What seemed highly unlawful under Rufus was commonly taken for granted later. Rufus wanted gold, not horses and armour: this was the novelty.

Henry I's charter to the barons shows, however, that what the barons considered to be legitimate feudal custom in 1100 was still far from according to the lord all those rights that later feudal law would take for granted. In particular, the rights of the mother, or the nearest male relation, to wardship of the children of dead tenants-in-chief, and their right to make bequests for a tenant who had failed to do so in his life-time (to the exclusion of the lord, and the king) prove that the family was still stronger than the lord. But lordship was becoming more powerful. Rufus was one of the lords who campaigned for more authority for lordship against the family, and wanted his rights calculated in cash terms.

8 Norman Government

The Barons

When he was crowned in 1100, Henry I promised his barons to give up the evil customs of Rufus and return to the ways of his father and the 'law' of Edward the Confessor. In one respect, however, Henry's own charter shows how far the Normans had moved from the conceptions of the Anglo-Saxons. Many of the abuses Henry listed were connected with feudal rights: reliefs, wardship, marriage; the king makes concessions to his barons, but they in turn must do justice to their men. Norman society is governed by the feudal hierarchy for matters of civil law, particularly for inheritance. The men who held land by feudal tenure may have been few amongst the whole population but they were men to be reckoned with and their own habits and their ideas of what was right created a type of government that could not restore Anglo-Saxon society after years of tyranny. Government as the Normans understood it required each lord to play his part loyally and obliged the king, even if he was lord of all lords, to allow them their due share in it. Society was based upon the mutual understanding of the king and his barons.

Rufus angered his barons by disregarding their interests, but it would be a mistake to think either that the king planned a type of government opposed to baronial power, or that the barons themselves disapproved of his authority. Rufus was able to win support in England and Normandy because he was successful and the barons needed a lord who knew how to command. The king himself narrowed his vision of government to the exploitation of his royal rights, and the administration he used attended to the two principal sources of revenue: his estates and his rights, particularly from his vassals. Henry I hardly improved on his brother's government.[1] In spite of his coronation charter, he was not in later life very deferential to the barons; but it is not necessary to believe that his concessions in 1100, before he had captured his elder brother, were repudiated when he became stronger, and that the whole charter was a mere *pronunciamento*. Like Rufus, Henry I was unprincipled and unjust. In his political struggles he did not have a baronial policy as such, but he knew how to keep his friends and destroy his enemies. He relied consistently on the Beaumont family and pardoned the hot-headed Waleran after he had come out in favour of the Clito in 1124; whereas many of Robert's supporters in Normandy were kept in prison, like Robert himself, after 1106, and tearful entreaties to release them, even when stiffened with gifts, failed to dissuade him from his purpose. His father similarly had been implacable against his brother Odo of Bayeux till his dying moments. Henry could temporise, if he thought it expedient: in 1106, Robert de Bellême made his peace with Henry and recovered all his father's possessions, which made him more dangerous than he could have been in opposition. Only some years later, did Henry seize him and keep him locked up. Henry's liberality to his relations, his bastard, Robert of Caen, earl of Gloucester and his nephew Stephen of Blois, count of Mortain, created rivalries which burst into civil war after his death.[2] Intelligent though the Norman kings were, they rarely mastered their passions.

The barons of Norman England, who invariably appear in monastic chronicles only when they rebel against the king or oppress the monasteries, derived their place in society from their relations to the king. They were not, however, the king's puppets, and by Henry I's time, they were capable of tracing their position not to the king, but to their own family and claiming consideration by virtue of the family's long possession of its estates. When Domesday book was written, twenty years had not been long enough to confer distinction on the lords who came over with the Conqueror. Many of the Conqueror's supporters failed to hold on to their lands in his reign. The king was bound by no sentiment to his companions in arms. If they were disloyal, they were driven out. His sons adopted the same attitude. Rufus exiled some of Robert's supporters in 1088, and others after the rebellion of 1095; Henry's enemies were more quickly eliminated between 1100 and 1106. These confiscations inevitably weakened the old Conquest families most for it was the Conqueror's own brothers, Odo and Robert, who felt most strongly about their nephew Robert's claim to the inheritance. The families with the biggest stake in Normandy considered their loyalty to the duke first. The families that had made their fortunes in England, and had less to lose in Normandy, were fortunate that the English crowned king could defeat the duke.[3] After 1102, only one of the Conqueror's earldoms, Chester, remained. New families thrust their way to the fore: Beaumonts, Giffards, Clares, able in their turn to acquire the title 'earl', and retain it longer. Admittedly, they were not allowed to take the role of a Robert of Mortain, or a Roger of Shrewsbury. As far as their collective power as barons went, they were just as formidable, because as families they were important enough to be appeased: the king had not made them as the Conqueror had made his barons. Over the generations, their estates descended in the same family and they expected recognition of their hereditary status. What were the signs of family pride? The foundation of religious houses in Norman England indicates powerful families: Hugh of Chester, Roger of Shrewsbury, Eudo Dapifer all founded important houses, as Norman barons had done before the Conquest. More interesting is the beginning of heraldry[4]: the use of family devices to make ancestry immediately plain to the observant knight. The earliest attested shields in Henry I's reign enable the device to be traced to the French court in the late eleventh century. The Bayeux Tapestry gives no hint that the shields used at Hastings bore distinguishing marks of this kind. Knights may have had individual markings, but their concern to adopt family devices is new. No doubt the use of heraldic shields may owe something to a change of battle tactics. As knights become persons of social importance, battles cede to duels as occasions for displays of gallant combats. It is the sophistication, or the sport, of war that matters more than conquest and loot. The men who dominate are not hired soldiers fighting as a professional duty but gentlemen who cover themselves in battle with their family distinction.

One other sign of baronial interest in the past may be Robert of Gloucester's patronage of the historian, William of Malmesbury, who dedicated his *Deeds of the Kings* to Robert, and which traces Robert's illustrious forebears. Oderic Vitalis, the Englishman who became a Norman monk, devotes a great deal of attention to tracing the family relationships of the Normans in Henry's day. At the time of the Conquest the families were too new to have troubled about their obscure ancestors; by the reign of Henry I, the baronial families are looking back with pride to their family past, and have acquired a comfortable feeling of the place in society which their birth has given them.[5]

The king's and the barons' interests could cause friction between them, but, when the political disputes were stilled, their concerns as great landlords, and lords of vassals gave them much common ground. Their major problems were to make their estates and their men serve them. They desired liquid wealth and had to find means of making their estates in land yield silver. Though the Conqueror left a bad name as a lover of money, his sons had an even worse reputation for being extortionate. Their offence was chiefly to find untapped resources; they showed how the relationship between lord and man could be calculated in money and did not simply raise heavy taxes on land, in the traditional manner. Their personal failings are less interesting than the fact that so much cash was being spent so freely in this period. Even Robert of Normandy was a notorious spendthrift, of whose generosity the frivolous entertainers of his court took every advantage. Rufus spent lavishly on warfare, soldiers and castles, and the great hall at Westminster, which he built, seemed a prodigal display of royal magnificence. Henry I also spent his money freely, subsidising Cluny with imperial bounty. The desire to have money was not in order to hoard it, though mere desire of ostentation could have been sufficient to make the kings harsh in wringing money from others. The important aspect to stress is the existence of a money market and the availability of goods of all kinds. Money had become hard to come by and all landlords, in particular, were trying to convert their lands to cash.

The fact that the problem was general, and that individual wickedness can not explain the prevalence of money-mindedness in England, may be seen by consideration of some continental monastic estates.[6] At Cluny, despite the monks' great estates, they were dependent for their grain and wine as well as for cloth, spices and church ornaments on cash revenues. This enabled them to buy necessities as well as pay for church ornaments and building materials. This worked well as long as the money came in regularly, did not lose its value, and the prices of goods in the market remained stable. By the beginning of the twelfth century, these conditions no longer obtained and the monks experienced occasional shortages of bread before 1109, which became chronic after 1125. Similar conditions prevailed at Molesme. The monks there became obsessed with the problems of estate management to the neglect of all spiritual concerns, and the saintly abbot retired with the more ascetic monks to the waste land of Cîteaux where they established a new type of monastic society. There the monks drew their own livelihood from the land and allowed the humblest farm-workers to become members of the community as lay-brothers. This solution to the problem, small subsistence farming, was not open to secular landlords, but it does suggest that one of the major problems of landlords was to find, or pay, agricultural labourers. By the twelfth century, all landlords were aware of the difficulties of finding labourers to cultivate their lands.

The examples of these monastic estates demonstrate two aspects of the late eleventh-century economy. First, where possible, landlords prefer to turn the profits of their estates into money, with which they can buy on the market a variety of goods that they cannot obtain from their own property. Second, either tenants from the estate were able to pay cash rents, or speculators offered a lump sum down in return for a long lease, in the expectation of making a profit by their own careful management. The importance of both these aspects of the economy were shown in 1095, when many landlords desired to go on Crusade. They mortgaged their estates to those who could give them the money they needed for their journey.[7] Estate speculators, offered many opportunities to invest their money, got favourable terms; landlords with less than the value of their estates found that the price of equipment, horses, armour, weapons and stores had gone up with the demand. There is no knowing about all the local circumstances that caused landlords to find themselves short of money at any one time; it is sufficient to realise that, where men have become dependent upon cash revenues to live and buy what they want, fluctuation in the value of money will cause hardship somewhere. In England, men did not depend directly on what they grew locally for all their needs; the great landowners, more than others, dealt in the market, and were least content with the resources of their lands, wide though these were. It was this group that was most interested as a whole in squeezing silver out of a stone.

England had one great advantage over other lands of Europe at this time, in that it did not suffer from fluctuations in the price of money due to a corrupt currency. Whereas much of France was disturbed monetarily by the issue of local and debased coins, or by a dearth of silver, England enjoyed the advantages of a standard, stable coinage. English kings before the Conquest[8] had changed the dies of their coins every two or three years. Over his last fifteen years the weight of the Confessor's coins was adjusted so that it consistently declined: in 1051–53 there were 27 grains of silver to a penny; in 1053–56, 21·5 grains; in 1056–59, 20·5 grains; in 1062–65, 17 grains. This effective devaluation was a source of profit to the king. By contrast, the Conqueror maintained his coins at a standard weight: in 1066–80, 21·5 grains; in 1080–87 22·5 grains. At this weight the English penny was stabilised for centuries. Nevertheless, the Conqueror continued to change the dies frequently. Probably for foregoing the opportunity, presented by the change of dies, of adjusting the weight as well, the Conqueror imposed a *monetagium* tax, of which all that is known is that Henry I abolished it in England, though it survived in Normandy. The Conqueror's steady coinage and Henry I's[9] fierce punishment of moneyers who struck debased coins both gave England the special advantages of a sound money in difficult times, and the wealth of English kings enabled them to play a dominant role in Europe. Henry deserved some of the credit he was given abroad for assuring peace and justice as the basis of prosperity. Together with England's own natural riches, this sterling made England seem very wealthy to neighbouring peoples. At the beginning of Rufus' reign, the monks of St Ouen, who had enjoyed a small share in England's prosperity since 1046, came to England with their relics when they were in need of money, and toured the country working cures, especially for blindness, and tempting money out of fat English purses.[10] Some twenty years later, the canons of Laon made an even more extensive tour, in search of money to pay for their cathedral. The report they made frequently refers to English commerce in the Channel and with Ireland.

They could see goods turning into cash before their very eyes. When the king and the great lords considered their own resources in a world whose veins coursed with silver, their greatest asset was their landed property. In England (possibly in Normandy as well but certainly to a lesser degree) this property was scattered over great distances. Some lords were very wealthy in one county, a few had an even distribution of land; only the least important had estates entirely concentrated in one locality. By marriage and enfeoffment their estates tended to grow, but there is no detectable desire to acquire a single compact holding. The advantages of having estates in different parts of the country were more than political. Some regions were stronger in cereals, each region had its own specialty. Barons with manors by the sea, on the downs, near woodlands and marshes could enjoy a variety of natural products for their personal consumption or adornment, or for profitable disposal elsewhere.

There were obvious drawbacks. The produce had somehow to be collected and transported to where the baron could use it, or he had himself to move round his estates constantly both utilising the produce and checking on the management of the property. Only the great lords were mobile enough to do this. Monks, for example, could not as a community, perambulate round their estates, near or far, and had to arrange for the grain to be transported from their manors to the monastery. The monks of Rochester were deeply aware of their debt to bishop Gundulph, who gave the monks one of his own manors near the cathedral and took one of theirs in Cambridgeshire, so that 'he himself and his successors as bishop should seek their substance (*victum*) every year at such great distance by riding (*equitando*)', rather than make the monks or the poor men of the vill wear themselves out every year carrying the corn to Rochester.[11] Lords who were free to do so toured their estates, making endless progresses from one manor to another, having no fixed abode. Their several headquarters, honorial castles, in the centre of their chief areas, could only support them temporarily. The king made similar journeys. These barons were always in the saddle and never at rest.

The management of the whole estate was no easy task, even when the lord was free to make personal tours of inspection. In taking stock of his property, he might well decide that isolated manors, beyond his normal tour might more usefully be leased to a tenant or let at 'farm' to someone prepared to offer a money rent. A lord had in each case to decide whether it was in his interest to negotiate a new farm every year and adjust the rate according to value, or instead to allow a perpetual farm, which would give him a steady revenue, whether prices went up or down. The possibilities of the estates varied from decade to decade if not from year to year. In Domesday book great tenants-in-chief,[12] like Hugh de Port, hold lands from the king and from other barons, take lands at farm as rent payers and grant other estates to their own vassals. To help the lords in their estate problems it was inevitable that they should rely on a household of officials and servants whom they could trust.

Lords needed to be shrewd business-men when it came to seizing their opportunities. The saintly Gundulph of Rochester appears in this unfamiliar guise when he acquired an estate in Gloucestershire, nothing daunted that it was so remote from Kent. He began by allowing Ralph, the son of the priest of Hedenham in Buckinghamshire, to succeed his father as incumbent in return for three hides of land in domain. Ralph and his brother-in-law had another property, the Gloucestershire estate, which, because the king's demands were too heavy, they soon found to be unprofitable. They first suggested to Gundulph that he might be able to get a concession of the manor from the king, which the bishop did for £15 and a mule worth £5. The two men thus became the bishop's tenants and the bishop had to bear the brunt of the king's demands, if any. However, the two men were soon complaining that this estate was too far from Buckinghamshire and that the customs of the county of Gloucester were oppressive. The obliging bishop granted them one hide and a half of land in their own county and became direct possessor of the four hides in Gloucester, from which the community at Rochester could be fed for eight days.[13] The bishop's influence with the king, his ready cash, his overlordship, his ability to travel and to offer lands in exchange for others enabled him to profit from a situation that impoverished smaller landlords. These advantages were open to all great barons in Norman England.

Gundulph's original influence over Ralph was derived from the cathedral's patronage of Hedenham and the bishop's power to waive the impediment to the inheritance of churches, for a consideration. The lord's rights were perhaps even more valuable to him than the property itself. Their value was not limited by nature; it would depend on how much the weaker party was prepared to pay. The uncertainty in the landlaw gave lords numerous opportunities to try what they could make out of their claims. When the earl of Warwick received from Rufus the estates of Turkhill of Arden, he discovered that Turkhill had made a grant of land to the monks of Abingdon. The earl protested that no landowner could make alienations of property that diminished the expectations of his successors, and tried to recover the estate. The monks had to buy his consent for £6.[14] The monastic cartularies are full of documents of the same period, showing the more common case of the son who contested his father's grant until bought off. The wish to explore the potential of an estate comes out well in an unusual case from Normandy. Robert de Beaumont obtained the castle of Brionne from duke Robert and then pretended that the abbey of Bec, which was on the domain of the castle (*in fisco*), ought to be subject to him. Anselm, then still abbot, only prevented the abbey from losing the duke's protection by pointing out to the unsuspicious Robert that Beaumont had no right to the abbey because he held the castle only as a temporary concession and not by hereditary right. This important distinction shows that there were two types of tenure still distinguished in Normandy about 1090.[15] It appears that hereditary possession gave complete rights to the owner; over temporary cessions by the duke, the latter retained 'sovereign' rights. Beaumont clearly hoped to assimilate Brionne to his other lands and make them yield the maximum.

There was a considerable danger that hereditary possession would obliterate older conditional tenures and men who acquired lands in good faith expecting to enjoy complete ownership were in a strong position to resist ancient claims. The constable Eadnoth, possibly before the Conquest, held Shippon, a suburb of Abingdon, which passed with his other property to earl Hugh of Chester. When the monks of Abingdon claimed that Eadnoth had in fact held Shippon of them, the earl was naturally discontented to be threatened with the loss of the property and grudgingly returned it to them for only £30 and a share in the spiritual benefits of the monastery for his whole family.[16] The lords of the estate in this case had to buy out the occupier to recover their land. But lordship was worth it.

The King

The exploitation of his estates and his rights by the king followed the same pattern as that of his barons on an unprecedentedly large scale. By 1086, the king had twice as many estates as the Confessor, with a stake in nearly every county and varied rights and customs. As a just man, the Conqueror decided after twenty years of government that he wanted to know what his resources were. Domesday book could have told him. Arranged neatly so that the king could consult each county record separately and find the property he held in each shire and trace the possessions of his own principal vassals, Domesday book was a work of reference, the like of which has no parallel. The mere conception of such a digest stamps the Conqueror as a man of rare imagination. That the material was collected and compressed to its actual proportions within a matter of months shows that the king had a remarkable staff of household officers. The arrangement of the material was so simple that it could be as easily consulted by sheriffs as by tenants-in-chief. Though there is no evidence of its use in shire administration, the numerous abridgements of the material for particular counties and estates show that the idea of Domesday had caught on.[17] The king's servants and vassals also wished to take stock of their resources. The Anglo-Saxon chronicler thought it undignified of the king to take note of every ox and pig on each estate, and in fact, though the information was collected, at least in some places, these details were omitted from the great record. But the particularity shows how thorough the king could be. Not the least thing would escape his net.

His sons, no less than he, imposed their personalitites on government, with equal determination to wring the last penny out of their rights. Rufus and Henry I are too often contrasted as men. As kings, they stand together as doctrinaire students of their father's

7 Protest of Clergy (above) and Henry I caught in a storm (below), early twelfth century
Oxford, Corpus Christi College, MS 157, f. 383 (see p. 301)

spe facit reges summus pervertere leges. Si reus est meritus dampnari debere coartis. Nummos plenis da quoque decenter talenta. Tolea
c. Lii, Anno decennovenalis iii · xiii · Cycli solaris iii · xxiiii · Bissextilis vi · annus · i · Romanorum imperatoris · MCX
tenus Lotharii · et anglorum regis heinrici tempore; quidam comes erat in partibus Alamannie · cui nomen Hermannus
erens et ducis · habitans in oppido Honburch nomine · habens filiam vocabulo Odiliam a nativitate cecam · Hanc cum
ter parvula · misit ad quandam villulam suam longe remotam · ignominiosum valde reputans · si in eadem villa qua
se manebat nutriretur · Que cum adolevisset · lasciviam modis omnibus fugiens · et honestis moribus prout poterat ·

power with few of his virtues. Rufus seemed indifferent to public opinion. He relied on his soldiers, or force, to take what Henry more circumspectly acquired by some legal nicety. Rufus's lack of hypocrisy makes him seem a less repellent character than Henry, in spite of his faults. To his contemporaries, his frantic activity seemed inspired by the evil one. He obviously enjoyed shocking conventional people and his dare-devilry was probably intended to convince himself what a great man he was. His sudden appearance at Barfleur, unannounced, was sufficient to excite popular wonder to his own satisfaction; his mischievous boast that kings never drowned was ambiguous: was it himself or pious belief that he mocked? His homosexuality is commonly alleged, but, perhaps not surprisingly, only circumstantial detail supports it: he was unmarried, had no bastards (as his brothers had) and Anselm reproached him for it. His irascibility, his swift repartee and his sardonic remarks establish the outlines of a man unsure of himself, for all his kingship. He was a good soldier and liked soldiering; he could see that he governed men of military temper and that they needed war. His administration was focused on the need to find soldiers and provide for them.

Henry I paid more attention to what people thought of him, except in respect of his sexual immorality. William of Malmesbury thought so well of the king in general that he excused even Henry's amours because they were inspired by love of procreation: his self-indulgence was not therefore that of the servant giving in to his lusts, but that of the lord generously pouring out his nature. Monastic and modern writers normally praise his capacity for government, but this is the least personal of his virtues. Henry I, though he reigned nearly three times as long as Rufus, is an enigmatic figure. His personality has been effaced by his image as a politician. His most personal characteristic, apart from his love of his family, particularly boys, is his interest in animals. He kept a menagerie at Woodstock, stocked with exotic beasts, camels, leopards, lions and lynxes and the famous porcupine sent by William of Montpellier. Other rulers sought to please him with gifts for his collection and the same interest may explain why the first French bestiary was translated and illustrated in his reign. Henry was also interested in the lands beyond his immediate dominions and this awareness of the outside world explains the importance of diplomacy in his political life. Whether his alliances reveal more of his capacity to plan and think ahead than a blunt pursuit of his advantage against all odds is a matter of opinion. Henry has such a reputation for cold calculation that his Norman passions are allowed to smoulder unnoticed. His fondness for favourites, his sexual athleticism into old age, his obstinacy, his love of display, as on the occasion of his daughter's marriage to Geoffrey of Anjou,[18] proclaim a man of more blood than the usual benevolent despot devoted to business. Henry was conservative: he patronised the monks of Cluny, not the new clerical movements of his day; he disliked the modern notions of monarchy and tried to restore the ways of his father and uphold the power of the empire, which the papacy had knocked off balance. Henry calculated all that he was entitled to in England, and explored the possibilities of his power in France. He feared that valuable powers had been let fall by negligence. His account-keeping suggests the device of the youngest son who is suspicious that he is not getting as much as his elders had done.

In England, Henry's government has seemed like a marvel of business management for the twelfth century.[19] Was Henry responsible for it? It became desirable for the king to have a regular form of administration because of his normal absence from the country. After 1106, only three times did Henry spend as long as two consecutive years in England (and then he may have paid brief, unrecorded, visits to Normandy). His presence in France focused trouble there; as the Caen annalist commented wistfully, 'England had peace in his time'. How much responsibility Henry may take for the perfection of the English administration in his reign will depend upon the general assessment of his character, for there is nothing in the records themselves, or in legend, to suggest his personal intervention in any field except the punishment of criminals.

If the Conqueror appeared to be sole director of his realm, the Anglo-Saxon chronicler already remarks that under Rufus his avarice was the fault of evil counsellors. These evil counsellors and their influence have a long subsequent history in England. The reason why they are not also supposed to have disturbed the Conqueror's judgment is that the Conqueror, for all his faults, did discharge all his responsibilities as king. His successors betrayed the popular trust in kings by treating their office as one for their personal gain only. If the king manifestly ignored the functions of kingship he could not himself be to blame; it had to be attributed to the influence of evil men. Under Rufus and Henry I the functions of kingship were discharged by ministers exploiting the king's rights, while the king engaged in warfare or diplomacy. This was because Rufus and Henry no longer saw their office as a personal responsibility in the public interest, but as a personal estate for private profit, and they expected to be allowed the same freedom in the royal domain as they allowed the barons in theirs.

This being the case, the men needed in government were those skilled at management, not those wise in public affairs. These counsellors commanded no general respect, though they were feared, and stories of their abuse of public trust are too indicative of their attitude. Under Rufus, the most notorious was Ranulf Flambard, who became bishop of Durham; under Henry I, the principal minister was Roger, bishop of Salisbury, whose family fattened in the royal service.

Flambard's family is not known,[20] but several members of it were connected with St Paul's where he was also dean, so he probably belonged to a clerical family. He had already emerged from the background common to many such families, by 1086, when, as the clerk under the royal chancellor who kept the king's seal, he held numerous small estates that added up to some twenty-five hides. With the promotion of his superiors in the administration to bishoprics, Flambard rose under Rufus to be the king's principal official. At the beginning of the reign, he went to Norwich to examine the site Rufus proposed to give for the building of a new cathedral in East Anglia. In 1091 he went to Ely on a judicial commission intended to help the abbot recover lands from local barons, but he used the occasion to acquire vestments and money for himself. He took the administration of the entire abbey into his own hands, and scandalised the monks by drawing up rates of food and clothing for each monk to be assigned from the estates, taking the surplus for the king. His precise arithmetic must have been appreciated by his master at the time, but it is the protests of the monks of Ely, Abingdon and Bath that have blackened his reputation as a loyal servant.

There was no part of the royal administration where his prying eyes, cool temper and twitching hand could not be used to the king's profit. He sat on roving commissions of justice that visited East Anglia in 1095 and the south-west counties in 1096. He went down to Essex to give his fellow counsellor Eudo Dapifer seisin of a manor there and more frequently witnessed royal mandates to the sheriffs. Orderic Vitalis called him *summus* or *capitalis justiciarius*, the title used by the chief minister under Henry I. His actual role in the government as bureaucrat and judge corresponds to this title.

Flambard seems like the first of a new type of royal servant; for this reason it is worth stressing his apparently conventional rise in the administration from junior to senior office. He may be more typical of his own age than the chroniclers suggest by singling him out for odious mention. He took the normal run of royal favours. Beginning with the mastership of St Martin's College, Dover, he became dean successively of Hastings, Christ Church Twynham and St Paul's before finally becoming bishop of Durham. At Christ Church he began a new church in the grand manner of Norman prelates. The charge that he cut down spending on Durham cathedral when he became bishop probably underestimates the true motive. The monks had planned a building on a scale that they could have had difficulty in completing, and his modifications would be typical of his nice sense of calculation. He was not popular with the monks, though he is said to have defended them against arbitrary despoilers. He presumably knew how to get round regulations he had applied himself. His personal capacity may have justly focused attention on him, but he differed little in outlook from his fellow-clerks of the period. The learned Gerard of York excited unfavourable comment for reading the obscure theologian Julius Firmicus[21] in his leisure hours, which was attributed to an interest in necromancy, and Gerard's death at evening in the cloister garden while his servants were at supper seemed to express divine disapproval. If such trifles excited comment, Flambard's fame was easily come by.

Roger, bishop of Salisbury served Henry I as Flambard had served Rufus. He was Henry's justiciar in England while the king was in Normandy, and he even tried to take the archbishop of Canterbury's place at Henry's second marriage. The bishop of Norwich was frightened of him and tried to use his own influence with queen Mathilda to regain Roger's good graces. The bishop believed that

Roger thought him too poor to be worth taking notice of. He was also disturbed that Roger had heard he had been speaking ill of him behind his back. Without trying to deny the whole story, Herbert admitted that what he had heard about Roger had made him anxious to take Roger aside for a word in private. His bad personal relations with the justiciar were, in his view, the reason why a fine of £50 for legal fines and £60 for military service had been levied on the lands of Norwich cathedral. Herbert was certain that Roger could have arranged matters otherwise if he had wished, for Roger had seen the charter of exemption which showed that Herbert's neighbours had no rights to customary dues from him. If Roger was not to be moved himself, he had at least the power to grant a delay until Herbert had seen the king.[22] Was Roger really the brain behind Henry's government? He was the typical servant, advancing his son and nephews in the administration and falling an aged victim to the fury of king Stephen, who would have known if he was indispensable to the royal administration. Henry's admiration of his brisk talents would be understandable if he had been looking for a sharp agent. That Roger created a new type of administrative machinery is not suggested by the records.

The importance of the royal clerks in administration can obscure the preponderant part still played by the king's secular barons. Flambard's fellow-officials, who regularly witness Rufus's writs, were Eudo Dapifer, son of a great landowner in the Bessin, Hamo Dapifer, who had risen through his connection with Odo of Bayeux, from the same region, and Urso d'Abbetot, sheriff of Worcester. Rufus also had the counsels and support of Robert Fitz Hamon and Henry, earl of Warwick. A similar list of laymen in the service of Henry I would include Vere, Bassett and Robert Beaumont, count of Meulan. The laymen at court had been influential with the Norman kings since the Conqueror's period as duke, when he had lacked the rudiments of a clerical service (though he had a chancellor probably in imitation of the king of France, his overlord).[23] The king normally consulted his great tenants-in-chief about policy and drew them to his court at the feast days of the church. Henry I gave up the crown-wearing ceremonies and perhaps the regular consultations as well, but his *curia regis* met as a more general law-court for settling disputes between the king's own tenants and of such others as petitioned for royal justice.[24] Even without these formal occasions the king normally surrounded himself in his household with laymen. Apart from the clerical Chancery, whose principal functions were to conduct the royal religious services (not to write his charters), his household was divided into four. The stewards attended to supplies of food, the butler provided liquor, the chamberlain and treasurer supervised the king's money and spent it on his clothes and linen and the constables and master of the horse commanded the soldiers and the huntsmen in whom the king was probably most interested.[25] They understood figures and warrants as well as the clerks of account, using wooden tallies to keep records of their expenses. The local administration was still in the hands of the sheriffs some of whom were likewise laymen. A few of the shrieval offices, as under the Conqueror, were hereditary, as in Worcestershire, Gloucestershire and Devon. Generally speaking, Henry I, like his father, used persons from the middling reaches of the aristocracy as sheriffs.

Orderic Vitalis in a particularly rhetorical passage describes the great power of Henry I, which enabled him to hurl many of noble birth from their summit of honour and riches, and contrariwise to raise to noble rank others of low origin—'from the dust'. Orderic's list includes men who are so obscure that their elevation by Henry I did not suffice to bring them into prominence, except in Orderic's account. Geoffrey de Clinton, Henry's best known sheriff, was a person without distinction of family, but it is hard to understand what Orderic means by saying that he was ennobled by Henry, for he was a master chamberlain and a sheriff who remained in royal service. Ralph Basset, whose family had been minor gentry of the Côtentin at least in the Conqueror's reign, served Henry I from his earliest years, and his connection with the king may date from Henry's original possession of estates there under Robert. Hugh of Buckland was probably the canon of St Paul's of that name. His origins might have been humble but his connections were good, or he would not have been admitted to the chapter. The kind of people who were useful to the administration were those with experience in running estates or households. This can be shown if Orderic's list of new men is put aside and attention focused on those of Henry's ministers whose origins are known. When the Montgomery estates were confiscated at the beginning of the reign, the Montgomery sheriff of Shropshire,

Richard de Belmeis, passed into Henry's service and from being royal sheriff was promoted to the see of London, where his numerous children and family established themselves. Likewise, Hugh of Leicester was seneschal of the countess Mathilda's household before becoming royal sheriff of Northampton, Warwick, Lincoln and Leicester.

The men Henry needed were persons of experience who were trained to attend to other people's business and to give accounts of their stewardship. He may not have been very particular about the social origins of his men, and social distinction by birth was anyway a relatively new concept. To obtain a royal office it was necessary to be well connected to reach the king's notice, or to have money to buy the concession.[26] Sheriffs sometimes paid a 'gersoma' to be allowed to take the shire, and other offices, down to that of gatekeeper of Appleby castle, were sold, but not necessarily to the highest bidder. Those who succeeded their relations in office, and this was the most usual case, paid a relief to obtain the position and the lands that went with it; others bought permission to marry the previous holder's widow. This aspect of the administration under Henry I is hardly consistent with the spirit of Orderic's account, which is designed to emphasise the king's power. Even Orderic stresses that the new men made their fortunes, like their predecessors, by using the opportunities of their service. Though Henry probably kept his men on a tighter rein than the Conqueror had done, there was only marginal improvement in making the demesne lands yield a profit to the king.[34] They did their best for the king, but they also looked out for themselves. Entrusting several shires at once to reliable officials, like Hugh de Buckland in 1110 or Basset and Aubrey de Vere in 1128, may have been connected with an attempt to revise shrieval administration; if so, it suggests that even with his new sheriffs the king could rely on only very few to be loyal servants.

The king's treasury had long been located at Winchester. Here the geld money was stored and the king's reeve made his annual reports, bringing with him even in the eleventh century actual produce from the royal manors to be valued by treasury officials. The treasury had technical experts, like the man who weighed the coins to test their soundness, and the melter who tested the purity by blanching. In Domesday book, there are references to some of these officials, including the chamberlain, who as keeper of the king's chamber was responsible for the king's treasure, which was kept there.

Over this treasury a court of law came into session twice a year at Michaelmas and Easter to go over the sheriffs' accounts.[27] To simplify procedure, the old system of tallies was supplemented with the use of a device, based upon the principle of the abacus, which came to be called the 'exchequer' from the type of chess-board used. It was a court of law as well as an accounting office, because the sheriff had to answer for any discrepancies between the sums he paid and the sums he owed. To justify his expenditure on the king's works and payments to officials and individuals, which he expected to be deducted from his debt, the sheriff had to produce the royal writs of authority. These might have to be closely scrutinised at law to prevent fraud. The meetings of the exchequer under the presidency of the justiciar imply a greater complexity of fiscal administration than anything suggested by Domesday book. The origin of the court under Rufus cannot be proved but four kinds of argument may support this assumption. First, the close supervision of sheriffs is unlike what is known of the Conqueror's sheriffs' vice-regal powers. By 1129, the sheriffs, though they still sometimes farm the shire, have also to account separately for particular items of revenue from judicial proceedings.[28] Second, Flambard presided over the king's business as Roger of Salisbury did later, and decisions reached by the king's barons, as in 1095, in connection with the reliefs charged against the bishop of Worcester's tenants, suggest that the barons of the exchequer are implied. Third, Robert Losinga, bishop of Hereford, expounded the use of the abacus in Rufus's reign and was himself used as a judge by the king. Fourth, to cope with the exchequer, existing literally at two levels, the Upper for legal business, and the Lower for counting, weighing and blanching, the treasury officials had to be doubled. There was already a second chamberlain under Rufus and the two chamberlains had charge of the accounting under Henry I.

The Conqueror had no such Exchequer. In his day the treasury, later the Lower exchequer, had been sufficient to collect and store the money brought by the sheriff's farm of the counties and royal rights, and for payments of the geld. In Domesday there is record only of the lay, official members of this body. Domesday itself might have revealed how close was the connexion between the royal income and judicial disputes. A group of 'judges' like those who had presided over the inquest and other judicial commissions of the Conqueror, could have sat regularly under Rufus, certainly at Michaelmas and Easter when the sheriffs presented their accounts at Westminster and paid in what they owed to the crown. As the sheriff presented his bundle of writs, his authorities for payments and allowances which went to justify his accounting, so the judges of the Upper exchequer, the barons, could check the validity of his statements or arraign him for fraud or embezzlement. This court of law was the place where the king's interests were most searchingly brought into the open. The Conqueror may have had, or needed, such a committee; but, however it may have existed in his time, it did not have these later and distinctive marks. The use of a board, like a chess-board, to make arithmetical calculation easy and obvious, enabled laymen to participate on equal terms with clerks.

By the end of his reign Henry I kept a record of the money coming into the treasury from the shires, of which one roll, for the year 1129–30, has survived.[29] How long the treasury had been keeping pipe rolls is not known. The roll for this year shows that experiments in administration were still being tried; the fact that eleven counties were in the hands of two treasury officials was surely unusual. The roll records payments made separately for each shire, and earlier sheriffs who still owed money from their period of office were still being held to account. The auditing of the accounts at the exchequer must go back many years. The name exchequer itself is first recorded in 1110 when it was still something of a novelty, but it is difficult to suppose that there was no earlier form of account-keeping.

Through regular accounting and scrutiny of expenditure the king kept an eye on all those who looked after his interests. At the lowest level, the king's concern for all his rights may be judged in the matter of a meadow called Kingsmead near Oxford, which the men of Hinksey (tenants of the abbot of Abingdon) required for the pasture of their beasts. The king's bailiff only allowed them to use it if they gave him a bribe, and when the abbot complained to the king, the king bargained with him for twenty shillings a year, flat rate, in order to keep the sheriff and his subordinates out of the matter.[30] The king was personally interested in the improvement of all his estates. The sheriff of Oxford who failed to keep buildings in repair, land in cultivation and animal stock at the right level was held strictly to account. The king attended to breeding farm animals and horses; he accepted many hawks as payments, since they were valuable for sport; he enforced his rights in the forest even against the greatest barons of the kingdom. Henry intended to lose nothing from his due.

The king did not insist on having a single manager in each county for all his rights. As in Domesday book, the pipe roll records that some royal estates were farmed by others than the sheriffs. The most valuable parts of the royal demesne, the towns, could be leased out separately; local barons, for example, farmed Wallingford, Northampton and Colchester. In Henry's reign, two towns themselves took over the responsibility of farming the revenues directly from the king. The burgesses of Lincoln gave 200 marks of silver and 4 marks of gold (more than £150 in all) for this privilege. The citizens of London gave a mere 100 marks for the right to pay a farm of £300 a year, but Henry may have thought this a paying proposition, because the succession of four sheriffs who had taken the farm at £525 owed the king more than £300 in 1130. The king dealt with each case on its merits and such opportunism precludes system. The examples of the towns indicates the degree to which the king recognised the realities of power and tolerated innovations, that might have been considered dangerous elsewhere. Typically, it was the towns that benefited by Norman royal protection, for the Normans had shown from the beginning that they appreciated the value of trade.[31]

Justice

England's special advantages in early twelfth-century Europe enabled an unknown writer to summarise lawful custom for the whole of the realm, over which the king himself guaranteed that justice would be done. In his long preface, the author lists the misfortunes and corruptions that law must put right. The untroubled times of great Henry have brought back the joys of peace: the liberty of the church, the security of the country, the respect for virtue, the grace for work, joy to the deserving, mercy to the suppliant. Neighbouring peoples have experienced his triumphs and his personal enemies have been humbled. Above all, his greatness is established by his victory over rebellion and his confirmation of good government with peace as an act of majesty, given by the advice of his God-fearing wife and by the discussion of his counsellors. What raises him so high is his lawgiving. He has restored the law of king Edward, with the amendments of king William, but has also added new rules of his own, so that his predecessors' trickles of learning have been drawn into an oasis of goodness, where his children may provide shade to the weary and refreshment to the parched.[32]

This lawbook is the most remarkable document produced in Henry's reign. It was not written by a native English speaker; but the Norman, or half-Norman, lawyer who wrote it goes further than any English writer in trying to reduce the variety of English legal practice to the proportions and coherence of a legal treatise. There can be no doubt that the need to record legal practice became more necessary as men's memories began to fail and as new men, without experience, took over responsibility. Inevitably, some English legal customs were becoming obsolete and the treatise represents a state of law in rapid decline, which would never again reappear in the texts. For Henry I's reign, however, these considerations only reinforce the argument that it was essentially the English system of law that the Normans preserved, reinterpreted and interpolated, and that the Normans had no difficulty about adapting themselves to its forms and finding a place in it for their own.

The originality of this treatise lies in the fact that it was the only work on customary law composed in Europe at this time, though churchmen were making an original effort to codify church law. The work itself is based firmly in precedent, and only one third of the material is peculiar to this text. But what is important is not that the author shows how English law was responding capably to the challenge of a new social order by creating new rules, but that it was possible for a contemporary of Henry I to attempt a codification of a mass of traditional rules and to claim that the law was standard for the whole of England. Only England had a king-given law which imposed order and provided a principle, whereas other countries of Europe had only local customs differing from region to region. Traditional respect for kingship was being challenged, even in England, but the English king was more than a lord of all lords, he was the heaven-sent giver of justice, to all his people.

The king's justice re-established the unity of England, broken by regional law, feudal loyalties and spiritual ideals. The fearful rule of royal majesty is above all other laws; the uses and customs of the pleas of the royal court provide an Olympian uniformity by comparison with the variety of customary law. Though the king does have his own *curia regis* for his feudal tenants, his royal cases are normally heard in the public courts, where they are attended to first, except that courtesy demanded that ecclesiastical cases, if any, should have precedence. The list of royal pleas under Henry I is largely traditional, but to the pleas declared in Canute's law, others had been added, equally unsystematically. The king reserved judgment on those who broke his personal peace or his peace accorded by writ, those who fought in his household or who killed his servants; he defended his writs, his coins, his good name and his law; he extended his protection over travellers, highways and places of public execution; he punished those who failed in their military duties, unfaithful or treacherous vassals or those who fortified houses without authority; serious theft, housebreaking, arson, manslaughter that offended God, violence done to virgins and widows and murder were his pleas; he had ancient rights to the repair of town defences and bridges and newer ones to Danegeld, forest fines, baronial reliefs, treasure trove and goods washed up by the sea; lastly, he had jurisdiction over procedural offences: unjust judgments, surety breaking, harbouring outlaws and excommunicates. These miscellaneous crimes were not all equally serious. The king might collect a fixed fine of £5; a condemned man might be liable in his goods or his life or be at the king's mercy. There is no rationalisation of offences. The king is not interested in accidental slaying or unaggravated homicide; he does not pursue those who do violence to wives. Justice may be had against such criminals by the parties directly offended, the family or the husband. The king's concern is to obtain the punishment of those who would otherwise escape: the secret slayer, the deserter, the corrupt court-keeper.

Henry I was the first king to appoint local justiciars, later called coroners, to keep records of local cases that touched the king and local panels of jurors who would present the cases in the ordinary courts. The king's officers will attend the execution of criminals in other courts to keep an eye on the way in which justice is done there. The king therefore presides over justice, but he does not have special courts to enforce it.[32] Many of the royal pleas may be heard by lords with the appropriate privilege from the king, in their own courts, or in public courts, like the hundred, which the king has granted to their supervision. Special cases, like contempt of the king's writ or his protection and cases of outlawry, are never ceded to others but must be heard in the public, shire court, and sheriffs have to keep records of what they collect as fines and account for them separately to the exchequer.

The scheme of law that this treatise assumes is the one prevailing in England before the Conquest. The list of tariffs for wounded and amputated limbs, the payments of fines and personal values are taken directly from the old laws. How much this represents mere antiquarianism on the part of the author depends on what explanation is given to the fact that within another generation all these tariffs will have vanished without trace, and that private or family presentment of crimes will have been superseded by royal accusations. The treatise indicates how this could have come about by relegating private suits to the end of court proceedings. When the cases of the church have been heard, the king's long list of pleas will absorb attention, so that men with private suits were well advised to attract royal interest. When the abbot of Ramsey countered Pagan Peverel's hereditary claim to two of the monastery's vills,[33] the case was heard in the churchyard of St Ive's, Sleep, and the normal suitors on both sides were supplemented with skilled men of judicial authority sent down by the king. Cases of homicide would tend to be presented by the king's jurors as cases of murder, before the time for private suits arose; a family that was determined to obtain the blood-price of their slain relative would have to prove Englishry to the king's satisfaction, before the murder charge could be dropped, and then they would have to wait till court proceedings in the king's interest had been finished. Why families did allow their monetary interests to be prejudiced by the king cannot be explained: but the old scheme of law was passing away.

In the actual conduct of trials, it was important to establish, from the legal point of view, whether there were one or more accusers and defendants, whether the accused or accusers were of equal social standing or whether one were under age or whether one were a dependant of the other or of another man. It made a difference if a woman, clergyman or an unfree person was involved. In the most serious criminal cases the accused was obliged to make an immediate answer to his accusers, in others a special time was appointed for his statement; for others the accused needed to make no defence. The man who was caught in the act did not benefit from the same legal procedures as the man who was accused on suspicion. Some matters had to proceed to trial by battle, others by oath-taking (even here the differences in form of the oath were significant), and other matters went to the ordeal, which was God's judgment on the accused.

The public character of the court also remained, and this is the most surprising survival of public spirit in a society dominated by feudal lords, who did not disturb the old legal pattern. The king expects the bishops, sheriffs, earls, hundred men, tithing men, reeves, barons and landlords to attend shire courts, and, if cases came up by appeal from hundred courts or a manor was the subject of dispute, adequate representation of the hundred or manor would have to be produced in the normal court of the shire. Lords could accuse their men and bring them to the public court. They also had the right to summon them and do justice to them in their own, feudal, court except for such crimes as theft, murder and ecclesiatical cases. Vavassors with freeholds could judge such minor matters that involved punishments by fines and wer-payments. The extent of court-holding of this type may be exaggerated and it was necessarily confined to minor crimes[34]. Some privileged barons could also settle disputes between their vassals by the privilege of English peers, if they had a royal grant to do so. The English, not the Norman, character of such a 'feudal' court is emphasised by the English expression 'sake and soke' for such jurisdiction. More important were grants of jurisdiction by the crown, and these privileges could be forfeited if the king were dissatisfied with the way the court holder managed his cases. The kind of private court that is best understood was the hundred court in private hands. This was a normal hundred court which the king allowed a private individual to run and take the profits of. In some cases the privilege was extremely ancient, even preceding the organisation of regular hundred courts in the tenth century. There was no reason to regard the system as reprehensible because there was no difference in theory between the position of the court under the sheriff and that under a private lord, like the abbot of Bury. Court proceedings were designed to establish justice by securing monetary penalties and it made no difference to the condemned whether his money went to the king or the abbot.

Lest money fines may seem to have been the sole purpose of enforcing justice, rather than the best deterrent, the example of abbot Rainald of Ramsey (who drew the sheriff of East Anglia, and the sub-sheriff, and many Englishmen and Frenchmen and the witnesses of nine hundreds to Woodwell) emphasises that the defence of privilege was a matter equally, if not more, dear. No lord will allow his right to be diminished, even if he gains nothing from it. The abbot claimed the privilege of taking what was washed up on the shore at Bramcester and found witnesses to testify that his predecessor had been accorded possession of a fish (*crassus*) washed ashore there. On the strength of their testimony, he was awarded what he claimed, a barrel of wine. He graciously decided to give it to the priests of the region so that they could sing masses for all the people, who should therefore always remember the abbot's claims to drift at Bramcester.[35] The more tragic case of Bricstan of Chatteris, the pawnbroker who was accused of stealing from the king, shows that money was not the chief consideration here either. He was sent to London and kept in irons for five months in a dark prison until in a vision he saw St Etheldreda, the patroness of the church at Ely, near his home, command St Benedict to release him from his irons. As a result of this intervention, the money lender was sent back to Ely by the queen and Ralph Basset, without further hindrance.[36] Gruesome though Bricstan's long confinement may have been, the injury to the king's interests demanded better punishment than making a money-lender pay.

English justice continued to respond to the new society of which the king was the chief innovator. The king's interest in justice was not to destroy the old elements of law. For this reason, what are most characteristic of that law—its blood-price, its oaths and ordeals, and its popular assemblies—were not abolished. The Norman Conquest did not 'feudalise' England: it strengthened the traditional resources of the king. Instead of introducing a confused network of conflicting jurisdictions as feudalism did in France—even in Normandy—the Norman kings preserved the clear distinctions and mutually exclusive jurisdiction of hundred and shires. The royal inquests in the Domesday shires and the judges of assize under Henry II both found the shire an ideal unit and a self-contained, coherent unit of administration on which their own authority could depend. The survival of the local courts was not a mere chance—it was essential to the Normans' work.

What was the motive of Henry I's special concern for justice? It is sometimes suggested that financial interest in the profits of justice, fines and forfeitures amply encouraged royal interference. This is needlessly cynical. Henry could have been more successful as a ruthless tyrant if money had been his principal end. His occasional heavy fines were far more remunerative than the general run of judicial profit and the whole apparatus of justice was not necessary to excuse the few cases of extortion. Henry's principal resources of money were in land and his grants of lands, although not lavish, would quickly have counteracted the value of judicial profits garnered with great labour. Contemporaries had no doubt that the work of enforcing justice was arduous or that Henry did this as part of the faithful discharge of his royal office. Nor do we need to suppose that the king merely gained in 'prestige' by enforcement of order and law. The king did not need to consider his popular reputation, because he was without peer in the realm; against his barons Henry needed more solid weapons than prestige.

To enforce the law by confirming custom and punishing transgressors was to fulfil the work of God in human society, which God himself exercised directly in the world of nature. Here, if anywhere, Henry fulfilled his royal duty to the general advantage.

8 Christ and Isaiah, twelfth century
Oxford, Bodleian MS 717, f. 2 *(see p. 300)*

9 Conclusion

Anglo-Norman Achievement

Before the Conquest England had a fine school of manuscript illumination and pictorial art. While it is no longer believed that the crude Normans stamped out English sensitivity to the arts,[1] it cannot be denied that the Norman achievements in these fields were greatly inferior to the English. What is characteristic of Norman painting is its emphasis on ornament rather than figure composition and it was expressed almost exclusively in embroidering the illuminated initial. The first letter of books or chapters of the numerous Norman manuscript copies of standard works was often a bold capital, but it did sometimes take the form of beasts or birds stretched and bent to shape. At their most elaborate, the initials could become cages of wildly contorted animals and men. Over their antics, the outlines of the letter itself imposed a formal discipline with uncompromised authority. Although this variety of fauna and scene indicates vivacity of spirit, this vitality hardly ever obscures or distorts the formal character of the letter: the Normans did not forget their main purpose. The contrast with English drawing of the same period is marked. The English enjoyed portraying individuals in action, using flowing lines and allowing for blank spaces that show they did not require every corner to be crammed with incident.

For more than a generation, artists concentrated on the initials, as a purely decorative feature of the manuscripts, creating exciting, but controlled, patterns from a variety of subjects, but rarely com-

8 Christ and Isaiah, twelfth century
Oxford, Bodleian MS 717, f. 2 (see p. 273)

posing free pictures to illustrate the texts or to tell stories, as they had before the Conquest. How fascinating it would be to know the reasons for this psychological change during the period of the Norman settlement. Without arresting or stifling the native skills, the Normans appear to have carried the English artists into a manner of composition that had previously had few exponents in England. Before the death of Henry I, however, the art of English illuminators had once more produced pictorial compositions that heralded a new important school of English painting.

Changes in style and subject matter cannot be neatly related to political or social changes. Individual talents are more significant,[2] because one artist may show a new way to a whole generation. The master of St Albans, the leading painter of the reign of Henry I, probably found his inspiration on a journey to Italy, and such personal experiences must be allowed for in trying to explain the development of a new painting tradition in England at that time. But the renewed interest in figure composition and set scenes indicate that much was derived from the old English school as well. How this was so it is difficult to say. The monasteries where most of the work was done had been changing slowly since the Conquest, and the new schools were not in the old centres. However, the artists had access to manuscripts with the old models of composition, with their traditions in the use of colour and subject-matter. Many of the manuscript sources cannot now be traced, but in the monastic libraries of those days, painters who looked back to the past found the materials needed for founding a new school.

This recovery and assimilation of the past indicates that the period of the Conquest was over. Norman and English elements combined to produce one of the most brilliant periods of English history. Credit has been given to both sides for the major share in this creation and cannot be nicely divided. Neither the English nor the Normans remained the same after they had come into contact with one another. The English contribution, however attenuated and weakened by the Conquest, had vitality enough to flourish. Even the dead retained their power.

In 1104, the monks of Durham translated the body of St Cuthbert into the new cathedral. The report wastes no words describing the Norman building, then completed as far as the crossing, and concentrates on the excitement with which the monks considered the prospect of examining the relics of their famous saint. The prior and nine monks fasted all night to prepare themselves to open the stone tomb and were deeply gratified to find the body lying as in deep sleep after more than four hundred years. Though some neighbouring abbots, with less durable saints, were as incredulous as the bishop, Ranulf Flambard, the belief in the miraculous survival of the body was not confined to the English monks. Ralph d'Escures and William of Corbeil, both later archbishops, three abbots, of St Alban's, York and Selby and the prince Alexander, later king of Scotland and others, nearly forty persons in all, were allowed to see the body and all alike shared the same faith in the saint. Only Flambard persisted in scepticism and was discomforted when rain dispersed the crowd to which he had preached without referring to the great event of the day.[3] Most Norman bishops in his position naturally accepted the ways of the English church and sponsored the old cults.

The Norman prelates were conscious of their role as church builders and nothing was in more obvious contrast to their predecessors than their magnificent conception of the churches they built.[4] The abbot of Glastonbury tore down his immediate predecessor's church, because it was not fine enough. Even the modest Wulfstan, however reluctantly, could not resist the desire to build. The movement began with the Confessor's church at Westminster; the Conqueror had founded the abbey of Battle on the site of his victory; the monks of Canterbury, first at Christ Church, after the devastating fire of 1067, then at St Augustine's needed new buildings. The cathedrals and monastery churches of England were all remodelled or rebuilt after 1066.

In Rufus's reign, seemingly so wanting in positive achievement, hardly a year passed that was not marked by the laying of foundations or the consecration of a new major church. Rufus laid the foundation stone of St Mary's York in 1089, in which year Gloucester abbey was begun. In 1092, the cathedrals of Salisbury, Worcester and Lincoln were consecrated; in 1093, Winchester cathedral was ready and Durham inaugurated; the next year Battle abbey was dedicated and in 1095 a magnificent band of prelates gathered at Bury to translate the incorruptible body of St Edmund into the new abbey. For all their pomp, the Norman buildings embodied a conservative idea: the old saints from before the Conquest were rehabilitated and given a monumental sepulchre. Never had such weighty and sumptuous buildings been seen in all parts of England. The grandeur of these churches survives today as the most obvious and widely appreciated achievement of Norman England. Symbolically, a Norman building encases an English saint.

Whatever else the Normans changed in the English church after the Conquest, they certainly did not much affect English intellectual life. Lanfranc's own eminence as a scholar may have been justified, but Lanfranc himself seems to have outgrown his interests in learning and to have turned competently to the government of the churches of Caen and Canterbury. His longest and most learned discourse as archbishop was a long correspondence with archbishop John of Rouen, himself the author of a work on church services, about the proper vestments to be worn by bishops at consecrations and about the proper symbolism to be observed at clerical ordinations.[5] Both John and Lanfranc may have encouraged the diffusion of elaborate rituals devised for the monastery in other cathedral churches, but this does not amount to an intellectual renewal. Lanfranc and other Norman prelates carried through a massive programme of stocking English libraries with good, plain texts of Patristic theology.[6] The significance of this is uncertain. Many manuscripts from England were carried to the continent both by those who fled from the Normans and by the conquerors themselves.[7] Libraries, therefore, needed to be replenished. The most valuable and prized English manuscripts had been those elaborately painted and gilded, and the Normans evidently had learned to admire them before the Conquest and had begun to imitate English drawing styles in several particulars. Some of the manuscripts written at this period show by their designs that the Normans did allow themselves a little room for fantasy in initial letters, but the more usual practice is for ornament to be eliminated in favour of the plain texts. The introduction of standard editions of the Christian Fathers would be typical of what was best in Lanfranc's convervatism, and no doubt marks an improvement on the old-fashioned authorities, like Bede and Isidore, whom the English scholars had respected. It did not however provoke a new zeal for study.[8]

The abbot of Abingdon in Henry I's reign could not trust his monks to copy theological works but found professional scribes for this purpose and left the monks to copy service books.[9] The monks' real interests were bound up in popular religious belief. By the 1080s the Normans had given up their hostility and indifference to traditional cults. Anselm's friend, earl Hugh of Chester, who founded an abbey on the site of an old collegiate church dedicated to St Werburga, one of the pious Anglo-Saxon princesses, saw no reason to change the dedication. The Norman abbot of Evesham, Walter, though he had formerly been sceptical about the virtues of the saints of his house, found that their relics could be used to obtain the money he needed for rebuilding the church, once he had exhausted his predecessor's legacy. The cult of St Egwin was a recent one in Walter's time. Egwin, the bishop of Worcester who had resigned his see to found the abbey of Evesham, obviously proved Evesham to be a place of greater dignity than Worcester, and it is not surprising that his cult was revived after the death of abbot Aethelwig, during whose abbacy the monks had been content to rely on his worldly wisdom and not to invoke spiritual powers. For Walter, however, Egwin worked wonders, especially in curing the sick son of Hugh de Grentmesnil, the greatest landowner of Leicestershire.[10]

In each place they stopped on their tour of the country, the monks proclaimed the holiness and the virtue of their saint. The more miraculous cures and coincidences became popular stories, passing from lip to lip, and were rapidly incorporated into the written store of legends that gathered round the shrine. Eventually the stories were put in writing and the reputation of the saint travelled as far as manuscripts could be carried. The fame of his sanctity drew crowds from very great distances and their offerings helped to pay for the larger church that their visits and veneration made a necessity. As the churches went up, so the stories multiplied.

The first writer to satisfy this demand for more information about the old saints of England was Goscelin, the monk of St Bertin who had settled in England before the Conquest and who was therefore ideally fitted to explain the customs of his country of adoption to the Normans.[11]

He travelled from monastery to monastery, reading the records, listening to tales and questioning story-tellers; he committed to writing the lives and miracles of the old English saints: St Edith of Wilton nunnery, the early Saxon abbesses of Peterborough and Ely and the lives of other pious Saxon ladies collected at Barking which he dedicated to Maurice, bishop of London. His most substantial work was done at Canterbury, first at Christ Church where he wrote up the lives of Anselm's predecessors for the new archbishop, and then at St Augustine's. Here he wrote several accounts, major and minor, to celebrate the first archbishop who had been translated in 1092, on which occasion the monastery's independence of the archbishopric had been vindicated. As late as 1109 he was still living, for he wrote a life of St Osyth, a patron of the new canonical life. Goscelin was not the only writer of such lives. His successor at Canterbury was Osbern who wrote up the life of St Alphege whose memory Anselm had defended before Lanfranc, and the lives of other famous archbishops like Dunstan and Oda. Eadmer also wrote saints' lives. Canterbury was the real heart of the revival because Canterbury had the most venerable traditions of Anglo-Saxon saints, but in the West Country, at Evesham and Malmesbury, the lives and miracles of the monastic patrons received special attention. Out of this movement William of Malmesbury developed his interests and skills to the point of writing history. His method in the church history is peculiar as it proceeded from district to district recording the deeds of famous churchmen and ending with St Aldhelm of Malmesbury itself. Individual monasteries needed to conserve their faith in their patrons if they were to survive. They cultivated the legends of their patrons whose divine help was their real wealth; few men could rise above local loyalties and look longer at the accumulated achievements of the past.

The English revival, when it came, found England little changed by Norman churchmen. The thinking of Anselm, which very gradually spread beyond the group of friends and pupils at Bec, could hardly have been suspected in England until late in the Conqueror's reign; and his most famous work, *Why God became Man*, was not composed until late in his own life, when he was already in exile from England. The new kind of teaching that was becoming common and popular in northern France only achieved maturity in the early twelfth century. By that time the old and the new learning were known in England. The exceptionally erudite Herbert Losinga comments on the fact that one of his monks, Felix, at Norwich was versed in both.[12] Felix was a writer of martyrologies, hymn books and prayers. He was also familiar with the writings of St Augustine. This appears to represent the old learning. The new was made up of grammar, to which Felix began to apply himself. How far he advanced is not known, but the monastery was not an ideal place to pursue such studies far without a master in the arts of disputation. Felix seems more typically monastic by his dabbling in monastic memoir writing.

The study of logic and philosophy from France did not penetrate far into the monasteries and the new learning had a much more direct influence on the secular clergy of England and Normandy. The new houses of canons were especially receptive to it.[13]

William of Corbeil, prior of St Osyth, had been a pupil of Anselm of Laon, the most famous teacher of theology of his day. When the canons of Laon visited England about 1113, they found several men who knew their cathedral school: William himself, and the relations of the powerful Roger of Salisbury, Nigel and Alexander, both later bishops; Robert the archdeacon of Exeter; the clerk Ansgard, later bishop of Coutances, who founded a college of regular canons at St Lô. The canons of cathedrals and regular houses had their own schools. Thomas Becket was educated at Merton priory; at Exeter, Robert Pullen, former student at Paris, taught scripture before going to Oxford and Paris, where he was master of theology; the prior of Smithfield was learned in the liberal arts; at London, under Richard of Belmeis, there was a succession of masters of the School with their own quarters, who looked after the books of St Paul's cathedral. Richard's successor, Gilbert the Universal, was a distinguished scholar and theologian. Though his achievements now seem minor, in his own day his glosses on the Pentateuch, the four major Prophets and the Book of Lamentations, difficult works from the Old Testament, placed him high in the world of scholarship.[14] Persons of learning and sophistication were as lost in the monastery as Abelard was at St Denis. If they sought to live by a rule of life, it is understandable if they preferred the life of canons offering better conditions for the pursuit of learning. In a document concocted at Colchester to pass under the name of pope Paschal II, the canons tried to flatter their order, and emphasise its discipline. They were not subject to the arbitrary rule of the abbot, as in the old Roman rule of St Benedict, but allowed a place for wise persons to be chosen by the canons from amongst themselves who could be sent out as need arose to enforce discipline in other places. The purpose of the clause was to secure the claims of Colchester to the direction of the other houses of canons, but it is indicative of a different approach to the problems of discipline and allows more influence to the canons themselves.[15]

The centre of English intellectual life was already in Oxford, where there were no less than three houses of canons: St George's in the castle, St Frideswide and Oseney. Easily approached from all sides by its position in the upper Thames valley, at the head of the limit of navigation, where a new stone bridge linked the north of England to Southampton, principal port for Normandy, Oxford was one of the most important cities of the realm and in the twelfth century the only rival to Paris for its intellectual life. There was no bishop to tread heavily on its beginnings, but the royal court was frequently in the vicinity to give it occasions for meeting those who came from all over Europe.

The secular clergy promoted studies that were quite outside the range of monastic intellectual interests. The clergy had the great advantage over the monks, that they were not in theory pledged to one house, but could move from place to place to hear famous masters and to make personal researches. The scholarly world was not static as the monastic one had been. For all the signs of new learning in England in the twelfth century, scholars were not content with what they found, and took their interests abroad. Certainly Paris, with its variety of schools, attracted not only scholars but teachers in search of greater fame or the opportunities of personal contacts with other men of their level. Robert Pullen went back as a teacher, not thinking Oxford important enough to hold him. Many men went on from their studies to Rome. Pullen became Eugenius III's chancellor. A man associated in its early days with Merton priory, Nicholas Breakspear became not only cardinal but pope. Scholars moved in a very wide circle of acquaintances.

Other subjects of most interest to them were connected with the effort to provide basic theological understanding and the problems of organising the diocese helped to stimulate a knowledge of law. William of Corbeil was at Canterbury when the Decretum of Yvo of Chartres was copied there;[16] another collection of canonical texts was copied about the same time by a house of regular canons. Learning was not, however, confined to a narrow range of practical studies as may be seen in the career of Adelard of Bath. He studied at Tours, the home of his diocesan bishop, and at Laon, in traditional subjects, but he went on to travel widely in Mediterranean lands, preparing the scientific translations that made him famous. In a variety of ways, the mobility of scholarship stimulated new interests as well as new ideas.[17]

The world the Normans lived in touched the extremes of Latin Christendom: Ireland and the Mediterranean. Henry I's Normans were intrigued by the Celtic world and it was in the 1120s that the legend of King Arthur, the Celtic hero, first emerges in Norman sources. William of Malmesbury tried to evaluate the evidence for him as an historical figure by collecting information at Glastonbury.[18] Rather earlier, the more gullible canons of Laon were shown King Arthur's chair and oven and witnessed a fight between some British men and one of their own servants who had presumed to doubt that Arthur was still alive.[19]

Strange places and remote time had an exotic appeal to the Normans and they were particularly curious about the Moslem world. The Normans of Sicily were their best source of information, but Normans also served in Spain against the Moslems. Henry I had a physician, Peter Alfonsus, a converted Spanish Arab.[20] Henry's French court had an easy contact with the French courts of France, Sicily and the Holy Land and accumulated impressions of a very large world, just as Henry I collected exotic animals from friendly princes in his menagerie at Woodstock. This mixture of peoples, languages and cultures produced a superficial eclecticism but the interest in what was strange in the known world stimulated a curiosity that could lead to profounder studies.

Adelard of Bath's travels to the fringes of the Moslem world in search of scientific knowledge were prepared by more conventional studies in the north. John of Tours' own practical interests and love of learning were shared by other bishops of the west of England in his day. Robert, bishop of Hereford, wrote about the use of the abacus and was interested in the problems of measuring time, and therefore in astronomy. Walcher, prior of Malvern, like Robert a Rhinelander, was the first man in England to use an astrolabe. He witnessed an eclipse of the moon in 1092 and his scientific curiosity was fed on notes translated from the Arabic, which Peter Alfonsus provided him with.

Peter was chiefly esteemed for his translation into Latin of a collection of moralised stories and fables from the Moslem world called the *Disciplina Clericalis*. In these vignettes of daily life in Spain and Egypt, the Western readers could glimpse the sophistication of manners in a strange society that was yet close enough in spirit to show how their own lives might be enhanced. When they read that the true arts of life were riding, archery and falconry, they might have been more ready to learn that swimming, boxing, chess-playing and versifying were also worthy accomplishments.

The horizons of noblemen were transformed by the influences that came out of the East in the crusading period. Their interest in literature and learning begins to soften the rough virtues that Normans had cultivated. William of Aquitaine's coarse or refined love-poetry has no Norman rivals, but Robert of Gloucester enjoyed reading and being read to, when he was not out of doors, and his tastes were probably limited to hearing about great deeds of valour, worthy of imitation, and preferably done by his kinsmen and ancestors. The nobility may have been more generally educated. The sons of the earl of Chester were taught by William of Corbeil, the pupil of Anselm of Laon. Orderic Vitalis's great history gathered information about Normans from Spain, Apulia and Syria, and the Normans who travelled and told tales about their adventures could have stimulated many different sorts of interests in their kin. The Normans no longer lived in a closed society or a poor province. They had contacts from one end of the known world to the other. How superficially they understood the Moslem world they lived so close to, is best guessed by reflecting how little modern armies of occupation in India or Germany may learn about the people they live with. It was, however, an Englishman, Robert of Ketton, whom Peter the Venerable found to translate the Koran into Latin. This may mean that the Normans, with their traditional curiosity and their unabashed willingness to learn from those they conquered, could even stimulate a faint interest in the religion of Christendom's greatest enemies.

Once the terrors of the Conquest had subsided, a new society comprising several different ethnic groups was taking shape. The settlers included Bretons, Flemings and Frenchmen from Blois and Champagne as well as Normans. Everywhere in England, and in parts of Wales and Scotland, they were closely allied with the local populations. They did not live apart from one another; by marriage and alliance the customs and cultures of neighbours could be adopted and absorbed. Henry I understood English and it seems likely that some of his children, legitimate and bastards, learned English from their mothers. Uninstructed Englishmen could pick up some French[21] and the priest Brichtric of Haselbury could regret without absurdity that he spoke none. There were some Norman peasants in England[22] to bridge the language gulf between social classes and it would be normal, in conditions of the day, for Normans to have acquired some English words from the lower classes, through hunting or in childhood. The hermit Vitalis came to England to preach under Henry I quite undeterred by the prospect that he would not be understood, and he was able to make his meaning clear with Divine help to those who had no French but who nevertheless flocked to listen to him.[23]

The babel of languages had disturbing effects on the spoken vernaculars.[24] The French of Norman England was already evolving in a different way from the French of royal France, in Paris and the Loire valley. Anglo-Norman was modified particularly in its sounds through the invention of new diphthongs and in the decay of morphology. In the written language, Norman verse was composed with an odd number of syllables to the line and in less strict metre than the French. By use of stresses, it evolved a metrical pattern quite distinct from the pure French forms of the late twelfth century. This stress pattern could have been derived from the accented English poetry that was evolving out of the old alliterative metre. The decay of standards and corruption of traditions in both English and Norman speech and literature argue that the languages were spoken or written by persons not well instructed in them.

In a community of mixed traditions the Norman English evolved their own characteristic culture. Even when the Normans came to England, French was much less developed as a medium of literary expression than English. The Chanson de Roland was admittedly already in circulation, for a version of it stimulated the Normans at Hastings. The Normans' own earliest writer in the vernacular, Tedald de Vernon, had already rendered the Latin life of St Wandrille and other saints in rhyming verses. But of French prose there was nothing comparable to the remarkable translations and compositions in English going back to the time of Alfred. The English example of prose translation into the vernacular could have inspired the inter-linear translations of the Psalter and the first four Books of Kings from the Old Testament made into French under Henry I. Whether or not these had been preceded by earlier efforts, they played a part in starting a new tradition.

The Anglo-Norman literature was strong in didactic and fabulous works, and the English before the Conquest had also used the vernacular for purposes of instruction and for recounting marvellous tales. This may represent nothing more than what the uninstructed laity normally looked for in literature, whether they were English or Norman. Nevertheless temperament plays its part, for the Normans produced no vernacular epic poetry as might have been expected in an early literature; instead they prefered to chronicle their deeds in poetic histories. The earliest Anglo-Norman work known is Benedeit's poetic version of the Latin *Voyage*[25] of the Irish saint Brendan, who journeyed in the Atlantic ocean and encountered many marvels with a band of companions. Benedeit omits the more tedious information of his source to concentrate on improving the dramatic adventures, but at the same time he emphasises the moral of each episode. Quite apart from his actual treatment of this theme, it is interesting that he should take this work from Celtic Britain and present it for French speakers. It reveals what the Normans found so fascinating in Wales and Ireland. The other early Norman work written under Henry I was Philippe de Thaon's *Bestiary*.[26] This is a version in metre of stories taken from the Latin *Physiologus*, an ancient collection of anecdotes about animals, real and fabulous, with appropriate moral conclusions, each beast presenting an appopriate character. Philippe's version is not particularly remarkable, except that it was the first French one, and that he gives instructions as to how illustrations should be drawn for each beast. If Philippe derived his ideas about what the animals looked like from an existing manuscript, that manuscript cannot now be identified. His text of the Latin[27] version had already been annotated with extracts from Isidore of Seville's *Etymologies*, and such an early text can be traced to England.[28] It is at least possible that Philippe found the text he used in England, for picture books, Isidore and curiosity about the symbolic character of animals can all be shown to have interested the English before the Conquest, whereas Normandy's intellectual revival in the mid-eleventh century had been confined to patristic theology.

On the English side, the Conquest has usually been deplored for its disastrous effects on English literature. Chambers[29] believed that the dearth of correct alliterative poetry at this period was due to the loss of its original home in the Anglo-Saxon hall, when the hall passed into Norman hands. This assumes a cataclysmic view of the Conquest. There are, however, a number of English prose writings of the twelfth century, lives of the saints Katherine, Margaret and Juliana, the tract of *Holy Maidenhead* and *the Soul's Ward*. These suggest that pious aristocratic ladies were the most consistent patrons of English writing and do not support the view that English literature was abandoned to the patronage of unlearned peasants or impoverished gentlefolk. The explanation for the break in the composition of poetry must lie elsewhere.

In this connection, it is instructive to compare the use to which English and Anglo-Norman were put in twelfth-century literature. If English was rich in pious works, it continued the tradition of writing vernacular works of religious instruction and edification for the laity. By the twelfth century, this field seems to be worked specially for the needs of ladies. By contrast, French works served the needs of the educated but un-Latined gentleman, who wanted handbooks of instruction. The earliest work of this sort was Philippe de Thaon's French versification of a Latin work on calculation. This had been composed by an Exchequer clerk, but Philippe made it available to a wider public interested in the times, the seasons and the Zodiac, with their mystical interpretations. His other work, the *Bestiary*, which gives information about birds and gems as well, may be regarded as a popular encyclopaedia of nature. The educated classes who used books in the twelfth century still understood both vernaculars; inevitably, one fell into disuse. Apart from its traditional hold in mystical writing, English succumbed, even in the monasteries, late conservers of English culture.[30] By 1170, a monk of Ramsey translated into Latin the charters of his monastery '*ex Anglica barbarie*'. In Henry II's reign, French was the polite language of society.

This apparently abrupt break in English literature has created a profound impression on modern writers. Some critics have interpreted the last words of the *Peterborough Chronicle* entry for 1154 as the extinction of an ever feebler flame of post-Conquest vernacular learning. For centuries, English lay uncultivated in the mouths of the illiterate English population, until it emerged triumphant in the poetry of Chaucer. Thus, the demise of Old English prose and the delayed birth of its legitimate successor could both be attributed to the centuries of foreign domination.

The Conquest did not brutally interrupt the achievements of English culture, for the age of great prose writing under Aelfric and Wulfstan (archbishop of York) did not continue beyond the latter's death in 1023. The succeeding hundred years of disturbance nevertheless witnessed an enormous effort to preserve what continued to have relevance and value; the Normans assured the survival of essential Anglo-Saxon documents by organising the copying of manuscripts. The homiletic tradition of the past, Anglo-Saxon translations of the Heptateuch, the West-Saxon version of the Gospels, Alfred's translations of Boethius and of St Augustine's *Soliloquies* were copied in precious post-Conquest texts. Those who lived under the Normans copied the Anglo-Saxon laws,[31] including two major manuscripts, without which we should know much less about pre-Conquest England.

The vernacular was also used for original compositions. Colman, chaplain to Wulfstan, bishop of Worcester (1061–95),[32] wrote a biography of the bishop, which is unique in European literature as the life of a bishop written in the vernacular. There was no pre-Conquest precedent for this, however varied English vernacular literature had been. The original version of the life is no longer extant. It was almost immediately superseded by William of Malmesbury's Latin life, essentially a translation from Colman. It has been argued that this proves there was no reading public for vernacular works in Norman England. If such an unprecedented work can prove anything, it must surely be the contrary. As the bishop's chaplain, Colman must have known Latin, yet he deliberately wrote a life in the vernacular, not apparently following any Anglo-Saxon tradition, but providing for literate men an account of the last Anglo-Saxon bishop. His work displays the continued vigour of the vernacular; its fate does not prove that the Norman Conquest inhibited vernacular writing.

Other writers have argued that a vernacular work of this sort indicates how English traditions and writing survived in isolated pockets, under the protection of an English bishop. Yet version D of the *Anglo-Saxon Chronicle*, written at Worcester (Cotton MS. Tiberius B iv), shows the occasional use of Romance words at a time when West-Saxon could still be written correctly elsewhere, as in the fragment for 1113, 1114 of the otherwise lost version of version H (Cotton MS. Domitian A ix). There is no reason to believe that Worcester under Wulfstan was an isolated stronghold of Anglo-Saxon traditions. At Canterbury, where the monks had been disciplined by Lanfranc, they had no difficulty in maintaining their English traditions and in profiting from Norman influence. It is ludicrous to explain every vestige of English culture in Norman England as the pathetic adherence of some author to a culture that was being trampled on by ignorant soldiers. At Christ Church, Canterbury, an early twelfth-century writer copied version F of the *Chronicle* down to 1058 (Cotton MS. Domitian C viii) and at St Augustine's the author of version E (*Laud Chronicle*) added some striking historical judgments about the Norman kings, that show he was not afraid to commit his impressions to the vernacular or compare the Conqueror to his English predecessors. When this manuscript went to Peterborough, a new compiler went on writing about developments after 1121, though it is scarcely credible that Peterborough should have become the sole haven of English writers by that time. The lapse of the *Chronicle* after 1154 had nothing to do with the decline of writing in English in the twelfth century. It was the result of the general cultural renaissance and the appearance of a new type of historical writing for which Latin was the proper medium. William of Malmesbury, who collected whatever Anglo-Saxon antiquities he could, wanted to give them a wider currency than they could have in a vernacular literature and to gain a reputation for himself in the literary world, by writing a history of the English, in Latin. No subsequent historian could be content to make the bare annual entries of the *Chronicle*. The changing tradition of historical writing is not to be regretted for its slight damage to the national culture. It lifted knowledge of English history out of the narrow world the English had conserved it in, and by raising it to European status re-established it on the lines laid down by Bede.

Epilogue

If the Norman Conquest is still the best-known date of English history, it is no longer regarded as the first event of memorable importance. Until recently it has been convenient to take 1066 as a point of departure, particularly for the history of English government. The Normans, although foreigners, were adopted cheerfully as the heroic founders of rational, centralised and disciplined government. Even Bishop Stubbs, for all his sense of the popular Anglo-Saxon background to English institutions, believed that the Norman monarchy was essential to the creation of modern government, and inevitably the sharp definition of its powers under the Normans made 1066 a date more memorable than the 'uneventful' centuries of Anglo-Saxon culture. The Victorians were content to accept Stubbs' interpretation of the Anglo-Saxons' contribution to English history, because it appeared to incorporate the recent studies of Anglo-Saxon antiquities into the tradition that the Normans had laid the foundations of all modern institutions. And so for generations schoolchildren have learned that England was peopled with various races, concluding with the Romans and the Anglo-Saxons, and that with the Normans alone began the regular history of the country.

Since Stubbs' death, Anglo-Saxon scholars have laboured to produce an unparalleled appreciation of the pre-Conquest English. Never, since Anglo-Saxon studies began in England, has the reputation of the Anglo-Saxons stood as high, not on the basis of unreasoning faith amongst a few enthusiasts, but argued with intelligence, skill and sympathy, particularly by Sir Frank Stenton, for a public that is completely convinced by his measured arguments. English history, least of all in the field of government, can never again be taught continuously only from 1066. A period as long and varied as that which extends from the Conquest to Elizabeth I has been added to English history before the Conquest itself; the Anglo-Saxons are no longer for us, as they were a hundred years ago to Freeman, a robust peasantry, a race of William Tells with love of freedom in their blood and simple homespun garments on their sturdy bodies—the people of myth—but people of many sorts and attainments, who themselves had their history, their development over five hundred years. They are no longer a simple race with a simple story—but more complex and varied than any other invading group that we know of.

The new assessment of the Anglo-Saxons has thrown Norman studies into great confusion. The Anglo-Saxons had clearly enough native resources to solve their own problems; their traditions were longer and richer than those of the Normans: they had proved their resilience and offered hope for the future; they certainly taught the Normans as much as they learned, if not more. Maybe they were not the great liberals or 'parliamentarians' that they once seemed—but they triumphed where formerly the Norman reputation seemed least in need of defence. Militarily, the English victory at Stamford Bridge balances the defeat at Hastings; in government the Anglo-Saxon kings, masters of coins and writs, tower beside the Normans, ruthless and ceremonious; in the religious field their piety and pastoral concern rival the Normans' devotion to monasteries. The reputation of the Anglo-Saxons in these fields throws a deep doubt over the traditional view that the Normans were necessary to save the Anglo-Saxons from their own incompetence and their vices. The rectification of the injustice to the Anglo-Saxons has tended to revive the more extreme Freemanism: the Norman Conquest was an unmitigated disaster which rapidly destroyed the old culture as irrevocably as the Spanish discoveries wiped out American-Indian civilisation.

Yet there is one big problem: if the Anglo-Saxons were so superior, how could they have sustained such a defeat at the hands of the Normans? It is possible that the conquered conquered in their turn: if the time span allowed be long enough, it could be argued that with the reappearance of the English language, transformed and simplified, the native English triumphed over the alien French culture. But this process took centuries and it is more realistic to interpret this movement as a fusion of cultural traditions rather than the rebirth of a native English one. Even from the point of view of language alone there is a great difference between Old and Middle English and from the social point of view there was no revival of Old English culture at all. If it survived the Norman Conquest, there is no doubt that it withered and failed in time as a result of events which the Conquest inaugurated. The Normans did therefore succeed in suppressing a culture that was superior to their own.

The innate weakness of historical explanation is that what is well explained appears to happen inevitably. Short of saying that the Norman success is miraculous, the historian is obliged to show that the Normans must have been superior at least in what counted for success. However wonderful the Anglo-Saxons seem, they must have had flaws which explain their defeat. This confrontation of the two peoples has been made by historians for centuries, because this was how the first historian of the Conquest posed the problem for himself.

William of Malmesbury lived in a world divided socially into two classes: the Normans and the English. The English held no positions of responsibility, spoke no French, and constituted the bulk of the population of England. Without leaders, their culture, expressed in the vernacular, tended to remain backward and to lapse into crudities. The Normans, associated in government by their importance as land lords, appeared to monopolise positions of influence everywhere both in secular and in clerical affairs. To Malmesbury these two peoples appeared in striking contrast. Although he himself belonged to both worlds by birth and probably spoke both languages (and was not necessarily exceptional in this respect), Malmesbury shows that no reconciliation of the two cultures could really be achieved. Perhaps a certain type of snobbery made those of mixed 'race' insist on their English lineage, but it was as a mark of antiquity not of culture that the claim was made. Malmesbury belonged to the Norman world and mixed in Norman high society. The English leaders and heiresses were adopted into Norman society, leaving the English without spokesmen. English language and literature were neglected by the new leaders who, whatever their racial origins, took up French language and literature. English, which had held its own in some places till Malmesbury's own day, disappeared totally a little after his death. It is certain therefore that the two cultures were more alien to one another and moving apart from one another more rapidly in his time, because a new aristocracy which spoke French and was 'Norman' by culture was established over a leaderless English population. This new aristocracy was keenly interested in its ancestry and its members identified their position with that accorded to their fathers and grandfathers after the Conquest. The sense of family loyalty and class solidarity assumed a new importance socially, just when social mobility was being reduced and new codes of chivalrous rituals made it less easy to be admitted to the higher ranks of society. This was the world Malmesbury lived in and understood and it is natural that he should have assumed that the cleavage between these two worlds dated from the Conquest itself; that the Norman lords of his own day behaved like the Conqueror's companions and that the dispirited English were the faithful replicas of their old English kin. Nothing could be more natural for Malmesbury than to use the 'racial' divisions of his own day as a clue to understanding the past—the Normans on one side, the English on the other.

Yet even a casual acquaintance with the events of the Conquest will show that this racial theory is not sound. The Conqueror himself and his successors never speak of the Normans in the sense that William of Malmesbury does. They use instead 'French-born' because the Conqueror's companions were indeed far more 'racially' heterogeneous than Malmesbury implies. Nor is this a mere quibble. The differences of Frenchmen are insisted upon by the Conqueror's own panegyrist William of Poitiers. Flemings, Normans and Bretons, to name only the most important, were not alike in language, culture or institutions and were far from sharing a common 'Norman' mentality. Without making a similar analysis of the Anglo-Saxons—because it would be hard now to show in detail how a Mercian differed from a West Saxon, however important that difference once was—it is sufficient to reflect on the other aspect of the problem: the great difference between the English position in government after the Conquest and in the reign of Henry I. In

1066 William had too much to learn from the English to replace them immediately with Normans. The English knew how the country could be governed and William needed them. He came as Edward's heir and there is no evidence that William ever regarded his position as anything else. Continuity with the past was the theme of his government and remained the watch-word of his successors. Even after the rebellions of 1069 there is no incontrovertible evidence that he intended to rule by some other principle. Domesday Book assumes that the customs and rights of Edward's day are still valid—although it recognises that usurpations have taken place. For all these purposes the English remained important. By 1130 they had become useless. Those who cooperated with the government were those who forgot their Englishry and looked like Normans. It was too because the Normans had learned what they needed, that the English could be relegated to a second place in the social order. In this sense the English and the Normans of Malmesbury's descriptions are fit labels for the divisions of his own time, but no guide to the differences of the Conqueror's own reign.

Malmesbury's analysis of the peoples was intended to explain the great problem that broods over the Norman Conquest. How could the English with their traditions in secular and clerical affairs have been defeated by the Normans? Malmesbury as a monk, whose ideas of history had been formed by a study of the Old Testament, naturally looked for a moral explanation. God had deserted his people because of their sins—their gluttony, their drunkenness, their lasciviousness. God had sent the Normans—sober, dedicated and dutiful—to punish them. Whether this explanation was a faithful reflection of his own convictions or whether it was designed to impress and please his Norman patrons, like the king's bastard Robert of Gloucester, the type of historical explanation is the same in either sense: a story of vice chastened. The Normans may be the mere instruments of Divine vengeance who will correct the failing of the children of Israel and prepare them for their greater future; or they may themselves be the children of Israel triumphing in the land of Canaan and taking over the land of milk and honey. All modern interpretations of Malmesbury's theme opt for one side or the other. Either the Anglo-Saxons lost because of their corruption, pride and disunity, or they lost because the Normans were superior in virtue, battle, wisdom and leadership. Until Anglo-Saxon scholars recently rejected Malmesbury's approach outright, it held sway over historical explanation. Now that the Anglo-Saxons no longer seem the corrupted and damnable people of Malmesbury's account some other view will have to be taken.

The corrective to Malmesbury has long been available in the pages of Orderic Vitalis, his unassuming contemporary. Orderic's picture of the Normans is the very reverse of Malmesbury's. For the latter the Normans reintroduced primitive virtue into corrupt Anglo-Saxon England; for Orderic, the Normans themselves were corrupted by the Conquest which made them greedy, and factious. Orderic's picture of them is in itself sufficient to suggest how much Malmesbury's is an intellectual device to justify the Conquest itself. Orderic is a much less pretentious historian than Malmesbury, with no desire to leave behind him a name as Bede's successor. His history grew slowly out of his enthusiasm for writing the history of his own monastery, St Evroul, and he added voluminous accounts of what the local Norman families and the dukes were doing, with no concern to present a continuous narrative. He takes up old themes, repeats himself, not always exactly, and the work remains rambling, repetitive and naïve, suggesting that he never revised it. As such, it is more revealing than the polished reflective work of Malmesbury. His picture of the 'pure' Normans, with their ferocious family quarrels, narrow outlook and unscrupulous morals, is a picture of the violent Normandy of Henry I's reign, annexed but never crushed after Tinchebrai. Orderic thought of himself as an English exile in Normandy—although his father was a priest from Orléans and he had been sent as a boy of ten to St Evroul. He kept his sympathies for the English saints and helped to diffuse their cults in Normandy, but he is not aware, as Malmesbury was, of the great social cleavage in England; in Normandy he was not involved in it. His environment is a Norman one and his curiosity caused him to record Norman doings from Apulia to Scotland—a chaotic chronicle with no historical explanations, only moral lessons. Orderic's naïvety therefore suggests a different dualism from that of Malmesbury: the real Norman world, hardly aware of a Channel barrier, that regards the Normans of Italy as the close cousins of those in the North on the one hand and on the other a superior romantic world of English legend—a fast vanishing, heroic age of saints, scholars and monks.

Malmesbury and Orderic for all their differences are equally great writers. Can it be a mere coincidence that they are almost contemporaries? Both are unqualified admirers of Henry I and have given him his reputation as founder of a type of government which was efficient, ruthless, profitable, and popular. Henry I figures as a kind of Augustus—he preserved his empire from civil war between Norman brothers, and made possible the survival of the valuable Anglo-Saxon traditions into the future: he gave stability in a world that threatened to change beyond comprehension. Without the efforts of Malmesbury and Orderic to remember and record (even as partisans) it would be much more difficult for us to understand what did happen after the Conquest. And the reason they both strove to write histories in this period seems to be that they were both aware that the world they wrote about was vanishing. This effort to record a way of life before it was altogether too late is reflected in other ways during the same period, notably in the effort to establish on paper in Henry I's reign what were the laws and customs of Edward the Confessor. Yet there is no doubt that the original impulse came in the purely religious sphere—an effort to reassert the sanctity of the old saints. The Normans themselves stimulated this defence by subjecting the relics they found in English monasteries to various tests, and out of their pragmatic approach developed a spiritual zeal that vindicated not only relics but reputations—collections of miracle stories and edifying lives of the saints. All this effort was conducted locally. But there were those who were more skilled conservers than others, like the writers Goscelin and Osbern who settled at Canterbury by the end of the century and produced a series of lives of saints designed to boost the reputation of Canterbury. This effort at writing history to assert the validity of historical links was necessarily local. It is in fact from such local histories alone that the attitudes of men of the times can be discovered. Hugh the Cantor is the spokesman of York as Eadmer is of Canterbury. Events seen from the viewpoint of such great religious centres may seem less parochial than the chronicles of such a house as Abingdon, but the spirit remains the same. Without the spade-work done by these local historians, it would have been impossible for Malmesbury or Orderic to stand even at such a distance as they did from their own monastic houses and to see events with a greater degree of unity.

This is only to say that it was technically impossible for an historian to write about the Norman Conquest until the reign of Henry I, for its consequences had only then shown that event in its proper proportions so that an historian could see his own particular party-interest in perspective. Yet, in reading back, we are now in the position of those who can see how great those local interests remained, until such time as a greater unity could be imposed. Malmesbury and Orderic could not see this, because they were less aware than we are of the process of change itself. Until now, historians have on the whole been content to take up the same position before the Conquest as these two twelfth-century historians; our only hope of seeing the events as they happened is to reconstruct the situation as it occurred.

Understanding the Conquest is not for us an effort to explain the achievement of Henry I, but to explain its course in its own time. Eleventh-century witnesses had no sense of the great religious drama that Malmesbury found in the event. Even the enthusiastic Normans saw the Conquest as an achievement of the Conqueror rather than a racial victory. Our nearest observer, in point of time, the author of the life of the Confessor, trembled at the undecided fate that awaited England in the months after his death. But this anxiety is not a prophetic expectancy before the most decisive moment of English history. Dangers threatened from all sides: there was no natural lord to turn to; the lamented king had himself prophesied the worst. All in positions of responsibility must have been aware of this. Yet we too easily forget that England had an experience of calamities of this sort that stretched back a century. Since Aethelred II there had been several kings unable to rule, swift to die, brave or shiftless. In a century of turmoil and bloodshed only two kings, Canute and the Confessor, had ruled more than eighteen years to assure regular government and a degree of order. Yet Canute at his succession had been a Dane and the Confessor, for all his ancestry, had lived abroad for twenty-five years after his adolescence. Every year in which a king had died since Aethelstan had been fateful in the same way as 1066. The English can have had no sense in that year that the House of Cerdic was spent and a long era of foreign rulers about to dawn.

That year was full of uncertainty, as so many previous years had been.

Even after Hastings or William's coronation there could still be no reason to think that the Old English monarchy was over. This was not merely because contemporaries were blind to change or not given to our sense of drama which salutes turning points in history at every bend in the road. In a sense, the Conqueror's reign was a struggle to preserve the Old English monarchy in a new social situation, the Norman settlement, that was unfamiliar with its workings. It is certainly true that the monarchy had to adjust itself to this new situation and that in time all that was characteristic of the Anglo-Saxon community disappeared totally. By emphasising what is new to the scene after the Conquest it is possible to misrepresent what in fact happened. It is the interest of the Norman period that it preserved as well as innovated. What finally triumphed was not the Norman element, but a compromise between the various contenders in the arena. The Conqueror did not change his policy after 1069 but time itself successively removed old counsellors and those familiar with an entirely different world that had come into being since 1066. Of course the old order had not itself been static, but it had served a social situation that disappeared with increasing rapidity. Ever more frenzied efforts to record that old order before it passed away entirely are themselves evidence of change that occurred in spite of, rather than because of kings, lords and churchmen. It was not on the morrow of the Conquest that the ways of Edward were committed to writing, for they were familiar to everyone except the invaders; by the time of Henry I living memory had become hazy and only writing could save some of the traditions for the future.

It was only at this point that the historical significance of the Norman Conquest impinged upon the more reflective, and by that time the need to put recent events into intelligible perspective could only distort the interpretation. It was the beginning of continuous English historical writing, but also of English legend, and it is necessary for us to try to get beyond that legend to an assessment of just how England was affected by the Norman Conquest. It is a story of a policy of conservation that was sabotaged without malice; it is emphatically not a story, as it is too often represented, of the triumph of a new order—a Norman ideal—a powerful, wilful monarchy that created the basis of subsequent law and institution. It is easy to see how this view could arise; by the mid-twelfth century it was a commonplace. The twelfth-century aristocrats claimed their right by inheritance from their Norman ancestors, companions of the Conqueror. So did the monarch: was not Stephen himself the Conqueror's grandson? Domesday Book was a source of reference: it contained the names of the original landlords, names written as in the Golden Book. The law of fees and of the land was already dated by Richard de Lucy to the Conquest—it was the classical view held by Edward I. The continuous history of the state began with the theory that England was forfeited to the king by its rebellion against him—and that by an act of mercy the Conqueror restored and confirmed all rights and customs and enforced them by royal grant, not by virtue of their power as custom. At one stroke England had renounced its powers to Leviathan.

The logic of this autocratic theory may be attractive, but it is not history. For the Conqueror did not claim by Conquest but by heredity, and was not known as Conqueror to his contemporaries. For all the attention that the Norman period has received, its deepest currents have still not been charted, because it has been studied more for what it is supposed to have resolved and achieved, than for its slow and painful manner of achieving.

Notes on the Illustrations

1 *Rouen Bibliothèque Municipale MS 456, f. 1 (facing p. 48)*
This is a Norman illuminated initial B from an eleventh-century manuscript of St Augustine's treatise on the Psalms, formerly at the monastery of St Evroul. It forms a very striking contrast to figure 2, both in the compressed character of the composition and in the absence of linear delicacy. The animation of the different scenes is conveyed by the extravagant gestures of the figures which overstep the formal edges. The foot of David, as harper, just stretches beyond the border, as the sword in the bottom left-hand corner reaches up towards the main figure of Goliath. The harper's left leg is at an awkward angle and the young David's arms in the main scene are theatrically posed and coiled in the shape of the letter itself. Too much weight should not be attached either to the similarities or differences of military equipment in the illustrations of 1 and 2, for illustrators habitually relied more on previous drawings than on contemporary costumes. The similarity of the standards, shields, swords and helmets may represent such borrowing. The Norman Goliath's armour resembles the texture of that shown in the Bayeux Tapestry, though here it is a knee-length, skirted garment. Even if the Norman artist had access to an English model, his different conception of the composition is very plain here. This initial resembles another in Evreux MS 131, made by a monk of Lire. See F. Avril, *La Décoration des Manuscrits dans les Abbayes Bénédictines de Normandie au XIe et XIIe siècle*, chapter 5. Position des Thèses. Ecole des Chartres (1962).

2 *British Museum Cotton MS Tiberius C VI*, f. *8v. (facing p. 65)*
This is a pre-Conquest representation of David and Goliath from Winchester. The expressive lines and gestures of the figures and the involved folds of the draperies are characteristic of English drawing of this period. It is a sketch of part of a larger scene. See F. Wormald, 'An English Eleventh Century Psalter with pictures', Walpole Society, vol. 38.

3 *Alençon Bibliothèque Municipale MS 11*, f. *1 (facing p. 96)*
This initial A from an eleventh-century manuscript of St Ambrose's letter to the emperor Gratian shows the bearded emperor, flanked by lions, seated on a throne with two lion-headed arm-rests. He wears a characteristic eleventh-century crown, as in the scene of David the harper in figure 1. The picture is lively and imposing, and though the initial is less

elaborately ornamented than the B of figure 1, it is completely dominated by the figure of Gratian.

4 *Pierpont Morgan Library MS 736, 22v. (facing p.* 113)
This figure of St Edmund crowned by angels was painted by the St Alban's master about 1130. It is interesting from two different points of view. First, it shows sainted kingship, in which the symbols of authority, the crown, the staff and the palmette (of martyrdom) are conferred by heavenly beings, while the monks, as mortal men, kiss the king's feet from outside the picture. Here it is both their patron and their king they bow down to. Second, this picture stylistically shows the revival of the English tradition of animated story telling. The angels are seen in the act of vesting the king; their robes have characteristic convoluted folds. The king's dignified presence suggests how Norman influence could have added weight and substance to the English style. The influence is not only Norman: Edmund is notably stiffer than Gratian in figure 3. See F. Wormald, *Bulletin of The John Rylands Library*, vol 35 (1952); O. Pächt, *St Albans Psalter* (London, 1960).

5 *Le Havre Bibliothèque Municipale MS 332, p.* 78 *(facing p.* 208)
This full-page picture precedes a text of the life of St Ansbert, co-patron with St Wandrille of the abbey of Fontenelle, from which this manuscript came. It is probably eleventh-century. In the life of Ansbert, the abbot, St Wandrille, ordered books to be given to the monk Ansbert in order to help him forward in the religious life. This seems to be the scene represented here. Ansbert's humble posture also recalls the episode when, as a layman, he asked to be taken into the monastery, and fell at the abbot's feet, humbly honouring the Christ who was embodied in St Wandrille. Whatever the particular reference, the general respect of monks for their patrons and abbots is symbolically presented in this picture. See W. Levison, 'Vita Ansberti. Scriptorum Rerum Merovingarum', *M.G.H.* t.v. (Hannover, 1910), 613–41, especially 622, chapters 5 and 6.

6 *Florence, Biblioteca Laurenziana MS Plutarch 12:17,* f. *2a (facing p.* 225)
This illustration is from a manuscript of St Augustine's *City of God*, executed at the monastery of St Augustine's, Canterbury, about 1100. The survival of the English linear style is very clear; the delicacy of the colouring can only be admired in the original. The formal border of imperial Roman heads may symbolise the walls of the city of Rome, within which the animated debate of the first chapter of the *City of God* was being conducted. The precise significance of the gestures of these distinct, individual figures has not been worked out. Most of them carry books or scrolls, which they appear to use as authorities. Only one is beardless, and he wears a cap that suggests he is a bishop, perhaps the

bishop of Rome, or St Augustine himself. The division of the scene into two parts, six figures above with six others and the bishop below, has no obvious symbolic importance. Whether the bearded figures are prophets or disputatious pagan philosophers is difficult to decide. The bishop is not at the centre of the picture and the most masterful of the figures in the lower scene appears to be in the act of bidding him leave. This very lively composition is almost the last of its kind in the traditional English style, which has obviously lost none of its vigour or imaginative power. See C. R. Dodwell, *The Canterbury School of Illumination* (Cambridge, 1954), 28.

7 *Oxford, Corpus Christi College MS 157, f. 383 (facing p. 256)*
These illustrations are two of four drawn in the chronicle of John of Worcester, apparently by the chronicler himself, about the year 1130, when Henry I was said to have had visions of his people protesting about his oppressive government. The upper scene shows the different orders of clergy protesting against the king's exactions and the lower scene shows the king returning to England from Normandy and caught in a great storm, during which he became so fearful of his ultimate fate that he called on God and decided to amend his government on his return. See J. H. Weaver, *John of Worcester, Analecta Oxoniensa.*

8 *Oxford, Bodleian MS 717, f. 2 (facing p. 273)*
The manuscript of St Jerome's commentary on the book of Isaiah was written in the early twelfth century and comes from Exeter cathedral. The manuscript is typical of the many patristic texts written for use in England at this time, but it is unusual in having several elaborate illustrations, not all by the same man. One of them actually shows the artist, Hugo Pictor, who also worked for the monastery of Jumièges, but he was not responsible for this picture. This is an extremely ornate example of a Norman initial and is painted in bright, but not strident colours. As in the other illustrations shown here, the outline of the letter is used as a mere excuse for the composition. As compared with figure 1, the scene is much less constricted and suggests that the painter had become more interested in spatial relationships between the scenes than in the interlacing patterns that dominate figure 1. Here the interlace is confined to the edge, except that the upper-inset of the seated Christ is revealed by a hanging drawn back between two painted pillars and draped in intricate folds on the left. In the foreground, Isaiah, with awkwardly crossed arms, holds up a scroll on which are written words from his prophecy (Isaiah 2 : 3). Some attempt has been made to present the Jews realistically, as in the beards of Isaiah and his first hearer and in the curious cloche hats. The folds of the draperies are much less agitated than in figure 6, but are more involved than in figure 1. See O. Pächt, *Bodleian Library Record*, IV.

References

These notes are intended to provide essential references and some bibliographical guidance ; controversial discussion of debatable points has been largely avoided.

Abbreviations

Annales	Annales Ordinis S. Benedicti (Paris, 1703–39)
A.S.C.	*Anglo-Saxon Chronicle*
B.M.	British Museum, London
B.N.	Bibliothèque Nationale, Paris
B.S.A.N.	*Bulletin de la Société des Antiquaires de Normandie*
D.B.	*Domesday book*
E.H.R.	*English Historical Review*
Gesetze	*Die Gesetze der Anglesachsen*, ed. F. Liebermann (Halle, 1898–1916), 3 vols; references to vol. I (text)
Hemming	Hemming, *Cartularius*, ed. T. Hearne (Oxford, 1723)
Jaffé	P. Jaffé, *Regesta Pontificum Romanorum* (Leipzig, 1885)
Malmesbury, G. P.	William of Malmesbury, *Gesta Pontificum Anglorum*, ed. N. E. S. A. Hamilton (R.S., London, 1870)
Malmesbury, G. R.	*ibid*, *Gesta Regum*, ed. W. Stubbs, (R.S., London, 1887–9)
M.G.H.	*Monumenta Germaniae Historica*
Orderic	Orderic Vitalis, *Historia Ecclesiastica*, ed. A. le Prévost (S.H.F., Paris, 1838–55), 5 vols
P.L.	*Patrologia Latina*, ed. J. P. Migne
Recueil	*Recueil des Actes des Ducs de Normandies anterieurs à 1066*, ed. M. Fauroux (M.S.A.N., 1962)
Regesta	*Regesta Anglonormannorum Regum*, I, ed. H. W. C. Davis (Oxford, 1913); II, ed. C. Johnson and H. Cronne (Oxford, 1954)
R.H.D.F.E.	*Revue d'histoire du droit français et étranger*
R.S.	Rolls Series
T.R.H.S.	*Transactions of the Royal Historical Society*
V.C.H.	*Victoria County History*
William of Poitiers	William of Poitiers, *Gesta*, ed. R. Foreville (Paris, 1952)
Worcester	*Chronicle of Florence of Worcester*, ed. B. Thorpe (London, 1848)

CHAPTER 1, Pages 13–41

1 *Liber Confortarius*, ed. C. H. Talbot, *Analecta Monastica*, III (1955), 49
2 *Abingdon Chronicle*, ed. J. Stevenson (R.S., London, 1858), II, 98
3 B.M. Harley MS, 3908, *f* 10
4 Hermann of Laon, 'Miracles of Our Lady of Laon', *P.L.*, 156, col. 973–88
5 *Miracles of Fécamp*, ed. A. Långfors (Helsinki, 1930) story no. 21. The negotiations with the pirates were subsequently conducted in English
6 William of Malmesbury, *Vita Wulfstani*, ed. R. R. Darlington (Camden Society, London, 1928), 43–4
7 *Gesetze*, Cnut II, 3
8 Nevertheless, the Domesday customs of Chester indicate that careful watch was kept on ships entering that port, if only to collect valuable and variable harbour dues for the king. *D.B.*, *f* 262, b.1
9 *Ramsey Chronicle*, ed. W. D. Macray (R.S., London, 1886), Appendix, xvii. 'Goscclini Miracula Sancti Ivonis'
10 F. M. Stenton, *Norman London*, Historical Association pamphlet. The Pipe Roll of 1130 ed. J. H. Hunter, (London 1833, reprinted 1929), 143–150 contains interesting information about London. Canute was the first king known to have been crowned in London, perhaps at St Paul's
11 L. Musset, 'A-t-il existé en Normandie au XIe siècle une aristocratie d'argent?', *Annales de Normandie* (1959), 285–99
12 William of Poitiers, 6
13 F. M. Stenton, 'The Road System of Medieval England', *Economic History Review*, VII, 1–21. The shire courts were responsible for punishing breaches of the peace on roads between cities and markets; *Gesetze*, *Leges Edwardi Confessoris*, 12, 9
14 *Gesetze*, *Leges Henrici*, 80, iii
15 *Simeon of Durham*, ed. T. Arnold (R.S., London, 1882), vol 1, 100
16 *Acta Sanctorum*, May, vol VI, 375; 'Vita S. Augustini', chapters 1 and 2
17 O. Lehmann-Brockhaus, *Lateinische Schriftsquellen zu Kunst* (1956), II, no. 4484. There is plenty of evidence for the plunder of these splendid churches after the Conquest
18 The best summary analysis of the distribution of wealth revealed by *D.B.* is by W. Corbett, *Cambridge Medieval History*, vol V, chapter XVI. A more elaborate discussion is provided by R. Lennard, *Rural England 1066–1135* (Oxford, 1959)
19 *Anglo-Saxon Wills*, ed. D. Whitelock (Cambridge, 1930), no. 39, 1066/8
20 *Memorials of St Dunstan*, ed. W. Stubbs (R.S., London, 1874), 245–6; C. H. Haskins, *E.H.R.* (1910), 293–5
21 K. Leyser, *T.R.H.S.* (1960), 61–83

22 W. G. Henderson, *York Pontifical* (Surtees Society, 1875), vol lxi, 279–83. Litany for Queen Matilda: 'Poscimus anglorum nostrum salvet basileum'
23 *British Numismatic Journal*, X, 111–46, cited by F. Barlow, *E.H.R.* (1958), 649–55
24 E. John, *Land Tenure in Early England* (Leicester, 1960), 119–21
25 C. W. Hollister, *Anglo-Saxon Military Institutions* (Oxford, 1962)
26 William of Poitiers, 198
27 *Gesetze, Edmund* (940–6), III, 1
28 *A.S.C., anno* 1016
29 B. Wilkinson, *Bulletin of The John Rylands Library*, XXIII, 504–26
30 P. Grierson, *T.R.H.S.* (1941), 71–112
31 *Liber Confortarius, op. cit.*, 41
32 *A.S.C., anno* 1051
33 *Ibid.* See the interest of the chronicler in the reactions of the Carolingians to the Vikings in Gaul
34 D. Whitelock, *English Historical Documents*, I, (London, 1955), 823–24
35 William of Jumièges, *Gesta Normanorum Ducum*, ed. J. Marx (Société d'Histoire de Normandie, 1914), 85–7
36 *Encomium Emmae*, ed. A. Campbell (Camden Society, London, 1949)
37 *The Life of King Edward the Confessor*, ed. F. Barlow (Nelson's Medieval Texts, 1962), quoting C. F. Wright, *Cultivation of Saga in Anglo-Saxon England*, 67
38 William of Poitiers, 6
39 B. Wilkinson, *Bulletin of The John Rylands Library*, XXII, 368–87; D. C. Douglas, *E.H.R.* (1953), 526–45; T. J. Oleson, *E.H.R.* (1957), 221–8
40 William of Poitiers, 172, 174

CHAPTER 2, Pages 42–68

The fullest recent account of the duchy before 1066 is given by D. C. Douglas, *William the Conqueror* (London, 1964). The analysis of institutions under the Conqueror was first made by C. H. Haskins, *Norman Institutions* (Cambridge Mass., 1920), a study not yet superseded.

1 *Mont St Michel Cartulary*, Avranches MS 210, introduction. A Rouen writer in the 1070s or 1080s wrote of his province that it was favoured by heaven with a mild climate, fertile soil, 'nemorum suavitate' and was rich in milk and herds: *Acta Sanctorum*, August IV, 829, II, §22
2 Dudo of St Quentin, *De moribus et actis primorum normanniae ducum*, ed. J. Lair, *Mémories de la Société des Antiquaires de Normandie* (1865).

Cf. Richer, *Histoire de France*, ed. R. Latouche (Paris, 1930), i, 156 and ii, 293, for their bad reputation in northern Gaul

3 *Gallia Christiana* XI (Paris, 1759), instrumenta 217–24. The visit of bishop Geoffrey of Coutances to his former parishioners settled in Calabria and Apulia

4 Wace, a contemporary of Henry II Plantagenet, cited by C. H. Haskins, *Norman Institutions* (Cambridge Mass., 1920), 41–2, 173 n.

5 L. Musset, *B.S.A.N.* 52 (1952–4), 148–9

6 J. Yver, *B.S.A.N.* 53 (1955–6), 28–115

7 D. C. Douglas, *E.H.R.* (1946), 129–56

8 J. F. Lemarignier, *Recherches sur l'hommage en marche et les frontières féodales* (Lille, 1945), 67–8

9 *Recueil*, no. 36. Bishop Odo of Bayeux ceded the right to settle criminal cases by inquest procedure to the abbey of Caen, at the duke's request. Therefore this right must have been the bishop's, not the duke's. It is probable that the bishop here exercised the powers of the Carolingian count. J. F. Lemarignier, *Etudes sur les privilèges d'exemption* (Paris, 1937), 295–6

10 A. Le Prévost, *Mémoires de la Société des Antiquaries de Normandie* (1840), 1–59

11 D. C. Douglas, *William the Conqueror* (London, 1964), 33-35

12 *Ibid.*, note 7 above. *Cf.* S. Painter, *Speculum* (1956), 243–57, esp. 247

13 Ralph of Ivry's lands were divided amongst his sons (the bishops of Bayeux and Avranches) and his daughter Emma, mother of William Fitz Osbern

14 J. Yver, *op. cit.*

15 L. Musset, *B.S.A.N.* 56, 5–41

16 The basic assumptions about Normandy were stated by Haskins, *op. cit.*, 5, (i) it is plain that Norman society in 1066 was a feudal society and one of the most fully-developed feudal states in Europe; and, 60, (ii) it is a feudalism which is held in check by a strong ducal power. Since Haskins wrote, concepts of feudalism have been radically revised

17 G. Bessin, *Concilia Rotomagensis Provinciae* (Rouen, 1717), 39, 67. The Truce of God was referred to in England in the *Leges Edwardi Confessoris* of about 1130, clause 2. *Gesetze, op. cit.* M. de Bouard, *Annales de Normandie* (1959), 169–89

18 D. C. Douglas, *William the Conqueror* (London, 1964), 52

19 *Recueil*, nos. 93–233

20 By 1034, the duke (Robert the Magnificent) had a seneschal, a butler, and a chamberlain as well. In fact he had a miniature royal court

21 Orderic, II, 81–2

22 C. H. Haskins, *op. cit.*, Appendix D, clauses 1–3, 11–13

23 L. Musset, *R.H.D.F.E.* (1960), 483–84. For the ducal treasure, see Haskins, *op. cit.*, 40–4

24 M. E. Bridrey, 'La chapitre du monnéage', *B.S.A.N.* 48 (1940–1), 76–519. The border regions (under the counts), the fief of Breteuil (former domain of the count of Ivry), the Val de Mortain (possession of the count of Mortain), the chatellenie of St Jacques (possession of the *vicomte* of Avranches) and the Passais (on the Maine border) were exempt. 'Similiter omnis justitia de exercitu vel de moneta ad solum ducem pertinent. Hec autem supradicta fuerunt generalia per totam Normanniam nisi solummodo in marchis ubi moneta non currebat.' *Très Ancien Coutumier*, ed. E. J. Tardif (Paris, 1881), LXX, 65. The duke's authority was therefore limited where the counts were most powerful. For the Rouen merchants see S. Deck, *Annales de Normandie*, VI (1956), 245–54

25 J. F. Lemarignier, *Revue du Moyen Age Latin*, IV (1948), 191–6

26 A *vicomte* announced the ducal 'bann' at St Ouen in 1073: Bessin, *op. cit.*, 63–4. A *vicomte* was present in the court that settled disputes about Taisson property in 1074, *Gallia Christiana XI, instrumenta* 96–8. Though they acted in a legal capacity, there is no evidence that there were regular meetings of courts of law in their jurisdictions, as the shire courts in England met within the sheriff's shires. The *vicomtes* of Bayeux have been studied by E. de Laheudrie, *B.S.A.N.* 46 (1938), 183–225

27 Cnut II, 12; the duke conceded ducal customs to the monastery of Préaux about 1050: they are stated to be 'hainfara', 'ullac', 'rat', 'incendium', 'bernagium' and 'bellum': housebreaking, outlawry, rape, arson, feeding dogs and war. *Recueil*, no. 121

28 C. H. Haskins, *op. cit.*, Appendix D, clauses 9, 10

29 J. Mabillon, *Annales*, V (1713), 635–40, from B.N. MS Lat. 2342, *f* 185v. 'Hic venerabilis abbas Heluinus nulli unquam hominium fecit de rebus ecclesie sue quia de patrimonio proprio pene omnia possidebat et cetera de elemosinis baronum terre illius'. This text, written in the 1130s, is remarkable for assuming that those inheriting their estates would not normally do homage to a lord. Roger de Montgomery, in a charter for Jumièges (1045–8), says of an allodial tenant that he was 'in mea ditione', not that his holding was a fee. *Cartulaire de Jumièges*, ed. J. J. Vernier (Société d'histoire de Normandie, 1916), no. 22. *Cf. ibid.* nos. 39, 37

30 L. Musset, *B.S.A.N.* 56, 5–41

31 *Gallia Christiana XI*, instrumenta 96–8. *Cf. Cartulaire de Jumièges*, nos. 52–3

32 *Recueil*, no. 188

33 D. Bouquet, *Historiens de France*, XXIII, 693–705

34 C. H. Haskins, *op. cit.*

35 Oxford, Bodley MS e Mus 93, *f* 15v.

36 *Recueil*, no. 229. *Cf.* P. Marchegay, 'Chartes Normandes de l'abbaye

de St Florent près Saumur', *M.S.A.N.* (Caen, 1880) no. 9, *c.* 1082, 673–4. St Ouen had a barony and owed service from it for the 'bourg' at Rouen. Its houses, in and out of the vill, were confirmed to it by Charles le Chauve in 876. P. Le Cacheux, *B.S.A.N.* 47 (1939), 63–81

37 H. Navel, *B.S.A.N.* 45 (1937), 137–65, 'Les Vavassories du Mont St Michel'

38 *Antiquus Cartularius Ecclesiae Baiocensis*, ed. V. Bourrienne (Societé d'Histoire de Normandie, 1902–3), no. 21

39 *Ibid*, nos. 1 and 3

40 Orderic, III, 249; *Recueil*, no. 224, *cf.* no. 218, p. 412

41 William of Poitiers, 88, 104. J. F. Lemarignier (*Recherches, op. cit.*, 32–33), argues that all men did 'ligeance' to the duke and cites the *Summa de Legibus Normanniae* of the thirteenth century: XII: 'Ligantiam . . . de omnibus hominibus suis totius provincie debet habere dux'; XIII: 'Fidelitatem unde tenentur omnes residentes in provincia duci facere et servare'. *Coutumes de Normandie*, ed. E. J. Tardif (Paris, 1896), tome II, 38–9. There is no proof that these rules were known in the eleventh century

CHAPTER 3, Pages 69–85

1 J. F. Lemarignier, *Revue du Moyen Age Latin*, IV (1948), 191–6. Raoul Tortaire described eleventh-century Caen in verses. For its connections with England note these two lines:

'Insula diversis quam mercis Anglia ditat
Et quacunque mari cingitur occidus'.

Archives Annuelles de Normandie (1824), 209–25

2 D. C. Douglas, *William the Conqueror* (London, 1964), chapter 3

3 Mathilda was seventh in descent from Alfred of Wessex. See also F. Barlow, *E.H.R.* (1965), 225–51

4 Oxford, Bodley MS Mus. 93, printed in J. A. Giles, *Scriptores Rerum Gestarum Willelmi Conquestoris* (London, 1845), from a later copy

5 P. Grierson, *E.H.R.* (1936), 90–7

6 *Bayeux Tapestry*, ed. Sir Frank Stenton (London, 1957)

7 William of Poitiers, 104

8 *The Life of King Edward the Confessor*, ed. F. Barlow (Nelson's Medieval Texts, 1962), 32. *Cf.* Hyde Chronicle (R.S.), 291

9 In 1172 there were fewer than 600 (581) knights owed to the duke; the Norman barons had about 1,500 knights at their own disposal

10 List summarised from Bodley MS e Mus 93, *f* 15v. in Orderic II, 124, n. 1

11 D. C. Douglas, *William the Conqueror* (London, 1964), 192

12 The best contemporary sources for the battle of Hastings are the *A.S.C.* and William of Poitiers. Col. C. H. Lemmon has written a concise modern account, *The Field of Hastings* (1960). Harold's fate has fascinated many, since the making of the Bayeux tapestry. One of the earliest attempts to link the unhappy fate of England to Harold's personal tragedy appears to be in the *Ramsey Chronicle*, written about 1160. Here, the Confessor is said to have appeared in a vision to abbot Ailsy (then in Denmark) and to have promised victory to the English. But the Confessor's prophecy was not fulfilled because Harold became so proud after his success at Stamford Bridge that he forfeited divine approval; in this way the glorious English liberty was lost. Ed. W. D. Macray (R.S., London, 1886), 179–80

CHAPTER 4, Pages 89–128

The fullest single study of the Conquest and the reign of the Conqueror was written by E. A. Freeman, *History of The Norman Conquest* (Oxford, 1867–79), 6 vols. The basic work on feudal institutions is still Sir Frank Stenton, *First Century of English Feudalism* (revised ed., Oxford, 1962)

1 The rite supposed to have been used was printed by W. G. Henderson, *op. cit.*, 270–7, and by J. Wickham Legg in *Three Coronation Orders* (Henry Bradshaw Society, London, 1900), 53–64

2 *Cf.* the installation of the duke in the *Très Ancien Coutumier*, ed. E. J. Tardif (1881), 1 (not written earlier than the reign of Richard I, (1189–99): the Norman duke swore to protect the church, to preserve the peace and to maintain justice. A similar oath may have been taken in the eleventh century. The *Anglo-Saxon Benedictional* (Rouen MS Y 7, *f* 181) which Robert of Jumièges sent to Normandy *c.* 1050 contains the Anglo-Saxon coronation rite and a religious ceremony used for inducting a new duke based on that rite was subsequently copied into the manuscript. It is unlikely that William himself had been inducted as duke by such a ceremony. His personal interest in the rite of coronation seems assured by the existence of a manuscript containing an amplified version of the Anglo-Saxon rite, assigning a place for music. P. E. Schramm, *A History of the English Coronation* (Oxford, 1937), 28. This service may never have been used, except for Rufus in 1087. 'Laudes' were sung for William and Mathilda at Winchester in 1068. Imperial kingship and regal dominion ('imperiale et regale') are phrases that occur in the coronation rite, and they are emphasised both in the English *Vita Edwardi*, ed. F. Barlow (1962), and in the Norman poet *Serlo*

3 *A.S.C. anno* 1086

4 Orderic, IV, 12
5 *A.S.C.*, *anno* 1086
6 J. A. Robinson, *Gilbert Crispin* (Cambridge, 1911), 141, n. 18; B. W. Scholz, *E.H.R.* (1961), 466–73, discusses the later papal forgeries of Westminster
7 *Cartulaire de Jumièges*, ed. J. J. Vermier (Société d'histoire de Normandie, 1916), no. 29
8 F. M. Stenton, *T.R.H.S.* (1944), 1–12
9 *Worcester*, 228
10 C. N. L. Brooke, *Cambridge Historical Journal* X (1951), 111–132. *Textus Roffensis*, ed. T. Hearne (Oxford, 1720), chapter 201. Odric, son of the English thegn Edric, is described simply as the king's thegn in *D.B.*, *f* 87. Likewise, Alwin Wit still held 20 years later the lands he had enjoyed in 1066, though he held in *Domesday book* as a subtenant of Milo (*f* 50, b 1)
11 *Textus Roffensis*, *op. cit.*, chapter 104
12 J. A. Robinson, *op. cit.*, 47
13 There were ten Flemish tenants-in-chief in 1086 and many small men, knights and others: F. Stenton, *First Century of English Feudalism* (revised, Oxford, 1962). For the departure of the Bretons, see Lanfranc, *Letters*, ed. J. A. Giles, no. 38. There were few important Bretons left by 1086
14 *Regesta*, 6, 40
15 Orderic, III, 44, says that one Norman lord refused to take anything. For Eustace, see *D.B.* II, 9, 26 b; for Hugh de Montfort, II, 100
16 J. F. A. Mason, *T.R.H.S.* (1963), 1–28. Roger de Montgomery had £2,000 p.a. in land
17 C. F. Slade showed for Staffordshire (*V.C.H.*, IV 1958, 26) that the king's manors in that county were more valuable than those of any tenants-in-chief, and other evidence proves that the lands of the richest Anglo-Saxons passed to well-favoured Normans. It seems the king could easily acquire information about the best estates. For *Spirites* see *D.B.*, 252 b; for Edric of Laxfield see *D.B.*, II, 304 a
18 F. Lot, *Etudes Critiques sur L'Abbaye de St Wandrille* (B.E.H.E., Paris, 1913), 81–2, no. 36
19 D. C. Douglas, *Economic History Review* (1939), 128–43. Lennard, *op. cit.*, 170
20 *Red Book of the Exchequer*, ed. H. Hall (R.S., London, 1896), I, 333
21 *Regesta*, no. 1404
22 For Evesham see B. M. Cotton MS Vespasian B XXIV and Harley MS 3763. *Red Book of the Exchequer*, *op. cit.*, 301. See also J. Kemble, *Codex Diplomaticus Aevi Saxonici* (London, 1845), vol III, no. 630. Bishop Oswald of Worcester granted one 'mansus' at Compton in the tenth century 'libera praeter arcis pontisve constructionem et communem contra hostes expeditionem'; no. 637—a similar grant

by him of five 'mansus ruris' at Lench, 'libera ab omni mundiali negotio praeter pontis arcisve restaurationem et communem publicae rei expeditionem'. The expedition is a public duty of the same order as bridge and fortress construction

23 *Regesta*, no. 462

24 *Regesta*, nos. 1428, 1527

25 Introduction by F. M. Stenton to *Lindsey Survey* (Lincoln Record Society, vol 19, 1924). This survey, like that for Staffordshire (*V.C.H.*, IV, 2–4) suggests that five hides were grouped together to form a unit for geld-paying

26 *D.B.*, I, 69. The Abingdon assessment was reduced from 500 to 300 hides

27 R. S. Hoyt, *Royal Demesne* (Cornell, 1950). Oxfordshire and Northamptonshire paid as counties for three knights' farm

28 'Northamptonshire Geld Roll', ed. A. J. Robertson, in *Anglo-Saxon Charters* (Cambridge, 1939); *V.C.H.*, *Northamptonshire*, I, 269

29 J. F. A. Mason, *op. cit.*

30 This is in dispute. See Sir F. Stenton, *V.C.H.*, *Oxfordshire*, I, 394, n. 1

31 *D.B.* does not suggest that its use of 'milites' is the same as that of other contemporary records. The 'milites' of Hemming's *Cartulary*, ed. T. Hearne (Oxford, 1723) (from B. M. Cotton MS Tiberius A xiii), at Westbury, are styled 'homines' in *D.B.* Similarly, Domesday's 'homines' of Peterborough (*f* 221 b) have become 'milites' in the *Peterborough Chronicle* ed. T. Stapleton (Camden Society, London, 1849), 168–75

32 B.M. Vespasian MS, Bxxiv, *f* 41v.

33 *D.B.*, *f* 173, b 2

34 J. A. Robinson, *op. cit.*, 37–41. According to *D.B.*, I, 986, thegnland at Withypoole in Somerset, that ceased to provide service, reverted to paying geld

35 *Abingdon Chronicle*, *op. cit.*, II, 3

36 V. H. Galbraith, *E.H.R.* (1929), 353–72

37 *Domesday Monachorum*, ed. D. C. Douglas (Oxford, 1940). There was great unevenness of obligation. Sixteen men owed 63 knights; 25 men owed only fractions amounting to a mere 10¼ knights; 25 men owed only one knight each and could therefore have discharged the whole service personally. As many as 13 of these 25 cannot be traced as land holders, and were therefore probably landless, household knights. Anselm refers to the land which English 'milites' were said to have held from the archbishop of Canterbury before the Conquest; when the knights died without heirs, Rufus claimed the right to give the lands to whom he liked, 'vult assere se posse iuste quos vult eorum haeredes constituere'; Anselm thought that this was the archbishop's right. They are apparently in disagreement about an Anglo-Saxon custom. *Anselmi Opera*, ed. F. Schmitt, IV, 59, *ep* 176.

According to an all English charter of Anselm's time (*ibid,* V, 358) there were two separate groups of knights at Canterbury: the hired retainers and the 'cnihts' of the 'cepmannegild' under the borough reeve, William Cauvel. Gilds of knights are also known to have existed at an early period in London (*Ramsey Chronicle, op. cit.,* 256) and Winchester. The Canterbury gild was, by implication, not made up of retainers; there was also a thegn gild at Cambridge (B. M. Cotton MS Tiberius V *f* 75) and at Exeter (B. Thorpe, *Diplomatarium Anglicum Aevi Saxonici,* 610–613)

38 W. Somner, *A Treatise on Gavelkind* (2nd edition, 1726), Appendix 209–110, cited by F. M. Stenton, *The First Century of English Feudalism* (Oxford, 1932), 145–46

39 *Feudal Documents from the abbey of Bury St Edmund's,* ed. D. C. Douglas, British Academy (Oxford, 1932)

40 *D.B. ff* 172 b 1, 174 a 2; J. Kemble, *op. cit.,* vol III, published 71 charters for the Oswaldlaw. They are arranged chronologically and fall between charters nos. 529 and 683

41 Hemming, 80–3

42 *P.L.,* 155, 79. *Cf. Vita Wulfstani,* 46, 55. A messenger Gilbert, going to Normandy under Henry I, sent bishop Herbert Losinga a present of five pears and five quinces. Losinga, *Epistolae,* ed. R. Anstruther (Brussels, 1846), no. 50

43 *Simeon of Durham,* IV, 9

44 Vespasian MS, *op. cit.*

45 *Red Book of the Exchequer, op. cit.,* 397; *D.B.,* II, 85, 258b, 428b

46 *Domesday Monachorum:* Lanfranc built an archiepiscopal palace at Westgate, for which 27 houses had to be destroyed before 1086. *D.B.,* 3 b

47 *Feudal Book of Bury,* no. 122, dated 1121/1148. 'Ut melius possit facere . . . servicium unius militis'.

48 *The Red Book of the Exchequer, op. cit.,* 413. The thegnlands of Abingdon, granted on leases for three lives before the Conquest, passed to Normans (*Abingdon Chronicle, op. cit.,* 3–4). The English knights and French thegns of *D.B.* also suggest that the two classes overlapped (*D.B.,* 66, 130a; II, 54a; IV, 428). The evidence for Worcester is discussed below at note 60

49 *Feudal Book of Bury,* nos. 168, 132 (1134–48)

50 G. J. Turner and H. E. Salter, *The Register of St Augustine's Canterbury* (London, 1924), II, 462

51 *Abingdon Chronicle, op. cit.,* 64–5; *cf. Regesta,* no. 958

52 *Burton Abbey Surveys* (*Historical Collections of Staffordshire*) (William Salt Society, 1916), 262–4. Abbot Geoffrey granted to Robert de Ferrers land in fee at Ticknall, in return for ten shillings a year at Martinmass, 'et debet diligere et manutenere nos et ecclesiam nostram et per se et per suos sicut amicus et tutor ipsius ecclesie per omnia et heredes ejus succedentes sibi'

53 R. Lennard, *op. cit.*, 107–8; *Ramsey Cartulary*, ed. W. H. Hart (R. S. London 1886) II, 259–60

54 'The Introduction of Knight Service', in J. H. Round, *Feudal England* (London, 1895). This essay, which has been most influential in crediting the Conqueror with the imposition of fixed quotas of service, is fundamentally a study of the 'servitia debita' of Henry II's reign. Round believed that Henry was investigating what service was owed to the crown (though this is nowhere explicitly stated in the returns themselves) and that the 'servitia debita' were already ancient in 1166. Since these services were, on his showing, utterly arbitrary and bore no relation to the wealth of the tenants-in-chief, Round decided that they had been imposed by a tyrant, and the morrow of the Norman Conquest seemed the most probable occasion for such an abuse of power. The contemporary chroniclers never denounced William for this injustice (particularly against churchmen), so Round was forced to back up his argument, based on Henry II's reign, by citing chroniclers of very doubtful authority. He used the *Liber Eliensis*, written under Stephen, which only proves that enfeoffments had been made by the Conqueror's reign, not that fixed quotas of service had been imposed. He cited the thirteenth-century chronicler Matthew Paris, whose testimony for post-Conquest England is valueless. The *Abingdon Chronicle* account (3, 4) is not unambiguous and belongs anyway to the late twelfth century. Recently Round's theories have been vigorously assailed. For example, H. G. Richardson and G. O. Sayles, *The Governance of Medieval England* (Edinburgh, 1963) give very useful and radical criticisms of Round's approach. C. W. Hollister, *The Military Organisation of Norman England* (Oxford, 1965) prefers to salvage what he can of Round's work, but he is not very critical of the sources e.g, 25–27

55 B. M. Cotton Vespasian MS, Bxxiv, *ff* 10v.–11; *D.B.* I, 177 b 2

56 For example, Geoffrey Mandeville had the lands of Ansgar and those of the men commended to Ansgar. *D.B.*, II, 412 b

57 I. J. Sanders, *Feudal Military Service in England* (Oxford, 1956), 17, n. 4

58 *D.B.*, I, 56 b: 'unus miles de quinque hidis tantum unus miles ibat et ad eius victum vel stipendium de unaquaque hida dabuntur ei iiij solidis ad duos menses'. C. W. Hollister, *Anglo-Saxon Military Institutions* (Oxford, 1962) argues that this custom of Berkshire was widely, if not universally, known in eleventh-century England. There is no general agreement that the 'miles' was a foot-soldier rather than a knight or mounted man. The distribution of the military burden resembled that of geld-paying: see note 25 above. For Canute's law, see *Gesetze*, I, 456

59 Bengeworth was given by bishop Oswald in the tenth century to the knight Aelfweard, and after his death it was to pass to the knight Eadwine 'libera ad omni mundialium servitute tributorum exceptis

sanctae dei ecclesiae necessitatibus atque utilitatibus'. J. Kemble, *op. cit.*, no. 625

60 The Worcester evidence is considerable and has excited much comment for its indication that the pre-Conquest English had been familiar with 'feudal' relationships and that earlier dispositions of property continued to influence Norman Worcestershire. The most remarkable work was done by F. W. Maitland, *Domesday Book and Beyond* (Cambridge, 1897). M. Hollings, *E.H.R.* (1948), 453–87, used documents unknown to Maitland. E. John, *op. cit.*, has revised and restated Maitland's views

61 Another example of the king holding the land of a knight may be seen in a charter of Henry I, granting the estate to a knight to be held on the same terms as he himself had held it. *Regesta*, 1062

62 *Peterborough Chronicle*, ed. T. Stapleton (Camden Society, 1849), 168

63 *D.B.*, 66

64 *Abingdon Chronicle*, *op. cit.*, II, 129; Adam of Domerham, *History of Glastonbury*, ed. T. Hearne (London, 1727), 318

65 Vespasian MS, *op. cit.*

66 Simeon, IV, 9. *Analecta Monastica*, II (1953), 46; Elmer of Canterbury: *Epistolae*, XI, XV: letters to the 'miles' Hugo

67 Henry of Huntingdon, *Historia Anglorum*, ed. T. Arnold (R.S., 1879), 237; *Regesta*, 959

68 Orderic, IV, 7

69 *Cf.* W. E. Wightman, *E.H.R.* (1962), 6–17

70 *Regesta*, nos. 976, 1499. Pipe Roll, P.R.O. E 372/69, Salop, cited by I. J. Sanders, *op. cit.*, 18

CHAPTER 5, Pages 129–166

In addition to the works of Round, Stenton and Hollister previously cited, two extremely important recent studies deserve special notice. R. Glover, 'English Warfare in 1066', *E.H.R.* (1952), 1–18; J. O. Prestwich, 'War and Finance in the Anglo-Norman State', *T.R.H.S.* (1954), 19–43. Mr Prestwich has also criticised Hollister and others in *Past and Present* (1963), 39–57. A more technical debate between Professors Hollister and J. C. Holt has recently begun in the *Economic History Review*.

1 Simeon IV, 9

2 *Regesta*, nos. 515, 941

3 *Textus Roffensis*, *op. cit.*, chapter 26: a band of up to seven men would be 'latrones'; seven to 35 men would be a small force ('hlaf'); 35 men and over constituted an army

4 *Gesetze*, *Cnut II*, 71, i–iv

5 William of Poitiers, 40

6 'Winchester Council penances of 1070', in D. Wilkins, *Concilia Magnae Britanniae*, I (London, 1737), 366 proem and clause 6
7 B. D. Lyon, *E.H.R.* (1951), 161–93
8 This view is further expounded in chapter 8 below
9 Malmesbury, G. R., II, 314
10 J. H. Round, *The King's Sergeants* (London, 1911)
11 The kind of evidence available has to be used with much ingenuity to yield information of this sort. See C. W. Hollister, *op. cit.*, In the Assize of Arms (1181) lords had to provide the equipment for the men of their domain. *D.B.* proves that some archers were enfeoffed. The king's crossbowman Reginald held Fambridge (*D.B.*, II, 97b); Berner the crossbowman held Cavelly of the abbot of Ely (*D.B.*, II, 214 b)
12 *D.B.*, 179, 181, 190; Worcester *anno* 1074. A reference to the ancient obligation to serve is made in *Regesta*, no. 1083
13 C. W. Hollister argues that the English fyrd and the Norman knights provided a combined force for the Norman kings: *The Military Organisation of Norman England*, chapter VIII
14 Orderic, II, 180; 254; Malmesbury, G. R., II, 316
15 This appears to be the drift of Hollister's arguments
16 *Textus Roffensis*, chapter 88. For castles in general, E. S. Armitage, *Early Norman Castles* (London, 1912) is still not superseded
17 J. Yver, *op. cit.* (note II, 6)
18 William of Poitiers, 210
19 J. Yver, *op. cit.*; Orderic, IV, 336–7
20 J. A. Beeler, *Speculum* (1956), 581–601
21 *Worcester*, II 20
22 Raoul Tortaire, monk of Fleury, wrote verses on Bayeux:
'Huic eo Bajocas, ubi vidi culmina clara
Turres excelsas aedis honorificae'.
Archives Annuelles de Normandie (1824), 209–15
23 B.M. Cotton MS Nero A i. *Cf. D.B.*, 44 b: the men of Berkshire do not wish to recognise any law but that of king Edward, until the king should modify it. F. Pollock and F. W. Maitland, *A History of English Law* (Cambridge, 1898) give the best discussion of the effect of the Normans on English law. Vol I, chapters III and IV
24 *Gesetze*, 279–371. They are printed in parallel columns with the Anglo-Saxon text
25 The longest account of a trial by ordeal is in *Archives d'Anjou* I (1843), 433–78. It was already being criticised by churchmen, as by Yvo bishop of Chartres, for tempting God: *v.* F. Patetta, *Le Ordalie* (Turin, 1890), 390–2. The ordeal is frequently referred to in *D.B.*
26 Battle was not allowed between members of the same family, or to settle disputes about inheritance; where the case was presented and there was no challenger, battle was not a possible procedure. It

occurs in *D.B.*, II, 146 b, 176, 190, 213 etc.

27 *Pipe Roll*, ed. J. H. Hunter (London, 1833, reprinted 1929), passim

28 J. Goebel, *Felony and Misdemeanour* (New York, 1937). Outlawry is described by *D.B.* as a royal right (*D.B.* 262b, 298b, 376b, etc.). *Cf. Très Ancien Coutumier*, *op. cit.*, 36, 7; *Gesetze* II, *Cnut*, 13, 30, 36, and *Leges Henrici*, 43, 7. Nevertheless, when Roger de Lacy forfeited his lands in 1095, his brother Hugh succeeded to them

29 E. John, *op. cit.; Abingdon Chronicle*, *op. cit.* 483. The estate at Fifehide, granted for three lives to sheriff Godric, was acquired before the lease expired by Henry de Ferrers

30 Orderic, II, 405. Robert de Beaumont obtained Henry I's permission to divide his estates between his twin sons (born in 1104): G. H. White, *T.R.H.S.* (1934), 19–48

31 A. Freeman, *op. cit.*, vol IV, Appendix G

32 *Evesham Chronicle*, ed. W. D. Macray (R.S., London, 1863), 96–7

33 *D.B.*, 280 b: *Gesetze*, *Leges Henrici*, 19, 3

34 W. A. Morris, *The Frankpledge System* (Harvard, 1896). This obscure subject has not received much attention since

35 C. Petit-Dutaillis, *Les Origines franco-normandes de la Forêt Anglaise* (Mélanges Bémont, Paris, 1913), 59–76. F. H. Baring, *Domesday Tables* (London, 1909). Note on Hampshire, the New Forest. 194–205. This is still the best discussion. Also useful for a local survey is W. H. P. Greswell, *Forests and Deerparks of Somerset* (Taunton, 1905). Professor M. de Bouard says Norman peasants preserved some Danish forest customs: *Bulletin of the Institute of Historical Research* (1955), 5

36 D. Stenton, *English Justice between the Norman Conquest and the Great Charter* (London, 1964) 15–16. In the Cambridge inquest in 1086, four Frenchmen and four Englishmen were summoned; at the enquiry into the Taisson property in 1074 there were also four appointed to investigate: *Gallia Christiana XI*, instrumenta 96–8

37 R. Besnier, *R.H.D.F.E.* (1950), 183–212

38 *P.L.*, 150. Lanfranc's letters nos. 45–7. For the king's work of justice, see *Worcester*, 210

39 *Liber Eliensis*, ed. E. D. Blake (Camden Society, London, 1962), 424–5

40 *D.B.*, 65 b 2; 264 a 2

41 *Inquisitio Cantabrigiensis*, ed. N. E. H. A. Hamilton (Cambridge, 1888), 459–60, xvii-xviii, *D.B.*, II, 450. R. Welldon Finn, *E.H.R.* (1960), 385–409

42 C. Hart, *Early Charters of Essex: the Norman Period* (Leicester, 1957), no. 77, p. 5

43 *Regesta*, no. 50

44 *Memorials of Bury St Edmund's*, T. Arnold (R.S., London, 1890–96), Vols I–III, 63, 65; *Regesta* I, 138, 139

45 *Worcester*, II, 8; *Regesta*, no. 220. There are numerous references in *D.B.* to such suits; i.e. for the king and queen's part in them, 48 b 2,

238 b 1; for the activity of the bishops of Coutances and Bayeux, 151 b 1, 175 b 2; for Lanfranc, II, 381; for sheriffs, I, 66 b, 377, 450, II, 98, 423 b

46 Hemming, sub. Charlton
47 *Regesta*, no. 221
48 Hemming, 77
49 *Liber Eliensis*, *op. cit.*, 206, chapter 125
50 For *D.B.* see R. Welldon Finn, *The Domesday Inquest* (London, 1961); V. H. Galbraith, *The Making of Domesday Book* (Oxford, 1961); *Domesday Rebound* (H.M.S.O., 1954); for the social picture see R. Lennard, *op. cit.*
51 T. A. M. Bishop and P. Chaplais, *Facsimiles of English Royal Writs to A.D. 1100* (Oxford, 1957)
52 W. A. Morris, *The Medieval English Sheriff to 1300* (Manchester, 1927)
53 *Textus Roffensis*, *op. cit.*, chapter 91
54 *V.C.H.*, *Suffolk*, i, 427
55 The abuses of sheriffs are frequently noted in *D.B.*, *ff* 58 a 1, 132 a 2 132 b 2, 133 a 1, 148 b 2, 181 a 2, 186 a 1, 190 a 1, etc.
56 Losinga, *Epistolae*, no. 35
57 Hemming, I, 278; *D.B.*, 133 b 1; *Regesta*, no. 187. Those who did not pay the geld due within three days lost their lands to those who paid the dues
58 See note 53
59 H. R. Loyn, *Anglo-Saxon England and the Norman Conquest* (London, 1962); J. Tait, *Medieval English Boroughs* (Manchester, 1936)
60 *Inquisitio Eliensis*, 143, 189. *D.B.*, 421. Ely wanted a house in Ipswich, *D.B.*, II, 421 b. For a demand for a house in Norwich, see *Regesta* no. 153
61 C. H. Talbot, *Life of Christina of Markyate* (Oxford, 1959), 10–12

CHAPTER 6, Pages 167–215

The most recent work on the state of the pre-Conquest English church is by F. Barlow. *The English Church 1000–1066* (London, 1963). There is no similar work on the post-Conquest period except H. Böhmer, *Kirche und Staat in England und in der Normandie* (Leipzig, 1899)

1 *The Life of King Edward the Confessor*, ed. F. Barlow (Nelson's Medieval Texts, 1962) 75–78
2 *Evesham Chronicle*, *op. cit.*, 335
3 *Vita Wulfstani*, *op. cit.*, 16–18
4 *Worcester*, *anno* 1066. The Worcester connections with York at this time mean that this authority is good. It is apparently contradicted by the Bayeux tapestry which shows Stigand present at the corona-

tion, but its evidence is tendentious and, probably intentionally, ambiguous. F. Barlow, in *The English Church 1000–1066* (302–6) argues that the papal objections were raised against Stigand's usurpation of archiepiscopal rank, and did not involve condemnation of his episcopal orders. His position after the Conquest was based on his submission to William at Berkhamsted: William of Poitiers, II, 28, 35, 40. Malmesbury, G. P. 36–7

5 This view is not stated by any early source

6 *Giraldus Cambrensis*, ed. J. Dimock (R.S., 1877), vii. 151–2

7 William of Poitiers, 234

8 *English Historical Documents 1042–1189*, 632

9 Ethelric had been consecrated by Stigand, but so also had been Siward of Rochester and Remigius of Lincoln. Leofwine, bishop of Lichfield and former monk of Coventry, being accused of keeping a wife and sons in public, was summoned by the papal legates to their synod, and was excommunicated for failing to appear. The legates gave the king permission to appoint another bishop in his place, and Leofwine decided to attend William's Easter assembly in 1071. He would not answer the charges, preferring to surrender his bishopric 'spontanei voluntate', and retire to his original monastery. Lanfranc was, however, too unsure of himself, either to consecrate another bishop or to authorise other bishops to do so, until Alexander II pronounced on the question. This scruple illustrates both Lanfranc's diffidence at the beginning of his pontificate and his exaggerated respect for the pope: *P.L.*, 150, letter 4

10 *Vita Lanfranci*, *P.L.*, 150, chapter 40; Orderic, II, 516

11 A. J. Macdonald, *Lanfranc* (2nd edition, London, 1944)

12 Eadmer, *Historia Novorum*, ed. M. Rule (R.S., London, 1884), 11

13 *P.L.*, 150, letter 23

14 D. Wilkins, *Concilia* (*op. cit.* I, 363,), 'regia munificentia et synodali auctoritate'

15 Register of Gregory VII, ed. E. Caspar, *M.G.H.* (Berlin, 1955), 443, 600–1; Lanfranc, *Epistolae*, ed. J. Giles, *ep.* 65. *Cf.* G. Bessin, *op. cit.*, 74: Gregory complained that the archbishop of Rouen also did not visit Rome. Absolution was given by the papal legates in 1088; *ibid*, 75

16 *Worcester*, II, 29. Referring to the existence of two popes, the chronicler comments: 'Quae res per plures annos ecclesiam angliae occupavit, ut ex quo Gregorio qui et Hildebrandus [as Gregory was called by the supporters of Henry IV] defunctus fuit, nulli loco papae usque ad hoc tempus subdi vel obedire voluerit'. See also the remonstrances of Urban II in 1088: Jaffé, 5351

17 Trinity College, Cambridge, MS 405. This manuscript is discussed by Z. N. Brooke, *The English Church and the Papacy* (Cambridge, 1931), chapter V. Yvo, bishop of Chartres, the learned canon lawyer,

was said to have heard Lanfranc at Bec; Robert de Torigny, *Chronicle*, ed. L. V. Delisle (Société d'Histoire de Normandie, 1872), I, 253. Herluin, the founder and first abbot of Bec, was also skilled in law: 'peritus in dirimendas causarum saecularium controversii legum patriae scientissimus praesidium suis erat contra iniquos exactore'. For Anselm's legal distinctions see also, from the same manuscript, *infra*, p. 323, n.15

18 *P.L.*, 150, Lanfranc letters nos. 12–14, 24–7, 30–2, 34

19 Hugh the Chantor, *History of the Church of York 1066–1127*, ed. C. Johnson (Edinburgh, 1961), 3–4

20 Gregory VII, *Register*, *op. cit.*, 499–502. Z. N. Brooke, *E.H.R.* (1911) 225–38

21 *Libelli de Lite*, III, *M.G.H.* ed. H. Böhmer (Berlin, 1897), 642–687, (34–5); P. E. Schramm, *op. cit.* The king remained king of England. He did not become king of England and Normandy

22 *Anglia Sacra*, ed. H. Wharton (London, 1691), I, 55

23 Simeon, *op. cit.*, I, 134

24 Malmesbury, G. P., Book V. *Register of St Osmund*, ed. W. H. Rich-Jones (R.S., London, 1883), I, 198–200

25 *Vita Wulfstani*, *op. cit.* He was on joking terms with bishop Geoffrey of Coutances, 46

26 Hemming, II, 391, See N. Ker in *Essays Presented to Sir Maurice Powicke* (Oxford, 1948), 49–75

27 *Evesham Chronicle*, *op. cit.*, 88–96

28 D. M. Knowles, *The Monastic Order in England* (Cambridge, 1940), 132, suggests that Remigius may at one stage have intended to transfer the monks from Stow to the nearby cathedral at Lincoln

29 *Ecclesiastical Documents*, ed. J. Hunter (Camden Society, London, 1840), 16–21

30 Goscelin, *Liber Confortarius*, *op. cit.*, 102. *Cf.* the interesting order at the synod of Caen in 1061, requiring abbots and other prelates staying in the country to move into towns near monasteries, lest it seem that they were wandering hither and thither and incur public censure; G. Bessin, *op. cit.*, 48

31 H. W. C. Davis, *E.H.R.* (1909), 417–31; V. H. Galbraith, *E.H.R.* (1925), 222–8; *Memorials of St Edmund*, *op. cit.*

32 *Christina of Markyate*, *op. cit.*

33 After Rufus' death, nine abbots (but no bishops) were deposed, including six for simony

34 A. Morey and C. N. L. Brooke, *Gilbert Foliot and his Letters* (Cambridge, 1965), 196, note 2. Archbishop John wrote *De officiis ecclesiasticis*, ed. R. Delamare (1923)

35 C. N. L. Brooke, *Cambridge Historical Journal* (1951), 111–32

36 *Commentaryon Lamentations*, ed. H. Farmer, *Studia Monastica*, IV, ii (1962)

37 *P.L.*, 156, cols. 982–3 chapter 13
38 D. Wilkins, *Concilia*, *op. cit.*, 408, canons of 1126, clause 3
39 The synod of Rouen in 1074 denounced those who claimed to have copulated before marriage, with blood relations of their unwanted wives in order to get annulments: 'Quod ore profitentur, judicio probent'. G. Bessin, *op. cit.*, 65
40 Innocent II complained to the archbishop of Rouen as late as 1131 about laymen calling themselves archdeacons. G. Bessin, *op. cit.*, 21–8
41 For the use of the ordeal of iron in Normandy, see G. Bessin, *op. cit.*, 39, 76; *Gallia Christiana XI*, instrumenta 17; *Archaeologia* (1838), 26–7; *Regesta*, I, xvi; B.N. MS Lat. n.a. 1243, *ff* 80–1; B.N. MS Français 4899, 292–3
42 *Gesetze*, 485. It is dated by C. N. L. Brooke to 1080–6 by the names of the sheriffs to whom the London writ is addressed
43 *Gesetze*, *Leges Henrici*, cl. 7, iii. 11. The clergy were judged by the bishops, but not if they were married men or farmers of lands, that is, pursuing a secular employment. *Gesetze*, *Leges Henrici*, 64, 8; 57, 9. Priests used the process of compurgation to answer charges against them: Eadmer, *Historia Novorum*, 194: decrees of 1108
44 *Vita Gundulfi*, *P.L.*, 159, 813–36. *Textus Roffensis*, *op. cit.*, chapter 212. He was Lanfranc's deputy 'tam in conversationibus regum quam episcoporum'; when he went to the archbishop, he was allowed 20 shillings a day and his expenses, in candles, wine and beer, for himself and his retinue
45 Eadmer, *Vita S. Anselmi*, ed. R. W. Southern (Edinburgh, 1962), 101
46 *Abingdon Chronicle*, *op. cit.*, 30–1
47 Eadmer, *Historia Novorum*, 143, quoting canons of 1102. *Cf.* *Abingdon Chronicle*, *op. cit.*, 142–3, for the division of tithes at Uffington
48 Losinga, *Epistolae*, no. 2; *Cf.* *Gloucester Cartulary*, ed. W. H. Hart (R.S., London, 1863), vol 1, 13–14
49 *Anselmi Opera*, ed. F. Schmitt (Edinburgh, 1946) vol IV; *ep.* 170
50 J. A. Robinson, *op. cit.*, 24
51 Malmesbury, G. P., 289, admitted that the gluttonous bishop of Worcester, Samson, also fed 300 poor men every day. Eadmer wrote of a later Worcester election: 'Cogitate in quantam invidiam quorundam malignorum hominum ordo monachicus hoc tempore venit et quantum nitantur eum saltem ab episcopalibus extirpare'. H. Wharton, *Anglia Sacra*, II, 238
52 Eadmer, *Historia Novorum*, 137–8
53 Losinga, *Epistolae*, nos. 59, 60
54 D. M. Knowles, *The Monastic Order in England* (Cambridge, 1940), is the standard modern work
55 *The Monastic Constitutions of Lanfranc*, ed. D. M. Knowles (London, 1951)

56 *Gesta Abbatum S. Albani*, ed. H. T. Riley (R.S., London, 1867), I, 51–66: a fourteenth-century work presumably drawing on more ancient local traditions or materials
57 *A.S.C.*, *anno* 1083
58 *Evesham Chronicle*, *op. cit.*, 336
59 *Abingdon Chronicle*, *op. cit.*, 284, from an account of the late twelfth century
60 J. Mabillon, *Vetera Analecta* (1723), IV, 450
61 Losinga, *Epistolae*, nos. 14, 16, 17, 23, 43, 51, 52, 57. B. Dodwell, *T.R.H.S.* (1957), 1–18. The monks kept many servants to attend to their physical needs. See Vespasian MS, Bxxiv, *f* 41v.: the 67 monks of Evesham had 65 *servientes*
62 Lanfranc revised the Anglo-Saxon ecclesiastical calendar, but introduced no Norman saints
63 Losinga, *Epistolae*, nos. 3, 36
64 D. Wilkins, *op. cit.*, 408, clause 15
65 *Abingdon Chronicle*, *op. cit.*, 10–11: the clerk of Sutton church, Alwin, 'legibus patriae optime institutus', was succeeded by his son. The priests represented their vills in the public courts. *Gesetze*, *Leges Henrici*, cl. 7, vii. Not all the churches built by 1086 can be mentioned in *D.B.* C. F. Slade concluded for Staffordshire, a backward county, that few men could have been more than eight miles from a church. *V.C.H.*, *Staffordshire*, IV, 24
66 D. Wilkins, *op. cit.*, 365
67 Simeon of Durham, I, 131–32
68 *Textus Roffensis*, *op. cit.*, chapters 183, 187, 207
69 *Libelli de Lite*, III; G. D. Williams, *The Anonymous of York* (Cambridge, Mass., 1951)
70 *D.B.*, II, 118
71 Anselm obtained authority from Paschal II in 1107 to dispense with the canons forbidding the sons of priests to succeed to their fathers' churches. Eadmer, *Historia Novorum*, 422
72 In 1075, buying and selling of sacred orders and ecclesiastical offices with cures of souls was forbidden. In 1126, more general objections were raised against taking money for specified spiritual gifts: Wilkins, *op. cit.*, 363, 408, 410
73 The council of Clermont had declared in 1095 that no priest was to become the vassal of a layman ('homo laici'), because it was unworthy that the hands consecrated to God and made holy by sacred unction should be placed in unblessed hands (as they would have been in the ceremony of homage). If a priest held a fee, which did not belong to his church, from a layman, he should do such fealty as guaranteed his trustworthiness: 'talet faciat fidelitatem quod securus sit'. Orderic, III, 473, cl. 7
74 J. C. Dickinson, *Origins of the Austin Canons and their introduction into*

England (London, 1950); C. Dereine, *Revue d'histoire ecclésiastique* (1946), 365–406; *ibid* (1951), 534–63
75 Jaffé, 5763
76 The Norman church was affected by the same movement, but later. L. Musset, *B.S.A.N.* 55, 5–38

CHAPTER 7, Pages 219–246

The reign of William Rufus was treated amply by E. A. Freeman (Oxford, 1889); Henry I has still not received adequate attention, though his charters have now been calendared. R. W. Southern, *St Anselm and his Biographer* (Cambridge, 1963), discusses many of the crucial problems of the generation.

1 A point made by L. Musset, *B.S.A.N.* 56, 5–41
2 J. E. Lloyd, *History of Wales* (London, 3rd ed. 1939). J. G. Edwards. 'The Normans and the Welsh March', *Proceedings of the British Academy*, 1956. Harold Hardrada's son, Magnus, ravaged England with the help of the Welsh, of Irishmen from Dublin and of men from the Hebrides and Orkneys in 1058. The Welsh raided as far east as St Ives (Hunts) in the eleventh century: *Ramsey Cartulary*, *op. cit.* lxxii–iii
3 Turgot, *Vita S. Margaritae*, *Acta Sanctorum*, II, 324–331; R. L. G. Ritchie, *The Normans in Scotland* (Edinburgh, 1954)
4 J. Yver, *B.S.A.N.* 53, 28–115
5 K. Leyser, *T.R.H.S.* (1960), 61–83
6 G. Bessin, *op. cit.*, II, 24
7 *P.L.*, 179, col. 150: Jaffé, 7585
8 Jaffé, 6450, 6453
9 See R. W. Southern, *op. cit.* His works have been edited by F. Schmitt (Edinburgh, 1946–56), 6 vols. Eadmer's *Vita S. Anselmi* is edited by R. W. Southern (Edinburgh, 1962)
10 Eadmer, *Historia Novorum*, 82–3
11 *Anselmi Opera*, *op. cit.*, V, ep. 319
12 *Ibid.*, nos. 222, 224
13 W. Holtzmann, *Papsturkunden in England* (Göttingen, 1930–52), vol I, nos. 10–17; vol II, nos. 5–15; vol III, nos. 5–15
14 K. Leyser, *op. cit.*
15 R. W. Southern, *E.H.R.* (1958), 193–226
16 This subject is unlikely to be much clarified. The chroniclers who write about the prevalence of sodomy may be referring discreetly to homosexuality, or only exaggerating the evils of soft, effeminate living. The excessive attention paid to elaborate fashions in shoes, clothes and hair-styles suggests the latter. Hair was grown long, over

the eyes and ears, and was curled; beards were common. The Normans had been known for their short hair and shaven chins and the Englishmen taken by the Conqueror to Normandy in 1067 excited comment there because of their long hair. The clergy were corrupted by the secular hair-styles, and priests neglected to keep their tonsures shaven: Orderic, IV, 472, cl.6. The vehemence of churchmen against such fashions would be understandable. It is not usually believed that beard-wearing goes with homosexuality; it seems simpler to interpret all these fashions as expressions of a less austere society. Henry I had many—and his brother, Robert, a few—bastards; on the other hand, Rufus' name is never linked with any woman's, and he had no children. His homosexuality may have encouraged it in his own immediate circle. Losinga, *Letters*, no. 6, suggests that it may have been more common in the monasteries too, at this time

17 Abbot Reinald of Ramsey gave the church of Wells to Folcard, son of Godric, son of Kingulph, who became the abbot's liegeman and had to settle on the estate: 'effectus est homo ligius . . . residens'. *Ramsey Cartulary*, *op. cit.*, II, 276

18 H. S. Offler, *E.H.R.* (1951), 321–41; William of St Carileph used legal distinctions of this sort in his trial: Simeon I, 174

19 *Abingdon Chronicle*, *op. cit.*, 35–7. When Lanfranc offered £60 to Rufus to acquire Hedenham for Rochester cathedral, the king waived half of it completely: *Textus Roffensis*, *op. cit.*, chapter 87

20 *Gesetze*, 521–23

21 *Abingdon Chronicle*, *op. cit.*, 34–5

22 J. H. Round, *Feudal England* (London, 1895), 309

CHAPTER 8, Pages 247–272

1 R. W. Southern, 'The Place of Henry I in English History', *Proceedings of the British Academy* (1962), Appendix

2 Malmesbury, G. R., II, 520: the author addresses his patron Robert of Caen, earl of Gloucester, as early as 1125, as though he were eligible to rule: 'Beata est igitur secundum sententiam Platonis, respublica cujus rector est philosophus, cujus princeps non delectatur muneribus!'

3 This was not the only way lands could be lost. Ivo de Grentmesnil mortgaged his English lands to Robert de Beaumont to go on crusade, and never redeemed them

4 *G.E.C. Complete Peerage*, X, 352 b, 350 *f*; XII, i, appendix J

5 Malmesbury, G. R., II, 519. The author's remarkable address to his

patron: the *Gesta Regum* would enable him to see himself as in a mirror, to find heroes for imitation. Robert's nobility derived from his outstanding (English) ancestors, kings and earls, just as his distinction as a soldier came from his Norman ancestry, his physical beauty from his Flemish blood, and his noblemindedness ('generositas') from France

6 G. Duby, *Annales* (1952), 155–71; J. A. Raftis, *Estates of Ramsey Abbey* (Toronto, 1957). Abbot Aethelelm of Abingdon raised £30 on his Culham estate 'mutuandae necessitate pecuniae': *Abingdon Chronicle*, 21. The *Leges Henrici*, cl. 56, refers to the need to supervise the farmers of estates: *Gesetze*, 575

7 For mortgages, see A. Allix and R. Génestal, *Vierteljahrsschrift für Sozial und Wirtschaftsgeschichte* II (1904), 616–640

8 P. Grierson, 'Sterling', *Anglo-Saxon Coins*, ed. R. H. M. Dolley (London, 1960), 262–83

9 *Worcester*, 57, 59; Malmesbury, G. R., II, 467, 487; *A.S.C.*, *anno* 1124

10 *Acta Sanctorum*, August IV, 839

11 *Cf.* E. Miller, *The Abbey and Bishopric of Ely* (Cambridge, 1951). The monks' estates were near the monastery, the bishop's further away. *Textus Roffensis*, *op. cit.*, chapter 86

12 R. Lennard, *op. cit.*, 27

13 *Textus Roffensis*, *op. cit.*, chapters 207, 208. *Cf. Abingdon Chronicle*, *op. cit.*, II, 10–11: the king's bailiff used the abbey's oxen to take lead to the king's court at Sutton

14 *Abingdon Chronicle*, *op. cit.*, 8, 20–21. *Cp. Regesta*, no. 200.

15 J. Mabillon, *A.A.O.S.B.*, tome V (1713), 635–400: from B.N. MS Lat 2342 *ff* 186 and v. D. Wilmart, *Revue Bénédictine* (1932), 21–46

16 *Abingdon Chronicle*, *op. cit.*, II, 19–20

17 J. H. Round, *op. cit.* 169–224; D. C. Douglas, *E.H.R.* (1929), 618–625

18 *Historia Gaufredi comitis Andegavorum* (S.H.F., 1856), 234–6

19 Men still went to Normandy to get decision from the king: *Pipe Roll* of 1130, 90. H. G. Richardson and G. O. Sayles, *The Governance of Medieval England* (Edinburgh, 1963) chapters VIII–XIII, take a more sanguine view of the omnipotence of Henry's bureaucracy

20 R. W. Southern, *T.R.H.S.* (1933), 95–128; *Regesta*, nos. 321–2, 420; Orderic, IV, 107–10; *Ramsey Cartulary*, I, 149

21 Malmesbury, G. P., 256

22 Eadmer, *Historia Novorum*, 292; Losinga, *Epistolae*, nos. 21, 26

23 The royal treasurer was a layman. Until 1133 there was a single master chamberlain for England and Normandy, the head of the Tancarville family. The king's butler ('pincerna'), Ralph Buarius, was also a layman. After he went blind and had to retire to Winchester, his son replaced him. *P.L.* 156, 978. D. C. Douglas thought that there were many small ministerial estates in Wiltshire (*Feudal Book*

of Bury, xcii) but Professor Darlington disputes this: *V.C.H.*, *Wiltshire*, vol II (1955), 76. Both Professor Southern (note 1 above) and Sir Frank Stenton (*T.R.H.S.* (1944), 1–12) illustrate the way Englishmen of middling rank found posts in the royal administration

24 Richardson and Sayles, *op. cit.*, 188-90.

25 G. H. White, *T.R.H.S.* (1948), 'The Household of the Norman Kings', 127–55

26 *Pipe Roll*, *op. cit.*, 18, 31, 37, 43 etc.

27 R. L. Poole, *The Exchequer in the Twelfth Century* (Oxford, 1911); C. Johnson, *Dialogue of the Exchequer* (1950); G. H. White, *T.R.H.S.* (1925), 56–78. Weighing occurs in *D.B.*, i, 2 b, at Dartford. Henry I extended blanching to payments other than those from the domain, but it was still unknown in 11 counties in 1129

28 *Gesetze*, *Leges Henrici*, clauses 10, 4; 19, 1. Some of the king's lands were leased directly to the tenants of the manor itself. *Pipe Roll*, 6, 23, 24

29 Ed. J. H. Hunter, *op. cit.*

30 *Regesta*, no. 970: 1102–1110

31 Because Geoffrey de Mandeville later made a determined bid to recover possession of the shrievalties of London and Middlesex, which his ancestors held, it has been argued that Henry I had tried to weaken the aristocratic families by taking the shrieval offices from them. These two shrievalties were no doubt a source of special profit, and no general argument about Henry I's shrieval policy should be based upon them: e.g. J. H. Round, *Geoffrey de Mandeville* (London, 1892), 107–8

32 *Gesetze*, *Quadripartitus argumentum* 533–5. Herbert Losinga compared Henry I to Constantine, Theodosius and Gratian: *Epistolae*, no. 11. Abbot Hugh of Fleury dedicated to Henry his *Treatise on Royal Power and Priestly Dignity*. *M.G.H.*, *Libelli de Lite*, Vol II, ed. E. Sackur (Hanuores, 1892), 465–494

33 *Ramsey Chronicle*, ed. W. D. Macray (R.S., London, 1886), lxxvii. *Goscelini Miracula S. Ivonis*

34 Not every lord had sake and soke over his own men: *D.B.* 11b. Wye; *Gesetze*, *Leges Henrici*, 9, 11; 19, 2; 20, 2

35 *Ramsey Chronicle*, *op. cit.*, 266–8

36 Orderic, III, 123–4

CHAPTER 9, Pages 273–297

1 F. Wormald, 'The Survival of Anglo-Saxon Illumination after the Norman Conquest', *Proceedings of the British Academy* (1944), vol XXX

2 O. Pächt, 'Hugo Pictor', *Bodley Library Record*, iii (1950), 96–103; *St Alban's Psalter* (London, 1960); *The Narrative Tradition in English*

Art (Oxford, 1963)

3 Simeon, I, 247–61; *Miracles*, chapter VII

4 C. Cheney, *Bulletin of The John Rylands Library* (1951–2), 20–36; A. W. Clapham, *English Romanesque Architecture before the Conquest* (Oxford, 1930); also *English Romanesque Architecture after the Conquest* (Oxford, 1934). L. Salzman, *Building in England* (Oxford, 1952)

5 *P.L.*, 150, letter 16

6 N. Ker, *English Manuscripts after the Conquest* (Oxford, 1960)

7 P. Grierson: abbot Seiwald of Bath took his manuscripts to Arras in 1065: *Revue Bénédictine*, 52, 117–40. Bishops Leofric of Exeter and William of Durham were remembered for important bequests of books. Sixty-five manuscripts were written at Salisbury before 1100

8 At Fécamp, the eleventh-century library catalogue was not arranged systematically: Mme Geneviève Nortier, 'Les Bibliothèques Médiévales', *Revue Mabillon* (1957), 1–33

9 Cited by N. Ker, *op. cit.*, 11; B.M. Cotton MS Vitellius A XIII, *f* 87

10 *Evesham Chronicle*, *op. cit.*, 56–7

11 Goscelin: G. H. Talbot in *Analecta Monastica*, III (1955)

12 Losinga, *Epistolae*, nos. 23, 24

13 R. W. Hunt, *T.R.H.S.* (1936), 19–42. William of Corbeil taught the sons of the chamberlain: *P.L.*, 156. *Miracles of Laon*, chapter VI

14 B. Smalley, *The Study of the Bible in the Middle Ages* (Oxford, 1941), 41

15 W. Dugdale, *Monasticon Anglicanum*, VI, 106; J. C. Dickinson, *Origins of the Austrian Canons* (London, 1950) 99–101

16 Corpus Christi College, Cambridge, MS 19

17 C. H. Haskins, *Studies in the History of Medieval Science* (Harvard U.P., Camb. Mass., 1927), chapter II

18 J. A. Robinson, *Somerset Historical Essays* (British Academy London, 1921) 1–25

19 *P.L.*, 156, 983

20 *P.L.*, 157, 671–706

21 *Wulfric of Haslebury*, ed. M. Bell (Somerset Record Society, 1933), 28–9

22 *Ramsey Chronicle*, lxxx–lxxxi, Miracles of St Ivo: 'natione transmarinus opere hortolanus ope permodicus, . . . laetus plaudit manibus atque more exultans Gallico, mirabilem Deum in sanctis suis vocis benedicit publico'. (1133/1160)

23 *Analecta Bollandiana*, I (1882), 379

24 O. H. Prior, *Romania* (1923), 161–185; J. Orr, *Words and Sounds in English and French* (Oxford, 1953), 28–42

25 *The Anglo-Norman Voyage of St Brendan*, ed. E. G. R. Waters (Oxford, 1928); D. Legge, *Anglo-Norman Literature* (Oxford, 1960)

26 *Philippe de Thaon, le Bestiare*, ed. E. Walberg (1900)

27 F. Lauchert, *Geschichte der Physiologus* (Strassbourg, 1889)
28 B.M. Royal MS 2 C xii
29 R. W. Chambers, *The Continuity of English Prose* (Early English Text Society, 1936)
30 *Ramsey Chronicle*, *op. cit.*, 176
31 *Textus Roffensis*, *op. cit.*, Corpus Christi College, Cambridge, MS 383; *v.* N. Ker, *Catalogue of Manuscripts containing Anglo-Saxon* (Oxford, 1957)
32 *Vita Wulfstani*, 2

Index

Note. Wherever possible, *persons*—popes, kings, earls, counts, dukes, bishops, abbots, priors etc.—have been indexed under the *places* with which they were connected.